MARYAM

Maryam

A WOMAN'S JOURNEY OF HOPE & COURAGE FROM REVOLUTIONARY IRAN

Mary Shafa

Mary Shafa

Contents

SUMMARY

With one-foot firm set in pre-revolutionary Iran and one foot in modern America, Maryam's life draws a picture of the cultural clash between old and new, East and West, and men and women in the time period before and after the Iranian revolution of 1979. Maryam grew up as a beauty pageant queen who believed that a wonderful life would open to her, but instead found a world that was determined to clip her wings at every turn. Thwarted at her every attempt to move up and move on, she agreed to a marriage of convenience that offered her a ticket to the United States. But little did she know that no matter how far away she flew, the restraints of her culture would never let her fly free. Yearned-for escape became a prison in her new country, when she found that distance from Iran alone could not liberate her body or her mind.

Traveling between America and Iran with the mystery and promise of the open the road, Maryam's natural optimism, perseverance and self-worth are severely tested during her immigrant's journey. Growing up the daughter of a wealthy business owner in Tabriz, Maryam is shocked to find herself living in poverty when she arrives in the land of opportunity. As her life and identity become lost in the battle between hope and despair, Maryam must find a middle ground between the oppressive country she can no longer endure, and the American dream that is far from her reach.

With the romance of her first love, the embarrassment of acquiring a new language, and the danger of helping two American families escape Iran during the Revolution, readers will follow Maryam's journey as they anxiously wait for the drama of every turning page. Filled with love, mystery, abuse and hope, this novel captures the story of a struggling immigrant, told in engaging and touching events.

PROLOGUE

Last night I dreamt again about one of the cold winter days that I spent in Tehran in 1979. I remember the day being dreary and overcast, with gray clouds adorning the sky, leaving behind a sullen and dark mood. The tree branches looked skeletal; their leaves stripped off from the harsh winds of winter—their beauty completely gone.

I called a cab to take my American friends, Debbie and Kristy, to the airport. Their husbands worked for a large American aviation company and were waiting for their arrival at the Tehran airport - ready to escape the political chaos in Iran and return home safely to America. "If you take us safely to the airport," I told the driver, "I will double the money." He nodded and pulled into traffic. I feared for my life and the lives of my friends as we descended into the unruly streets of Tehran. Islamic Revolutionary guards were taking over every street by setting up checkpoints at every corner of the city, making it difficult for anyone to travel, especially foreigners.

The back seat was silent as we weaved our way through the streets, making our way toward one of the main roads that would lead to the airport. Never before had I felt so on display inside a car, so exposed to the world. Behind the walls of my apartment, I had been certain I could keep my friends safe. But out here with nothing but the glass of the windows between us and the outside world, it suddenly seemed very treacherous to be seen. I scrutinized the faces of pedestrians and tried to look at other drivers without catching their eyes. Every person was possibly someone who was against us, who would turn us in. Every moment, I thought I might hear gunfire and must duck for cover.

Although the driver tried to avoid all soldiers and check points, the cab was funneled toward a line of revolutionary guardsmen with long, black rifle barrels slung over their shoulders and army colored ski masks on their faces. We slowed down as if in a traffic jam and the driver turned toward me with a look on his face that showed both apologies and nerves.

We got a little closer, to the point where I could make out the faces of individual guards. Two of them were carrying something down the line in our direction, although they were still at least a dozen yards away. As they turned slightly to move around a car, I was shocked to see a middle-aged woman, not wearing a cover but clothed modestly in the sort of long-sleeved dress older ladies wear when going to the market. One guard had her arms and the other grasped around her ankles. Her head was thrown back and there was blood all over her forehead. The red blood was more than a smear. In fact, it was flowing through her hair and had dripped into a path along the guard's route. The guards hailed an empty taxi. They opened the back door and placed her in the backseat like a bag of rice. The way her body responded to their touch, I knew she was either completely unconscious or dead, and I tried to get myself to believe that it was only the former. One of the guards got into the front seat of the cab and the car drove away. I quickly glanced in the back seat of our own car and saw both Debbie and Kristy looking pale and slack, their eyes following the wounded woman, too. Kristy had covered one of her kid's eyes and Debbie had one child pressed to one shoulder and the second pressed to the other.

Was that woman talking back to the guards or trying to smuggle something? Was she someone important in the time of the Shah, someone close to the former regime? Was she simply in the wrong place at the wrong time? And where were they taking her? Would her family and friends ever hear from her again or know what became of her?

Although I knew that Debbie and Kristy's husbands were waiting for their arrival at the airport, fear took over my mind. "Turn around, driver," I said softly, not having enough breath to speak above a whisper. "Please turn around." I could hear my heartbeat pounding in my chest due to the overwhelming fear...

June 1978 – Tehran, Iran

The air is warm and there is music in the streets. There is traffic everywhere. My husband and I pull up to a glitzy hotel and are parked by valet. Women in ball gowns and men in tuxedos adorn a red carpet-like walk into the hotel. On the rooftop, the lights of the city glimmer in the distance as guests mingle and partake of appetizers and champagne. Movie stars, business executives, government officials; a who's who of Tehran.

My husband and I are both dressed at the height of fashion. We mingle with guests. I recognize different faces, famous people and friends and talk to an Iranian movie star. I notice my American neighbors Debbie and Kristy, who are living in Tehran with their families and we talk.

I also recognize someone else. At first, I am not sure how I know him, but then I realize that I have seen him on TV. He is the bodyguard of the Shah. Of all the famous faces at the wedding, I am most impressed with the bodyguard. I reveal to him my love and fascination with the Shah and his family.

February 1979

One morning, I turn on the TV and everything has changed. There are new Islamic newscasters and new radio broadcasters. I call my friends and relatives to find out what has happened. The regime has collapsed. The revolution is victorious and Ruhollah Khomeini, who has returned from exile to the celebration of millions, establishes political and religious control of the country.

March 1979

Debbie and Kristy finalize their plans with their husbands to leave the country on a cargo plane. My family's friend Parviz helps us to take them to the airport. We must turn around several times to avoid roadblocks. After a tense ride, we finally arrive to the airport where Debbie and Kristy reunite with their husbands, then they walk together through a back door into the cargo plane. "Let's go," Parviz says, I ask him to stay and be sure the plane take off. **While they were flying, I smiled and said "Parviz, I think this is the beginning of a beautiful friendship".**

September - October 1979

My husband's cousin Behrouz, a professor at the Iranian university, led us to his American friend Mr. Michael J. Metrinko in the US Embassy to help us regarding obtaining US visa. I arrived to meet Mr. Metrinko personally. We walked together through the Embassy garden and he advised me of two essential choices: either waiting on line for a visa, but that would take a lot of time because many Iranians were urgently trying to leave Iran to the US, or fly to Canada and get the American visa from there. I really appreciated his advice and him being so generous with his time.

Fortunately, my brother helped us to get a visa number from the Embassy to make an appointment for a visa. Few days After meeting Mr. Metrinko, we were able to get our document together and hand it to an American lady named Cora, asked us to check back for the result if we have been approved for a visa to America.

Three days later, my husband called home, I picked up the phone and asked him any news from our Visa? He asked me to pass the phone to John "My little son", I hand the phone to John, I heard him saying my son ... we are going to Disney world ... my son and me, we both were so happy and start jumping and dancing.

But few days later, exactly in November fourth, The US embassy and all the employees were taken as hostages. Few years later I watched a movie, I realized that the lady who interviewed us in US Embassy "Lady Cora" was able to get out of Iran with the help of Canadian embassy. While Mr. Metrinko remained as a hostage for 444 days.

December 1979

On day 44 of the hostage crisis at the U.S. Embassy, we left Iran. Me three months pregnant, my husband and my seven years old son finding our way to the US. First, we took a flight to Paris, then we took the second flight to New York.

Chapter One

I was born in the city of Tabriz in the East Azerbaijan province of Iran. Mapped on paper with the Caspian Sea to the north and the Persian Gulf to the south, Tabriz lies near the borders of Turkey, Armenia and South Russia.

In fact, my grandfather was a businessman who traded goods from Turkey and Russia. He was a well-respected man often given the title *Mir* by others: Mir Yusuf or honored Yusuf. He was only 39 years old during World War II when a Russian bomb fell within a few yards of him in a Tabriz street. Though the bomb did not explode, his heart simply could not handle the shock. My grandmother was left a widow in her late 20s with three children to take care of, including my mother, Monier.

My grandmother's home was large, consisting of several levels for living and expansive back gardens, and was located in an affluent and international area of the city. The Russian consulate was in the neighborhood, and Russians, Armenians, Muslims and the local Jewish population frequented each other's shops, played with one another's children, and invited each other over for tea and dinner parties.

Next door to our home was a family also of affluent stock but without as prestigious a family name as my grandmother's. Given the fact that a bride moved out of the house of her birth and into her husband's home upon marriage, my Grandmother could think of no better arrangement than to ally with this neighboring family, thereby keeping her daughter only a wall's breadth away. So at the age of 17, a husband was agreed for Monier in this house next door, and the groom, my father, was 30-year-old Mehdi. The two houses were connected via an inner door, meaning neither my mother nor grandmother would need to travel outside to share household duties or visit over a cup of tea.

My grandmother lived with her other two children and several girls hired to help with domestic duties in her more old-fashioned home, with remnants of my grandfather's trading business lingering in the rooms and hallways: imposing furniture and antique Persian rugs. She'd host gatherings, mostly for women but also for mixed company on the moon patio, a raised platform above the kitchen where cooler air kept guests more comfortable on steamy afternoons.

My father's home was large enough to house two families. His brother, my uncle, as well as his wife and children had separate living quarters in the rear, while my father, the older brother, claimed the choice living areas in the front of the home. Huge trees dominated the back gardens along with water ponds and lush greenery.

My father worked for the police force in an administrative capacity, though I never saw him in uniform outside of old family photos taken before I was born. When the province's administration was shaken up by another revolution, he found it expedient to abandon any job within the city or state. This time, Russia had annexed the cat's head of Iran, declaring the area to be under the control of the communist Azerbaijan People's Government, with Tabriz as the capital city.

The government led by Jafar Pishevari, held power for a scant year, with Iran reclaiming the area in 1947. It must have been a somewhat unstable and nervous time for my family, though you would never know it from their stories. They shunned politics in general and took up the attitude of taking what came.

Looking on the bright side, my mother used to gush about the good fortunes we reaped from the brief revolution. After all, the Russian Embassy was right around the corner. Therefore, the Russians prettied up the neighborhood by paving the streets, digging new wells and burying modern pipes for the neighborhood's water system. My mother always told me that it boded well for my life that our home received its first electricity from the new Russian electrical system the day I was born on October 25.

My mother was enthroned in a bed in the largest room of the house, which contained many windows and was painted a light blue with a border of pink and blue entwining near the ceiling. Propped up on pillows and in pain, she was attended to by a midwife as well as her sister, mother, cousins, aunts and in-laws. Most of the ladies, after drifting in and out of the labor room, adjourned to an adjacent parlor for tea and gossip. Persian women, after all, will use any excuse for a party.

Being that birth was strictly ladies' business, my father and the other concerned men waited outside in the street, far enough to avoid the unpleasantness but still within shouting distance. Even so, they could not pretend that such events did not concern them. They smoked cigarettes and paced, wondering if my father's first child would be a son. Out of excitement and the generosity for which he would become legendary, my father spread the rumor that the bearer of good news — meaning the first to tell him when the baby was born and what sex it was — would receive a token of his gratitude, a large and most likely shiny token.

After a short silence and a gentle pat on the back, I was told that I cried like any newborn baby. Her braid swinging wildly as she rushed to my father, it was my mother's younger sister, still only a young lady, who pushed the other hopeful messengers aside and ran out the door. "It's a girl!" she said to my father, proud to claim the promised prize. She bragged about the small gold ring she received for years afterwards.

They wrapped me in a blanket and slid me into a traditional newborn pillow, a silk cushion with a baby-sized pocket to keep babies swaddled tight. The blanket was pink satin, of course, because of my sex. They then carried me out in the street to my father, his chest puffed with pride at bringing home a wife and now creating his first child.

"You had tiny little eyes," he told me later, "and when you opened them the sun shined into them and you squinted and closed your eyes again. We all laughed."

I later found out exactly what occurred on my birthday when two years later, on July 14th, my first sister, Mahnaz, was born. Though warmer with the heat of the season, the labor took place in the same room, in the same bed, light filtering from the windows onto my mother's straining face. Partially interested in the strange things going on with my mother and more interested in chasing my cousins around in the other, I ran back and forth between the spaces. I remember no fear for my mother despite her cries, for the family and friends attending made the occasion feel so joyful and safe. A home birth didn't happen every day, but it was definitely a regular occurrence. I think it would have been the possibility of a hospital birth that would have been frightening.

Running back and forth, I transferred the news between parties. "Grandmother says soon," I told the men loitering outside in the heat. "Grandmother is walking with her now to help things along," I told the ladies drinking tea. "Auntie says it will be a boy," I said to the midwife. "Fetch some water," she replied.

When Mahnaz came into the world, I was too young to hold her immediately but I remember exactly what she looked like: a chubby baby, with wrinkles of flesh around her legs and neck that were simultaneously plump and incredibly tiny. Her hair was dark and curly, and her skin was flushed and damp from her ordeal.

With me trailing behind, the women took the baby to the backyard and propped her up in a sitting position on a stone in the shady corner of the garden. A garden pitcher filled with warm water was gently poured over her, splashing off her head and making her close her eyes and sputter slightly. They then wrapped her in a blanket and placed her in the pocket of another pink, satin pillow to present to the world. Or rather, to show the now tidy and calm baby to the male world who had been sequestered outside.

I was two and half years old and I'm amazed I recalled my sister's birth in such detail. But such is memory: unpredictable, uncontrollable and very personal. I believe her birth is the first vivid memory of my life.

In some ways, we — especially the women — were incredibly cut off from the outside world, living as we did in a smaller, less cosmopolitan town with no television, little in the way of mass media and only a few Western influences. But on the other hand, I felt incredibly in tune with the people and things going on around me, and with the seasons of the year, thanks to the multiple traditions and ceremonies that punctuated our lives. Some rituals, of course, related to the standard rites of passage (like weddings, births and funerals) of friends and family, and some were seasonal (mostly related to food). No matter the reason for the occasion, these ceremonies would cause family, friends and neighbors to gather around a certain task or celebration, usually around my grandmother. And looking back, my memories of such times spin back to me like a colorful, buoyant and musical Hollywood film.

Colorful, for certain, are my memories of tomatoes: delivered at the peak of summer by a truck, which unloaded a mountain of the red fruit in our walled back garden. Enough tomatoes to make a preserved tomato paste for two families, mine plus grandma and my uncle's family, and enough for an entire year of cooking and eating. From the bed of the truck, workers my family hired brought baskets of fresh tomatoes, basket after basket, the round produce tumbling and shining in the sun. In this age before plastic, clean sheets of canvas had been laid out on the ground for the tomatoes to rest upon, and they eventually mounded up to cover a large portion of the incredibly large yard. In my mind's eye, it was always a sunny day and the kids would be playing, running back and forth between the legs of busy but good-humored adults.

A hose would run from the house to wash the tomatoes, and then every bowl in the house — big, small and gigantic, most locally-made ceramics — would be filled with the bright red spheres and doled out among those in the yard. To the hardy working women with their large hands and large smiles went the large bowls. My mother and grandmother and the other women brought more medium-sized bowls onto their laps. And we eager children were allotted the tiny bowls for our tiny hands, to keep us from whining to be included and also to keep us out of trouble.

Side by side, the women sat with their skirts furled around them, happy conversation and huge vats of salt between them. The soft and ripe tomatoes were crushed with the hands, kneaded and kneaded into smaller pieces, salt sprinkled over the lump mixture at intervals. Sometimes an adult would come across a baby tomato, the size of a grape or walnut, and jokingly toss it into the bowls of the children as we industriously worked away, looking to be just like the adults. Of course, by the end of the day we'd be tired and cranky and in tears due to the discomfort of so much tomato juice on our hands. The hard hands of the adults seemed able to withstand anything.

Hour after hour, finished bowls of crushed tomatoes began to line up in rows on one side of the yard. My aunt and my grandmother made lunch for the crowd of 60 or so people, perfuming the air with spices as well as the aroma of the bruised fruit mixed with salt, which always smells of summer to me. More and more rows of full bowls lined up like soldiers, spanning 30 yards and growing to four rows deep, then five and six. And when the sun began to sink in the sky, the mountain of tomatoes would finally shrink, too, showing that there was an end to the work in sight. The workers and various friends and family would drift homeward, leaving the army of tomatoes in the garden. The smooth surface of the liquid in the bowls shined in the starlight, reflecting the moon.

For the next day or two, the army of bowls soldiered on, checked on and stirred occasionally by my grandmother and monitored constantly by us kids. Curious as I was, I would lie on the grass on my stomach with my nose perched at the level of the bright red juice, and watch the tomatoes bubble, popping in the slow cooking heat of the sun. Tiny bubbles that I'd watch as if Mother Nature was speaking through them.

Once the tomatoes reached the right, saucy consistency, the party would rev up again as all the friends and family and workers returned to finish the job. One by one, the bowls would be poured into a wooden box with a screen on the bottom, filtering out the larger pieces and the skins. The thin red juice was then placed in wooden trays, the size of large round tables. The red army of juice reassembled on the patio, covering every available surface. From the aerial view provided by any of the back windows of the house, it looked like there was a whole palette of red paint laid out, just waiting for some master artist to dip his brush and create a masterpiece.

Again thin, the tomatoes sat in the sun for another three or four days, bubbling happily and thickening. My grandmother would make the rounds of the dozens of trays with a wooden spoon a few times a day, stirring and monitoring with her expert eye. Once the tomatoes met her exact specifications, the juice was poured into dozens — if not a hundred — waiting clay jars and pots. Butter was melted and poured in to fill the top half inch of the jars' necks; when it cooled and solidified, it formed a flexible but firm seal.

The memories of listening to the tomatoes pop and seeing God's paint arrayed in the garden will always remain in my memory. And for the remainder of the year, every time a dish called for tomatoes, the seal of the jar would be cracked and a scoop of the still-bright, still-fresh tomato paste was added to the pot.

In these days, after all, there was no such thing as a grocery store, where you could pick up the ingredients to complete an entire meal start to finish. There were butchers and bakers. There were spice shops and produce stands. But canned tomato paste was something strange and unknown to us. We'd never heard of such a thing, and even if we had, my traditional grandmother would never have allowed it.

I can't imagine all the wonderful memories I'd have missed if life were as simple as in the modern grocery store age, when the mystery and the celebratory qualities of food preparation disappeared.

Whatever we needed and whatever we wanted was created through one of these picturesque and fun ceremonies, events I'd look forward to watching or participating in. And the fruits of our labors lasted all year round.

Tabriz, wedged so close to Turkey and Russia, has a hefty dollop of winter in its seasonal schedule. Winter storms raged through the city streets, turned frigid by the wind coming off the mountains, and could dump 30 or 40 inches on the ground in one swoop. And because it wouldn't warm up for months at a time, the snow failed to melt, instead collecting on the ground in higher and higher mounds.

The roofs of our homes, however, provided a different challenge. Tall and spacious, most homes in Tabriz also included flat roofs. Unlike the sloping variety, moisture didn't easily flow off, but instead collected, which was especially dangerous when the snow fell. Too much snow on the roof could become very heavy, caving in onto the upper level.

That's when the men who plowed the snow came in. I affectionately referred to them as the "snowmen."

Bundled up in coats with wool mittens on their hands, they'd appear after a snowstorm as if they sprung from the ground.

"We clean the snow," they called out, singing the words to a tune of their own. With wooden paddles planted on their shoulders, they sang, "We clean the snow."

We'd hear the voices from blocks away, echoing through the city alleys.

"We clean the snow!"

Wandering their way through town, they'd appear on our street, happy groups of men and boys singing together. Their breath clouded in the frosty air and they carried the tools of their trade: a long, wooden oar-shaped paddle, not quite a shovel. They looked like a jolly group of sailors looking for their boat. They were most likely the same workers who visited these affluent neighborhoods during the summer, taking care of gardens or cleaning out the fishponds popular in backyards. But in winter, they were the legendary snowmen, transformed by snow into jolly neighborhood jokesters.

"We clean the snow!"

The women of the houses would come to their front doors as the men drew near, paying their small fee of half a toman or so. A long ladder would be angled against the house and the men climbed up like a row of ants. They'd smile or wave as I watched them from a second-story window, the only feet away but on the opposite side of the wall.

Once they arrived on the roof, they took up positions and started slinging the snow with their paddles, creating arcs of white powder flying in all directions, appearing like a dust of diamonds as the rays of sunlight shined on them. And all the while they would sing, both the song advertising their services and any number of other things: traditional tunes, Western songs from movies, whatever they all knew.

They always seemed to be in a splendid mood. Perhaps because they were happy for the extra income. Maybe because the physical exertion felt good after being cooped up during a snowstorm. I don't know. But I do remember their songs of casual joy, their joking, even snowball fights which broke out among the workers. Sometimes you could look down the length of an entire street and see snowmen on every roof, the snow falling down like splashed water. It looked like the city was cleaning house, running fingers through its hair and shaking out all the snow.

Grandmother's house held so many mysteries. Its formal but welcoming rooms were stuffed with antiques, especially items from Europe leftover from my grandfather's merchant career. There were many corners and dark cubby holes for playing hide and seek — or just hiding from the adults. There were tea parties to be had and fantasies to spin out among the cushy furniture and ornate Persian rugs.

Grandmother's house was simply a different world and she was a blessed figure. In my mind, she glowed like a holy person in a painting. She was a little chubby, but in a way that makes a woman look content rather than lazy. She had straight hair that she hennaed to a wine-colored red. In rare idle moments, she would let me play with her hair, running it through my hands and using my clumsy young fingers to braid it or fashion it into some (I'm sure) outrageous design. She wore long, shapeless dresses of different fabrics, all created with the same patterns by her favorite seamstress. She smelled of the kitchen and of flowers when I hugged her tight or rested my head on her chest when I was upset. Braless, soft and warm, her chest was the ideal place of comfort in my youth. Her hand stroking my hair and rocking me slightly back and forth, that was my safe spot, cuddled against her beating heart.

As a widow, my grandmother had survived and thrived over the years by selling the remainder of my grandfather's wares — rugs, china and other artifacts — one by one, and also through certain wealth she had from her own family. For instance, she inherited several acres of almond fields in Tabriz on land that is now the modern railroad station. In the hungry days of World War II, there were stories of my grandmother slipping almonds under the doors of those who lacked food to fend off starvation.

Peasants farmed the land throughout the year, where my father or other male members of the family would check in from time to time. I still remember going to the workers' small houses, seeing their rural ways with their animals and farm tools. It seemed very normal to me at the time that their lives were very different from my own, their hands rougher and their women dressed in long and colorful floral fabrics, sometimes using the beautiful fabrics to tie their children to their backs as the worked. I remember passing through the fields and always finding myself surprised at the joy they exuded while they worked, completely content with their lives despite their circumstances.

Middle men used to sell the almond harvest and bring my grandmother the profits. However, she also used a small portion for herself to make baklava and to eat plain as snacks. Once a year after the harvest, they would arrive. Taxis and trucks very, very rare in the city of Tabriz in my early childhood, a group of villagers would arrive on horses with lumpy bushels of the nuts hanging off the animals' hips. There would be a line of 10 or 20 horses lumbering up to the house, swinging the bushels as they walked. The men dismounted and took almonds and chopped wood for heating onto their shoulders, carrying them into the store rooms on either side of the main doorway. I'd watch from the upstairs window of one of the family's houses as the men came and went, thinking of the sweet baked goods the almonds would help create.

Because of her success in life, the good name of her family and the traditional deference shown toward elders, my grandmother was considered to be one of the most respected women in our community. There was no question of where the tomato paste would be made or who to turn to when you had a dilemma. My grandmother was sought out for advice on whether to accept a proposal of marriage, whether an expensive purchase would be a wise course or how to please a husband whose eye had begun to stray. There is no doubt in my mind that my grandmother was extremely wise and experienced in life, often giving me the best advice. Whenever things ran a different course than I expected, or I felt that life was being unfair to me, my grandmother always said, "If you have patience in your life, you can witness sour grapes turn into sweet raisins someday."

She knew a lot just being the eyes and ears of the neighborhood that others might not be aware of. Or perhaps her wisdom was innate, something pure within her heart and forged through the adversity of raising her kids alone.

My grandmother was also an excellent cook — a skill she somehow never passed on to my mother. She made the best baklava for the New Year's celebration, and she gave it to me as a sweet snack for the rest of the year. She'd make me sandwiches of feta cheese and a form of clarified butter on hungry afternoons. But she was also known for lavish meals, either for the family for a normal, weekday dinner or for a large group of friends and neighbors.

Though I enjoyed eating her food immensely and she repeatedly tried to get me into the kitchen with her for some formal lessons on how to cook, I mischievously avoided her, scurrying out of her grasp to go play in the garden, climb trees or find one of my neighborhood friends. When she did catch me by the neck of my shirt, she'd ask, "You will have a husband one day, and then what will you cook for him if you don't learn how in my kitchen?"

"A fried egg," I replied, wiggling away.

"And what will you cook when you have important family visits or company is coming to dinner."

I paused to think. "An omelet," I proclaimed.

She'd sigh and shake her head in seeming disapproval, but I could see that she was trying to suppress a smile as she let me go on my way.

Cooking wasn't the only form of female education and socialization, however. Because I was a girl and therefore tuned into the semi-private lives of the women around me, I particularly remember my grandmother's female gathering on the moon patio. I'd watch and listen in wonder, looking up to the women around me, pondering what it must be like to be so adult, so beautiful. That backyard patio was the ideal place for ladies to flock in the afternoon or early evening because it was outdoors — located on the roof of the kitchen — surrounded by the cool vegetation and trees of the gardens, and also secure from the wandering eyes of the outside world.

A Persian rug would be unfolded to make the ground comfortable. The nearby leaves of the garden, with its grape vines and fruit trees and water ponds, would be wet with a hose to cool the area. Neighbor ladies would step up to the patio, pour hot tea from the waiting samovar, munch on grapes and feta and bread, and spread gossip: who was taking a second wife and how the first was pulling her hair out, whose son was going to the most prestigious university, who was starting or expanding a new business, whose husband was making money, which engagements were good matches and bad, who was pregnant and who they suspected was permanently infertile. Such talk had constantly been in my ears since the time I was born. The musical talk of the lives of others was present in the air like the scent of incense: something you forget is surrounding you once you become accustomed.

Sometimes the ladies would go through their beauty rituals on the moon patio. As in any culture, it was often a hideous path women walked on to the road to beauty. Not only was it popular to henna the hair, there were also certain styles with eyebrows. I remember the ladies mixing a pungent herb with steaming water from the samovar into a small bowl. They then used the equivalent of a cotton swab to paint a wide and inky line across each other's eyebrows. After 30 minutes or so, they'd take turns walking down the garden and rinsing the paste off in a garden pool, leaving their eyebrows very dark and thick, which (don't ask me why) was the fashion of the time.

During such female gatherings, no one wore cover of any sort. Granted, my grandmother did wear a strip of fabric around her waist most of the time. If a man outside of her own family happened to arrive, she could untie the fabric and place it around her head as a makeshift veil, thereby hiding herself from male attention like a proper Muslim lady. However, many of the younger ladies like my mother didn't even bother with cover of any kind, inside the house or out, with males of their own family or complete strangers. They went freely into the world with their faces naked of fabric, and no one seemed to mind or raise much fuss except the older ladies, steeped in the traditional ways like old women of any generation and any country. Even the younger women, though, felt the freedom of the female-only get-togethers. They just giggled and scoffed when on one occasion my father stumbled into their midst before they'd washed off their eyebrow paste. "Why do you look like monsters?" he'd asked in horror, before the ladies shooed him away from their private party.

Of course, the moon patio wasn't just for women. Often on the hot summer nights, it would be the scene of the evening meal to avoid the stifling heat of the home's interior, warmed up with the heat of the food cooking. Or, special dinners for visiting family from out of town took place under the stars on the raised platform.

A special tablecloth would be smoothed over the short, knee-height tables surrounded by soft carpet and pillows to sit upon. Only used for special occasions, the big copper tray with the zig-zag border was brought out, piled high with steaming food from the kitchen: various meats and vegetables seeped in and sprinkled with herbs and spices. From the communal tray, we'd portion food onto our own matching copper plates and enjoy the bounty of grandmother's gourmet kitchen. Family and guests would sip strong and slightly bitter tea, which was always accompanied by something sweet like raisins or pastry, and watch the stars come out over the Tabriz sky.

Chapter Two

During the tail end of World War II, my father left the police force to follow in the path of many of the men of our social class: He went into business. He had worked for law enforcement not as an officer, but in administration. It is a function I cannot imagine my father doing, knowing him later in his career and life, when his well-kept suits always had the sheen of respectability and his reputation was of an outgoing, social and generous man who attracted the company of other people of both sexes.

His first venture into the business world — where he fit so smoothly — was in sugar rations. The supplies of food being scarce due to the war, he was the middle man who made sure that bulk supplies of sugar filtered all the way down to individuals holding out their ration tickets, hoping to sweeten their tea or baklava. Soon after, he bought a shop that sold the minor luxuries of daily life, much like a basic department store. He was always the sort to have lots of friends and associates gathered around, with a group of four or five men often meeting for laughs and tea in his shop room — the Iranian male form of social networking.

My mother, on the other hand, led a much simpler and more cloistered existence. She was educated only through the equivalent of fifth grade, enough to help her children with homework. Her one skill and passion was knitting. Alone or with a group of other ladies, her hands were constantly tangled with yarn and a growing piece of fabric that would become a sweater, a blanket, a wall hanging. She thought of herself as in competition with other women in her knitting, and she and my aunts would often hide their current projects from one another, hoping to unveil something more unique or skilled than anything the others had ever conceived. Like my grandmother, she had a young lady helping her around the house with laundry, dishes, ironing and some marketing.

My mother did a lot of work around the house, the female jobs that were simply expected to get done. This included things like planning meals, marketing, laundry, producing and mending clothing, organizing holidays and special events, and keeping tabs on the lives of others in the community through tea parties and gatherings. While it may seem that the latter was only gossip and fun, it is amazing how many business transactions, weddings, jobs and many other important deals were arranged at such get-togethers. The women were the glue that kept communities connected and vibrant. Even so, I never saw that my mother did any of this work with any joy or relish. She seemed to go through the motions because it was what was expected and she never wanted a bad remark said about her housekeeping skills. She had a no-frills professionalism about her as a mother, treating it as more of a job than a labor of love for her children.

Rather than having an education or any money-making skill, my mother's real talent was in control and manipulation. My father left the house early in the day, returned for lunch and then returned again at about eight in the evening for dinner. His natural inclination was to sweep into the house in a jolly mood, lightening the meal hours with jokes and good-hearted teasing. However, my mother, perhaps feeling isolated from the things of "real" significance to the family at the store, would pepper him with questions.

"How was the morning's business, Mehdi?" she would ask, shaking her head and telling him it needed to be better no matter what his answer was. Or, she'd needle him by saying, "Has Mrs. So-and-so, who borrowed 100 toman last week, paid you back yet?"

I don't believe her manipulation of the conversation was ever malicious, but she simply needed to be needed. She sat like a queen spider in the middle of her knitted web of yarn, talking loudly and puffing herself up to feel important. The insignificance of her other contributions to the world may have overwhelmed her otherwise.

I know that a lot of her self-doubt stemmed from her womb. After my sister and I were born, my mother gave birth to yet another girl, my youngest sister, Azar. There were no sons to give my father a male heir and no where to lay this blame except squarely at the woman's feet, which I know kept my mother up nights worrying about her worth as a wife and what father might do or say if the sonless situation continued. Under marriage law, he would have a right to divorce her for such an offense. And under social conventions, she was not yet a true woman, for a true woman needed at least one son.

Perhaps this is the reason my parents chose to raise me in such an unorthodox way in my early years. Though I cannot remember the source of their beliefs, my parents were convinced that if they shaved my head as a little girl, my hair would grow in thicker as I got older. You see, hair was a very important beauty indicator in Persian culture, especially the amount and thickness of a girl's hair. It was also a sign of youth, because women often dealt with hair thinning and loss as they aged. So, to make me more beautiful, they made me quite ugly, shaving my head down to a shiny ball. To make matters worse, my mother also slathered egg yolks over my scalp all the time, I suppose because she wanted me to have healthy hair. To cover up my bald head, my mother wrapped a chiffon scarf around my head and fashioned it with a bow on top.

On the other side of the coin, I was allowed quite a bit of freedom in those early years. As I said, they wanted a boy and, whether because of that yearning or not, my early wardrobe consisted of several pairs of brown pants, suspenders and white shirts, not skirts and dresses. This allowed me to play outside in the cul-de-sac with the boys, including some of my cousins and a few neighbors. In games of tag and running matches, I was the lone female, which was a good thing in my opinion. I didn't feel very comfortable among the pretty girls with a scarf on my head and pants on my legs.

For a time, I had a pet lamb to play with around the neighborhood, though I have no memory of where the animal came from or why it was put in my possession. With her big, dewy eyes, the lamb adored me and followed me around everywhere I went, which made her very easy to train. If I ran, she would run behind me. When I stopped, so would she, even if I didn't turn around to make sure she did. I sat the other children down in a row on the street and did performances. Raising my hands like a lion tamer, I'd lead the lamb around in circles and when I'd clap, she'd jump on cue.

A short while later, my father bought me a horse. Not a real horse, mind you, but a wooden one about the size of a pony, painted red and black, which he purchased from an Armenian toy shop. "Everyone knows the Armenians make the best toys," he said, pointing out the horse's real eyebrows and eyes whose pupils moved. Four legs tapered down into four wooden wheels. Always the big spender, my father allowed me to take the horse out into the street to play with the neighborhood kids, providing I told everyone who had been so generous with me — my dashing dad. As soon as I brought my new wooden horse out, the neighborhood boys and girls would help to booster me up onto the horse and push me around on it, hoping to ride the horse themselves. Of course, I would make sure that only those who pushed me around the fastest got a turn.

When I came of the age where I was headed off to my first year of schooling — about 6 years old — I was sitting in our family's main living area, looking down into the street. The afternoon sun was warm, making the boys in the street appear sharp and clear and fun. I pushed off from the blue-painted window to head across the cushy Persian carpets to the front door, and my mother stopped me.

"Why don't you sit?" she said, her tone affectionate and calm. There was music playing on the radio and a samovar with boiling water had just been brought to the table. She had nested onto the couch and was assembling her yarn around her. The sun pooled on the couch, making the cushions warm and drowsy.

She patted a spot next to her and I sat down. She then handed me some thick yarn. "Here you are," she said. "I will show you how to make a chain." She handed me crotchet needles and my hands awkwardly tried to follow her instructions with the yarn. After some time, I had created my first chain with the sun on my neck, my mind no longer with the boys I could still hear playing in the street.

And that was the end of my boyish freedom, the end of childhood games where my sex didn't matter. Ever after, my femaleness was an elephant in the room — it changed everything, though no one ever explained why.

The rhythm of daily life in Azerbaijan had households rising early and eating dinner late but with a long break in the middle of the afternoon for lunch and naps. Even the adults, such as my father the businessman, would leave their jobs and close their shops, returning to their homes for food and rest. Such naps weren't formal sleeping, where one changed clothes and climbed into bed. Instead, people would grab pillows and lie down in the living area on the Persian carpets or recline on sofas. If on the bed, one would just lie across the surface rather than snuggling in under the covers for the night. Even though the nap was not "formal," however, sleep was definitely expected and enforced, especially by parents for their children.

These two hours of the day were incredibly quiet, both within the house and outside in the streets of the city. But the one person who wasn't, at least that I knew of in my little world, was me. The quiet entered my ears and woke me up rather than calming me, and I was unable to close my eyes. I would lie still and stare at the ceiling, waiting for the house to begin breathing regularly, snoring lightly. Then, I would tip toe away from the house and into the garden, where there was still the noise of the world living: winds in the leaves, the calls of the birds, water trickling.

Very quietly, making very little noise other than the scuffle of my feet, I would play in the garden. Even when I was so young, it felt like stolen time, time where I was free from interference and restrictions. Especially as a girl, there were few other times for me to be completely alone and unwatched, and I felt as if I was truly myself and ruler of my world when I was alone in the garden. Those hours were exploring time, dreaming time, research time, a time for being nosy and figuring out how the world worked.

I remember being only five or six years old and meticulously learning about the lives of the ants. I crouched down with my nose in the dirt, watching them march in formation hither and thither with seeds and other goodies on their backs. I would block their path with a pool of water or a branch, only to see them find their way around the obstacle. I found it fascinating that they seemed to talk to one another, sing to one another. I laid on my stomach under the rustling of the sour cherry blossom trees and hummed to them.

On lazy summer afternoons, my grandmother had taught us girls how to make ice cream, or at least what we called ice cream. It was partially a sweet treat and partially a way of keeping us troublesome girls occupied when there was nothing else to do. She'd sit us down around a table in the kitchen or on the patio, lining up tea glasses, spoons, sugar and eggs. We'd separate the eggs and put a few yolks in a tea glass with some sugar and then beat the mixture like mad. The spoons would clank on the sides of the glass tea cups for what seemed like hours for a six-year-old little girl, which was why our grandmother loved suggesting the activity to keep us out of her hair for a spell. After much clinking and beating, the mixture would become fluffy and light like a cloud. It wasn't cold, but the light mixture was sweet on the tongue with no discernable taste of egg and I loved it.

Independent girl that I was, I used to steal into the kitchen to get the ingredients to make ice cream by myself, often times when everyone else was sleeping the afternoon away.

In our family's garden there were huge trees of white berries, beautiful and sweet white berries that popped on your tongue. I'd become very adept at climbing those trees to get at the plumpest untouched berries on the upper branches. I could climb up as high as the roof of our house, then straddle myself between two branches and kick back, reclining and resting and looking at the sky. If it wasn't nap time, I would sing to myself at the top of the tree, feeling as if I was alone in my own little world.

Often, I would grab the ingredients for ice cream before heading up the tree, cradling the spoon and tea glass under my arm or between my teeth as I climbed. Once I was done with all the stirring, I would eat the sweet treat and throw down the glass from the top of the tree. Climbing down was harder, after all, and I wasn't about to chance it with the glass. Besides, it didn't always break. OK, most of the time it did shatter, but they were inexpensive glasses and my mother and grandmother didn't seem to care for them too much.

Whenever my mother would see me so far up in the trees of our garden, she'd clutch her chest and yell, "Maryam! Come down right now or you are going to fall down on your head." She'd shake her fist, looking small as an ant down on the ground. "Do you hear me?" She'd shout. "Maryam!"

I'd wave my hand at her and come down in my own good time, never once falling on my head as she predicted. Eventually, she would still yell but the threat of falling seemed like a remote possibility to both of us and her threats lost their impact. I'd sit up there happily for hours, eating and thinking and looking at the sky, imagining all the possibilities of the world and what place I might have in it.

I wasn't the only one who saw the spot's appeal — I also had a tree friend, a little red bird that was attracted to the white berries of the tree. He was very small, what I assumed to be a baby, with a red chest and beautiful grayish green feathers which shined in the sun like some rare metal. He must have had a nest nearby because he appeared so regularly, it was as if we had a standing appointment. He'd hop out of the green leaves fluttering in the wind, chirp prettily and peck at the berries with that quick, sharp manner of all bird's movements when they're not flying. Quick, sharp hops around and around the tree, sometimes a few feet away and sometimes only inches.

As we grew more and more used to one another, I rather thought he was singing solely to me, trying to have a little conversation, something like, "Beautiful weather up here today, don't you think?" Little by little, I started singing back to him, whatever tune or made-up melody popped into my mind. My singing didn't frighten him. Sometimes, I'd even throw berries for him to catch, although I didn't have the nerve to see if he'd eat them directly out of my hand. He might pause in his berry collecting to look at me with his head cocked, but he didn't seem to mind, so we continued the strange conversation until he moved on again.

It was not my intent to tame the little bird, but I think I may have done so unintentionally over time. We grew used to each other's presence and at one point, I felt as if my little friend was trying to teach me how to fly. He would stand next to me and flap his wings continuously, as if he was waiting for me to take flight with him. So, during those warm summer afternoons in Tabriz, on top of the berry tree, I mocked my little red friend as I spread my arms, moving them up and down, showing him that I too could fly. So, whenever I saw him spread his wings, I imagined myself spreading my own wings and flying with him.

It was no wonder that I didn't want to come down from the tree when my mother called, even if she was frantic with worry. I'd created the secret and somewhat magical place that every child dreams of, and I had a secret friend to keep me company, someone I imagined liked me as much as I liked him. After the overwhelming closeness of our house, where I seemed to have little privacy, the tree was my house in the clouds.

Unlike my mother, who eventually started sighing and shaking her head when she saw me perched up in the berry tree, her admonishments growing more halfhearted, my grandmother thought my tree climbing was much more alarming, perhaps because it was usually her tea glasses that wound up fractured on the ground. Also, she was an extremely protective woman and I think an injury to her first grandchild would have broken her heart. She decided that only a crazy girl would spend so much time with her head in the clouds, singing at the top of her lungs to no one in particular and throwing glasses to the earth as if she had no cares in the world. And being a very practical woman, she thought the only thing to do with a potentially crazy person was take her to the doctor and have her mind put right.

We walked into downtown Tabriz near the city hall to a doctor recommended by a friend of my aunt's husband, where we sat in a waiting room. The doctor's offices were adjacent to his home and the whole environment was very peaceful and domestic. In fact, when we went in to see the doctor, I could see his home and its garden through the window behind his desk, where a little boy that was probably the doctor's son played by himself in the sunshine. Like most doctors and professionals we knew, he had been educated abroad, getting his medical training in Germany.

My grandmother and I sat in two chairs facing his broad, wood desk, while he sat behind in a big leather chair. He knew my grandmother socially and by reputation, and he began the appointment by asking after our family, my mother, her brother, my father.

Addressing her with a title of utmost respect, he then got down to business, saying, "And what brings you here today?"

"I am here about my granddaughter," she replied in a serious tone, her hands folded neatly in her lap.

The doctor's eyes leaped over to me in my chair, a girl of six or seven years old at the time. He nodded and said, "What seems to be the problem?"

"I think she's crazy," said my grandmother, looking at me with a mixture of worry and unconditional love. "You see, any time of the day on most days, she climbs into the trees for hours, where she sings for the whole neighborhood to hear and she makes ice cream for herself. Then she throws down her ice cream cup like its nothing, and comes down whenever she feels like it, despite the fear that she will fall and break her head." She shook her head slowly as if envisioning my injuries in her mind. "We do not know where this compulsion comes from to be up in the trees, and I am afraid for her mind."

The doctor was silent for a moment, looking us over. He leaned back in his chair with his hands pressed together near his beard, his salt and pepper hair curling over his forehead and his kind eyes.

He directed his gaze at me. "Why do you do this?" he asked. Both the adults in the room looked to me expectantly.

I shrugged. "I get bored," I said. They continued to look at me, wanting more of a reason. The doctor played with his pen, flicking it between his fingers. I added, "And I like ice cream."

The doctor leaned forward to put his elbows on his desk, an authoritative moment that seemed to mean he had an answer for us. After all, this man was worldly and had a foreign education and experiences, things that raised him in our esteem. He knew about televisions and popular music and movies and the modern world, things that had sidestepped our hidden corner of the continent.

He looked pointedly at my grandmother and, still with the utmost respect, said to her, "You know what? I think it is you, madam, that might be crazy." He smiled at me and winked.

My grandmother's jaw dropped open in shock, and she made a few noises that were almost words, but didn't quite cohere. "But... I... but you don't... why..."

He continued smiling and spoke just in my direction. "You should try not to worry the women who love you and take care of you, you know?" I nodded. "And do try not to break so much glass, yes?" I nodded again.

"Now," he said, "what do you think we should give you as a remedy for this illness, Maryam?"

Rather than thinking of painful shots or disgusting medicine, it seemed as if he was offering me a present and I began to think about what kind of present a doctor would be able to give. In my head, I tried to think back to other things I had heard people say about doctors. I remembered a friend of mine in the neighborhood who was much older than me, a teenager, who had a big orange tablet she said was very good for her. It came in a tube which one opened and stirred into water, and it created a bubbling and sweet drink. I couldn't read except to see the letter S on the tube's side, and the girl explained that it was Sandoz Vitamin C. In a world where beverages were usually either tea or water and soda was unheard of, I coveted her bright orange drink and asked the doctor if I might have some Sandoz Vitamin C drink.

He laughed and agreed, giving me a prescription for the tablet and shooing us off home. My grandmother shook her head and mumbled to herself most of the way back. She kept reminding me that the doctor may not have said I was crazy, but he did say that I was to be very, very careful. And if the doctor said it, she thought, it would mean more than when she or my mother lectured me.

Of course, I continued to climb the trees, and my mother and even my grandmother eventually sighed and gave up on me.

It was my uncle, my Javad, who was finally able to succeed where others had failed, who brought my head out of the clouds as well as my body out of that tree. Javad, my mother's younger brother by five or six years, was unmarried and was the spoiled prince of the family, the boy child that the family revolved around. His ego was enhanced by his position at an oil company, a position that was notoriously well paid and respectable in our oil-rich country. Javad was a shadowy figure in my childhood: always present because he lived next door with my grandmother, but also always unexpected. Tall and imposing, he had sharp eyes and a smile that often looked more like a snarl than a sign of happiness. One minute he could be climbing up a tree like a jaguar at a family get together, the next he would be yelling at one of the kids because of the slightest, accidental disrespect. On the one hand, his large and powerful hands could be violent. I knew that personally. But on the other hand, he was also the careful caretaker of birds — mostly parakeets and canaries— which he bred, raising and gave away as lovely living presents to people he knew.

Raising birds was a popular hobby in Iran. In my Javad's case, there were two unoccupied and unneeded rooms on my grandmother's side of the two-house complex and she allowed him to take them over for his hobby. The walls and the floors were bare and unfinished, but he added all sorts of greenery and branches and shelves for the birds to perch on and covered the open windows with netting. The birds could fly about the room in perfect freedom but were unable to escape. Javad did keep a row of cages along one wall but used them solely for breeding.

I much preferred my treetop hideaway and my little red friend, who visited me in friendship and in freedom, both of us dreaming the afternoon away among the leaves.

One such afternoon, I came home from school and immediately walked through the house to the back garden, flinging aside my school things along the way. I approached the tree and climbed, a now very familiar action that I was quite good at. Straddling the large branch that I found the most comfortable, I positioned my back against the trunk and kicked up my feet, balancing easily, and let the breeze caress my face. After a few minutes, I still hadn't seen my friend. Nor had I heard him, which was usually possible even if he didn't stop by to say hello in the white berry tree. I carefully looked around, scanning all the trees in the garden for movement and trying to listen carefully for his song.

"Are you looking for your bird, the little red one?" I heard a voice from down on the ground call up to me.

Javad stood under the canopy of the berry tree shading his eyes with one hand, seeming like a large man even from this distance above. Like the rest of the family, he knew that he could often find me in this spot, but I had no idea how he knew about the bird or its absence.

"How did you know that?" I called down to him, brushing my hair behind my ear.

"Come down and I'll tell you," he replied, taking a few steps away to allow me to do so.

I stared at him a moment, thinking, before I grabbed the tree and made my way down. I jumped when there were only two feet left to go and then smoothed my skirt and my hair. I looked at him, waiting for an explanation, but it became clear that he was waiting for me to speak.

"What is it, Javad?" I asked. "How do you know about the bird that I watch in the tree?"

He didn't answer, but instead took one hand from where it hung at his side. I hadn't noticed that his hand bulged as if he was holding something. He brought the closed fist in front of him and my stomach started crowding up my throat in fear, realizing that something was going on. As his fingers began to bloom, I saw the shape of my tiny bird friend, easily dwarfed in my uncle's large hand. The bird's head was pulled back at a strained angle, its beak open and its red chest rising and falling as if he was having trouble drawing breath.

A strangled sound escaped my throat and I instinctively reached toward his hand, the frail and scared arm of an elementary-school girl, still in her school clothes. He quickly closed his fingers and returned his arm to his side, then turned on his heel and headed toward the house.

"What are you doing?" I weakly shrieked, unable to control my voice but also unable to raise the volume of my voice to this man I feared. "No, give him to me. Give him here!"

When I caught up, he started to hold the hand above his head, like a kid playing the keep away game, a small but stern smile on his face. I was too scared to hit him or pull his jacket, but I continued tailing him, pleading and begging, as he went into our house and then through the connecting hallway into my grandmother's.

"Let him go, let him go, let him go," I begged. He was silent, allowing me to tag along.

We eventually came to Javad's bird room, where he carefully opened the door so none of his canaries escaped and closed it quickly behind me.

"Now Maryam," he said, the hand without the bird held up in front of me like a stop sign, keeping me three feet away. I sobbed and blubbered, "No, no" repeatedly. The sight of the bird and the feeling that something horrible was going to happen made me lose my words. "Maryam, calm down. Maryam!" He gestured with his hand to stop one more time and I obeyed, showing him, I would stay where I was.

He walked to a table and picked up an evil-looking pair of curved scissors, which I knew he used to clip the birds' wings. I moaned and he looked at me firmly. He grabbed the small red bird between his hands with a practiced gesture, spreading one of the wings with his large, square fingers. For such a small bird, I was amazed at the size of the wingspan and frightened at the delicacy of the bird's tiny bones and fragile feathers. The scissors came nearer and I could not bear to close my eyes, but also didn't want to watch, but I had no choice. Javad maneuvered the clippers into place and then squeezed on the grips with a firm gesture. There was a crunching noise and the bird, who had been trying to chirp in alarm but had been held too tight, shrieked in alarm, its beak thrashing around in Javad's fist.

The clipped wing started to bleed.

"Damn it," said Javad, but he wasn't upset, only miffed in the way of a man who drops a coin and must bend to retrieve it.

The blood dripped in a regular rhythm to the floor, where it had already created a pool the size of my young fist. I screamed. I saw that blood and the thrashing bird — the bird I had fantasized had known and loved me — and I thought about how tiny he was. How little blood he probably had in him in the first place, and here it was dripping away, his beautiful aerodynamic wing crushed with the squeeze of my uncle's hand.

I couldn't bear to see anymore and I raced out of the room, flinging the door open and not thinking of the birds who could escape. Tears streamed down my face and I quickly ran into my grandmother, who had heard some commotion. I flew into her arms and buried my face in her chest, sobbing deeply.

"What happened, honey?" she asked in a worried tone. Her arms went around me automatically, then she reached for my shoulders and pushed away trying to see my face. I shook my head against her chest, resisting the force. All I could begin to say through my tears for my secret friend was, "Javad... he... Javad."

"What did he do?" she asked urgently. "What did he do to you?"

"He's... he's killing my bird," I finally said. "And it couldn't bleed and he cut the wing and there was blood..."

"Shhh. Calm, child. It will be OK," she whispered into my hair, kissing the top of my head. She sat down and pulled me into her lap, rocking me until my shoulders stopped shaking.

That night I dreamed of a bird in a jungle, a tangle of greenery and a jumble of noises made by strange animals. The bird had a red chest and metallic greenish-grey feathers, and he hopped along the ground pecking here and there. But he was looking over his shoulder, always jerking around to look behind, as if he was being followed. But it wasn't a he: I somehow knew the lonely, clipped winged bird was me, without my other half and I could no longer fly.

I was never told for certain, but I know that my friend died, whether of his wound from this botched wing clipping or because Javad did away with him some other way. There would have been no way to return him to the outdoors, his wing in that condition, but I also didn't see his familiar face or shape when I poked my nose in the bird room the next day. After a quick peek with my heart thumping out of my chest and tears about to return, I never went back to that bird room again. And outside a few isolated times — when I thought I could find comfort but only found fear — Javad broke me of my habit of escaping up the white berry tree.

I don't know if that was his goal.

I don't know what he planned to do with the bird in the first place.

For a long time after that incident, though no one else ever mentioned it, every time I looked at Javad and thought about the bird sticking his tongue out of his strangled beak, I rubbed my own arm, the right one, the right wing being the one that was stretched out to be cut.

Chapter Three

After Azar was born, the world began to look at my father differently. A few years earlier, he had been a young married man who had no problems getting his wife pregnant with children and growing his young family. But after three births where the children were shown to the neighborhood on their pink satin pillows, they began to shake their heads and sigh, their hearts pulling sadly for him. It was a faltering of hope, really, that the creation of sons would be possible in the marriage. The possibility of such a barren and sad future made pity flow in gossip channels around our area of the city.

Most of this sighing and hand wringing happened behind my father's back and hidden in the world of women. It was his older sister, Hajar, who one day came to my father's shop — where he was sure to be away from my mother — and said, "Mehdi, I feel sorry for you."

He stopped in what he was doing around the shop in confusion. "Why?" he asked. He was a humorous and mostly content man, who attempted to make the best of whatever life gave him. Nothing seemed incredibly out of place to him.

"You have no sons, Mehdi," she explained. This was no news to him, of course, and he waited to see what the crushing bad news was going to be. "And I don't think you will ever have any from Monier," she continued.

This, on the other hand, was something my father had not considered, or if he had thought on it, had not believed. And coming from the mouth of his sister, it was as if the inability of my mother to beget sons was now a proven fact, or at least a likely hypothesis. Though he had not seriously thought of doing anything about his sonless marriage before, it now seemed imperative that he do something — anything — right away.

"She is getting older, Mehdi, and she has had three female pregnancies now. Three!" Hajar said. "You need to think about taking a second wife, a woman who has proven her ability to sire a male child."

Though the ability to take a second wife was lawful in Iran — Islam allowed up to four, actually — it was not necessarily the norm. I don't know if my father had ever considered it before his sister inserted the notion like a seed into his mind. But once in that fertile and impetuous ground, the idea sprouted quickly into action.

However, the course of his action was due largely to Hajar's suggestions, too. Behind my mother's back, she invited my father over to her house to meet a woman she thought would make an excellent second wife: a young widow with two sons who came from a respected and decently wealthy family, but had little money of her own and was searching for another man to protect her. She was pretty though not beautiful, her name was Aziz and she was actually a few years OLDER than my mother.

With Hajar as a witness, my father signed a contract with Aziz that specified she would be his wife on a trial basis for the period of one year. If within that time she could become pregnant and eventually give birth to a son, the marriage would become permanent. If not, the marriage would be dissolved.

In order to seal the deal and make the marriage official, my father and Aziz had their picture taken in a professional studio in town. He was dressed sharply as usual with an American-style suit, his hat at an angle and a silk handkerchief in his pocket. He had on one of my mother's beautifully knitted vest. Next to him was Aziz in a 1950s-style, velvet dress and matching handbag, very thick lipstick and her head leaning on his shoulder with a knowing smile.

The only thing left was to make the arrangements of where she would live and how he would support her, and father was in the process of making ready the house in back of his own for Aziz and her sons. At that point, my father was doing very well in his business and had purchased a few more stores and properties, so he could afford the extra expense of a second wife. In fact, he'd recently added onto the second level of our own house, creating some large, beautiful rooms with expansive views of the nearby mountains.

My father did not tell my mother he was considering a second marriage or that he had gone through with it, though I have no idea when and how he was planning to. Lord knows, he must have been aware there was going to be a lot of drama when she found out and perhaps, he was trying to avoid it for as long as possible.

Because of his timidity and attempt to keep it a secret until the last moment, it was a non-family member who broke the news to my mother, someone who had gotten hold of the picture of my father and Aziz together and given a copy to my mother. There he was — in her vest, no less — with another woman's head on his shoulder, the shoulder that belonged only to my mother. And our house erupted into tears, where it stayed for many, many months.

My mother had always believed that Hajar was a clever and manipulative woman, which is just to say that Hajar was adept at influencing my father, sometimes better than my mother was able to. But I don't know what my aunt's motives were. Perhaps Hajar had introduced my father to the idea of the marriage in the first place to help this woman — a friend of hers. Or perhaps she saw two people who could solve each other's mutual problems and thought she could do some good in the world. Either way, Hajar worked against my mother in my father's heart, an unforgivable sin against my mother.

There was crying all the time in our house after the second marriage had taken place. My mother was often to be seen on the sofa with her head buried in a pillow, my grandmother sitting beside her and stroking her back. She was a woman who knew she had very little in this world to recommend her — no education, no training, no financial support— and would be lost if my father decided to divorce her. So on this one side, she had a feeling of low self-worth and wanted desperately to please him and endear herself to him more than the second wife could.

On the other hand, she was also incredibly mad at him for proving that he was the one with the power in the family, despite all her attempts at manipulation and control, which usually kept her feeling in the loop. He could do as he pleased, and she could do nothing about it. With all these emotions boiling around inside of her, she alternately wept and screamed, sometimes angrily weeping to combine both at the same time.

"Where will I go?" she asked the walls, God or the universe. "What will I do? I have three daughters, and what will I do?"

I was only a little girl of about seven years old, and when my mother cried, I would cry, too. Sitting there in our parlor, her face was buried in one pillow and mine was in my hands, both of our shoulders heaving up and down with the injustice of the situation. She raised her head.

"Why are you crying?" she asked me, her own eyes red and puffy.

I tried to open my mouth but gagged on my tears. She reached for me and placed an arm around my shoulders.

"Don't worry," she said. "If I get divorced, I will take you with me."

I sobbed harder then, wondering what would happen to my sisters if such truly became the case. Somehow, I knew she'd only meant me alone, and that made me think that I didn't want to go with her after all. Repeating the words of my mother in a different context, I thought to myself, "Where will I go? What will I do?"

Around this time, a lot of friends and neighbors came around our house to call on my mother. Many wanted to support and commiserate with her, others wanted to know more about the juiciest bit of gossip circulating at the time, and most wanted to do a bit of both. One such visitor was a friend of mine from down the street and her mother, who was a very large woman. She was both tall and wide, with a mouth that could intimidate anyone but that also spoke the truth, wisely and loudly.

The mothers sat on silky couches in the newer section of the house, where the brightness of the sun was beginning to fade into evening.

From a bag she had brought with her, my friend's mother brought out a small bottle of make up to show my mother, some of the first Elizabeth Arden foundation that had ever come into the country of Iran. They both took a small amount of the expensive cream (the woman claimed it was 60 toman) and rubbed it into their faces.

"I can't believe it. How beautiful," my mother remarked. The smear of make up was very pale, far too white for her skin tone, and that was just the way she liked it.

"I cannot believe it either," the other woman replied. Before the introduction of such American products, women used a fine powder they shook together with a liquid for make up, and it was not as smooth or creamy as this new foundation.

"Let me put a little more on," my mother said. "Where on earth did you buy this?"

"I just love it. And my husband paid so much!" the lady said. In a normal situation among women, the expected reply to a remark about the generosity of husbands was to congratulate the woman on her husband's action and then to scheme about how the other woman could convince her man to do the same for her. But my mother was in no shape to respond in the expected fashion. Instead, my mother burst into tears, causing the pale make up to smear on the third of her face she had applied it on.

"Why are you crying, Monier?" my friend's mother asked.

My mother looked out the window at the setting sun, a window that looked down on the walkway beside our home. She sniffed.

"Every evening when he goes to visit that woman, he comes and he passes under the window right here," she said. Both women leaned further out to take in the scene of the crime, a narrow alleyway that led straight as an arrow to Aziz's house. "And he uses so much cologne that I can smell him all the way up here." She went on to explain that he had been taking care of himself better and dressing up very nicely lately, nicer than he ever had for her benefit.

The big woman shook her head and clicked her tongue. She called my father an evil name and asked, "You know what you do next time that man passes under this window?"

"What?"

"You boil a big pan of water and you pour it down on his head. That's what you do. And then he won't look or smell so nice for that second-place woman."

My mother laughed and the woman laughed, even we girls tittered a little bit because we naturally took sides with our mothers. But then my mother's laughter turned back to tears.

One evening during the beginning of this second marriage, my father was getting ready to visit Aziz and came through the family room to say goodbye to his daughters. He was dressed to the nines in a sharp suit and smelling of sweet cologne. During that time, he was spending one night with my mother and then one night with Aziz, rotating the two as if they were articles of clothing in his closet. Though the situation was not ideal for either lady, neither would they deny him when it was their night to have the man all to themselves. Those with no power are bound to be ingratiating.

The lights in the room were very dim, I remember, and my two sisters were sleeping on the couch. I was playing on the floor near the front door and my mother was ensconced in her usual place on the couch. I also remember that my father had his winter coat on, a shiny, silk white scarf around his neck, and I thought he looked very handsome.

There were some quiet words exchanged between my mother and father, and then some very loud words. I wasn't paying too much attention, as kids tend to do when their parents are upset. My father became very, very angry. He turned to walk to the front door and I was sprawled on the floor, blocking his way. So he picked me up under the armpits and threw me across the room at my mother, hardly glancing back to see where I landed before slamming the door behind him.

I was a very small girl, only about seven years old, and he threw me with enough strength to propel my body all the way across the room and onto the sofa, where I landed with an arch in my back. I immediately started crying. My grandmother was there and grabbed me to her chest, feeling all over my body for broken bones and bruises. Luckily, the more than 10-foot journey across the room had only sprained my back and caused a broken blood vessel in my eye.

The next day, my grandmother gathered me up and took me to my father's place of business. She stood in front of him with all the confidence of a queen, holding firmly to my hand. I didn't want to look up at him, focusing instead on where my shoes met the ground, so grandmother had to reach down and pull my chin up, showing him the pink splotches of blood in my eye.

"You see what you did to your daughter?" she asked. "You see?"

I didn't see his response because I was still too afraid to look up.

"You will give me some money now so I can take this child to the doctor and fix this. You understand me?" my grandmother continued.

My father said nothing but touched me lightly on the head and handed some money to my grandmother. I returned home later with some specialty eye drops and had no permanent damage from the incident.

Not all of my father's family was supportive in his choice to take on a second bride. In fact, battle lines were drawn with my father and his sister Hajar on one side and my mother and my father's younger sister on the other side. This second sister visited my mother often.

"Don't worry," she said to her on many occasions. This paternal aunt was married to a much older man, a teacher who was much respected in the community and thought he could help the marriage dissolve once the year trial period was over. "Just one year," she said. "I will make sure that after this one difficult year, this second wife will fade away. She will disappear and it will be as if she never existed."

My mother would sniff, half in sadness and half in hope that my aunt was correct as the other women patted my mother's hand.

"Besides," my aunt continued, "do you really think you can be supplanted by that woman? A widow?" She sipped her tea. "You know, I heard that her father, though wealthy and respected, wore cheap knitted socks?"

"No!" my mother replied and they laughed. Cheap, hand-knitted socks, they repeated, and laughed over the thought of such a tight-fisted father. Men, after all, were prized for having an open hand, being generous to a fault and — most importantly — showering their women with gifts of approval, of status.

On the other side of the line of loyalty, my aunt Hajar was on speaking terms only with my father. The other women, at least the ones who frequented our living room, wouldn't give her the time of day and avoided her presence at all costs. Being a woman in my mother's house, my mouth was also sealed against her. But I loved my father. I simply couldn't stop loving him on a dime, and tried to balance my parents' agendas as best I could.

One day, I went to visit my father's store, where he was in the process of building an addition. There were workmen and dust and banging tools everywhere.

"Would you like to see the new shop?" he asked me.

I nodded and walked through a doorway into the construction zone. He followed behind me with his hand on my shoulder.

"I have a surprise for you," he added.

Through the dust, I began looking anxiously for a toy or a doll, which were the best surprises my young mind could conceive of. Instead, I saw the shape of a woman — my aunt Hajar. She was sitting on a box amidst the chaos and, with his hand, my father led me to stand at her feet.

"Maryam," my father scolded. "Don't you want to say hello to your aunt?"

I scuffed my feet and thought of my mother, of the bad things that had been heaped in my mind about this aunt: traitor, creator of tragedy, schemer, and manipulator.

I shrugged, thinking, "Who cares about her anymore?"

My father's hand rose and slapped the back of my neck with enough force to send me sprawling face first in Hajar's chest, who sat silently on her box as if it was a throne. My mouth had opened in shock and I began to cry from the stinging pain.

"I'm sorry, Hajar, for her disrespect," I heard my father say above me. Remaining on my aunt's chest, she put her arm around me and began to comfort me, attempting to make the pain subside. As I remained in her arms, I was shocked at my weakness. I wanted to be strong for my mother, but instead, I was crying over my enemy's shoulder and taking comfort from the woman who was ruining my mother's life.

We children, I learned, were small battles to be won or lost by either side in this bigger war, forts to be conquered. Disrespect or disloyalty meant loss of face to my father. Though my mouth was still full of dust, I knew my father meant only to teach me where my obedience should lie. Like slapping a puppy on the nose with a rolled up newspaper, he was training me in the way of the world: Obey your father, despite your personal convictions.

He had less violent ways of wooing me, the oldest and most rebellious child, to his side, too. Once, he attempted reconciliation through one of my friends, a girl two or three years older than me from a Russian family down our street. Her name was Lulu and the freckles on her face were so numerous as to almost connect, and she was usually smiling, fun and excitable.

"I have a surprise for you," she told me one morning.

"What?" I asked her, my heart beating fast at the thought of something special just for me.

"You have to come to my house this afternoon."

"Why?"

"Well," she said. She looked around to make sure no one could overhear. "I'm not supposed to tell you too much, but I can say that your father set up a surprise, kind of a party, and it's just for you."

A party! At the age of seven, I wasn't quite sure about the date of my birthday, but I'd heard about surprise birthday parties. My mind spun with ideas of cake and other sweet goodies, music and friends. And I remembered standing with my father in the street, looking through a shop window at a beautiful doll with a lacy dress and lifelike eyes. He'd winked at me and said that perhaps that doll was meant for a good girl on a special occasion. I went home and dressed in my best outfit for the occasion, thinking about what it would feel like to hold such a lovely doll and how I would show her off and play with her.

That afternoon, Lulu ushered me past the door of her house into a room where a table had been set with tea and sweet goodies. My eyes took a moment to adjust to the indoor light and to recognize the children set around the table who greeted me. Once I saw them, it was one of the biggest shocks of my young life. There sat the two boy children of my father's second wife, Aziz. They were slightly older than me and were scrubbed into their best clothes for the occasion. Their hair was fair, almost blond, and they were good-looking boys, but their very presence signified evil to me. With all the bad thoughts that had been fed into my mind, it seemed that simply being near them betrayed my mother.

I turned to run back out the front door, but Lulu was behind me. Apparently, she had been prepared by my father that I was not going to like some of the guests at my party.

"They are just friends," she said, grabbing my hand and pulling me back. "They are friends here to enjoy your party."

She was older than me and strong, but I fought against her. Eventually, I had two hands clasped around the door frame and she was tugging me back toward the table with all her strength.

"No, Maryam," she scolded. "You have to come. Your father says you have to come." My hands gave way and she took hold of my shoulders, guiding me towards the table and forcing me to sit.

Beaten, I remained at the table but was silent and still. We all sat around the food, eating little and talking even less. We hated one another impersonally, hated one another for the adult we each represented. I came home in my pretty clothes disappointed and without a doll. Ashamed to have been tricked by my father in such a way, I quickly changed my clothes and attitude, afraid my mother might find out where I had been, why and who with. She, too, would have been angry at what she considered a public betrayal, a battle played out with children that my father had won.

There were power plays and games amongst the adults, too, and some of them were even light hearted, at least in retrospect. In Iran at that time, much was still made of magic. There were fortune tellers that would relate your future for a small fee, and such women of the dark arts would also offer spells and talismans. Most of their customers were women and, like women of any time and place, these females usually asked for help in snaring and keeping men or competing with each other. Most of the magic required the lighting of candles or the use of hair and other personal items.

Around the same time, one of the most notable "spells" of the bickering wives took place. I had been out in the neighborhood, coming home from school, and it was a very hot after noon. I had a sugar plum in my mouth, which was sticky and sweet but was doing nothing to relieve the heat. So I just let it hang in my hand, waiting to throw it out once I got home.

At our front door, however, no one answered my repeated knocks. The tall, red door stood quiet and unmoving, leaving me out in the beating midday sun. My mother must have been out, and my uncle's wife was out of hearing in the furthest quarters of the house, so I knew I had no choice but to continue banging and hope someone would eventually hear.

I tapped four or five times and then leaned against the door. Then tapped again and waited. After a few minutes, the sugar plum in my hand was getting unbearably sticky and I was about to throw it to the ground. Then, I saw the thick layer of dust covering the red door. I pressed the sugar plum, which was moist, against the wood and the candied fruit left a damp line in the dirt, almost like paint.

In between attempts to knock, I continued rubbing the sugar plum on the door, making circles and spirals and triangles and other shapes. By the time my sister came to the door after a particularly loud knock, the design covered the door from left to right and as far up as I could reach.

"What's wrong with you, knocking so hard?" she asked.

I tossed the sugar plum aside and slapped my sticky hands together. "Nothing," I said. "It's just hot and no one would come."

"Well come on, come on," she replied, motioning me inside.

I went out to play later in the day, forgetting all about my sugar plum. But when I came home from school they next day, I saw a large crowd gathered in front of my family's dirty, red front door. My uncle's wife had a bucket and a sponge and was scrubbing away at the tall wood, a stern expression on her face. Others in the crowd were talking about a strange charm.

"Like nothing I've ever seen before," I heard one woman say.

"It must be very bad magic," said another.

My grandmother, sisters and mother were huddled near the door and I heard the name Aziz and saw their heads shaking in anger.

"There is nothing for you to do but find a way to get that second wife," my grandmother said. I crept up to join the group of disapproving women, saying nothing and rather scared of my own role in this scene.

Meanwhile, my uncle's wife finished cleaning the door, which was redder and more sparkling than it had been since I could remember. But all the ladies knew the spell was not yet broken.

In Persian culture, only the urine of a little boy can cleanse away such an evil charm. Why a boy's urine? I don't know. Perhaps it has something to do with the innocence and hope embodied in male children. My uncle's wife grabbed her 10-year-old son, my cousin, by the shoulder and led him to the front of the door. The crowd of mostly women parted to create a small semicircle for him to stand in.

"You are going to have to pee on the door," she told him. He stood motionless, unsure if he had heard her strange request correctly.

She knocked him on the head. "You are going to have to pee on your uncle's door, do you hear me?"

He nodded and looked over his shoulder at the crowd behind him, his face as red as the wood he needed to aim for.

"What are you waiting for?" his mother demanded. "If you do not pee on this door, whatever bad charm was written here will come true. Your uncle, whose house we live in, could become poor and bankrupt. And the spell will be forever!" She knocked him on the head again.

He closed his eyes, scrunching his forehead in concentration. It took one more chorus of "Bankrupt, do you hear me?" from his mother before he was able to produce a small stream of urine that splashed on the door and into the dust at his feet.

The look of fear on my cousin's face mimicked my own, and I was unable to appreciate the humor of the situation because my own heart was equally scared. I saw a small bit of plum on the ground and quickly kicked it out of the way, down the alley. I promised myself that I would never tell anyone about my accidental magic.

The year of the second wife wore on, and my mother's constant supporter was my father's younger sister. They would sit and knit, and I remember her listening patiently to my mother's complaints and worries.

"The time is almost over," she repeated. "It is flowing even as we speak. She will soon float away with the wind. You'll see."

And so they whiled away the days and months.

Before the end of the contract, my mother became pregnant and my father was overjoyed. His visits to Aziz continued regularly, but it was obvious that his head and his heart remained back at home with my mother, me and my sisters.

When the appointed time came to dissolve the second marriage's contract, he signed on the dotted line with no hesitation and, as far as I am aware, he never saw the other woman again. Instead, the drama of our lives subsided and my father reverted to the kind and generous man I'd always known. We children sighed with relief, no longer torn asunder and pulled between parents, and we were excited to watch our mother's stomach grow.

The birth scene repeated itself nine months later, but this time my mother was laid out in a bed on the second floor of our home, in the new addition with a view of the mountains. The women gathered in the home, drinking tea and offering encouragement, while the men congregated outside. The atmosphere was joyful, and everyone seemed sure that this child would be a boy.

Sure enough, the baby was brought forth into the street on a blue pillow. The men erupted in cheers and my father raised his fist into the air with joy. I remember looking down from one of the windows at his happy face and all the men patting him on the back in congratulations.

A short while later, after the baby had been bathed and my mother tidied up, my father visited the birthing room. My mother was still lying on the bed, which had a velvet cover with a design of flowers and tassels my father had bought from Europe. Her head was propped up on pillows and she held the baby, who they named Reza, in her arms. With his face glowing with happiness and pride, my father sat next to my mother. He kissed her forehead and brought a diamond necklace out of his pocket which he fastened around her neck. The gold chain supported the sparkling stone, as large as a coin, between the curves of her collar bone. He then kissed her forehead again, along with the forehead of the baby.

Two years later, my mother brought my second brother, Ali Reza, into the world. My father fastened a matching diamond bracelet, thick as one of my fingers, around her right wrist.

Chapter Four

It was taken for granted that the boys received different treatment from the girl's in our family's house. From his birth, everything was ordered new for Reza. He had a blue stroller that my father imported from England whose tassels would swing when my mother walked him around the neighborhood. Later, Reza and Ali Reza would get first selection of the platter during family dinner and were showered in bicycles and boy's toys.

Honestly, though, none of us girls minded their preferential treatment in the least. We were all in love with Reza from the day he was born. He was a handsome miracle of olive-colored skin and deep, dewy eyes, thick hair hanging over his forehead. Then Ali Reza was born a fragile boy, sick in his infancy and in need of constant care. We all took turns watching over him, thanking God for every breath in his tiny lungs, where his thin ribs would rise up and down. The age difference between the boys and the girls also ensured that we older siblings watched out for our brothers, rather than seeing ourselves in competition with them. There was never a question of who received the thickest, juiciest pieces of kabob — we all rushed to feed, bathe, pamper, pet and otherwise spoil the family's miracle boys.

Once Aziz was banished from our minds and the boys lit up our lives, everyday routine returned to how it was before the second marriage. My sisters and I went to school, my mother knit, my grandmother entertained the neighborhood ladies on the moon patio and our family was no longer the center of whispered attention.

To rejoice Aziz's absence in her life, my mother invited all of our family and friends over for an annual ceremonial tradition—the making of rosewater. On one day a year, the air filled with the smell of red and pink stem cut roses, which, like the tomatoes, were emptied out by the truck loads. It was an enchanting and heavy aroma that drifted around you like you were walking in a romantic fairy tale. The making of rose-water, which required huge copper pots that, since they were too big to even keep in the kitchen, were laid out in the garden. The workers carried baskets and baskets of rose petals to meet the line of copper pots in the garden. Beautiful shades of pink and red roses were poured into the boiling water of the steaming copper pots to create a vision of heaven as steam traveled into the air, blending in with the earthy nature of our garden. Steam traveled up the neck of the oddly shaped bowls placed within the pots, and the liquid that collected at the top of the bowl was the rose essence, the strongest of the concoction.

When the rose water cooled down, it was poured in small glass jars that were sealed tight to ensure that the aroma of the roses wouldn't escape. Lined on the shelves of the cool basement, the jars were occasionally used to add flavor and essence into food and drinks and often times, for beauty enhancement. The rose water was also given to the children for luxurious scented baths later in the day. It was a treat for the girls, but the boys, like boys all over the world, must have hated the command to bathe.

My father could never live a life that wasn't in constant motion. His store, which has become several thriving shops, was prospering. Though we weren't the richest family in the neighborhood by far, his pockets were full of money, which he gave to my mother with an open hand. My mother wore a sable coat from Russia to formal events like weddings, her face made up with foreign cosmetics whenever possible. If she asked my father to give her 1 toman for marketing, he would give her 10. If she said the kids needed winter coats, he would bring home two for each child. He was even known to pay for weddings of associates who couldn't afford to have a nice reception, and he furnished more than one less fortunate expectant mother with everything she would need to raise her baby: blankets, a crib and money for food.

This spreading of wealth and generosity were part of the unspoken morality of our Persian culture. Not only was wealth a symbol of your status in society (meaning that the parties you threw, the gifts you gave and the jewelry you wore told others how important and respected your family was), wealth was also for sharing. A person with money or goods — usually meaning a MAN with money or goods — had to help his friends and family to prosper or his prosperity would not continue.

I went to an all-girls school with other girls of a similar social class, some of whom were much richer than me. Even in elementary school, we knew the importance of the clothing we wore, the jewelry we had or how far our shoes had come before they found our feet.

"It's from Germany," one girl might say when another asked about her shiny, purple purse.

"Oh this? My father brought it from France," another would explain, pointing out the gemstones on her new hair barrette.

I learned very early — about fourth or fifth grade — that being pretty and dressing well were a large part of how the world would judge me. So I did my best to measure up. I'd study the latest styles in a magazine called Bourda, which printed patterns that were popular in Germany. I made sure to walk, talk and act like a proper, alluring young girl. I was a stubborn, ambitious girl who always wanted to prove herself, and fashion became one of the arenas of competition. Of course, there was also the school plays, table tennis tournaments and other school activities to compete in, all of which I was very passionate about.

My father, though generous to fault, did some damage to my reputation at school, which was very vital to me at the time. I had approached him while he was grooming himself for work in front of the mirror, tying his tie and pushing his hat to sit jauntily at an angle on his head.

"Father, darling," I said, "I need one toman for school today."

"What?" he replied, distracted. I repeated myself, and he shook his head. "What for?" he asked.

I explained that the school currently had only one cabinet to keep school papers in for all the grades, a cabinet we called a commode. The school itself did not have enough money to outfit every classroom with a new commode, but had asked each student to bring in one toman to cover the cost. It would save the teachers lots of time and energy, I explained, and was not a large hardship on the students, most of whom could more than spare the small amount.

"No," he said curtly. "It is not right for the school to ask this of its students, who may not be able to afford it. No, we will not pay."

He turned to leave the room without saying another word and my heart broke in my chest. Here was my father, who'd provided the most expensive wooden horse for me to share with the neighborhood, who gave my mother 10 toman for marketing and threw about money as if it was his manhood. And he was denying me the smallest amount for the good of my school. I had to leave for class with only my books, empty pocketed, and I hung my head with shame.

Not 10 minutes after arriving for class, when all the girls were still chatting and rattling their pencils, I saw my father's hat stream past the window of my classroom. Even the teacher, who was standing at the front of the room ready to call the girls to order, turned as the noise of his loud footfalls turned the corner and headed down the school's hallway towards the main office.

"Who was that?"

"Maryam, was that your father?"

"What is your father doing at school?"

Whispers spread, halted only by a head peeking through the door. It was the school's caretaker, Arefeh, who lived in the building and took care of all the maintenance issues.

"You're wanted in the principal's office," she told my teacher, who cocked her head to the side in curiosity before leaving the room, telling us to read quietly until she returned.

"I wonder what's going on."

"It was your father. I know it."

"I know! He's going to take the teacher as another wife now."

The girls giggled and, unable to deny that my father was taking the school by storm, I stared at my desk and tried to become as small as possible. I hoped I might disappear beneath the desk and wake up in my own bed, as if from a dream.

Finally, the teacher returned with red eyes and slumped, rather defeated shoulders. The girls fell silent, waiting for an explanation. After a few deep breaths, she looked directly at me and said, "If some people's families are too poor to bring in one toman for our school's new commodes, they don't have to push too far to find it. Apparently, the school will have to find a way to pay for the new commodes without asking for donations."

She sat down in anger and I wanted to die. My skin went hot and then cold. I felt as if the stares of the other students were making my hair stand on end, and I could feel each and every strand on my head burning with shame. I went home alone, with none of the other students daring to walk next to me, and the next day at school, the girls spoke only to each other. They giggled and rustled their papers as usual, waiting for the teacher's command, and pretended I did not exist.

Just as the class was quieting down, I again saw my father's hat pass by the window and turn the corner toward the school's main office. But on this day, his steps were light and jaunty and he was not alone: Following behind his snappy steps was a line of porters. They hunched forward over ropes, which supported large and heavy cabinets on their backs, the very commodes that our school had asked for. There were six in all, for all six grades in the elementary, filing past our classroom windows as the girls exclaimed and pointed.

Our teacher made no excuses this time, but simply left the room to find out what the commotion was. When she returned, she brought one of the commodes, which a porter positioned in the corner of the room. My father came in a moment after them and my teacher said to the class, "Everybody say thank you to Mr. Mehdi for generously donating some much needed commodes for our school. Class?"

"Thank you, Mr. Mehdi," replied all the girls but me. My face was still red — with both anger and confusion — and I felt my father's eyes upon me. I looked up and he waved at me, as if his presence in the classroom was the most normal thing in the world. I didn't wave back, but sat frozen in my seat.

At lunch that day, I went home for my meal as usual to find that an identical commode to the ones at school had been placed in my bedroom. I wanted to kick the square cabinet until it shattered. I couldn't understand the reasons for the things my father had done, either the way he'd first reacted or his sudden generosity. Was he teaching the school a lesson about charity? Was he trying to say they needed only ask for a gift rather than enforce a draft? Was his lesson directed at me instead?

It didn't matter to me, a young girl. I only knew that he had chosen to prove a point about his own character and status to the community, not knowing or caring that what he had done had effected my reputation and character badly. I promised that when my father died, I would take the commode outside, burn it and jump over it several times.

Always the center of the social scene, it was about this time that my father was convinced (or so he said) by the community to take over the Tabriz theater where concerts and stage plays were presented.

The building was located in the center of Tabriz, within hearing distance of the bells of the Municipality building, where the traffic of the city circled around a dancing water fountain. Surrounded by green parks with a large water pond and manicured beds of flowers, the theater rose like an ornate wedding cake from the ground. The wide brick base was punctuated by windows and a grand, double-door entryway, while the second and third floors stacked on top were adorned with classical columns and arched windows. The top of the theater ended in a pointed roof with ornamentation of leaves, angels and other figures who smiled down upon the actors and theatergoers alike.

The famous Ark of Tabriz was adjacent, with its ancient and formidable strength: a large rectangular monument with a circular turret in the center and two arches to pass through on either side. All decoration had worn away from the Ark over time, exposing the solid rock structure and a few crumbling cracks, making it feel as old as the Persians themselves. The theater next door, while also representing our culture, stood out. Built by the Russians in the style of their famous theater in St. Petersburg, the theater was more European in style and spoke to Tabriz entering the world of art, theater and modern thought. I grew up between the two impressive structures, and also between the ideas behind both of them: the pull of Persian tradition and the glowing lure of the bountiful world of international, mainly Western, culture.

The inside of the theater was just as grand as its exterior. The semicircular stage was flanked by thick velvet curtains and a carved proscenium. The carvings and statues of cherubs and roses continued into the seats, where stacks of private boxes lined the walls. A grand chandelier with sparkling crystal hung over the main audience's seats on the floor. To the right side, several doors led into a wide hallway where guests would mingle, at the end of which was an elegant, shining wood bar that sold cakes and pastries, pumpkin seeds and other goodies. Sometimes during shows, there would be a woman outside the garden door offering bread filled with feta cheese for those who couldn't afford the high-priced snacks.

Being inside the theater was similar to being inside a plush and padded jewelry box, warm and fragrant. And it was always elegant, even when not full of well-dressed and jewelry-decked guests.

From the management's private box, I saw many plays performed in the theater. The actors and actresses were exotic beauties, most of them traveling from nearby Turkey, though one of the other manager's wives had a lovely voice and performed on occasion. The shows varied from musicals to dramas to folklore, but were often performed in the Azerbaijani-Turkish language. The public didn't mind because our Azerbaijani roots were so similar to that of Turkey and had, in fact, once physically been a part of our country. But the government interceded a few times, asking the theater to perform more shows in the Farsi language out of patriotism to Iran.

My family's position in society changed slightly due to the theater. My mother worried constantly about my father associating with beautiful actresses, sometimes at "business meetings" that went late into the night and that included alcohol. But the glamour of the theater was also social currency: We would invite friends and family to share our private seats, and I was allowed to invite friends and neighborhood kids, which made me feel very special and generous. It was like my wooden horse all over again, the girls and boys of the neighborhood envying my special toy and my father's generosity.

After school and on the weekends, I often reveled in sight of the vacant theater, presiding over all that glamour like the princess of a kingdom. And in a way, I was. I was management's daughter. In addition to having a private balcony for every performance, no one could complain when I tagged along with my father to work. It was my mother who would complain when he didn't because my constant bickering with Mahnaz and my continued excursions into the backyard trees drove her crazy on cloistered afternoons.

"Take her," my mother would say. "Just get her out of my hair." My father smiled at me, as if my unruliness pleased him.

My father and I would walk through the theater door in the morning and separate, him to the management office where he took care of business. Behind his desk in that office loomed a painted mural depicting a scene from Romeo and Juliet, surrounded by small curtains to mimic the real stage downstairs. He'd deal with actors, directors, funding and other details in front of his little faux stage, leaving me free to explore every nook and cranny of the building in my own quest for glamour and excitement.

I would sit in every one of the cushy theater seats and run through the empty hallways. I would stand on the stage and imagine the empty seats looking back at me, my everyday clothes transformed into an elegant costume of sparkling gems and gold. I'd marvel at the weight of the thick, burgundy stage curtains between my feminine fingers and give names to all the plaster angels and faces. The front of the theater, as a rule at that time of day, was basically deserted, with all the performers and other workers squirreled away in the maze of dressing rooms and production departments in the rear of the building. Basically, it was the isolated fort that every child dreams of on a grand scale and I loved every minute of it.

That's not to say that I was alone when I played in the theater on weekend mornings and afternoons. There were other children present some of the time, the kids of other workers or actors who came out of the wood work like the plaster angels that watched over us from the balconies. Some of the actresses, who mostly came from Azerbaijan and Russia to perform in our town, brought daughters about my own age with them. We'd frolic on the stage playing games of make believe, wishing we were as elegant and beautiful as their mothers.

However, it is not those little girls — who came and went with the actresses — that I remember as companions in the Tabriz theater. It was a boy named Arian, who was about six years older than me who I knew from our family's circle of friends. I knew his name and face since the time I remembered anything at all. He was part of the background of my life, a piece of the set that I gave little thought to. That is, until we formed a fast friendship in the echoing emptiness and pre-show excitement of the theater, the sort of childhood bond that is usually only found in movies or dreams. Due to that feeling of unreality, I always thought of him as my Dream Man.

Arian was slender and gawky, like most boys who are not quite men, and his mischievous sense of humor shined out of his dark eyes. His father also worked at the theater as the costume manager, and he tagged along to help. At first, I found him back in the maze of rooms for various staff in his father's costume studio.

It was a room with no windows full of the musty scent of cloth, racks of multi-colored garments taking up most of the floor space. The costumes were no order that I could discern, and I saw traditional Chinese garb hanging next to the puffy garments of Shakespeare's England. Lacy costumes meant to depict French characters shared space with intentionally worn looking rags that would cover beggars. In addition to the clothing, there were rows upon rows of shoes as well as drawers and boxes stuffed with costume jewelry, hats, gloves, stockings and more.

Actors and actresses would file in and fill out tickets to check out the costumes, thereby taking responsibility for the costume's condition when it was returned. There was a lot of bickering over ripped hems, small stains, lost articles and other normal wear and tear on the precious costumes, which always seemed to need maintenance or refitting.

Arian and I were thrown together on various errands to begin with. A rushed actor would motion for the nearest child, usually me and Arian, to run back to his dressing room and fetch a missing glove. Or, we'd be sent to find someone who could fix a performer's wig or an actress who hadn't yet picked up her dress for the evening. We'd get water and tea for the adults or transport messages we didn't quite understand between management and the performers. While it was certainly useful work to the adults, it was fun for us kids to feel involved and needed in the enchanting and somewhat magical world of backstage.

When we weren't "working," however, Arian and I would find ways to entertain ourselves around the theater, always finding fun activities that we both enjoyed despite our age difference. There were games of tag down the carpeted hallways where I would challenge him to catch me, which he usually could. We'd examine the various buttons and levers of the electrical room, where the lighting was controlled, scared to touch anything lest we break it.

One of my fondest memories was in the imaginative world of sets. Backstage, the various backgrounds for all the theater's performances hung from the ceiling in a row. They were toweringly tall, especially to a young girl, spanning more than 30 feet from their ropes at the top to where they hung a few inches off the ground. During performances, a special group of stage hands would wait for the curtains to close for a break, slide one background out and replace it with another, also moving furniture or fake trees and other props at the same time. They were always hammering nails and rushing around like the ants in my family's garden. But, when they weren't in use, all the various worlds of the stage hung quietly, waiting of us to bring them back to life.

On the rare occasions when Arian and I would grow bored of life in the theater — which was rare because, remember, we didn't have television, had very little radio programming and few movies — we'd venture out into the bright sunshine of the surrounding garden and parks. It was so beautiful in the summer: smelling of jasmine, sounds of twinkling water in the pond and fountains, plump roses blooming in the golden sunlight.

The ancient Ark watched over us as we ran over the grass, playing games, or as we climbed up and down the step of the Tomb of the Unknown Soldier. This tomb was a monument to the soldier of World War II and was inlaid with black and white marble and gold. Four poles reached toward the sky, one at each corner, and in the summer an awning was stretched between them for shade. Among the bushes, flowers and the marble steps, there were many places to play hide and seek.

Because the public tended to gather in the beautiful park among the monuments, there were often street performers to entertain us, too. I remember in particular one set of such performers. One man was dressed head to toe in red, with red make-up on his face as well. His partner and he would set up two poles with a tight rope in between which the man in red would climb up to, his more normal-looking partner staying on the ground.

The man in red carefully traversed the rope from one end to another, making a big show of holding his arms out to keep his balance. He'd occasionally pretend to tilt to one side, almost falling. His face would contort comically and his arms wave around just to make the crowd gasp in fear.

Meanwhile, his partner would shout criticism up at the red man to make him fall or make jokes about the talents of the red man to the kids in the crowd. To make the show even more exciting, the partner would hand the man in red a large pole to walk the rope with, then more and more difficult objects to try: a large tray he couldn't tilt, a chair he would try to sit on while suspended in the air.

The park had the air of a circus at such times and we found the performers fascinating. In fact, I never got bored when in the company of Arian, my Dream Man, whether there was entertainment at hand or not. The memories glow in my head as some of the easiest of my life, when happiness simply fell from the sky without an effort. I felt at home in the theater and in the garden, whether we were playing a particular game or sitting and watching the world go by.

When our energy ran down a bit and we were tired, Arian and I would sit in the shade of the garden, often by the large pond of water. We'd look at the clouds or the passing people and drown in the sun.

One day as we were lounging on the ground outside the theater, Arian started picking up small rocks from the garden beds, near the flowers. One by one, he gathered a pile of them in his hand and then, one by one, he started laying them out in the grass. He placed them very precisely, as if he had a plan in mind, and I sat up from where I was laying to spy on what he was doing.

There on the grass was a shape about three feet long, a little bit like a bird, with two wings along the sides and a pointed front.

"What is that?" I asked him.

"It's my airplane," he responded, pointing out the plane's nose and tail and tapered wings.

"You don't have a plane," I teased.

He pointed at the shape on the ground and smiled. "Yes I do," he said.

He repositioned some of the rocks a little bit until it suited his tastes. Then, he looked through his pile of rocks, obviously looking for a few larger stones. He settled on two larger rocks and placed them one by one inside the shape he had been creating on the ground.

"What's that?" I asked, pointing to a stone he'd placed in the front of the plane, perhaps in the imaginary pilot's seat.

"That's me."

"What's that, then?" I pointed to the rock lined up behind the first one.

"That's you."

I smiled at the plane on the ground and then looked up to the sunny sky, looking for real airplanes. "And where are we going?" I asked.

He laughed and said, "London. Of course."

I laughed and thought, "Yes, of course." I thought of the recent English movies that had been playing in Tabriz that I knew we had both seen, especially the films starring a comedian named Norman Wisdom. I thought of the smartly dressed women with their blond, styled hair and dainty shoes, of the apartments they lived in and the bustling, clean streets of London depicted in those films. "Yes, I'd like to go to London," I thought.

Arian and I began getting together outside of the theater and its surroundings. He introduced me to the birds that he kept as pets and trained, another symbol of his free spirit and urge to fly far away into distant lands. I fell in love with the animals, so much so that I used to come by his house when I knew he was gone. His older sister, who was a good friend of mine, would let me in. I'd play with his birds, once even setting a dove free by accident, and he'd get angry with me, though never angry enough not to smile a few moments later. As a special gift, he gave me a dove, a lovely little dove that I kept in a cage in our home.

I don't know exactly when it happened, but one day Arian stopped becoming just part of the background of my life, another face I saw often in the street and at holiday parties. He became my reason for going to the theater with my father. First thing, I would search out his usual haunts inside the theater, including his father's costume room. And if I couldn't find him, the plush interior of the theater, which always seemed so elegant and mysterious, lost its luster. I'd wander the hallways bored and dejected.

Though he got older and became a teenager, Arian always seemed to have time for me. The smile on his face when he saw me led me to believe that he felt the same ease of happiness around me that I did in his presence. He was 17 or 18, and I was about 12 years old and in sixth grade, when his family moved to Iran's capital city, Tehran. Though I know I didn't cry or cause a scene at the news, the move signified the end of a certain sunny chapter of my life.

The page had turned, but the memories remained sharp. Without a heavy heart, though, I continued to the future. Knowing that such happy times existed, I went in search of where else I could find them in what I was sure was going to be a fun and adventurous life.

Chapter Five

Even though I was a high-spirited and optimistic person by nature, it was impossible not to feel somewhat imprisoned being a good Persian girl in a good Persian house in Tabriz. Hemmed in, stitched into a pre-defined pocket of what was allowed and proper. Even when I had climbed the trees in the backyard to get the tallest view of my restricted world, there were still the garden walls keeping me from exploring it on my own.

During the afternoon nap, I still retired to the back garden, although now more concerned about my appearance, I didn't want to climb the trees like a wild child, and I was too old and mature, in my opinion, to talk to the birds. But sitting on the grass or on a bench, I'd write compositions for school amidst the noise of the birds and the trickling water fountains, dreaming of one day being a lawyer. I would be strong and loud and, of course, beautiful at the same time. I saw myself in a smart, Western-style suit waving my hand at a judge. Behind me, my clients were always women, women with bowed heads and more traditional clothing who needed help and protection. Knowing how much women fell under the thumb of dominating males — fathers, husbands, brothers and uncles — as well as the suffocating pressure of "tradition," I would be the one to gift these women with power to make their own decisions and choose their own lives.

I tried to ignore the fact that in order to pursue such a future, I would first have to find a way to get out of that repressive model myself, but day dreams are not limited by reality. That is what makes these daytime fantasies so alluring.

Years and years after my secret friend had created an airplane in the grass, I still looked to the sky. I traced the course of airplanes and wondered where they were headed, whose life the trip was going to improve. I felt in my own heart all the hope and joy that must be contained on that airplane along with the suitcases.

Many afternoons were spent staring out the window, pondering the limitless expanse of the world outside Iran, outside my own limited world. Thinking idly, like teenage girls do, about what Arian, my Dream Man, was doing, what I would do if one day he showed up at my door in a pilot's uniform, ready to follow through on that promise from long ago. London.

Such thoughts dominated almost every part of my life, especially my leisure time. I spent every penny I could at the movie theater, where I fell in love with Audrey Hepburn in the film Breakfast at Tiffany's. Her stylish and flippant manner, her independent existence. I even wore my hair in that signature style, all smooth and sleek and elegant. And then there was Doris Day, who lived the clean and stylish life I thought was standard in America, where the streets were as squeaky clean as her smile, where everyone lived in apartments with views of New York City and had a different dress for every occasion, sometimes three to wear in one day.

In fact, I sought out patterns to create dresses that I'd seen in the Hollywood or British movies. I corresponded with a friend in Tehran about fashion, she was Arian's sister. She was a very stylish girl who was older than me with green eyes and cheekbones like a model. We'd try our hand at any pattern we could find from international magazines, especially the German publication called Bourda. I'd make a smart outfit, have my picture taken and send it to her. She'd do the same in Tehran and send it back to me. It was not a competition. Instead, we were trying to create a community of style, to share our modern tastes with another person and to feel less like we were living in an isolated backwater of the world.

It was the same urge that made me collect postcards of foreign lands and movie stars. The cards were inexpensive and were one of the few Western things I could get my hands on. They each offered a sort of adventure, a very cheap day dream vacation into the world I wanted to be a part of someday. I took care of those cards as if they were made of gold and I placed them between the pages of my diary where I wrote about my life. They rested there with colorful chocolate papers I had pressed into soft, unwrinkled sheets. The treasures of a little girl.

Naturally, society at large had much different plans for me than the ones I concocted inside my head. My parents laid out their plan for my future in no uncertain terms: I would graduate from high school and, if I wanted to continue schooling, I would get a teaching certificate, which was a very respectable career for a woman. Of course, I would only teach until I was married, if I taught at all. The certificate — and this was my mother's thinking, I know — was only insurance in case a marriage turned out badly, a safety net that my mother would have loved to have during the rocky times of her marriage to my father.

Marriage was the most important part of their conception of my future. I would meet a respectable boy who lived nearby. My mother may have even dreamed of me staying directly next door to my childhood home, as she had with my grandmother.

Even my grandmother, who I adored, reinforced this narrow existence. She was the source of fairytales and mythical stories, tales that made me think that anything was possible, that magic could happen in my life, too. But she didn't believe in them. When I was upset about the obstacles in life or the setbacks I experienced, I cried on her shoulder. She would stroke my hair and say, "You cannot have everything in this life, Maryam." She said this with love, as if she was helping a child learn a necessary lesson. "There are things that are not possible, you know," she said.

"No," I told her with my tear-streaked face upturned. "Anything is possible, grandmother. Anything. I know it."

She clicked her tongue at me and placed my head back on her shoulder.

Anyone who faces such a preplanned existence knows how following that path is so easy, like floating in a river that is flowing downhill. You are just pulled along. And going against such carved-in-stone ideas is the opposite: You struggle against the current, walking uphill against tremendous pressure.

But I knew that I wanted a life outside the boundaries of the garden walls. I even knew that I wanted a life outside the borders of my native country. I was sure of this as I was of anything. I wanted to be abroad, where Doris Day broke into song at the drop of a hat and everyone fell in love before the credits rolled.

However, I was also only a girl. While I was young, I fulfilled my dreams of reaching beyond the ordinary in smaller, milder ways. In other words, I got my feet wet during small forays against the current.

I don't know where it came from, and I don't know why it's there, but if I held in my free spirit long enough, tight enough, it would accidentally burst out in a flash of rebellion. Especially around my mother. Like most mothers and daughters, there was always both love and tension between us. It often felt like we were sealed in the same prison on long summer afternoons, stuck in the sitting room with the noise of her clicking knitting needles and gossip. It was a prison with tea whenever it was called for, nice clothes and comfortable furniture, but it became stifling nonetheless.

On occasion, irritation would cause me to flare up, usually by accident, which would cause my mother to flare up just as hot in return. Proper behavior and respect were the first of the things my mother not only expected but demanded, sometimes with force. Her toughness was very evident on the occasion where I pushed the boundaries by saying a bad word one day in our parlor. I was mad at her for some reason, and I cussed at her to vent my anger and then I turned to storm upstairs.

Shocked into stillness in the middle of her knitting, her fingers frozen, she said, "What did you just say?" The tone of her voice made me suddenly frightened, and I hurried to leave the room more quickly. "What did you say, Maryam?!" she repeated, throwing down her knitting and darting across the room. She caught me by the shoulder and spun me around, shaking my body in her hands. "What? Huh? What?" she repeated once again. My body was picked up from the ground with her anger.

We were standing near the stairs to go both up and down. Where they led down to the front door, there was a little mat where people removed their outdoor shoes before coming in. She forced me to the ground at the top of these stairs, my neck over the first step and my head hanging downward.

"Fati," my mother said to the house girl, "go bring me the pepper jar."

Fati scurried away and brought back a medium-sized ceramic jar with a cork containing freshly ground black pepper. She continued to push me down and I was straining to get away, my neck beginning to hurt from the downward pressure. My mother scooped out a handful of the black pepper and stuffed it into my mouth, some of the spicy powder falling into my nose. Then she grabbed a slipper from the mat and began hitting me on the face with it to shove the pepper further inside, to make sure I would have to swallow it.

I gagged on the pepper, my throat trying to cough but with no where to cough to. I inhaled the flakes through my nostrils and into my lungs, which were burning from my throat into my abdomen. My chin was thrown back further and further as she continued to hit me with the slipper, landing blows on my chin, nose, eyes, cheeks and neck. Eventually, there was blood dripping from my face, forming a muddy paste with the pepper powder and staining the stairs below me.

The whole incident probably lasted a little more than five minutes, but it felt like forever to a twelve-year-old. And I was reminded for a week about it thanks to the pain in my face and the stain at the top of the stairs, a reddish brown blood stain that wasn't immediately removed.

Even now, it is my first instinct to speak very politely and properly, and I hold fear in my heart that I may say the wrong thing at the wrong moment, causing a reaction that I can't anticipate.

If there was one particular person who symbolized the boundaries of my life, it was my mother's brother. Javad had left the oil business to join my father in show business, becoming my father's right-hand man at the Tabriz theater. Although never dishonest in his business dealings with my father, Javad was certainly a shady character. His pockets — the pockets of his exquisitely tailored suits — were full of money and beautiful women. His big, square hands and sharp eyes exuded the aura of power, a power he knew of in his own ego, even if it wasn't always justified in the real world.

He may have been linked with my father professionally, but Javad was my mother's property. Again, she was a woman who felt powerless, and therefore became manipulative in order to get from the world what she needed. Javad was a pawn — a tool — of her manipulation. He kept an eye on my father at the theater during the day and after hours, where cards, actresses and even liquor abounded. And he kept an eye on us children. His evil looks, evil words and fists voiced my mother's displeasure in our actions. He came as warning and punishment, a symbol of my mother's indirect power.

Though I had run up against the wall of my Javad before, one major head-on collision came when I was in sixth grade. I had a Jewish friend in school with round, rosy cheeks and braided hair. She wasn't the smartest girl I knew. In fact, she was a few years older than I was, but had been held back in school to be in my class. But she was sweet and kind and friendly, and she was a favorite friend of many of the girls.

"Maryam," she said to me one day, her cheeks rosier and her eyes brighter than normal. She placed her hand next to her smiling mouth and whispered, "I'm getting married."

"What?!" I responded, my voice louder than I'd meant it to be.

She waved her hand at me, as if to calm me down. "Yes, it's true," she continued. "My father found a nice guy in the family, and I'm 15 years old now." I nodded my head in understanding. Fifteen was a womanly age and, after all, she was not meant to continue in school.

"But the best part is that it's to be a hotel wedding," she added, flashing a large smile.

"A hotel!" I said, amazed.

"The Hotel Palace," my friend said with a squeak of excitement.

I had been to weddings around my family's circle of friends that were Armenian, Persian, Jewish, all sorts. In fact, there were many Jewish women in my mother's circle of knitting friends, I'd played in the street with Jewish kids when I was young, and no one batted an eye to invite a Jewish family to a party. But no matter what the type of wedding, the ceremonies I'd been to were always held in the home — in large rooms with arched windows looking out at the mountains or more often in the large garden behind most houses, music and fountains sounding late into the starry night.

But to have a wedding in a hotel was an amazing occurrence. What glamour and style and extravagance! I had never stayed at a hotel, let alone stepped behind those glass and brass doors where elegant couples — often foreigners — went for dinner and were waited on hand and foot by uniformed waiters, doormen, bellboys and maids.

"And I am to come?" I asked breathlessly.

"Of course you are to come," my friend replied. Our enthusiasm bubbled over into girlish giggling, and we at once began to talk about all the dreamy details — the clothing, the decorations, the food — all the things that little girls think of idly when staring out the window. All the wedding details that change a little girl into a real woman.

As the news spread among the girls of our social circle, there was a core group of about six — three Jewish girls and three Muslim girls, including me — that planned and dreamed and helped our friend prepare for her wedding day. Together we visited the Armenian seamstress of the neighborhood who made most of our special occasion clothes. She fitted us bouncing girls with elegant dresses just for the wedding. Not only the bride, whose dress was naturally the most important, but all of us had new outfits tailored to the elegant occasion and worthy of the hotel we would visit. Mine was a form-fitted sheath of pink satin with a gauzy layer of white fabric on top. I could spin in a circle and the translucent white gauze danced around me. We did our hair and makeup, and tottered around in dress shoes.

All of this happened under the nose of my parents and family. My father had responded, "That's nice" when I told him the news and gave me some toman to purchase the new dress. My mother had nodded at the time, shooting me searching looks from where she looked down at her knitting. When the day of the wedding arrived, my mother was there to answer the door to the bouncing group of excited girls and say goodbye as we headed off to the hotel together.

The five of us girls headed off to the hotel together, because the bride naturally went to the ceremony with her family. Our shoes clacked along the pavement and I thought the sound was exactly the same as the signature beat of the high heels of "real women." I felt so grown up and so cosmopolitan. We all pulled at the fingers of our white gloves in nervousness, talking about what the hotel would look like and what everyone would be wearing as we walked.

We turned a corner and suddenly a man appeared in front of us. We all stopped for a moment because he appeared so suddenly and so near — he was less than four feet away — but my confusion vanished more quickly than the other girls. The square, wide shoulders, the hard eyes and the aura of confidence: It was Javad.

His eyes met mine and he took one step closer to me, his chest confronting my face. His body loomed in front of me like a brick wall. I looked up into his stone hard face.

"Where are you going?" he asked.

"We're going to the wedding," I said, my gloves clutched together. I mentioned the name of the bride and thought he probably knew about the big event through the family grapevine.

"And where is this wedding?" He placed his hands on his hips. I heard the whispers of a few of the girls behind me.

"At the hotel, the Hotel Palace."

The last word of my sentence was thrown out of my mouth by the force of his hand striking my face. It seemed as if the noise of the blow could have carried for miles. He'd slapped the knuckle side of his open hand across my cheeks from right to left. My eyes snapped shut and my neck snapped backwards, making the blow appear to have a color of its own: black, with shooting stars of pain. I fell back with the force of the blow, catching myself on my fancy shoes before I hit the ground.

"You are not going to a hotel."

He stated this as fact, his hand still hanging in the air as a threat.

"You are not going to a Jewish wedding at a *hotel*." He spit out the last word as if it was dirty in his mouth. A hotel was a public place, a place of many eyes and hands and ideas. And the very thought that they advertised rooms to rent, where we all knew what took place.

My hand flew up to my face, where I could feel the valleys of his fingers imprinted on my cheek. My jaw was open half to ease the cheek's pain and half in astonishment.

"You are going back home," he said. He grabbed my shoulder and spun me around to face the direction I had come. My hand still at my cheek, I looked back over my shoulder to the faces of my friends. Above their party dresses, they looked at me with a mixture of emotion: surprise, fear, pity. But I also saw hurry. They still wanted to go to the wedding, of course. I would have, too. I nodded slightly to one of them, who touched another on the shoulder. They turned as a group to walk away.

I didn't get to see if they looked back in my direction at all because Javad's hand thrust at my shoulder to get me going. We walked all the way back to my house with his footsteps following mine, his presence hovering above me. The white gauzy fabric of my dress was no longer flowing, but drooped over the pink under layer like my deflated hopes.

My mother was in the sitting room when we returned. She looked up.

"What happened?" she asked, in a tone that tried its best to be surprised, maybe with an added hint of worry. But I knew better than to believe her mock surprise. There was only one person who could have sent Javad to stop me, who knew when I left and with who and where I was going. My eyes didn't even meet hers and I sped away from Javad, up the stairs to my room.

"Nothing. Nothing happened," I heard Javad say as I ran away. His voice was confident, measured and perhaps just a bit triumphant.

I cried into my pillow for the whole night. The open window occasionally let warm air drift over my heaving shoulders, reminding me that there was a world outside where my friend was getting married, where there was music and dancing and food and fun. And a hotel, a hotel that I would never get to see. I looked out that window and wished I had wings.

The next school day, my friends who had attended the wedding could do nothing but gush about the wonderful time it had been.

"We had such a good time."

"It's a shame your stupid uncle wouldn't let you come."

"You should have seen it!"

I nodded my dejected head. Later, they brought in pictures of the bride and groom, the boys and girls dancing. My heart moved in my chest towards the pictures, as if it, too, physically missed attending the event.

It seemed to me that intimidation was Javad's job in our family. We had a girl to help with the housework, my father had men who helped with the theater, and Javad was the enforcer, the bodyguard and the doer of dirty work. He was part babysitter and part dictator. His role with the kids reinforced my mother's authority over us and created an aura of power and fear around him, and both of them liked that just fine.

Where Javad pitched his battles was often unpredictable. At times, he seemed to be protecting me and my siblings from danger. More often, it was warding off shame and dishonor. However, I also surmised that anything that gave us pleasure raised the hackles on Javad's back. Smiles, joy and fun: These were warning signs that Javad's wrath might fall upon you. As a man with something to prove, he wanted all of us children under his thumb, which meant inside the house and under the supervision of a family member. His fists were regular visitors at our house and he hit, slapped or verbally attacked every one of us children at one time or another. It was a relatively regular occurrence in my life.

I vividly remember one evening; the family was gathered in the dying afternoon light in one of the living rooms, sitting on sofas or ottomans or lounging on large pillows on the floor. My brother, Reza, still a toddler with a dark mop of handsome hair, was cross-legged on the ground, a few of his toys strewn about him. Javad was perched on one of the sofas next to the young boy with his arms crossed over his large chest, one of his ankles resting on the other knee.

He seemed to be watching Reza play idly until I saw a light come into his eyes, like the light bulb that glows over a cartoon character's head when they have a wonderful idea. With a smile, Javad turned to my mother.

"Watch this, sister," he said in a soft yet audible voice. "Watch the power."

Placing his elbows on his knee, he shifted his weight towards my brother and was only a foot or two away from Reza's face. Noticing the movement, Reza turned. He jumped at the shock of our uncle being so near and his hands went to his lap, his toys forgotten.

"Reza," my uncle said in an even and authoritative tone. He seemed to be holding Reza's eyes with the strength of his own, their gazes locked together. "Reza, don't move. Don't. Move."

My brother's eyes flickered, moving toward my mother. She sat on the couch with her knitting strewn about her, a cat's smile of amusement on her face. She seemed to be waiting to see what happened. Reza's eyes flickered once again, this time to my uncle's face. Javad raised a finger in warning.

"I said don't move, Reza. Did you hear me?"

Reza nodded.

Javad clapped his hands loudly in warning, as one does when training a puppy to sit and stay, and my brother started and caught his breath.

"I said don't move, Reza. Did you hear me?"

This time the boy remained still as a statue. Reza's eyes were firmly fixed on his hands, curled into a loose mass in his lap. His shoulders hunched forward. He was like a turtle, pulling in his extremities into the center of his body, retreating to the safest ground. His eyes were fixed on his hands as if to move his gaze would be to lose his grip on the world.

"Don't move, Reza." My uncle waved his finger back and forth in admonition, though Reza didn't look up to see it. Javad's face was aglow with a huge smile in the fading light of the day. He beamed over to my mother, who had taken up her knitting again. She shook her head and rolled her eyes, not displeased but also not very entertained by her brother's little trick.

And still Reza sat still, the deep pools of his eyes focused firmly on the floor. This was one of my uncle's favorite games, what he considered a fun power play over the little prince of the household, and it was a game that Javad played often. Sometimes, Javad would forget all about the frozen boy, losing himself in conversation or food. He'd leave without releasing the boy from the spell. Other times, he would intentionally pretend to be distracted and catch the boy moving with a mock-angry yell or a slap across the face. And the others in the room would listen to Javad's shouts of "Don't move!" and occasionally watch his open hand strike Reza's skull, saying nothing, not wanting to shift the focus of the game onto ourselves.

I came home after school one afternoon to find Reza in the entryway. In addition to a small Persian rug upon which we left our shoes on, there was a long, narrow table in that hallway with odds and ends on it. During certain seasons, there was a large bowl filled with goldfish, which were given to children in March during the New Year's festivities.

I had interrupted Reza, who was about three years old, in the middle of some solitary play. He was down on his hands and knees on the small carpet, which was lumped up in the middle as if it was hiding something.

"Don't move," he said. His small boy's face was all squinting eyebrows and serious mouth. "I said don't move."

He bent down to look under the corner of the mat and returned to his kneeling position. His tone became more sing-song as he repeated, "Don't moooo-ve."

He peeked under the carpet again, looking for something which, this time, he found. His little, tan hand shot under the rug and grabbed an object I couldn't make out. He held it gently and tossed it back and forth between his hands. He walked over to the bowl on the hall table and thrust his hand into it, only then loosening his grip. Out swam a panicked goldfish, gulping at the water as a suffocating human does at air.

His nose pressed against the glass, Reza scanned the school of fish for another likely candidate, who was then scooped up in the toddler's pudgy fingers. He held the poor fish in his cupped hands as he scampered back to the rug, placed the fish on the ground and covered it with the thick carpet. The fish bounced up and down beneath the fabric, making a mountain between the barriers of the boy's hands.

"Don't move, fish," Reza said. "Didn't I tell you don't move?"

After a few rounds of peeking under the carpet to check on his captive, Reza gathered the goldfish up and released him into the bowl from which he came.

He must have known I was in the room watching him at this game of fish domination, but it was only then that he acknowledged me. On his tip toes at the table, his head level with the fish bowl, he looked over his shoulder at me. He smiled.

I asked him what he was doing, and he replied, "I'm teaching them."

His eyes returned to the bowl, where they followed the fish tracing their lazy circles in the water.

Despite all the family and societal pressure to the contrary, I was not the type of girl to refrain from doing something simply because it was new, different, foreign, perhaps "inappropriate" or because of the consequences Javad laid down. In fact, such characteristics usually made the activity more attractive to me.

The Red Cross was one example. The local branch of the Red Cross had a girls group who would gather to assemble care packages to send around the world, to do other good deeds and perform community services. When the queen of Iran visited Tabriz, the girls' Red Cross group sang for her, bringing a smile to her royal face. It was a group I desperately wanted to join, something that would in my opinion build character while I had fun. Yet I had to sneak out to Red Cross gatherings as if I was meeting an illicit boyfriend.

My mother did not approve, which meant my Javad would physically prevent me from going. However, my grandmother, who had a special affection for me as her oldest grandchild, was my secret helper.

"Hurry, hurry," she would say. "He's asleep." The meetings took place in the afternoon right after the time of rest, and the "he" she spoke of was Javad.

In my grandmother's hand was my Red Cross uniform, which she'd procured the money for me to buy and helped me secretly wash and iron. There was a crisp white blouse, a navy blue pleated skirt and short white socks. I looked in the mirror and saw a modern, European girl peering back when I wore that uniform. The starched shirt, so unlike the flowing fabrics of my native country, and the pure white color of it, unlike the bright colors I was accustomed to, seemed smart and modern. And on this particular day, I was excited and anxious to quickly get out of the house as my Red Cross group had been invited to sing for the visiting Queen Farah, in the Tabriz City Hall building.

My grandmother led the way down the stairs and to the front door, making sure that no one would see me on my way out. I never stopped to think about how these little dramas and alliances played out. For instance, my grandmother would not stand up to her son — Javad — in person, perhaps because of his masculine place in the family, but would help me behind his back. My mother would not say no to me directly, perhaps because of her feminine place in the family, but sent a man to do her bidding.

I hurried out the front door, my pleated skirt swishing around my legs, and into the street, which was always deserted at that time of day. People were mostly indoors if they could help it, sleeping or otherwise resting. Only those whose work would not let them rest were about, hurrying here and there.

I ran through the block of my own street and turned the corner towards my meeting. Coming towards me across the pavement was a man on a bicycle. His skin and clothes were as greasy as his hair, which flapped across his shaggy eyebrows, and my first thought was that he was a mechanic on his way back to work after the lunch break. When he saw me hurrying towards him, his gave me a crooked smile.

We grew closer, and as his front tire came level with my feet, he turned the handlebars violently toward me, making me think he was aiming to hit me with the bike. But then his hand leaped out like a waiting crab and grabbed a handful of my breast.

He squeezed roughly, digging his dirty and greasy fingertips into my chest and compressing my teenage breast, which was small and tender. I cried out in pain and tried to slap his hand away, but he had already withdrawn his dangerous fingers. His hands were suddenly back on the handlebars and he circled his feet quickly, pedaling away as fast as he could.

He soon disappeared around the corner and I stood still in shock. I couldn't believe what had just occurred. The fading pain proved it had been real, I thought, but then I looked down at my blouse. Even more proof lay smeared there: a dirty handprint across the swell of my chest, four fingers and a thumb clearly imprinted in grease.

I cried out in surprise, and the pain was quickly replaced by the thought that my snow white blouse had been marked by this wicked man. I ran back to my home and knocked on the door lightly, hoping not to wake anyone. Then I knocked a level louder and continued until my grandmother opened the door. In tears, I pointed towards my shirt and tried to explain what had happened. She stood for a moment with her hand to her mouth and eyes wide.

Then she surged toward me through the door with her hands raised before her. "Where is he?" she demanded. "I'll show him."

"He's gone, grandmother," she said, throwing my arm out to stop her. "It doesn't matter."

"It doesn't matter?" she replied. "Of course it matters. I can't believe he would—"

"It doesn't matter to me," I said. "I just want to make it in time to see the queen and sing for her. If we hurry, I can make it. Will you help me?"

She looked at me hard and said, "Is that what you want?"

I nodded. She looked one more time out the door for the mechanic, called him an evil name and then shooed me through the door.

"Come on, come on," she said and took me by the hand up to the kitchen. "Let's get this taken care of." She started the iron heating and ran cold water over the hand print, scrubbing the wet blouse between her hands. As I sat shivering a little with no shirt on my back, my grandmother then used the iron on the wet shirt to speed its drying.

"Don't worry," she said. "It will all be fine."

Moments later, the slightly damp shirt was buttoned up across my chest once again and I was hurrying out the door. I didn't have to ask her not to speak of the incident to anyone else. She knew that if news of the attack had reached my parents or Javad's ears, I would no longer be able to go to the Red Cross or anything else outside of the house again. She knew that I would rather face the isolated streets, even if there was the possibility of evil mechanics on the prowl, rather than be so restricted.

Similar begging, pleading, insults, threats and fear surrounded my joining of the Girl Scouts when I was about 14. "These girl scouts are not good girls," Javad proclaimed when the subject was broached. "Only bad girls become girl scouts. The boys take the girl scouts behind the trees and do bad things."

The truth was that Javad, like a lot of the older population who hadn't been exposed to scouting when they were young, found the idea of taking girls into the woods a possibly dangerous and impure one. Javad was particularly superstitious: Anything new or foreign was intrinsically bad. And he imagined the Girl Scouts to be a place of sin and depravity, where they taught girls "new" things they didn't need to know. His negative outlook made him think that the unknown should stay the unknown, because what you didn't know couldn't hurt you.

Knowledge, after all, is power, and Javad wanted power only for himself.

Similar to the Red Cross battle, I thought that there had to be a way to circumvent Javad and my mother to make my wish of joining the Girl Scouts a reality. But this time I was not so lucky. My father was also dead-set against the idea, which made it entirely out of reach. But I continued to beg, day after day for weeks on end, saying please so often I'm surprised I didn't wear the word out completely.

It was my mother who finally broke down and decided to find out more about the group. She invited a woman who she used to go to school with over for tea, a woman who happened to be one of the leaders of the local Girl Scout troop. Blowing on their steaming mugs of tea and nibbling pastries, my mother grilled the woman about what the scouts did and what they stood for. When she was assured that the scouts only went camping, learned about nature and were never, ever unsupervised, I was given grudging permission to join the troop.

My heart did a cartwheel at the thought of all the fun and adventure — not to mention the cool uniform — I would have.

We had a few meetings at my school at first, a few trips outside the city and a large jamboree in Tehran. At this jamboree, which was a meeting of scouting trips from all over the country and the world, there were competitions in tent pitching, rope tying, survival skills and community service. It was good, clean fun, and it was amazing how hard I had to struggle for that minor amount of freedom, the freedom to hike with an adult chaperone and tie knots.

Next to my family's tall and stout, red-painted door — the one I had once smeared sugar plum on to create an accidental charm — was the chocolate-brown door of our neighbor. Behind it lived a somewhat ordinary family. A husband and wife with their children. However, the wife was much younger than her husband and her faithfulness to the old man was a regular subject of gossip and innuendo. If the whispers of the women were to be believed, she had a handful of other boyfriends she snuck out to (or snuck them into her, who knows). Even so, the rumors were only that, idle gossip, and no one had any proof of her un-wifely conduct, at least not that I was aware of.

One morning when I was in fifth or sixth grade, I awoke to the smell of burning wood drifting in my bedroom window. The smell of fire from our wood-burning stove was commonplace to me, but this aroma was different, stronger. I jumped up, thinking the house was on fire, only to see bobbing heads and raised hands through a haze of smoke outside my window, on the street. Something was definitely on fire: Our door! Our big, red, solid door.

I woke my parents. I ran downstairs and into the crowd, my eyes jumping around the damage. The door was charred, beginning at the ground level and working its way up. The fire had eaten through in some areas, splintering and curling sections of wood. But by the time I arrived, the flames were gone and only cold, ashy puddles on the pavement remained from the efforts to put it out. The red paint was hidden with the greasy stain of smoke, though small sections were still blazing hot and glowing red. The door let off curls of smoke, as if from a few scattered cigarettes.

Though I had never before seen a smoking door, my mind knew well what this symbol meant. A burnt door symbolized the unclean state of someone living behind it. While that person could be a man with bad dealing in business or evil motives, a burning door was usually reserved for a woman of questionable sexual character. It was a whore's door, and my young girl's heart leapt at the imputation.

A whore's door at my house? My mother? Me? My young sisters? It couldn't be.

I saw the gazes of the crowd upon me, their eyes searching my face and my clothes — my rumpled bed clothes with a jacket thrown over — for signs of wickedness. My cheeks flushed and my skin swelled with shame, shame for something I hadn't done, would never do, but shame nonetheless. Shame by association with a burnt, red door.

My father and mother, my uncle and aunt, my siblings, my cousins: We gathered around in shock in the pre-dawn light, our mouths open. Then my father turned his head, as if hearing a far away call, and froze in thought. He nodded his head, as if in decision, and stepped in the direction he was looking. He strode with an angry purpose towards the brown door next door.

Suddenly, I knew exactly what happened, the mistake that had been made. I knew for whom this punishment was intended. And my shame, so violently swelling in the blush of my cheeks and my flaming scalp, transformed into anger. Anger at this woman, this unclean neighbor woman who broke all the rules. This was her door, not ours! My little hands became fists at my side as I strode behind my father, followed by the other neighbors and my family.

The neighbor's door had been cracked open, a servant girl sticking her head out to take in the scene, but was quickly closed as the mob approached.

"Come out, now," my father shouted. "You know what happened out here? Come out, I say to you!"

The crowd behind him, of which I was part, jumped and shouted with him, moving as one creature.

"There has been a mistake," my father continued, knocking with his beefy fist.

After a short while, the door opened on the face of the husband of the house. He was an older man with graying hair with a small, square hat over it, dressed in his slippers and housecoat. At first just his nose appeared, but he was quickly swept out by my father and the crowd.

My father held onto the man's shoulder, forcibly angling him towards our family's home, towards the image of the burned door. "Someone made a mistake and burned our door," my father shouted at the cringing man. "This is meant for you, isn't it?"

"I know it is," came a shout from behind me.

"This was for your door, old man!"

"They burned our door," my father repeated, his nose only inches from the other man's face and his cheek blazing with injustice and dishonor and shock.

My uncle, my father's brother who shared our home, appeared behind him. "Take care of your wife! Everyone knows you need to take care of your wife!"

From there, the crowd surged, dragging the old man into it.

I was so insulted inside my heart, the tender heart of a little girl that cared immensely what the world saw of her. And now the world saw a burned door. I took the insult very personally, and wished that this man had taken up his husbandly duties and perhaps his fists to keep this horrible, horrible woman in line, in her place.

The passion inside of me — stemming from my wounded personal ego — welled up and erupted. I snaked through the mob and tried to hit the man on his back, though I was several feet shorter than him. The whole time I was repeating the angry phrases of the crowd, spitting the words out at the top of my voice. I jumped up towards his head, knocking his hat off into the street, where it fell into an ashy puddle.

He turned and saw me. His eyes filled with anger and he lunged at me, but my family and neighbors served as a barrier, fending him off.

"Go take care of your wife!"

"Take care of that wife!"

I was a young girl and, like most young girls, what was most important was my status and how I looked to the outside world. My mind could handle small rebellions, my own struggles against my family and society about what I could and could not do. My ideas of personal freedom — of Western dresses, Red Cross, Girl Scouts, visiting foreign lands and such.

But there were certain ideas — about what a woman was supposed to be, what a wife was supposed to be, the role of the husband as protector and enforcer, the shame of an unclean woman, that men took care of their women, that women were supposed to obey — that I never questioned. Some things just were the way they were, unquestionably.

Soon after this incident, with the shame of the burned door still fresh on my mind, I asked my father for a favor. If he was ever angry at me or if I had done something wrong, I told him, please discipline me at home, behind closed doors. No matter how mad you are, please ask me to explain myself first. Then you can hit me, yell at me, and punish me. But please, I begged him, don't humiliate me in the street, in front of all those eyes.

Chapter Six

Some parts of my life as a young girl in Iran were steeped in the past. Fortune tellers sold charms to attract a male suitor or to ward off the evil eye, marriages were arranged.

However, the outside world — from the news and trends of Iran's cosmopolitan capital of Tehran and out into the bustling, modern West — slowly began to filter in to Tabriz, tucked away in the cat's ears of the country. As I entered my teenage years, the oil industry, which had been present and productive for as long as I could remember, continued to prosper and forged international ties of commerce, diplomacy and — most important to me — social discourse.

There were the movies, the magazines, the posters and post cards of stars, the rising skirts and shaped, shiny hair. The Iranian version of pop music streamed over the air waves.

My high school years, while hardly similar to those of an American teenager, offered me more freedom, praise and inspiration than I'd ever known. And while I was still a relatively good, obedient and traditional Iranian girl — a daughter intent on making her father proud — I finally achieved my lifelong dream of seeing over the backyard's walls and traveling further from home than I could glimpse from the top of the garden trees.

From the very beginning, I had been educated in relatively high-class all-girls schools. Actually, there were no co-ed classrooms in all of Tabriz, or in all of Iran as far as I was aware at that time. But the female curriculum was on-par with the male version, I think, in that we learned history, literature, math and science.

In eighth grade, I had a unique art teacher that taught us young girls to harness the power of our imagination. We were provided with easels, brushes, and paints and told to close our eyes.

"Think of a horse," he'd say to us. "What does your horse look like? Show me what your horse looks like."

In previous classes, we'd been shown reproductions of famous art work and we were told that these stiff, ancient-feeling paintings were the pinnacle of art, the only thing that other art could aspire to be. But at the impressionable age of 14, here was a teacher who said we could all be artists, that anyone with a will could apply a brush to paper and create.

One afternoon in class, the art teacher made an announcement. There was to be a national art competition, a contest between all students. Each region of the country would hold its own competition in various artistic fields, including painting, drawing, singing, dancing, musical instruments and more. And the winners of all the regional competitions would meet for a young people's art festival in the city of Ramsar by the Caspian Sea.

At the name of the city, my head snapped up on my neck. Ramsar. This was a place of vacation post cards. Perched on the Caspian Sea, the city was white-washed in sunshine and shaded by lime-green palm trees. Ramsar, a beautiful beach city, filled with luxurious hotels and fancy cars, where tourists walked the streets with beach bags, were allowed to wear bathing suits, collected seashells, and ate fresh fish rubbed with spices grilled over an open flame. Such was the image of Ramsar in my mind, implanted there by stories of family and heard over the radio. There was a glorious hotel with ocean views seen through arched windows and a casino where the filthy and immoral rich could gamble away their cash. I was told Ramsar was the Iranian equivalent of California in America, with its sunny beaches, relaxed attitude and lush greenery. Like many cities on the Caspian Sea, it was a glamorous vacation destination, very different from the climate of East

Azerbaijan, which was blanketed in snow for at least four months a year.

I had never been on vacation to the Caspian Sea.

In fact, I had only been outside of Tabriz for afternoon picnics on the slopes of Sahand Mountain, the peak we had such a great view of from our second-floor windows.

While I was packing my suitcase in my mind, wondering if I could convince my mother to buy me a real bathing suit, the teacher continued talking.

"This Friday," he said. "In our very own school."

The contest for the state of East Azerbaijan would be held in our very own school!

"There will be boys and girls from more than a dozen schools competing right in our own classrooms," continued the teacher.

The girls began to whisper amongst themselves. Boys. This was to be a co-ed competition, which means the young people's arts festival would also be co-ed. The teacher was offering us a chance to paint, to travel to the Caspian Sea, to vacation at a fancy resort and to do all of this in the company of boys!

The girls left the classroom like a flock of excited birds, twittering to one another about the Caspian Sea and boys and paint brushes. But not one of the girls had signed up to compete in the contest, I found out.

I scurried back into the art room to find out more. It was true enough, the teacher said, that no girls had yet applied.

"Why don't you do it, Maryam?" he asked.

I hesitated. Was there something wrong that no other girls wanted to sign up?

"Can I?" I asked. "Is it OK?"

He laughed. "Of course it's OK." He clapped me on the shoulder and told me to bring my own canvas and paints, and show up on Friday. "Somehow, I knew it would be you," he said. "I know you."

My mother shrugged the event off and gave her permission for it, knowing that I was interested in art and it took place at the school. She probably didn't understand the height of my excitement because I kept the news of the art festival in Ramsar under my hat for the time being. Her approval didn't extend to her purse, however, and I had to resort to my usual source of illicit funds: the bank, my grandmother.

We snuck out of the house that Thursday afternoon to the Tabriz bazaar. This half indoor and half outdoor market was a bustling place of glittering gold jewelry, piles of fruit, spices in tied baggies, and books.

This time, grandmother and I hunted down some art supplies and carried home an easel, a selection of paints and brushes of all shapes and sizes. Seeing the look of joy upon my face, my grandmother was also glowing with vicarious excitement, imagining out loud the masterful picture I would paint and the admiration I was sure to elicit from all the judges. In my grandmother's mind, there was no other possible outcome and my heart swelled with her optimism and her pride of me.

Friday morning found me in a crowd of about 50 boys and girls from all over the state of Azerbaijan, sitting in front of their personal easels and arranging their paints just so. We were situated in growing circles around a central table. After learning that I would be participating in the painting competition, two other girls from my class had also signed up and I waved at them from across the room.

But I had placed myself next to a girl I did not know. She was smiling with nervous confidence with a neat braid hanging between her shoulder blades. Even her paints were positioned with expertise on her easel, ranging the colors of the rainbow from red to purple, and I thought her confidence might rub off on me.

A balding man in a suit with tufts of grey at his temples came into the center of the young artists and introduced himself as Mr. Nemaa, a famous Iranian artist of the time. He explained how long we would have and the excellence that was expected of us, the country's new generation of artists and leaders. Then he began arranging what we were to paint: a still life. He procured a plump watermelon and poked it with his thumb, pulling it into two juicy slices. Apples and pears were positioned around the watermelon like gossiping friends with a few leaves thrown in for more color. Then he stepped away and nodded his head, giving us the signal to begin.

I took a deep breath and closed my eyes, picturing the arrangement of fruit in my head like I had once imagined a horse, trying to think of how to begin crafting these shapes on my blank canvas. By the time I opened my eyes again, the confident girl to my left had already taken a pencil to the vast whiteness of the canvas and sketched out the basic shapes of the scene before us. Her fingers were lithe and skilled.

For a moment, I panicked. I looked down at my own fingers and wondered what I was doing here with my clumsy, unskilled hands. How did I think I ever had a chance of going to Ramsar? But then, I remembered my grandmother's voice telling me "you can achieve anything you put your heart to." With that thought, I grabbed my pencil and started.

I, too, sketched out the basic shapes I saw before me, except from the angle of my own vantage point. Then I saw the girl to my left adding deep purple and black shadows next, pooling the paint where the still life was darkest, and I followed her example in that as well. I mixed my colors, holding them up and squinting to compare the colors to the actual fruit. Next, I saw the girl adding the main body of the fruit, green for the watermelon rinds and red for the flesh, a lighter green for the leaves, and I again followed suit. She was truly masterful, and rather than copying her work, I followed her example as to the step-by-step layers of the painting.

At one point, I was trying to blend two shades of red onto an apple to give it the appearance of depth and I saw her taking a short break, glancing over at my canvas.

"Why, you're quite good," she said, flipping her shiny braid back over her shoulder.

I laughed. "No, no," I replied. "You are truly talented. I have seen the way you attacked that canvas."

"Well, my parents have given me a private art tutor for some time," she said, whispering conspiratorially. "They think it's very important."

I whispered back. "Well, his technique is now teaching me."

We both smiled widely and wished each other luck.

Next, she mixed some lighter paint, almost white with shades of pink and yellow. Her brush skittered over the tops of the paint on her canvas, highlighting the fruit where the light struck it. I was amazed to see the still life become three dimensional on the page and tried my own hand at completing the same effect on my own watermelon. Lastly, I took out my smallest brush and painted tiny crescent seeds, brining my nose close into the scent of drying paint.

When time was up and we were asked to step away from our easels, I took in the painting I had produced with pride. While I wouldn't have sold the simple still life to a museum or anything, I was amazed at the amount I had accomplished in so short a time. As the kids lined up in another part of the room, letting Mr. Nemaa and the other judges wander through the easels, I approached the confident girl again.

"That was so much fun," I said.

She nodded.

"And your painting is sure to win," I added. She blushed and tried to shoo my compliments away. "No," I insisted. "You may have a tutor, but now you need to tell him that you are quite a good teacher, too, on your own."

We shared a smile and anxiously awaited the results, which turned out just as I expected. My painting companion was awarded the number one position of all the girls who took part, and her smile lit up her whole face from chin to forehead. She would be going to Ramsar and a worthy representative she would be. However, I received second place for my watermelon still life, and I, too, glowed with happiness.

Whether or not I would be attending the young artist festival and experiencing the trip of a lifetime, I felt as if I had actually engaged the outside world in some way. Here were girls from all over East Azerbaijan and I stood out amongst them. Always a competitive girl, I thrilled at that feeling of being a big fish in my small pond. I felt that perhaps it was possible to make something of myself in the world — a world outside the close confines of my garden walls. It was a feeling of self-esteem and self-worth that electrified my girlish heart. The world seemed a little more open, a little more conquerable after all.

The feeling of self-esteem stayed with me, buoying my spirits for some time after I had mostly forgotten about the competition and the young artist festival on the Caspian Sea.

And then two months later, the phone rang and it was my art teacher.

"Maryam," he began, "You must be the luckiest girl in the whole world."

It turned out, he explained, that the talented girl who had won the competition had a very protective and prejudiced father who wouldn't allow her to attend a co-ed camp that took her so far from home. Because I was the second-place painter, the open slot on the bus to Ramsar had my name on it. That is, if my own father would allow me to attend.

My heart went flying and I believe I must have dropped the phone in my excitement because I surely don't remember hanging it up. I ran through the connected door to my grandmother's house, where I found her in the kitchen wearing an apron around her stout waist. She hugged me to her breasts and together we jumped up and down like two crazy people, making excited noises that weren't quite words and weren't quite screams.

Once the elation had worn off slightly, she held me by the shoulder and asked, "Well, what are you going to do?"

I nodded, knowing her meaning exactly. "Father," I replied.

In other words, I would run right past my mother and my uncle and apply to the highest household authority — my father. Never having been outside of the province herself, never having gone far in school and certainly never having won something of distinction, my mother was sure to give me an emphatic, "No!" Then she would bring out my Javad to prove the dangerous aspects of the trip: the distance, the separation from family, the fact that I would learn new things and meet new people, that I might develop too high of a sense of myself and, not least importantly, the boys. Boys! If the boys took the naughty girl scouts behind the trees to do dirty things, what on earth would he think boys did to the young artists? I was always sure to keep any information that could be deemed suspect to myself, sure that someone in my family would find a way to change good news into bad and rain on my parade. This trait had been ingrained in me since my days at the Red Cross and younger, so I planned out how to present this trip to Ramsar in the best possible way.

I approached my father when he was alone, finding him as he was entering the door from work that evening. As he took off his coat and hat, slipped off his shoes, I performed a set speech for him. I outlined the great prestige of the award I was given, how these children came from all over Iran, how the Shah himself supported the competition and festival. Then I brought out my arsenal of safety information. There would be the constant supervision of adults throughout the trip, boys and girls quarters would be divided, a professional bus driver would take us there, the schedule was typed out for the family to keep while I was away. And, I wouldn't miss any school and I would continue to get good grades and please and please and please and please?

My hands were clasped under my chin and my eyes wide with yearning. "I only need your permission and a bit of money to prepare the uniform they require," I said.

My father's eyebrows were bunched together in thought as he placed his hat on the entryway table. "And it will bring great honor to the family," I said, "as well as meaning a great deal to me. Father?"

He paused a moment more and then turned to me, fumbling for something in his back pocket. It was his wallet. My father glanced inside of it, his brows still knit together.

"I only have 50 toman," he said. "Will that be enough?"

I jumped up and flung my arms around him, trapping his hands and his wallet in between us. I squealed an answer and he smiled, handing me the few bills and patting me on the head. "I'll tell your mother," he said.

The next week was a flurry of excitement. In addition to the 50 toman my father had given me, my grandmother, my ever dependable bank, added 100 toman more. We shopped the bazaar to find fabric for the dark navy blue pants I was to wear, to which I added a pink and blue striped blouse whose pattern came from a Western movie. There were mounds of packing, lists of preparation and mountains of pride from my sisters.

One bright summer morning, my paintbrushes and blue pants packed, I boarded a bus to the Caspian Sea for a week away from home. The trip was nothing like I had imagined in my head, and I had imagined quite a lot in my fantastical teenage head. But at the same time, it was more than I had ever imagined.

The bus was stocked with not only graphic artists like me, but also musicians and singers. The joyful melody of the accordion filled the aisle and poured out the open windows as we roared down the road. In the city of Ardabil, representatives of the local government met us with music and festivities, speaking about the honor that we young artists were conveying upon our own country.

Once we reached Ramsar, I got my first view of the Caspian Sea, the largest enclosed body of water in the world. The sun glinted off the metallic water and the air was fresh and salty. I could smell the water and hear the rustle of the palm trees from my private tent on the girls' section of the campground where the festival was held. My own tent! It was a small triangle of isolation and independence that, while rustic, was the most romantic thing in the world for a girl who had never been away from home.

We were a crowd of excited and smiling faces from all over our great country, a flock of birds that were never still, never quiet and never calm. We gathered in the cafeteria, where boys did mingle among girls, and each state would chant their anthem and taunt the other states in a light-hearted competition. Every night, there were performances of dancers or concerts, and during the day there were workshops on painting and other art forms.

I joined the other East Azerbaijan kids in a traditional dance wearing the traditional costumes of our region, and I also remember painting a picture of such a dance, too. An older man spun around a pretty young girl, both smiling, and I learned that I could show the motion of the dancers in the strokes of my brush. When the judges came around this time, I received fourth place among girls pulled from the whole country.

If I had felt my chest swell with pride when I received second place in my hometown, I now felt that I was truly someone. I was a big fish in my pond. If I smiled wide enough, I thought it might just be possible to see the brightness of it from space. Instead of being lost in the shuffle of everyday life, I saw the world standing still. There was Iran, there was Azerbaijan, there was Tabriz and there was me. You see? There she is, and she is somebody special.

And I had done it all on my own. Alone. Independent.

I had the best time of my life so far on that trip to Ramsar for the festival. It was a memory that I smoothed flat, placed between the pages of my diary with my post cards and chocolate wrappers, and cherished. For the rest of my life, I would take out the memory now and then, dust it off and enjoy again the pure joy and feeling of self-worth I had on my first voyage to the Caspian Sea.

Chapter Seven

From the age of 14 on, I became a teenager with a vengeance and a passion. I giggled with my girlfriends from the time we met to walk to school in the morning until the late afternoon, having ice cream in the cafes of the bazaar. I put more time and effort into my make up, hair and clothing.

In fact, I continued to write letters to my friend in Tehran, the sister of my friend Arian, because she learned the latest trends and styles in the cosmopolitan capital city than I did in provincial Tabriz. We wrote of dress lengths and patterns and fabrics, sending pictures of our latest outfits back and forth. And she underhandedly fed me stories about her older brother: how he graduated high school with honors and was traveling to England for university. England! Just like we'd always dreamed.

Like most teenaged girls, I was in love with a new boy every day. In my head, that is. I could simply see a young man in the street and the shape of his eyes would melt my heart. My thoughts would be consumed with nothing but the quick glance I had of his profile and dreams of how we would get married, where we would live, how many children we would have ... until the next morning, when some other young man would strike my fancy.

I knew even then that such thoughts were harmless, meaningless fantasies. I knew because I saved the real ones for my Dream Man, Arian. When I stared out the window on sunny afternoons or climbed the trees to take in what I could of my neighborhood (now without the ice cream because I was always watching my figure), it was Arian I would think of. How much fun we had together when we were young! Would it be possible to reclaim that happiness? Would it be possible that he — so much older and now traveling to Europe — stopped to think of me now and then? Of his promise to take me to London?

Like most teenagers, I experienced a lot of angst during my teen years. I think a good portion of my time was spent crying into my pillow over my treatment at the hands of my parents, especially my mother. My heart yearned for so much and there were so many things I longed to do, all of which were apparently improper, immodest, un-womanly, disrespectful, dirty, too European, against religion or — the worst sin in my mother's book — too expensive.

It would be many years before I again felt my heart swell with such feelings of gratitude, hope and pride as I felt at during the young artists festival. But the experience never totally deserted me. I had learned that I was a special human being in this world. Crying on my grandmother's breast after childhood disappointments, she often told me that some things were simply not possible, and now I knew I was justified in my belief that anything — absolutely anything — was possible if you put your mind to it.

I was 16 years old and in my last year of high school when I was thumbing through a magazine and found my next opportunity for greatness. The thick and glossy publication was one of my favorites — and the favorite of most women in Iran — called Women's Day Magazine (Zane Rooz). Written in Farsi, the magazine contained everything a middle- to upper-class woman might find of interest including recipes for the kitchen, clothing patterns and other sewing instructions, fashion updates, news of the rich and famous, features about Iranian musicians and artists, fictional stories and — perhaps most importantly — up-to-the-minute news and photographs of the current queen of Iran, the Shahbanu, Farah Diba.

Lounging on a pillow on the floor, my eyes suddenly froze on an article calling for entrants in the Women's Day beauty pageant.

"The Annual Women's Day Beauty Contest," I said aloud to my sister, Mahnaz, who was on the sofa in the sun, similarly employed in reading. She was about 14 at that time and surly, always in opposition to anything of which I was in favor. "What?" she asked. "The Women's Day contest?

I turned back to the magazine page to analyze the contest's entry requirements. They wanted a girl in her teens, just finishing school and not yet married who epitomized Iran. She was to be lovely and graceful, smart, well-spoken and accomplished, with "accomplished" meaning in cooking, sewing, knitting, athletics or another "respectable" hobby. A few girls would be chosen from each state of Iran to compete in the semi-finals in Tehran, and the finalist's picture would be printed in the magazine, with readers' votes counting towards the final competition. Any entrant needed only to send a picture and a letter describing why she would be an excellent choice to represent her region and her generation in the pages of Women's Day.

"So, what about the contest," I said. "This is a new year and a new contest. They are still taking entrants."

Mahnaz laughed. "I wouldn't be caught dead doing that kind of thing," she replied. "You can try if you want to," she said, trying to stifle her giggles at the same time, "but I wouldn't hold my breath if I was you. You might just suffocate."

I shrugged off my sister's acidic attitude. What did she know?

The requirements didn't seem so hard. Besides, I'd learned in the past that many girls missed out on fabulous opportunities simply because they didn't have the nerve to put one foot in front of the other and try. I'd thrown my hat in the ring for an art competition I didn't have much of a chance at winning, and I'd wound up having the time of my life at the Caspian Sea. What was there to lose except a little time writing a letter?

As a teenaged girl without a television, not allowed to fraternize with boys or to go on dates, and with browsing the bazaar one of the few forms of entertainment available to me, time was one thing I had plenty of on my hands.

Soon afterwards, I got a return letter in the mail that stated my letter and photograph were chosen to represent the state of East Azerbaijan for a round of preliminary interviews. Enclosed was an airline ticket. It was a rectangle of thick paper with rounded edges that felt so foreign and exotic in my hand. Through my tears of excitement, I made out the blurry typing:

Depart: Tabriz

Arrive: Tehran

I was going to the capital. I was going to the capital to meet and greet the largest and most popular women's magazine in the whole country. And then there wasn't much time at all to prepare.

This opportunity came during a unique window of freedom in my childhood. My uncle had moved further away from our house and was rarely around to interfere in our lives. My parents were focused on their two sons. Plus, the pageant had the extra allure of being free of cost to me — airfare and other travel expenses were paid by the pageant — and also being respectable, because such a well-known magazine was hosting it and beauty was something to which any Iranian girl was expected to strive.

It was something my parents could really stand behind. Not that they did. Instead, both my father and mother approached the subject with an attitude of indifferent acceptance, saying, "That's nice" and patting me on the head. I suppose they didn't think the undertaking would lead anywhere. My emotions, however, were the opposite of theirs. My heart leapt around in my chest as if it could fly without the aid of the airplane. It was easy to feel graceful when every step was taken on a cloud of excitement and hope.

I packed a suitcase while my mother called her younger sister, who lived with her husband in Tehran, to see if I could stay with them during the course of the preliminary interview. My mother called me over to the phone to speak with my aunt. She was always the relative I looked up to the most, partially because she was young and closer to my age and partially because her spirit was so light and buoyant, akin to my own.

"I am so proud of you, Maryam!" she exclaimed. "This is so great!"

My cheeks blushed to hear her praise, the first excited words I had received about the competition.

"We are going to be right there to pick you up at the airport," she continued. "I can't wait."

"It's only the preliminary interviews, Auntie," I said. "Don't get too excited."

"Oh hush," she said. "I'll get excited if I want to. Besides, I know you are going to go far in this, Maryam. I just know it."

As far as my excited heart was concerned, I was going far as it was. All the way to Tehran.

From one letter sent to a magazine, a whirlwind fell about my 17-year-old ears. There was a flurry of clothes strewn over my bed and around my floor as much as in the suitcase. There were many hours in front of the mirror brushing my hair into different styles, different positions, or just brushing it repeatedly until it shone.

Then there was the airplane, which was whirlwind in itself, tossing me up and down on with the air currents, yanking me about by my seatbelt. I stared out the window and felt no fear, only nervous anticipation.

At the door of the plane, where the passengers poured into the airport proper, a cloud of smiling people with flowers and happy voices crowded around me, introducing themselves as representatives of Women's Day. They pinned a sash diagonally around my shoulders: silver, with scrolling letters noting the girl it adorned was from Tabriz and was a guest of Women's Day. My chest swelled against the sash with pride. There were a few pictures snapped — for the judges and for the readers, I was told.

As I walked — in a ladylike and graceful manner, or at least I hoped so — up to the familiar face of my aunt in the waiting crowd, I waved as I had seen the queen do in the glossy pictures of the press, some of which were sandwiched in my diary. I felt like I was walking into the smooth and silky pages of the magazine itself, walking into a life of glitz and glamour in Tehran. Then my aunt's familiar arms enfolded me and we jumped up and down in our excitement, squeezing one another.

Once the spell of excitement passed, her hands grasped my shoulders and she held me at arm's length.

"Look at her," she said, directing the words over her shoulder at her husband. "Isn't she beautiful?"

"Oh auntie!"

"No, really. You are. The prettiest in Tabriz. I know it." She winked at me. "Isn't she, dear?" she asked my uncle, who nodded absently, his eyes looking elsewhere around the crowd of people.

"Now what is this?" my aunt asked, grabbing a piece of paper from my hand.

"I don't know. The Women's Day people — over there — gave it to me," I said. "I haven't had a chance to look."

My uncle grabbed my suitcase and my aunt took my arm as we turned to leave the airport. Her eyes grazed the paper as we walked.

"Well, well. It's your agenda," she said. "It looks like they are taking you everywhere around town. The Golestan Palace, skiing in the Alborz mountains, museums, swimming — "

I stopped in my tracks, causing my aunt's arm to snag against mine, halting her, too.

"We're skiing in the Alborz Mountains?" I asked. "We're swimming? I don't have any clothes to do those things." I grabbed the paper out of her hand to check its accuracy. "How am I going to do all this?"

"It says you were supposed to receive a list of clothing to bring, honey," she said to me. "You see?" Her finger pointed out the pertinent sentence on the page.

"But I didn't!" I exclaimed. "I didn't get anything like that."

"Come now," she said, seeing my growing panic. "It will be OK."

"How will it be OK?" I asked. My voice was rising and tears were mounting in my eyes and clogging my throat. "I brought three beautiful suits, stockings, shoes. Beautiful suits. No winter clothes, no gloves, no bathing suit."

By then my uncle had turned around and looked at us nervously, my suitcase still hanging from his arm. My aunt gestured to him to wait just one moment.

She grabbed me again by the arms.

"There, there. It must have just been lost in the mail or sent too late or, well, who knows," she said to me. "But don't you dare cry, honey."

She smiled and began to walk again. The confident beating of her feet against the ground and her upturned chin turned around my mood.

"You're in my city now," she continued. "I'm going to make sure everything turns out fine. You'll see."

With a few phone calls placed to aunts, cousins, sisters-in-law and friends, my aunt had solved all my problems within hours. She tracked down a swimming suit easily, thanks to the fact that her daughter and I were about the same size. The ski suit was a bit harder to manage, but was found in the closet of a cousin on my mother's side. Then she tucked me into a bed in her comfortable home in Tehran. As she closed the door to let me sleep, she said, "Enjoy your beauty rest. Not that you need it." Then she gave me yet another wink.

The next few days were a blur of happiness and excitement. We were taken up to the top of one of the Alborz mountains, where the prosperous of the country came to carve down the ski slopes on their winter vacations. Boys and girls whizzed past us, laughing and racing, while many of the adults lingered at the top of the mountain, where a fancy restaurant served gourmet meals and hot tea to keep off the chill. Along with about 20 other girls from around the country, I huddled in front of the scenic abyss for a picture in my borrowed dark pants and matching jacket.

On the way back to town, we talked and giggled, comparing hometowns and hemlines and interests. In fact, I made a few friendships. We were just girls away from home, away from our parents in a fascinating location. Because we were all very aware that this trip was only the semi-finals, a spirit of competition was non-existent. We all knew and talked about the odds: Women's Day was hosting a group of girls every week for months for a total of 585 semifinalist contestants, a few from each area of the country. Only one in 10 would then progress to the finals, which would be held early the next year.

Therefore, we were teenagers on a field trip from school, many of us on vacation from our more rural, far-flung lives in smaller towns. We were princesses for a week, walking in a dream of magazine glamour for as long as we could before returning to the day-to-day life we'd just escaped. For one week, we were beautiful, graceful, adored, photographed, admired, enviable, complimented and pampered. I, for one, was set to enjoy every little minute of it.

After the skiing adventure, the days were filled with one new experience after another. In our swimming suits — one-piece suits that preserved some modesty but still showed bare shoulders, back and leg — we posed for the camera, knowing the pictures would go back to the judges. Then we splashed in the pool and shrieked like we were young children again.

Later, we were arranged in rows in front of the Golestan Palace, a line of us flowing neatly down the entrance stairs. I was wearing a smart suit with a shorter skirt and matching jacket. With hushed manners, we were then led on a tour of the historic palace by a guide, who pointed out the historical significance or unique beauty of certain features. Our heads were filled at Tehran's museums and our stomachs were filled at its restaurants, though I never was satiated with the busy beauty of the capital city.

At the end of the week, which passed all too quickly, we girls were again showered with flowers, thanked for coming and told about how we would be contacted if we were chosen for the finals. In my heart, I cherished hope that I might be recalled, that I might catch the attention of one of the judges. But I also looked around at the other girls — so lovely and sweet, some very smart or very funny, others so elegant and from important or famous families — and I knew I couldn't hold my breath over it.

Instead, I kept the hope as a small flame, like a candle one lights in hope of your dreams coming true, kindled in my chest. I smiled and hugged the other girls, exchanging addresses to write letters and stay in touch. I thanked my aunt profusely, though she just shook her head with her twinkling eyes, saying, "It was such a joy to see you. And I know the judges will be joyful at seeing you, too." She hugged me tight and, in my ear, she whispered, "Perhaps you will be back soon, yes?"

I laughed and said, "I hope so."

After I returned to my home and to Tabriz, I saw the life I had sampled in Tehran only in the pages of my magazines, including Women's Day, who printed more and more pictures of different groups of semi-finalists taking their week-long tour through the city. They were so lovely, so beautiful and I sighed.

So life went on. Until, much like the call that opened the door to the young artists festival, the phone rang. This time, it was Women's Day, letting me know that I was one of the 60 girls chosen from 585, one of only two girls to be picked from Tabriz, and that I would be headed back to Tehran for a more formal competition.

The excitement that flooded my veins was enough to stop my heart for a full minute. And when I finally caught my breath, I don't think there was a person in the house — perhaps in the neighborhood — who wasn't startled by the sound of a young girl's yell, the yell of a girl whose dreams had just come true.

So much about my second journey to Tehran went smoother than the first. The airplane trip was not as new to me, or at least I put on the air of the seasoned traveler. My aunt and uncle's house in Tehran, my cousins and the city had an air of familiarity about them. And my preparations for the competition didn't meet any snags on this second round. My clothing choices were perfectly fit to the agenda and perfectly tailored by my favorite seamstress in Tabriz. The only difference this time was in attitude, mine and of the other girls in the semi-finalist group. Though only a few scant months had passed, we had matured. Rather than a fun-filled fieldtrip for a bunch of giggling school girls, our mission in Tehran and with Women's Day was now much more serious. Being a finalist in this prestigious competition was a large honor, and the eyes of our friends, family and countrymen were upon us.

We smiled sweetly for cameras at all of our various destination and activities, posing carefully in our heeled shoes. We nodded earnestly when taken to historical sites and museums, making sure to show the right amount of interest and passion about our national identity. We played up our hobbies and interests when speaking to pageant representatives and amongst ourselves. All the blue ribbons, trophies and awards we'd received since childhood made their way into casual conversation.

The stakes of this contest may have appeared small. Yes, the winner would represent Iran at the international version of the competition and receive some prizes. But the real goal was the notoriety. A girl who won the Women's Day beauty pageant would be able to travel (even to America!), would have her pick of important husbands, probably living a more luxurious, rich and famous life than she could have without the distinction. The winner was a minor celebrity, a trophy for any husband and any family until the end of her days.

We didn't speak these thoughts aloud. Not yet. But we felt it. The spirit of competition was growing in our teenaged hearts, and we all thrust our chins out a bit further, held ourselves a bit more gracefully and grew up just a bit more.

Even so, we were teenaged girls whose main hobbies were giggling and gossip, like any young women. And despite the heightened pressure, I still made lots of friends with the other girls representing every nook and cranny of Iran. Many were daughters of titans of industry or famous oil men. Others dripped with family jewelry and ancient lineage.

The girl I bonded with the most was from such a lofty position. She studied in Switzerland at a prestigious boarding school along with children of European and Middle Eastern royal families. Her father was a rising star in the rising economy of the country. She was lovely, with creamy skin and shining hair.

And she was a lot of fun. Every time the girls were sent off in groups of two to explore a park or museum, to take pictures of some soaring ancient monument, it was her and I together. Cameras around our necks, we'd walk off in our knee length skirt and braided hair to whisper and gossip, talking about boys and clothes and friends. For once in my life, I met someone that I was happy to sit and listen to as much as

I wanted to talk myself. I wanted to hear everything about her school, about Europe, about the fabulous home I envisioned her family living in. This girl, Sherry, and I sat together on the short buses that ferried the 60 girls in the semifinals around Tehran and its environs. Over the span of the semi-finals trip to Tehran, there were many buses, many destinations and, therefore, many times to talk.

But there was still something in the air between us, a feeling that was related to the general spirit of competition. But this went beyond the feelings every contestant had. It seemed to me that the pageant co-ordinators went out of their way to please this girl, when the rest of us girls wanted only to please them.

With six buses of fresh, young teenage girls, we arrived for lunch one day at a famous Tehran restaurant called Naayab Cholo Kebab, where we tumbled off the bus and into the parking lot. We walked in clumps and groups towards lunch with adults from the pageant mingled in between. When I reached the doorway, the wife of the senator who founded the magazine and one of its editors were hovering around the threshold. They shook hands with the girls or placed a warm hand on their shoulders, asking how they were enjoying their time in the capital city.

But when I reached the front, it was the girl I had become friends with the important women paid all their attention to.

"Hello, Sherry," the senator's wife crooned.

"Are you hungry for their famous kebab?" the editor asked.

The girl laughed and flashed her straight, white teeth, assuring the women she was having an excellent time.

"And are you ready to become Iran's next beauty pageant winner?" The senator's wife took the girl's hand and sandwiched it between her dainty, gloved hands. At that moment, I realized I competed just to be in the finals, as the pageant winner was already chosen.

Again, the girl laughed, treating the conversation as mere pleasantries and walked on to find her seat inside the restaurant.

When it was my turn to walk through, the women were still smiling. I wondered if it was only my imagination that the smiles weren't quite as warm and soothing.

"Hello, honey," said the senator's wife. She failed to use my real name, I noted.

"Yes, are you enjoying Tehran very much?" asked the editor. "All the way from — " she paused to look at the sash strewn over my chest that labeled my home city — "Tabriz?"

"Oh yes," I replied. "I find it — "

"Good, good," said the senator's wife. "Enjoy the kebabs." And then she was on to the next girl, trying to keep track of all 60 of us.

We sat in the restaurant, famous for its gourmet version of traditional Persian dishes, and I examined the face of the girl I had befriended. The incident at the door had given me pause and left me thinking that there was something I had missed, something I wasn't privileged to know. But the girl was elegantly cutting up her food into delicate pieces, sipping at her water glass, making small talk with me and the other girls. She patted her napkin to the corners of her mouth with a practice grace that I thought she must have picked up from her European education.

Perhaps, I thought, she is accustomed to such shows of deference due to the exalted nature of her family name and her father's money. She brushes it off her shoulders like falling snow, I thought, oblivious.

Watching her smile and eat — and eating the delicious food myself — I came to the conclusion that I must be right. And the food was so good, I couldn't wait to go home and tell my friends what famous restaurant I had dined in. And the very important girl I had dined *with*. Such things were the bricks of one's social standing, after all, and social standing was very important to me.

At the end of three days in Tehran, the groups of girls were to attend a glamorous ball in the Women's Day Magazine Hall, where there would be food, music and dancing.

With my shining hair coiled on my head in my cocktail dress —
sitting up very straight with my ankles demurely crossed and my chin
lifted — all I knew was that I saw the judgments taking place.

The ball room was spacious but not echoingly large. The walls
were hung with rich fabrics and both ceilings and floors were adorned
with scrolling woodwork. There were round tables covered in thick,
starched linens, from which flowers arched upwards and glassware
twinkled in the light. One corner of the room was taken up by a raised
stage, where a beautiful woman of some renown sung into a microphone. Her voice and the music of the band flowed through the room,
overlapped with the soft tones of conversations taking place. An emcee, a well-known reporter covering the event for a newspaper, took
the stage to welcome us and to make other announcements.

"Let's all give a round of applause for these lovely girls, hand chosen
from all over our beautiful state," he'd said at one point. While the sentiment about our beauty and how special we were was flattering, we
all knew that some of us were more special than others. Some of us
would be chosen, while others would travel back to whatever part of
"our beautiful state" they came from.

When he retired from the stage and the music took up again, we all
saw the emcee return to the main table, the table of honor. Sitting at
that table, placed apart from those of the girls, was the emcee, the director of the magazine, the senator's wife and another reporter, a writer
who worked for the magazine covering news of the beloved and beautiful queen. If anyone knew beauty and glamour, it was her. After all,
she'd conversed one on one with the famous royal, attending exclusive
parties for the rich and famous. When they put their heads together to
speak, I knew what it was they were deciding. We all did.

But there was no announcement, no relief for our anticipation. The
night simply wound to a close and we gathered our belongings, tiptoe-
ing in our fancy dresses and shoes towards the exit. We all had plane
flights home the next day.

Much like other events we had been to, the judges were arranged at
the exit, greeting each girl as they passed through on their way to the

street, to their taxis. Handshakes and smiles and good wishes. As the crowd funneled through, I found myself face to face with the queen's reporter, a woman in her 30s whose dress was never flashy or trendy, but always startlingly elegant. She placed her hands on both my shoulders, which were bare in my cocktail dress.

"Maryam," she said. "From Tabriz."

I mumbled something about the honor I felt in meeting her, which was genuine. I followed her coverage of the queen regularly, like most other girls my age. She nodded and smiled. Then she bent forward to give me the traditional Iranian farewell: a kiss on both cheeks. Her face was cool and smooth next to mine. As she reached my second cheek, however, she paused and whispered, "Please go across the street. There is a meeting room with the number five on it."

She pulled away, her hands still on my shoulders, and said, "Take care, my dear." She was still smiling warmly. The same expression of good will had never left her face, even as she turned away from me to greet the next girl in line, the other contestant from Tabriz who I knew very well. But my own expression must have been shocked and confused. I didn't realize I had paused in the midst of the human traffic until my fellow Tabriz contestant bumped into me from behind.

She sighed, pulling on the jacket that matched her dress. "Let's go find our taxi, right?"

She had guided me out the door when I stopped, excitement finally overcoming my confusion. "Wait," I said. She turned to me. "I forgot something inside."

"Well, let's go get it."

"No!" I replied, perhaps too quickly. "You go on ahead. I'll get it and take a different taxi." She looked at my quizzically. "Really. It's OK."

The girl smiled. She lowered her voice and leaned in to whisper, "You've been chosen. You've been chosen, haven't you?" She smiled at me, genuinely happy.

"No, no," I scoffed, still unsure of what the queen's reporter's message truly meant, but hoping that this girl was right. "I just forgot something."

She nodded, still smiling, and stepped away into a taxi. I waited a moment, until I was sure that no one was paying particular attention to me in the crowd of ball-goers dispersing into the night. Then I dashed away as quickly as my excited heart would take me, across the dark street and through the puddles of light put off by street lights. The building across the street did in fact have several numbered doors, and I threw open the one with the number five on it, closing it quickly behind me just in case it was meant to be kept a secret.

Once my eyes adjusted to the light inside, I saw several other girls huddled at the other end of the rectangular room. They were holding hands, talking only occasionally in breathless whispers. I ran over and joined them. Seeing from their pale and expectant faces that they knew as little as I did, I joined them in their vigil. Other girls arrived one by one until there were more than a dozen, including the girl I had become so close with over the last three days. We hugged each other, smiled and then attempted to stand still, shifting our weight back and forth in anticipation.

Then a door opened.

The first figure through was the director of the magazine flanked by the other judges who had huddled together that night at the main table. The director's chest was puffed up with pride and excitement and he smiled down at us, as if he had a gift to bestow.

"Ladies," he said. I could have sworn that every person in that room could have heard my heartbeat in the silence. "Congratulations! You are Women's Day's finalists."

The girls exploded with tears, shouts, squeals, sighs and screams of excitement. Sherry and I faced each other and linked both hands, jumping up and down in unison with joy.

We were to come the next day to the Hilton hotel for a final round of photographs, the most important round of photographs. These were for a special section of Women's Day magazine, a full-color spread with at least a page for each girl, in one of their biggest editions: The March New Year's issue. In a knee-length red gown, I stood on the plush stairs of the hotel — a hotel! At one time in my life, it was a luxurious place I thought I would never be allowed to go. Across my chest was the next sash the magazine had given me, a thicker and richer sash, which read: pageant finalist, Tabriz.

I left on the plane back to my home thinking of that sash in my suitcase, my heart soaring with joy. I envisioned in my head the looks on the faces of my family, how shocked and amazed my classmates would be. Our sitting room was going to be constantly busy with the stream of people who wanted to know more about the competition, wanted to see me and gauge if I had what it took to win. This experience, which had begun when I took a risk and wrote a letter to a magazine, had become something life-changing for me, something that could break down the sheltered walls of my home life and show me the world.

I just couldn't wait for the plane to land and the glamorous life to begin.

Unlike a lot of things in life, for once the fantasies of my imagination came true. The fact that I was the Women's Day finalist for our region was the main gossip on the lips of both my female classmates and our male counterparts.

"Oh, Maryam," one said. "This is so exciting!"

"Our Maryam, in the national competition! I can't wait to see you on television."

"You are going to be famous. You are going to have all the men wanting to marry you now," another pointed out.

Having my own positive thoughts echoed back to me was wonderful. However, a portion of the girls I had known all my life were not so glowing. Well, they would mouth the same words of happiness and encouragement to my face, and then glower and whisper behind my back. On one side stood the women who were proud of my accomplishment, and on the other were the women who saw my success as a blow against them. Jealousy and scorn turned them against me, and caused them to spread rumors about me in tea rooms and sitting rooms all over the city.

The boys were a different matter all together. I was never allowed to date. I had never so much as touched the hand of a member of the opposite sex to whom I wasn't related. No one of my group of friends had either, and most wouldn't even think of doing so. Instead, we were left with a rather strange ritual as a way of sizing each other up.

The boys would research which girl went to which school or where they lived in order to place themselves along the girl's normal route of travel. They would slouch against buildings, talking amongst themselves, or pretend to be reading a newspaper. And then the girls would walk by, pretending to be equally oblivious of the boys' presence. Despite the act of nonchalance, the girls would sneak looks at the boys and giggle. The guys would glance back, point out one of the girls to their friends and make remarks.

Now that I had my picture published in a national magazine — which also listed which school I attended, of course — these parade-like meetings became much more common. There were boys of all ages — starting at 17, my own age, and up into their 30s — lining the streets outside my school, several of them each day. Unsure of what I was supposed to do or how I was supposed to act, I continued walking past them with my friends, holding my books close to my chest. Sometimes, a boy would toss a note or a flower or some other token towards me, where it landed on my books. I'd simply tilt my books towards the ground, making sure it would slide off, and pretend I hadn't noticed.

Of course, I did notice the attention. Like any girl of that age — that shy, unsure, awkward and dreamy age — I relished the feeling that men found me attractive, that I was seen as worthy in their eyes. It went no further in my head, however. I was 17 and I wanted to see the world. I was not about to marry some man simply because of his attraction to me. All the attention meant I could be picky, that I didn't have to marry right then, right there. I had options, which was the most freedom a girl in my place could have ever expected. And the dreams of my active imagination — of airplanes, of London, or of the rainy yet romantic New York City I saw in Breakfast at Tiffany's — stoked the warmth of my heart.

Many of the men, on the other hand, had other opinions and had marriage on their minds, much to my surprise. Soon after the New

Year when the magazine was on the shelves, my school day was interrupted by a call to the principal's office. She sat me down in front of
her big, imposing desk and I wondered if I was in trouble from the serious look on her face. She seemed stern and worried. I asked her what
I could do for her and she responded by taking out a stack of mail from
one of her drawers.

"Maryam, I think it is most wonderful that you have done so well in
the Women's Day competition. And it's also wonderful for the school,
because it shows the country the kind of quality education we give our
girls here," she said. "But because all the country knows we are your
school, the whole country knows to find you here, too."

She began sifting through some of the envelopes and postcards on
her desk and her stern look softened into an expression of amusement.
"From Tehran, from Mashhad and from here in Tabriz. You even got
a few from abroad: Kuwait, for example." She handed me a postcard to
look at and I reached forward for it.

Sure enough, it was addressed to Maryam, care of my school, and it
was from a hopeful suitor. He noted his age and profession, the status
of his family and how he believed I would make an ideal wife. I reached
forward and my principal handed me more letters from the stack, all
very similar. There was a boy from a nearby oil refinery who spoke of
how my picture and description touched his heart. There were gifts of
poetry books with notes about undying love. Other books and small
presents emerged from the stack, along with pictures of the men who
hoped to be my husband.

"I have opened them, you understand," the principal said, "because
there were some that had content not fit for a young lady's eyes. But
these are your letters and they belong to you." She paused. "You have
made quite a stir, hm?" She leaned back in her chair and smiled at me,
her hands crossed in her lap.

The situation was quite funny and I understood where the amusement in my principal's eyes came from. I took none of it seriously — the
words of love and devotion or the proposals of marriage. But the words
nonetheless were warming to my heart and made me feel very special,

as if I was engaged in something important. I felt as if it was possible to be someone in the world, that no one and nothing could hold me back. That maybe the beautiful movie stars in my favorite films, like Audrey Hepburn and Doris Day, and I perhaps weren't so dissimilar after all. That perhaps my mother and my uncle were wrong: I could achieve anything I wanted to, go anywhere I wanted to, and no one was going to tell me what my limitations were.

While we contestants were busy preparing for the finals, which would be broadcast on national television, the readers of Women's Day magazines were busy voting for their favorites. Part of who won the competition, the pageant said, was based upon which girl drew the greatest percentage of the votes from the magazine's readers.

My family's reaction to the possibility of me winning was mixed. My mother shrugged to my face, but gossiped about my chances (in her opinion, slim to none) to her girl friends over tea. My father asked if there were lots of prizes: "Cash?" he asked. When I told him that the prizes were mostly intangible — fame, prestige, etc. — he shrugged, too. He was excited that his little girl was excited, and if it brought the family some notoriety, that was always a good thing. Javad, however, was on the receiving end of some of the public excitement. Officials from the magazine and the local government had apparently visited his office about the possibility of me winning.

"They said it probably wouldn't happen," he related to our family one night. I was sitting in the corner, trying not to meet his face with my smile. "They said it is usually some girl from a big, famous family, who has a father with influence, that wins."

I could see some of my family nod and look over at me, as if sizing me up.

"But if it did happen — and I emphasize *if*," he continued, "they said they would be prepared to place lights and banners around the city and at the airport to welcome her home from Tehran."

Though I didn't gloat directly in his face about the sense of accomplishment I felt, an accomplishment that could bring even his attention to me, I think my face was bright enough with happiness to light up the dusky afternoon sunlight in the sitting room.

It was a blessed period of my life, an idyll. Each day opened up like a gift to me and my belief in myself was such that even the everyday worries of life failed to dash my high spirits. My pillow, often soaked with tears in the past, cradled my head gently as I dreamt of glamorous clothing, trophies and crowns, airplane trips around the world, and a faceless man who would one day be my husband, who would take care of me and place me on a pedestal, who could make my dreams come true. Sometimes the mysterious man revealed himself as my childhood friend, my Dream Man, and sometimes he remained cloaked in fog.

I know that at times my ego became over-inflated. I could have been nicer to the men and boys who tried to court me or attract my attention. There were conversations with my friends in which I may have lorded my accomplishments over them. And maybe I walked through the streets with my chin held a notch too high, my nose tilting into the air. But I meant no disrespect, and if I was self-important at the time, it was unintentional. As a woman living in a rather isolated, male-centric country, I knew that the sky was cloudy and quick-tempered. One needed to bask in light while the sun shone, for you never knew when the rain again would fall.

The evening of the final competition was a blur to me. The girls were bundles of nerves: irritable from dieting, powdered and pampered, glossed in lipstick and hairspray. I think the pitch of our voices raised an octave, because our giggles and screeches for joy or anxiety cut like whistles through the atmosphere of excitement backstage.

Backstage. How exciting! Only a plush, red curtain separated us from the lip of the semi-circular stage, which was bordered by a row of harsh, yellow lights shining towards you. Beyond that, in the murky dusk of the rest of the room, were rows and rows of seats. Once empty and expectant, the seats were filling with important people, strangers in fancy formal clothing. We could hear the wave of their combined conversations through the curtains. Even more frightening, however, were the non-human eyes that were watching us: the television lenses.

Big, black beasts of cameras were set up in three places — left, right and center — where they could record for posterity whatever triumphs, tragedies or embarrassments were about to transpire.

By now, all of the girls knew each other well. I sat at a table next to the girl I had become so friendly with during the semi-finals. We had caught up on each other's lives during the few days we had spent in Tehran leading up to the competition. Her experiences were so different from my own. Where my whole town, or at least the whole social circle my family belonged to, buzzed with excitement that I was involved in the competition, she said that her friends and family were, yes, proud but also nonchalant. It was as if they always knew she was destined for such greatness, and would be disappointed if she didn't win. I suddenly thought of my family's indifference as a minor gift in that sense: If I lost, there wouldn't be any shame in it.

From some of the other girls, I heard more negative opinions about Sherry. Behind their hands and in hushed tones, they spewed gossip about how she was preordained as the winner, before all the letters from girls around the country had even been collected.

"Of course," I heard, "Do you know who her father is?"

"I heard that the crown is a sort of present from her father to her. Happy Birthday! What a present!"

Others were less acidic in their comments, but still held the belief that the pageant was fixed in the princess' favor. These girls would sigh and say things like, "But it is an honor to even be here!"

"She is so lovely, though," I heard. "It is her destiny. Don't you think?"

Such gossip is so common among girls that I thought little of it. Nothing could put a damper on my enthusiasm. Even though my attitude was one of confidence and high esteem, I thought little of winning. Competing itself was enough. Look at what has happened in your life up to this point just because you have gotten this far, I thought. Anything beyond this would only add to my already large treasure chest of prizes.

And I was going to be on television! Only in the last few years did my family own such a thing and I was going to be featured front and center, in color on that glowing screen in my family's sitting room. It was this attitude that allowed me to genuinely wish the other girls the best of luck during the competition and yet still keep high hopes for myself.

With the make-up and grace of women much older than our teenage years, we traipsed back and forth along the stage during the various competitions. There was the presentation of the evening gowns, which we called soiree dresses.

The interview portion was one of the most intensive. We were brought — alone — to the center of the stage to talk with the emcee, who was prepared in advance with a question for each girl. And we had no idea what that question would be. When my turn came, the lens of the camera, not 10 feet away from where I stood as straight and tall as I could, stared at me, making the butterflies in my stomach flap their wings faster. But the only indication of my nerves was that my anxiety made my smile even bigger for the host. If all else fails, I thought, smile!

"Maryam from East Azerbaijan," said the host into his microphone. He was wearing a shiny black suit to match his shiny black hair. "You have said in past interviews that your favorite study is that of literature. Tell me, what have you learned of the great Iranian poets? Specifically, can you tell me of the famous poets Ferdowsi and Hafez?"

I had been looking directly into the emcee's eyes, trying to concentrate intently on what he had to say. Now, he started shifting his eyes from mine back to the camera, smiling expectantly.

"Of course," I responded. I swallowed, as if I had to bring down the air I would need to speak the words on my mind. "Both poets are ancient masters and are thought of as some of the best writers in Persian history. But they are very, very different in their styles." Taking a cue from the host, I looked at him and then out the audience, as if I was giving a presentation before my classroom back at home.

"Ferdowsi wrote epic poems about history and battles. They told stories of things that really happened or of legends. But Hafez wrote more about love and about people's feelings. They really couldn't be more different."

There was a smattering of applause from the audience, who I could barely see through the thick lighting of the stage.

"Thank you, Maryam," said the emcee. "That's very illuminating."

"Thank you," I replied. I waved to the crowd and bowed my head slightly to acknowledge their applause, then pivoted on my shoe and walked back stage. It was only later that I found out about the clapping and shouting that happened all over Tabriz at same time. The television broadcast was interrupted regularly by commercials, and my interview was one of only a few that was shown in its entirety, making mine one of the most memorable performances of the night.

At the end of the evening, the emcee announced that the judges had conferred. Their scores and the votes of the whole country — collected over the last few weeks from the magazine's contest — had been combined.

Standing in a line with the other girls, all of us frosted in different vibrant colors and smiling out the bright joy that was in our hearts, I felt as if I was standing on top of a cake, a towering multi-layered cake. I had been elevated above the teeming masses of people and told I was special, and here I was, on top of a mountain. It was a sweet emotion and I attempted to savor it as the emcee drew out the anticipation of the moment as far as the crowd would tolerate.

First place was announced and the theater erupted in applause to hear the name Sherry. I clapped as hard as the flowers in my arms would let me and jumped up and down as she came to join me on the winner's section of the stage. Our bouquets clashed together as we hugged, bouncing up and down in our excitement. There were a few tears in everyone's eyes, threatening to smudge make up, but they were tears of joy, a release after the long months of build-up and nerves.

Some of the girls were slightly bitter, saying that the end of the pageant had been decided in advance, but most were still happy to have taken part at all. We felt like princesses, pampered and prized and now forced to descend back to earth. The pageant was over, the dream completed. We held hands and hugged, promising to write one another and to never forget all the fun we had in Tehran, especially the events outside the competition. As when any good thing comes to an end, it was bittersweet. I yearned for the time of the pageant to return, even in the final moments of the experience.

As for the pageant's winner, I begrudged Sherry nothing. She was a very nice girl, very charming and very pretty. There may have been girls who were more purely beautiful than she. But the winner of the competition was supposed to represent the perfect, well-rounded Iranian girl who could be the dream of her parents, the love of her husband and an honor to her community. And I knew Sherry was all of that. Such was what drew me to her in the first place.

And if it was her family's position and wealth that won her the prize, I accepted that, too. After all, I had lived all my life in a culture of privilege and patrimony. When a man had wealth and prosperity, he dealt out presents to his friends and family. He showered them with gifts as a symbol of his status in the world, and these gifts could include jobs, prizes, marriage arrangements and more. When such a thing occurred, when such a thing was "bought" for another, the world shook its head and took note, but it was the way of things. It was no less valid, really, for being earned by privilege instead of merit. But perhaps the most telling fact in my mind what that this girl — my friend — went on in the competition, putting herself against winners from every country in the world at a contest held in the United States, in the city of Chicago. She earned our country a third place prize — third place in the world!

That time, I was in my family's sitting room in Tabriz, hoping she could sense the clapping and shouts I directed her way through the television screen.

Chapter Eight

Life after the pageant slowly resolved itself back into my normal routine — home and school, my friends, planning for my future. But life also opened itself to me in ways I hadn't seen before. While marriage had always been discussed as inevitable for me — the only route for a girl in my country, in my situation — it had always been a remote destination, a trip you dream about taking "someday."

After the pageant, I found myself taking on the role of a woman of marriageable age, a role that blossomed in front of me and that I blossomed into. Suddenly, my life was supplemented with the opposite sex, and I don't mean my brothers and cousins, who had been the most regular male components of my life before. I mean that I was finally allowed to mix and mingle with men, out in the open and in closer proximity than smiles tossed across streets or notes exchanged (and usually ignored).

I was allowed to date. Well, that's not entirely true. Just like it had been for years, the phone in our household was locked to only receive incoming calls, cutting off the chance that we three girls could have any contact with people (especially boys) outside of our parents' attention. And when the phone would ring with an incoming call and I or one of my sisters was called to answer, my mother would obviously be able to stand three feet behind us, her eyes and ears trained upon every word and every blush. It would have been shocking for a boy to ask a girl to spend an evening with him, for dinner or a movie, even if he met her parents and a curfew was established. There was no concept of "going steady" or the "first base," "second base" and other baseball analogies of American youth.

When I say I was allowed to socialize with the opposite sex, I mean that I was able to come as close as Iranian youths were permitted to dating: I was invited and allowed to attend parties of young people.

I was still in 12th grade when I returned from the glory of the pageant in Tehran, and I had a friend who was in a unique position. First of all, our mothers had known each other since they were girls themselves, which lent her family a respectability and trustworthiness in my family's eyes. Her mother was also educated in London and was therefore quite forward-thinking and modern. On top of that, her father was a very important General in the Iranian army, a rank called Timsar. That rank allowed them the wealth and privilege to entertain freely. All these factors combined led to my teenage self's greatest dream: co-ed parties with music and dancing, great food, late nights — all with parental permission.

Not that the parental permission was given freely and without reservation, of course. When told about the first of these invitations, my father was skeptical. A huge fan of parties and merry-making of all sorts, he didn't want to deny me or my sisters the chance to have fun. But he also prized his daughters' virtue and respectability. After much chin stroking and thought, he sat us three girls down and outlined how it was going to be.

"You will be allowed to go," he said, and smiles and bouncing joy began to bubble up from the three girls on the couch. Then he raised his hand to add that he wasn't finished. "It is OK for you to go where the boys are, it is OK to go anywhere we approve of in advance," he continued with one finger raised in warning, "if you are accompanied by Hassan."

Hassan happened to be an old man employed by our family to do various tasks. He worked around the house, ran errands, delivered messages and anything else that needed doing in exchange for a wage and a place to live. He was quiet and kindly, much like a distant cousin or an uncle to us girls. But he was also fiercely loyal to my father, meaning that my dad could trust the man not to let his girls come to harm.

The smiles remained on our faces, still threatening to erupt in happiness.

"And," my father said, "anywhere you go, if you go to these parties, you must bring your little brother, Ali Reza, with you, as well. After all, if the place is unsuited for a little boy's eyes and ears, it is unsuitable for you, too."

"So, we can go?" I asked, making sure I understood him correctly.

"Yes."

We girls hugged one another and immediately began talking about what to wear, wondering who else would be in attendance and otherwise scheming.

"And Hassan will bring you home by 12 o'clock. By midnight, do you hear?"

We heard and understood, but the curfew didn't at all inhibit our joy at the news that we would be allowed to be social creatures, girls with their own parties and functions outside those held at our own home or those of family members, outside of dry and dusty tea parties between women.

In the end, there were many parties thrown at this friend's home, so many that they blur together in my memory. That doesn't mean they weren't memorable, however. I would prepare for at least a week in advance by planning which dress I was going to wear. By this time, I was both buying ready-made dresses and also sewing my own or having them made by a seamstress, but they were all of European styles. Size 2 or size 4, cut slightly above or slightly below the knee, sometimes sleeveless but never strapless. One dress in particular I remember hugged my body, so effortlessly small in my youth, with blue fabric, flouncing with ruffles around the neckline and around the hemline. I wore pearls around my neck and, as with the rest of my life, no cover at all. Of course, I had coats and sweaters for the cold, but not once did I attempt to shield my face in the traditional veil common amongst some Muslim women of the country.

I was well aware of the fact that most of my city and country was religious. If asked, I would have said that I was Muslim, too, just like them. However, I grew up in a mixed neighborhood with a very open-minded father, who placed such spiritual concerns firmly in the background in favor of everyday life. And there were many others who felt the same, people in our family and that we socialized with who approved of parties where there was sometimes alcohol and always dancing. (The host parents kept a careful eye out for couples dancing too close together, though, something that was very daring and bold for young people at the time.) Most everyone at these parties knew one another or knew someone who knew your family. At the time, I took it for granted, but these free-thinking and open-minded people were often of the upper-middle to upper classes of society, to which we belonged. Once I became a finalist in the pageant, however, I began to mingle with those people who had been on the upper fringes of our social circle growing up, having friends that were from better or more prosperous families than even my father — the theater owner and business man — did.

The parties at my friend's house were a colorful and melodious blur to me. We started by munching on little bites of food, appetizers, set up on a corner table in the main room, where music would be playing on a stereo system. At that time, the young people listened mostly to music from the movies, both European and Eastern movies, though we favored the former. The soundtracks of "To Sir with Love" and "Love is a Many Splendored Thing" were scratched to pieces on record players all over the city in that year, if I remember correctly.

After a bit of talking and fun, the whole group of 30 to 50 people would sit down to dinner. A large table was set with painted platters heaped with traditional Persian fare, and glassware glinted in the light, both from electrical lights and candles. Soldier in smart uniforms, the troops of the Timsar General, stood at attention around the table, bringing in and out platters and refilling water glasses and teacups. (The Timsar stocked his house with servants from his troops, a common practice at that time.)

Positioned in the seats of honor were the Timsar's children: the daughter I knew and two sons. And except for a few adults — the Timsar and his wife, perhaps two or three others — the remainder of the guests were the children's friends and the children of the parents' friends, an always shifting but never unfamiliar group of vibrant young folks.

Once the roasted chicken and spiced lamb were consumed, the party really got going. The music was turned up louder and the furniture pushed out of the way for dancing. Not everyone danced to every song, but most made the rounds of the guests at least once, each boy dancing one song with each girl to be polite and social. But boys would also jockey to dance with the girls they fancied, and I found myself to be much in demand. I had to ask for a break when I got tired or found myself swept back up the next time the music began.

And the dancing! What a joyful release for young people usually so constrained and controlled, their every action monitored for correctness. To us it seemed so close together with one set of hands clasped and the other on his shoulder, his other on your girlish hip. It was thrilling in an almost illicit way, and I don't think I was the only girl who asked herself, "Am I really doing this? Is this really allowed?" We maintained a solid foot of distance between our bodies, swaying this way and that in formal dances — the Tango, the Paso Double, etc. — but it still felt prohibited. I would have described it as sexy if I had such a word in my vocabulary at that time.

But it was also exciting for other reasons, exciting because we were engaged in the activities we saw depicted in the movies and on television. The feeling was akin to doing a play, becoming someone else — someone special — for an evening, far away from your normal existence.

Then at the stroke of midnight, Hassan would appear in the doorway. My sisters and I would gather up our coats and sincerely thank our hosts. We'd wave goodbye to the boys whose hands still made our fingertips tingle, all boys of good families and reputations that our parents would approve of, and head off home with enough fodder for dreams to last us until the next party, perhaps two or three weeks in the future.

When someone from our family graduated high school, it was my father who usually helped them find their future. Of course, I was the oldest of his children, so this had only happened with cousins and other more distant relatives so far. Our culture put a great deal of emphasis upon schooling at that time. After all, the world was opening up to Iran thanks to plentiful oil money and good diplomatic relations, and Iranian young people were sent all over the world for education. Europe, America, England, Asia: Undergraduate and graduate educations were bought for kids in far-flung locations at prestigious universities. And the further and more prestigious a school a child went to, the more it reflected well upon his or her family and our country, where they could come back and use their smarts to improve things.

My father had financed the educations of quite a few of my cousins, my favorite of whom was in France at university. My final year of school, I tried to wrangle out of my father what was planned for me upon my upcoming graduation. I had always been expected to continue my schooling until I got married — being a teacher was one of my mother's common suggestions — so I was hoping and desperately dreaming that I, too, could go abroad for my studies.

Where I wanted to go in particular was London, the same destination I had dreamed of since Arian built me a plane out of rocks and promised to fly me there. And my father waved his hand at me and said some words of reassurance, promising me that if I graduated and everything went well, that dream could come true for me. But it was not a subject we spoke of too frequently, especially in comparison to the subject of marriage.

In fact, marriage — and who I was going to marry — became an almost daily conversation in my house. Not because of my insistence and not because my mother forced the issue, but due to outside pressure offers from men. Though I never thought myself a beautiful girl — thin and pretty, yes, but never beautiful — I seemed to incite a great deal of men into thoughts of matrimony and commitment. The teachers at my little brother's school, a local Senator, doctors, clergy men: all sorts of males of all ages, from their 20s to their 50s, suddenly wanted me for their own, for better or for worse, for the rest of their lives.

Of course, that doesn't mean I met a lot of men during this flurry of offers and hints and suggestions about marriage to various suitors. That's not the way things work in Iran, or at least in the Iran of my youth. It was complicated and formal dance with many steps, many layers, beginning with small gestures and subtle hints.

And most of these small gestures and hints are administered solely by and to women. While it did happen differently, outside of the traditional steps, on occasion, a Persian man usually began a proposal by recruiting the help of his closest female relative — his mother, or an aunt or older sister when the mother was not present or available. This female relative, knowing of the man's interest in the girl, would start the ball rolling by calling up my house and speaking to my mother.

"I have heard about your daughter from my son," she might say after introducing herself, "and would like to come to your house to have your daughter serve us tea."

To serve us tea: This meant that the family would like to take a look at the house of the family, to see what kind of background the girl had, and also to assess the girl herself. My mother would usually agree to this meeting and welcome the flock of women into our home, because if the family has decided that the girl is old enough to get married, the door is always open to these kinds of meetings.

Instead of the everyday sitting room, the guests would be escorted to what we called the "guest room," where the furnishings and fabrics were a level nicer than any other room in the house. (Mother would be sure to have it cleaned and dusted in preparation for such important meetings.) The potential groom's females were situated about the sitting area and pleasantries were exchanged, barbed pleasantries that were meant to deem how worthy both young people and their families were: the son's occupation, the daughter's level of schooling, the history of each family, the occupations of their fathers, the background of their mothers, if the bride cooks, sews, knits, sings, dances, paints, gardens or practices any of the other female arts.

Then, the potential bride would be called into the room to serve tea. She is supposed to carry a tray with the ornate tea pot, cups and saucers, and bowls of sweetness. Raisins or pastries or something else sweet was always thought to compliment the bitterness of the rich tea. Without saying anything unless spoken to and with eyes downcast, the girl would serve each woman tea, serving the oldest before the youngest, in a most respectful manner. Then the girl is supposed to turn around and leave, letting the other women talk about her while she is not present.

Somehow, the female delegation would assess from this brief meeting whether their son or nephew should pursue the women, whether his conception of her was correct and if they, as a family, would take the next step in the proposal process. All of this judgment made from the girl's appearance, the information her mother related, how she held herself and the one word she was expected to utter: Salaam, which means hello.

That's how the first visit was supposed to happen, anyway. It's not the way it always unfolded for me.

There were a few occasions where the match was too ludicrous to even consider, and even my mother was aware of it, so no tea came to pass. While I can probably assume that my mother refused in advance many times, it was only once that I witnessed it.

I was wearing a slinky, chiffon dress of bright red and had my hair done, earrings shining out from behind my careful curls. It was a large party, larger than those usually held at my friend's house, and my mother was in attendance with me. I was walking by, taking in the surroundings and the people, when I saw a woman I vaguely knew speaking to my mother. She was older than my mother by a few years, stout and reserved in a very traditional outfit, and she was wearing a cover. It was this last observation that reminded me that she came from a very religious family. In fact, her son was a clergyman, an imam. My heart beat nervously, hoping that they weren't setting up a marriage between me and her devout son, so I walked a bit closer.

"Maryam is lovely," I heard the woman say to my mother. "She looks more beautiful all the time."

"Thank you," my mother replied. She then went on to describe how I had done so well in the beauty pageant and did very well at school. Her prideful speech caught me off guard, as accustomed as I was to her negative opinions of what I did and said.

"I suppose if we asked you for her to be our daughter in law, you'd say no," the woman continued, keeping her voice very light and polite.

My mother paused, fanning herself a few times with her hand in the press of people at the party. "You would be correct," she replied. "Our families just don't match."

The woman nodded, as if expecting this answer. "I will tell him that I asked. Give our best to your daughter."

My mother also nodded and smiled as the woman left. She then met my eyes where I stood hiding, not wanting to be too obvious in my listening. As if she knew I was there all along. I smiled, and she made a motion with her hands as if she was washing them of the situation.

My mother grew used to my continued refusals, to the point where she would often take a phone call from a potential suitor and call to me from downstairs, "Maryam! Maryam, what about Mr. So-and-So. You know, he works at … "

I would wrinkle my nose and shake my head. Her hand over the receiver, she would sigh and tell the woman on the other end of the connection that she didn't think coming over for tea would be worthwhile. "But thank you very much," she would say, "and give my best to your son, Mrs. So-and-So."

Even with these preemptive refusals, I still said no in person to many, many men (or rather, their mothers) who came to our guest room for tea: the old Senator, who may have been a millionaire but was as old as my father; a pharmacist; a doctor; a butcher.

My mother never denied me my right to say no, but she did grow frustrated and tried to build the men up in my mind.

"He's so handsome," she said of the pharmacist.

"But he's a womanizer," I replied. "I've seen him around town making eyes at so many women, you wouldn't believe it."

"He has no parents alive," my mother said about my brother's teacher. "That means you won't have to deal with a mother-in-law or nosey family. You should marry him."

"Forget it," I responded. "I don't want to."

My mother readied the guest room one morning for a visitor that neither of us knew very much about but, as I said, the home was supposed to always be open for these kinds of things. To refuse too many invitations to tea is to set oneself up as too good for the rest of society; it's haughty and downright rude. I was walking down in the garden of the backyard, where my mother could see me from the guest room window. I was resigned that if she called me to serve tea, I could come inside and obey, but I also knew my answer was going to be no. Something inside me knew it wasn't my time, that my marriage wasn't going to happen like this, so my feelings were of imposition and annoyance rather than anticipation.

"Maryam! Maryam!" I heard my mother call from the window above me. I looked up to see her leaning out of the window, her hands clenched on the sill and eyes squinting into the sunlight.

"Ah, there you are." I could see the figure of a woman behind her, a larger and imposing woman I was sure I didn't recognize. My mother gestured at the figure and introduced her as the mother of the man who worked at the local car dealership, a profitable and respectable occupation when only the very rich had cars in Tabriz.

"You know the guy?" my mother asked. "He walks or drives by the house all the time looking for you, you know."

"I know him," I said.

"She's here for him, so … "

My mother knew I was a stubborn creature, and if she pushed for an answer, it would be the answer I thought she least wanted to hear.

When I remained silent, the car dealer's mother shouldered into the window to call out to me. "So, would you consider marrying him or not?" she demanded.

"Not," I said.

She made an angry, whooshing noise by forcing the air in her lungs out between her lips and threw her hands up in the air. "You know, I heard about you being so particular, so I shouldn't be surprised. What? You have a man in that head of yours already, don't you?" She pointed a finger down one story to where I stood on the grass, as if the finger could point to the secret thoughts in my head. "You're walking the garden thinking of the man who already has your heart, aren't you?"

I smiled and shook my head.

"Fine then," she fumed. "I don't need you to serve me any silly tea, then."

Her figure disappeared from the window and my mother frowned at me, turning away. I continued walking under the shady trees that were once my refuge from the world, my personal ice cream shop, and wondered if the woman might be right.

No, none of my suitors had struck my heart and I didn't think it belonged to anyone. But if I admitted it to myself, there was one man in my thoughts regularly, only one, especially when I was wandering out in the garden or when I sat during the quiet part of the day toward evening, watching the sunset. It was my Arian.

Somewhere in England, perhaps in London, he was still completing his studies. And once my father sent me there after graduation, perhaps I could find him there. Perhaps: The plan was only a perhaps in my mind. Maybe we'd bump into one another by chance and he'd be amazed at how much I'd grown-up and yet how nothing between us had changed. Perhaps: These were the fantasies of a 17-year-old girl, fleeting and passionate.

I never encouraged any of the suitors that came to tea. If it wasn't stated at the actual meeting, my mother would relate my disinterest to the family when if and when they called to set up a second meeting. If such a meeting were scheduled — or in my mother's words, if I wasn't such a stubborn girl — the boy would accompany his relatives to second meeting. The same ritual would be repeated with small talk and queries about me with my mother and, this time around, maybe my father. I would have been called in to serve tea, bowed my eyes, poured based on age and respect, said my one word, and left. If the boy was still interested and wanted to follow through with a proposal, he would leave a small, gold ring on the tray for me, for when I returned to carry it back to the kitchen. Or perhaps he wouldn't this time around, waiting for another visit to be sure. Or perhaps he simply wouldn't, having changed his mind.

Only if the ring was given and the girl accepts it — both parties had a right to refuse — would the engagement begin, and the next steps take place. A marriage contract would be arranged, which was a modern version of a dowry, laying out what the girl's bride price was in gold, antique Korans, apartments and other valuables. It also outlined what the bride's father would provide to help the newlyweds set up house in terms of furniture, pots and pans, and linens. Both gifts would be haggled over, and sometimes the family wouldn't be able to agree, calling off the union.

But if everything could be worked out, the bride's family began researching the groom by interviewing his family and friends and co-workers. The bride and groom would meet several times to get to know one another.

Again, if everything went according to tradition, a huge engagement party would be thrown, followed by a ceremonial presentation of the bride's gifts from the groom's family, a ceremony the whole neighborhood turned out to see. How well did she do?

Of course, then there was the actual marriage, a huge event meant to impress everyone invited, which was everyone the families knew, and a few strangers thrown in for good measure. There were florists and dressmakers and people to do hair and make-up. There were mixed seeds called Esfand burned for their scent and good luck for the future, sugar sprinkled on the couple's heads, butterflies let loose, and loads of gifts: gold, paper money, jewelry, watches and more.

In other words, this tiny, little tea meeting was the first step of a big, important cycle of tradition. My mother's frustration was understandable: She wanted to put on an enviable party, spending lots of money to make her and our family the center of attention. She wanted to make my wedding ceremony look great, setting up my sisters for even better matches in the upcoming years. All she ever wanted was a position of power and for eyes to be respectfully directed upon her. Therefore, she had been waiting for her first daughter to get married for years.

The only thing standing in her way was me.

Chapter Nine

Unlike the traditional engagement routines and marriage ceremony my mother was dreaming of for me, my high school graduation was rather anticlimactic. There were no caps and gowns or special music, no ceremony where your name is called and someone important shakes your hand. As far as I know, there are no pictures of me surrounded by my parents, glowing with happiness at the accomplishment.

Instead, there was a meeting between each girl at my school and each teacher, where they would test how much we had learned and hand out our final grades.

Although I was known as the beauty queen of the school, I had always done well in my classes at the same time. Social and outgoing — and still having a few jealous enemies — I was nonetheless confident that I had studied and paid enough attention to do well in all of my meetings, finishing up with good grades. Even so, any face-to-face meeting where a teacher sizes you up is a bit intimidating.

But my meetings were not exactly what I had expected, especially my conference with my literature teacher, Mr. Taher, who was about 40 years old.

We were in the classroom, where we were completely alone, and the door was closed for privacy. I sat down with my textbook in front of me, a paper and pen ready if I needed them, and I waited for him to begin. He was thumbing through a folder of paper in front of him, which I assumed was my school records or past grades, something of that nature.

After a few moments, he cleared his throat and looked up at me.

"Maryam," he began, "it's been a pleasure to have you it my class and at this school. You have done very well here and done well — perhaps even better — outside of school. Ah yes," he continued, "the beauty queen." He shot me an amused smile.

This digression confused me and wanting to get the testing and grading over with, I tried to keep him on track. Especially for a teacher at an all-girls school, Mr. Taher had a reputation for having a wandering eye. Not wandering hands — nothing was ever alleged or proved in that regard — but most girls felt he had a playboy side to his personality, an irreverence and sensuality he kept hidden under his brown blazer.

"Which page do you want me to read?" I asked him. This is what I had been told by other students that I would be expected to do.

"None of them," he said. In his 40s, Mr. Taher had curly hair and what I thought of as a smooshy face, with lots of smile lines around his eyes.

"Mr. Taher," I repeated, meeting his eyes, "what do you want me to read?"

"Nothing," he repeated.

"I'm graduating," I said, letting some of my frustration to be finished show through, "and you don't want me to read anything, like the other students had to do?"

He was quiet, as if composing his thoughts. He leaned back in his chair, playing with the pencil he held in his hand.

"I pity the man who is going to take you under his wing, Maryam," he finally said into the silence of the classroom.

"What?" I responded. My mouth stayed slightly ajar in shock, and I was not quite sure I heard him correctly.

"Do you want an A or a B then?" he said, bringing the pencil to hover over the paper to write down my answer.

I closed my mouth. "I don't care," I said. "You're the teacher. Shouldn't you know that?"

He nodded and smiled at me one more time, and I picked up my things. I left the room and I left the school, the door swinging shut as it always had behind me. But this time, I would never open it again. That was as much ceremony as there was to my high school graduation — the soft click of a door closing. Even so, that small action of opening a door and walking through it into my future was exhilarating, like crossing the line between practicing at life and living it.

This is now real, I told myself. Anything is possible now, I repeated in my head.

The only problem was, I wasn't quite sure which of the many possibilities I actually wanted to come true.

"It's time for you to send me to London," I told my father. I was approaching him in the place I often did, in front of the mirror where he was preparing himself for work. So many of our conversations took place there — with a tie being tightened around his neck, a suit coat smoothed over his European-style dress shirt. I suppose it was easy to speak to him alone during these times, because when he returned from work, we were usually in the common areas of the house, surrounded by the rest of the family. Besides, I loved to see him taking as much care with his appearance as I did with my own. It felt like a bonding moment in that way. I was so proud of how dapper and sharp he looked. That was my father, a generous, charming and handsome man. It was the picture of him that would remain in my mind for the rest of my life when I thought of my father.

"I've graduated, father," I continued. "It's time to talk about sending me to school, to England."

"No, I'm not going to do that," he said in a very casual tone, as if we were discussing the weather. But his eyes avoided mine, looking down or into the mirror instead, which meant he knew exactly how important this conversation was to me.

"What?" I asked. "You promised." I watched him avoid my eyes a few more moments before repeating, "But you promised."

"No."

"Why?"

"We are not going to talk about it, it's just a no," he said firmly.

Tears began to fill my eyes and I stood stock still, feeling shocked and betrayed.

"But..." I could no longer speak. There was a ball of tears rising in my throat, painful and throbbing and threatening to explode at any time.

"No," my father repeated, finally looking me in the face. He was ready for work, ready to turn on his heel and leave me stranded inside the house, in the land of women, for the day. A long, long day. And he needed me to move out of his way.

"Just go," he said. "Go. Go. Go."

It was only after he strode by me as fast as he could and had left the house that words came to my mind. "Why are you treating me like this?" Words I should have said, but couldn't have. Because girls don't say such things to their fathers. "Why are you betraying your promise? Tell me what is going on here." My head swam with all the words I wanted to say.

Because something was going on, something behind the scenes. I could see it in my father's downcast eyes. Something or someone had convinced him that his daughter should not be sent abroad for school, and though it broke his heart to tell me, there would be no changing his mind.

The open door I had walked through upon leaving my school for the last time had just slammed shut in my face. Nothing was going to change. Nothing was going to become better and no freedom was going to miraculously materialize simply because I had reached a certain age and passed a certain level of schooling. Here I was, in the same house as I'd been since my birth. The same walls and the same trees still surrounded me, and though the trees may have grown a bit taller, they still weren't high enough to help me escape into the great, wide world.

It was summer and warm, the time where children play in the street like I had once been allowed to do, until I was too old to play like a boy anymore and was taught to knit, told I *could* be a teacher and *would* be a wife. It was summer outside but I fell into the cold, emptiness of my future and fell also into a depression.

At first, I would not leave my room for stretches of 20 hours at a time, reading dark and heavy books like Charles Dickens and other classics that were as depressing as I felt. The magazines I usually read so avidly sat untouched, a reminder of brighter times and higher hopes. My pillow was my closest companion. For a few weeks after, I broadened my moping to the rest of the house and the garden.

Throughout this time, I tried to figure out the reason I was not allowed to go to London. Yes, there was the fact that I was a girl. I sensed that the flurry of engagement offers and marriage prospects had something to do with it, too. If I went away to school, perhaps my parents thought that flurry would end, that my prospects would become fewer and not as appealing. Or perhaps they just didn't want me to go away, to fly so far over the ocean and — like some roaming children — never return to my home country. Marriage to a foreigner, being taken advantage of, wasting their money on schooling I would never use once I was married: Were any of these the things my parents feared? Why? Why wasn't I allowed to go?

I had a feeling that my mother was behind the sudden refusal and change of heart, but of course I couldn't prove it. I just knew that I felt thwarted and controlled in the same way I used to when Javad was more involved in my life, when my mother used him to keep us docile and obedient. I certainly felt docile and obedient — against my will, of course — and that led to thoughts that my mother had blocked me from my future. Without any evidence, I still had my suspicions.

After this black mood had lasted a month or more after my graduation, however, my mother surprised me with her concern.

"I know you are upset, Maryam, but this is enough. This is it," she told me once morning. "You must snap out of it."

I kept my eyes averted, upset at being told once again what I was to do and feel, and able to do nothing about it. "So," she continued, "I'm sending you to my uncle's house in Tehran." Suddenly warm, she placed a hand on my shoulder and said, "You need to get away and have some fun, do the fun things you like to do. And you will feel better. I know you will."

"Yes," I said. "Tehran might be fun." I offered her a shaky smile, the weight of my bad mood lifting but still present on my shoulders.

My mother went back to her knitting. "Besides," she said, "you never know. There are lots of parties and lots of people. You might just meet an eligible man in Tehran."

I rolled my eyes at her comments about the eligible man, but with the thought of the parties and the people, I went to pack my bags.

Fun people lived in Tehran, cosmopolitan people who wore enviable, slinky dresses and sipped on wine or beer at parties. My mother's uncle had several children that were slightly older than me — so grown-up and confident, the way I hoped to be one day. Despite the crush of the city, with its traffic, high-rise buildings and the constant shuffle of people on the sidewalks, Tehran seemed incredibly open to me: open-minded, open to the world, open to me.

If my aunt and cousins weren't at home, hosting a stream of friends and family coming to visit, we were on the other end of the equation, traveling all over the city to visit acquaintances. Sometimes we would arrive for tea in the afternoon, sometimes for parties that lasted into the evening. Always a social and outgoing girl, this stream of new people was the medicine I needed to drag me out of the black mood I'd wallowed in since my graduation. Here were all sorts of vibrant young people about my age, some married but some single, and they did a remarkable variety of different things both for fun and for careers. They studied English and French. They were on holidays from schools in Europe and America, where they were getting degrees in business and engineering. They worked for oil companies or government ministries.

I was only in the city a few days when I met a woman who might have changed my life completely. She was older, but still very friendly and relatable to my teenage self with her stylish hair, red lipstick and sharp matching suit jacket and skirt. She enquired about my recent graduation and what my plans were, and I responded with my story of thwarted wanderlust and how trapped I felt living in remote Tabriz under my parents' thumbs.

"Have you ever thought about Iran Air?" she asked. Of course, I thought to myself. I had long fantasized about the planes of the country's largest airline taking me away, scrutinizing a sky full of such planes while pondering who they were carrying, where they were headed.

"They are hiring lots of girls just like you," the woman continued, "to be flight attendants, traveling all over the world. You know, it's really a quite respectable career for an educated young woman nowadays."

A stewardess, I thought, because that's what they were called in those days. How interesting! While teaching or nursing were careers that I had been told were suitable all my life, this path was completely unexplored in my mind and I asked the woman for more information.

While I don't know if she was affiliated with the airline herself or through her family, she was certainly knowledgeable. Apparently, the airline was taking on a great deal of new flight attendants to catch up with the increased travel to and from Iran due to the oil business and sunny diplomatic relations with Europe and the United States. After two years of domestic service within the country, flight attendants would then be considered for international routes to London, Paris, America and beyond. All it would take to be considered was to go down to the Iran Air offices and complete an exam and have an interview, and a girl could be walking down the road of a new future, as wide open as the sky.

The idea of this life lit up the circuits of my brain, setting all sorts of new ideas into motion. Here was something I could hold on to, something that no one could take away from me. By reaching out for a career of my own, I would no longer have to wait for someone else to allow me what I wanted — I could take it! To a woman of a different background, it may be hard to understand how liberating this feeling of empowerment was, because such women take for granted that they can choose the path of their own existence. But to a girl who had just spent weeks trapped inside her family home and inside of her own disappointed mind, the thought of a job was as dazzling to me as a diamond ring, which catches sunlight to create rainbows. Perhaps this could be my rainbow.

After a night spent tossing and turning in the light of this new idea, I went to the office of Iran Air the very next day. Test taken and interview concluded, I was told that I would be a perfect candidate for the job of hostess of the skies. I walked back to my mother's uncle's house on a cloud, and though I'd only been in Tehran for a few days, I called my mother to tell her I was headed home to Tabriz.

"But you just got there!" my mother exclaimed, confused.

I laughed. "But I found a way, Mother," I said. "I found something very important."

Giddy with excitement, I related the story about opportunities at the airline and how I'd been approved, how I wanted to head home and wrap things up before setting off on my new life in the clouds.

"But Maryam," she said, "I — "

"I'm headed home now," I interrupted. "I'll see you tomorrow."

When I arrived back home and had stowed my baggage up in my bedroom, I walked into the sitting room to find my uncle sitting with my mother. I hadn't seen Javad in our home for quite a while, at least not alone and sitting in this manner in the sitting room, as if waiting to pounce. When I met his eyes, his eyebrows were furrowed together, as if massing for an attack against me.

I saw him exchange a look with my mother. He raised his hand to indicate his desire to slap me across the face, and my mother shook her head no. He lowered his hand and sighed, returning his fierce eyes and attacking eyebrows towards me.

I was frozen only steps into the room, unable to either leave or sit down due to the adrenaline pumping stiffly through my veins.

"Hi, Javad," I said, trying to regain the feeling of power and independence I'd absorbed in the cosmopolitan atmosphere of Tehran. Trying to feel like an adult.

"So," he began, "You want to become a waitress in the sky, do you?"

He paused, rubbing one fist with the other hand. His gravely voice was strong with anger.

"You are going to be serving people in the air? Foreigners. Foreign men, even. You handle their dirty cups and pour their alcohol? Disgusting."

My mother nodded, for once totally engaged in the conversation instead of her knitting or other handy work. I looked down toward the floor.

"A waitress in the sky?" he continued. "It's bad enough that I see you walking down the streets with no cover, your brazen face out for any man to see. It's bad enough that your father allows you to be in the company of boys and men. It's amazing that you haven't ruined your reputation and the status of this family already with your disgusting ways."

Javad stood up and walked to the archway that led to the front door. He leaned against the door jam with his elbow and shoulder.

"This is completely against our culture and against your family," he said. "This is not going to happen."

I took a deep breath, hoping it would cool the growing heat of my blushing cheeks and give me strength.

"But I have taken the test already, Javad, and they have accepted me," I said.

"Well that doesn't matter if you are not able to go back to Tehran," he said. "Does it?" His bulk in the door way and his fists aching to be put into use made me feel like a rat in a trap.

I turned to look at my mother. She nodded and said, "That's the way it is, Maryam. That's how it is going to happen."

Tears were threatening to stream down my burning cheeks. My feelings of empowerment, that seemed so tangible and real to me just a day before, wavered and tumbled away. She was right. I had no way to go to Tehran without my family's permission: no money for a ticket, no uncle's house to stay at, no way to even force my way out of the house.

I was beaten. They had won.

"Fine," I said to my mother, trying not to give her the added victory of seeing me cry. "Fine! But I will find another way, Mother. I will."

I ran upstairs and smothered my face in my faithful friend, my pillow and once again saw my red-breasted friend alone in a jungle with no wings to fly, remaining trapped by the towering trees of the jungle, and unable to escape his misery.

This image was marked in my mind as I tried to find a way out of my situation. How would I find a way, another way to be happy and excited about the future?

This time, I decided not to wallow in my disappointment, but to actively seek another way into a bright future. To me, no future would be bright without the possibility of traveling abroad figuring into it somehow, and so getting out of Iran remained my number one priority. Knowing that my parents were unwilling to pay for me to make this escape, I hid my activities from them as best I could, exploring my options behind their backs.

During this time, I was accepted into a nursing program at the University of Tabriz, which was quite an accomplishment during the time. With over 18,000 applicants, the university only accepted 1800 students for placement in various studies including Engineering, Literature and Nursing. As one of the 1800 accepted, I was placed for study in nursing. However, while getting into the University was a huge stepping stone in my life, I also saw it as a huge weight on my plans of leaving Iran. In order to complete the program, I would have to remain under my parent's roof in Tabriz for at least four more years, which was something that I was no longer able to endure. So, I decided to reject the offer of admissions into the University and instead, focus on my plans of a bigger and brighter future, outside of Iran.

One person who seemed willing to help me on the side was one of my favorite cousins, a boy a bit older than me who was studying in France thanks to my father's generosity. In a letter from Paris, he outlined a new plan for my escape. He could secure a letter of acceptance for me from his university, which would allow me to get a visa. If I had that, all I would need was the money for a passport and I would be on my way. With the very little money my cousin had, he would help me out until I could get a job to help pay my way through school. And who knew? Maybe after they saw I could get by in France on my own and that I was determined enough to do it, my parents might change their minds and help me.

The only problem? I didn't speak French.

Luckily, it was relatively easy for me to convince my parents to send me to school while I was at home in Tabriz. My neighbor, an Armenian girl named Gohar I had known since childhood, was attending the French school in town, where they gave language classes to the growing group of Iranians who would need the language for their school or work. There were classes for all ability levels and all age groups, though the class I joined was made up mostly of young people my age, ready or at least willing to travel to France.

The classes weren't incredibly taxing — it was hardly a full-time schedule — but there were homework assignments, research, tests and oral presentations. The attempt was my first at learning a foreign language, and the feeling of wrapping my tongue around the awkward words was frustrating. But I remained committed and hopeful.

The French school was also the first time I had been in a classroom setting with the opposite sex, because my formal education through high school was sex segregated. Learning French was almost like a university experience in that way: working with boys on homework after school in the library, talking with male classmates in the hallways without anyone thinking it untoward or unseemly.

While my French language ability developed very slowly, the feeling of working toward something I wanted buoyed my spirits. Of course, I was still in the same situation — stuck in my parents home in Tabriz, without the money or permission to live the life I wanted, the life I had been promised — but this modicum of hope allowed me to resume my active social life. Parties, teas, the bazaar with friends: I resumed the parts of my life that made me the most happy.

I also was meeting lots of new friends at the French school. In addition to being co-ed, the students at the French school opened my eyes to the fact that there were many young people like myself in Tabriz, people who were trying to find ways to live the modern life they dreamt of. My heart and my hopes were similar to theirs, and I found a home amongst the light-hearted, open-minded group.

Suddenly, it was permissible to do some things that we had not been allowed to in the past, in addition to studying side by side with men. My favorite amongst these new activities was the Youth Palace, which provided a place for young Iranians to get together and mingle. There was a cafeteria and a lending library, a schedule of events and club meetings, and a stage where there would be entertainment most nights. Sometimes, the main act would be local musicians playing the guitar and singing. Other times, boys and girls would dance to music played from a nearby record player.

At the Youth Palace, I had a large circle of friends, including a girl named Fariba who still attended the school I just graduated from. She was three years my junior, and we had always been friendly, if not the best of friends. But at the Youth Palace, it was normal to work your way around the room, saying hello and talking to everyone in turn, getting to know new people. It was in this way I ran into this Fariba a few times in the company of her older brother, Ahmad.

I had met Ahmad one time previously when I applied for a government job in the water department. A girlfriend of mine had found a job as a clerk and typist, and told me I should give it a shot since I was sitting at home doing nothing. At least I could wear nice clothes and go out into the city each day, earning my own money and saving for my future.

"Do you know how to type?" the man who I spoke to at the water department asked, the man I later found out was Ahmad.

"No," I admitted. Though my knowledge of classic Persian poets was sharp, my practical skills in office work or even housework were slim to nonexistent.

"That's OK," he said, throwing me a wink where I sat in my nicest blue suit and matching high heels, my hair swept and patted into place. "Let's give you the typing test anyway."

He led me upstairs, where several girls were typing furiously away on a row of typewriters, the keys clacking up a musical storm. Smoothing my skirt, I sat down to copy the words on a page onto a new page with as few mistakes as possible. But the clacking of the other girls distracted me as I hunted around for the A or the G, and by the time I was finished, I was sure that I wouldn't be successful — or happy — typing in an office all day.

Ahmad took me back to his desk, where he sat in a neat but not overly stylish suit. He offered me the job. By his smile and his twinkling eyes, I knew he was offering it despite my lack of skills because of my appearance. I knew that admiring look, and I was flattered, but I turned down the position in favor of French school, which I began the next week.

"The job is just not for me," I said, thanking him for the opportunity nonetheless.

"Best of luck to you," he called to me as I left the building, obviously not wanting to let me escape the office.

And here in the Youth Palace was that very man with the twinkling eyes, who wanted a clerk who couldn't type.

"I'm Ahmad," he said, re-introducing himself to me and reminding me that we had met at a job interview. I said hello and that I remembered him. When he asked what I was doing instead of hunting and pecking away at a typewriter in his office, I told him that I was attending French school, hoping against hope that I would be able to fly to Paris to study at university.

He nodded and smiled, and I began talking to his little sister. Then I was pulled away into the noisy crush of the Youth Palace on a weekend evening.

Strangely, it was only a few days before I saw this mysterious Ahmad again. A man who seemed to pop out from behind corners, he appeared bright and early and eager in a desk in my French classroom the next week. His hands were clasped over a notebook on his desk and a sharpened pencil sat to the side. He glanced up at me and smiled before the class began, and I went about my French conjugation for the remainder of the period.

After class, he approached me where I was speaking to Gohar and explained that he would be very honored if we would allow him to study with us to catch up on the French he had missed in the beginning of the class.

"Gohar," I said, "This is Ahmad, the older brother of one of my friends from school."

"Sure," said Gohar, "you can join us in the library."

We retreated to the French school's library most afternoons to collaborate on our homework, mostly worksheets where we had to fill in the blanks with the correct form and tense of French words.

"I *am going* to the store today."

"I *went* to the store yesterday."

"I *will go* to the store tomorrow."

We compared notes and tried to speak the words aloud, asking the other if our pronunciation sounded really French. Imagine what it would be to be in France: wearing black, eating crepes, seeing the Eiffel Tower. How amazing.

Our routine continued for a week or so, Ahmad joining Gohar and me in our studies at the library. And it was about that time my grand plan to join my cousin in Paris shattered on the floor like an unlucky mirror.

"But it's only 2,000 toman," I pleaded with my parents across the dinner table. The fact that I was going to French school and the letters they saw me receiving from my cousin must have tipped them off, I suppose. "I only need 2,000 toman to get a passport and I will take care of the rest of the money when I get there."

"How? How will you take care of this money?" my mother had demanded. Having never worked a day outside the house in her life, she could conceive of nothing — or at least nothing respectable — a girl could do to support herself. After all, a girl shouldn't have to support herself if she obeyed her father and then her husband.

"I'll get a job. I'll baby sit. I'll work in a store," I replied, counting options off on my fingers, though I, too, knew it wasn't going to be quite as simple as I was leading on. "I'll make it work."

"Do you hear this, brother?" she asked my Javad, who sat across the table.

"I'll put myself through school if you don't want to," I continued. "I just need the money for a passport and that is it. My cousin had promised to help with everything else, including admissions!"

"Well, I'll tell you what," said my uncle. "You write to your cousin and you tell him that he has to send you that passport money, too, if he wants to be such a big help. We don't have to give you any money."

I couldn't believe that they were using money as a means of keeping me in Iran. My family had more than enough money to send me to France, but were using it as a road block to keep me from my goals. Perhaps what bothered me the most was that this very money that they were denying me of was so enthusiastically given to support the education of my male cousins in Turkey. I was once again being denied happiness because of my gender.

"It's a long way for a single girl by herself to go," said my uncle. "You would be safer here in Tabriz. I say if you cannot get the money from your cousin for yourself, then you have no choice but not to go, right?"

My father wouldn't meet my eyes and my mother nodded as if that decided everything, that one sentence from my uncle could determine my entire future.

I tried not to cry into my dinner plate.

Despite the scene, however, I was still going to French school, still hoping against hope that a new opportunity would assert itself to help my plan get back on track. I began composing a letter to my cousin, asking if it would be possible for him to send me the 2,000 toman as my uncle had demanded in addition to his kind offer of lodging and help with schooling. But I found myself fearful that the money for his own studies would dry up if he went too far with his help. Soon, the paper was transparent and soggy with tears, and I shoved the letter into the commode my father had bought for me so long ago. It seemed fitting, I suppose, to shove a disappointing thing into an embarrassing thing.

All of these thoughts were taking precedence in my head over French nouns or verbs as I sat in the library that afternoon. For some reason, I remember that Gohar was not sitting with Ahmad and me at the library table where our books and notes were spread out. In fact, I don't remember anything at all about that day up to the point where Ahmad turned to me and confessed.

"I don't think I'll ever get to go to Paris," I sighed.

He caught my eye and with a smile of accomplishment and said, "I'm going to America."

Four little words. Four little words sailed across the table, where I had been sitting with the brother of a friend to learn French.

I'm going to America.

Four words and I was suddenly in the company of a man. Poof! There he was! It was if he had been invisible to me before that very moment, but the mention of the United States turned on the lights to reveal him.

"America?" I asked. "When are you going to America?"

"When I get my admission papers and everything is settled."

"But, but," I sputtered in confusion. "What are you doing in a French school if you are planning to go to America?"

"Well, you were going to the French school," he replied, blushing slightly under his olive complexion. "And I am going to the English school, too."

"English!"

"Yes, I think I like English more than French," he said, pointing toward the open text book in front of him, scrunching up his face as if the book was something that smelled bad.

I laughed.

"So you are going to America," I repeated, leaning back and taking in this new man in front of me. America of the silver screen, of Doris Day and Audrey Hepburn. It wasn't the Eiffel Tower, of course, but it was a good trade in my mind.

From that point on, our French homework became the least of our shared activities. Finally paying attention to the man who had been following me around, I noticed that Ahmad was a bit taller that me, but not much. He was skinny, his skin a light olive color and his hair brown. He wasn't handsome, or at least I wouldn't have described him as such, but firmly average looking. Unremarkable — but having seen a few men that were remarkable distasteful, I knew that unremarkable could also be a good quality in a man. What I remember noticing the most was that his hands were very clean and clipped neatly — as if he'd rarely dirtied them with manual labor — and his voice was soft, as soft as a hand petting a cat.

I learned a few other material facts about Ahmad that endeared me to him, too. He was born in Tabriz into a very respectable family. His father was the managing director of a government bureau in Azerbaijan, the equivalent of the social security and birth records office — Hence Ahmad's job at the water department, where he had interviewed me for a typist's job. The family had a sprawling house and a driver to carry them around town.

He had graduated from the National University of Iran in Tehran, a school known only to admit the rich and powerful, not scholarship cases. His degree was in economics, and he was venturing to the U.S. to get his master's degree in the same subject. His uncle through marriage, a high-ranking General in the army who had married his mother's sister, lived in Tehran and had been a second father to him. In fact, he had lived at the General's house for his years of college and the General's education at an American university was what inspired the same goal in Ahmad. Once he got his master's degree, the likely plan was to come back to Iran and make a great success of himself, the same way his uncle had.

After following me to the French school and admitting his deceit, he began to follow me most everywhere. At the Youth Palace, he was at my side. At a Halloween celebration, he dressed as a knight because he knew I was planning on wearing a queen costume. Along with one or more of our siblings, we went to parties of mutual friends and acquaintances. He brought me sodas with extra bright red cherries in them, knowing they were my favorite.

He began to say that he loved me. Of course, I had heard those three little words from men enough times to know that men gave them out like candy. He may have been saying he loved me, but in my ears, that meant that he thought I was pretty and would make a good wife, not that we were soul mates. Even so, Ahmad couldn't help hiding his pride as he showed me off to his friends and family, guiding me around like a prized possession. He never failed to mention the beauty contest or that my father owned a theater.

It was the closest thing to a modern courtship possible in Iran at the time. My parents knew of him and knew of his family, knew that he was often at the parties and events I attended. He had often knocked on the door to pick me up in the evening, though usually with a group of other people, and he'd waved and exchanged pleasantries with my parents. We were never truly alone — in the library, perhaps, but in that case alone in public, under the noses of the other students and librarians. But we were able to get to know one another on our own terms, without the meddling of mothers and the traditional steps of courtship. Over time, he broached the subject of marrying him and accompanying him to America, and it was informally decided between us. There were no calls from his mother, no tea services or rings slipped onto trays.

I was not in love with Ahmad.

He seemed a doting fellow. In fact, like so many other boys I had met in recent months, he carried around one of my pictures from Women's Day magazine. He promised me that in exchange for helping him attend school in America for his master's degree, he would later support me in getting a university education, something I had always craved. But I did not love him.

In Ahmad, I saw a means to an end. It sounds cruel, I know. But this was the way of marriages: what can he do for my family, what can my family do for his, how will money be exchanged from father of the groom to the bride's father and vice versa. Such things were essentially business arrangements. Of course, the young people of my generation spoke of love, too, and we saw it depicted in the movies as a passionate, music-swelling moment to get teary eyed and emotional. But love was the stuff of the screen, not of marriage itself.

Marriage was a partnership for the raising of children and the furthering of a man's career, which benefited the entire household. It was the continuation of a family's good name and, hopefully, the aggrandizement of that honorable reputation. I had seen the partnership of my parents. I had seen them fight and argue, and I had seen them at peace, but I don't know if I ever saw that they were in love. The only love I witnessed that I could identify for sure was the love in their eyes when they looked at their children, especially the miracle child Reza.

Ahmad's allure was simple. He was going abroad and he would be taking me with him. Nothing else mattered. He wasn't ugly, he wasn't cruel, he wasn't poor. In other words, he met all the major prerequisites. Life with him, I figured, wouldn't be all that different than life with any other man of our religion, country and social group. At least that marriage would take place in America.

I had tried to fight marriage while I could. I had tried to find a way to break out of the country on my own, by myself. When Ahmad appeared in my life, I realized that marriage would be the only answer. So I sighed and accepted that.

The engagement was by no means final, and not only because we never spoke of it to our families. Even between the two of us, I considered the bargain informal and I thought that if something changed, I could change my mind at any time. In fact, I once did tell him over those first months we knew one another that I had decided not to marry him. He reacted passionately, grabbing my hand and pleading with me. He would kill himself, he said, if he could not have me for his wife. He explained that we could first live in his parents' home, in a new section of the house recently decorated with a pattern of wallpaper I would love. We would save for America and then we would go.

"America," he said. "Don't you want to go to America?"

I nodded to appease him and calm him down, telling him I would still marry him, though I did nothing to actually begin a formal engagement, something a serious bride would have done long ago.

Instead, my life continued as normal. We went to parties and to the Youth Palace. We studied English. I saw my friends and family.

One night, however, changed everything.

We had been at the house of Ahmad's uncle, where Ahmad's father and some other local big shots had set up an evening of cards. We played rummy late into the night, far past the midnight curfew my father had always demanded I adhere to. It was about 2 a.m. when Ahmad finally showed me to my door and headed home himself, and the minute my foot hit the steps to upstairs, my father was upon me.

"Do you have any idea what time it is, Maryam?" I heard his voice before I saw his form come stomping from around the corner. Wearing his robe and slippers, his hair was not as neat and stylish as usual but flying out at all angles. "What are you thinking coming home so late? What on earth have you been doing?"

"Playing cards," I said, telling him the name of Ahmad's uncle, who he was acquainted with, and the names of other partygoers, including Ahmad.

"No, Maryam," he said, his finger extended near my face. "It doesn't matter what you were actually doing. Does it? No! Because everyone knows what kind of girl stays out until 2 a.m., and everyone knows what such a girl will do. Do you have no care for your good name or the good name of this family?"

I saw my mother appear behind him, similarly rumpled due to the late hour.

"Mehdi," she said. "What you say is true, but you need to calm down."

"No!" my father screamed. "I am going to go over to the house of this Ahmad right now and tell him that he cannot so sully the name of my daughter and my family. This is not the way proper young people act."

My father cast around for his shoes, shoving his feet into them without tying the laces, trying to put on his coat with the hem of his robe hanging out messily from the bottom.

"Hush, Mehdi," said my mother. "It's late. Let us talk of this in the morning."

"Father," I said. "You're being ridiculous." While his frantic behavior was frightening me, I was also indignant at being treated like such a child. I had not been doing anything that could have been considered disreputable. I had been spending time with people my parents would have approved of, never alone with a boy, never without his family present.

"No, you are the one who is being ridiculous," my father replied. "You are ridiculously disrespectful and I will not tolerate it. I am your father."

"And I'm an adult, father," I yelled, meeting the volume of his voice with my own. "I have done nothing wrong."

"We can talk about this in the morning," my mother repeated, taking my father's coat away from him.

I stomped up the stairs, repeating, "I'm an adult."

"We will talk about this tomorrow, Maryam," he yelled up the stairs after me. "I will make sure of it."

I slammed the door to my bedroom and I wished — not for the first time — that I had wings to fly away.

"Why don't we just get married?" I asked Ahmad the next day.

"What?" he replied, furrowing his eyebrows.

"Let's forget about the mothers and the other problems. Let's just go down to the courthouse and get married."

"Really?" he asked, searching my eyes with his own to make sure that I was being serious.

"Yes."

"But only widows on their second weddings get married in this way," Ahmad said. "There will be no pretty dress and music and family, all of that stuff. It will be so simple and some may think shameful."

"I don't care," I stated, my voice even and confident.

"You don't think that you will regret not having all of that? Won't your mother be upset at not having an engagement and wedding?"

"Exactly," I replied. "Now do you want to do this or not?" I asked. "I'm not going to suggest it again."

He shrugged. "Okay."

We gathered up two of his friends to serve as witnesses and went down to the Iranian version of a Justice of the Peace. He said yes, I said yes, and the man stamped a page of a little book, which was a few pages of official looking paper with a red cover, our names printed by a typewriter on the inside cover.

With the book in my hand, I walked into my family's house that evening — alone, Ahmad having gone to tell his parents of the afternoon's adventure. Both of my parents were in the sitting room, and I strode right up to them and put the red book into my mother's hand.

"What is this?" she asked.

"It is my marriage certificate, Mother," I said, as if this was the most normal thing in the world. "I am now a married woman."

Her eyes grew wide looking at the book she held between two fingers. She took it in both hands to open it and look inside.

"Maryam, what are you speaking of?" said my father.

"Married," I repeated. "Today."

I was not happy with this news. In fact, I was extremely angry. Mad at my parents, mad at my culture, mad at being caged in such a way. I was even angry with myself for not having any other options, for my life coming down to this shameful sort of marriage ceremony, for this being the only option left to me. I was mad at the earth and the sky and the air in my lungs. I was mad at Ahmad for wanting to marry me, myself for marrying him. I was so mad that I didn't even want to put on a wedding dress, and I never did. The world was red with rage through my angry eyes. But still, I was married and that was that. That was the way it was going to be. So there.

My mother sighed. "Well, at least it cannot be thought that you are a bad girl anymore."

My father nodded. He was then holding the book to check its authenticity.

"You are probably right to put water on the fire in this way," he said after a short pause. He sighed. "The way you were acting... and now I know that his intentions were honorable." My father handed the book back to me and put his hands in his lap. "You probably don't think this way, but there are many men who would take advantage of a trusting young girl — convincing her to do who knows what — with no intentions of marriage. That is what we feared, you know."

"And what would we have done with you then?" my mother said, continuing his thought. "No one would marry you. You would be shamed and thrown away."

"I was not shamed. I *am* not shamed, and Ahmad is going to America. My husband and I are going to America," I said, trying out the new word "husband" on my tongue.

"I had such dreams of seeing you on your wedding day, in your wedding dress, though," my mother said.

"Well, you will just have to wait for my sisters then," I fumed.

No one said congratulations.

My anger was still strong and I left the room in a huff, finally feeling that I had a right to leave in such a way. I was an adult, a married woman, and they would no longer be able to treat me like a child.

That was my first and most important thought. Other than that notion, it seemed to me that everything else was the same. I got dressed and did my make up, getting ready to leave the house for whatever social engagement I had planned that night. It was the same as any other fun evening during that frivolous and fun time of my youth.

Only tonight, no one would be able to tell me when I had to be home. By getting married, I had pried the key to the chains I had worn all my life from my father, unlocked them, and stepped out into the night.

I didn't quite realize that another might now own that key.

Chapter Ten

For a few days after the wedding, everything except my curfew seemed the same. I slept in my family's house, I ate in my family's house and I continued all my normal social responsibilities. The main difference to me was the weight that had been lifted from my shoulders. I now had a future, and there was an airplane and a foreign destination in it. It felt as if I had broken through a brick wall and was now dusting myself off and taking a deep breath.

Perhaps it was this — my conception of the marriage as a hard-fought, destruction of a roadblock — that made me hate the idea of a traditional wedding ceremony so much. If I had put on a wedding dress, burned the Esfand, sprinkled the sugar and let the butterflies loose, I would have been expected to be exultant about my new husband, talking about all the children we would have and painting a traditional, rosy future. But I didn't feel that way about the marriage, so I didn't want to be married in that way. I would be married on my own terms, non-romantic terms. My whole goal was to break free from my town and the expectations others placed upon me. I was incredibly glad that I had broken free of the big wedding, too.

Also, I doubted my own resolution to Ahmad. I don't know if I could have gone through with it if we had to plan and carry out the big wedding. And I knew that going through with it was my only option at the time. In a way, getting married was similar to placing a blindfold over your eyes before a firing squad: What was about to happen wouldn't be pretty, so let me just close my eyes and get it over with.

Despite the overall lack of pomp and circumstance, there were a few arrangements that needed to be made between the families. The girl's father was supposed to outline how he was going to help the new couple get set up. Usually, he would provide a certain amount of money to buy or build a house if one wasn't already available, furnish the house and buy necessities like linens, pots and pans, and appliances. The generous man that he was, my father agreed to set aside 70,000 toman for us — or about $10,000 American dollars. We weren't going to use it right away because we were planning on leaving the country, but that amount was enough at the time to have built a beautiful house in Tabriz with most modern amenities.

Ahmad had spoken to me about moving into his parents' house, into a nice, big room that would give us some privacy while we were waiting for our American adventure to begin. But it seemed like a far off eventuality to me — as in *someday* we *may* move into his parents' home. But the wedding itself was so fast, that this change happened faster than I could have imagined, too.

After a few days of "normal" life post-wedding, the changes began with a call from Ahmad's sister, Fariba.

"I am picking you up tomorrow, Maryam," she said. "Papa is cooking a special dish for lunch today because he wants to meet you." Papa was the pet name everyone in the family used for Ahmad's dad, such was the affectionate and loving role he played in their lives. "Papa is very excited about it, about you," she added.

The next day arrived and I was shepherded into the family home, where I had been before for parties. But I had never before been treated with quite the ceremony and adulation that Ahmad's father ladled on me.

"Welcome! Welcome to our home, my daughter," he said in a booming and jovial voice, winking at my when he used the term "daughter."

He sat me down at their table, which was laden with steaming plates of special occasion food — several kinds of meat, rice with vegetables and spices, aromas of kebab spices and the pungent scent of brewing tea. Around the table were arranged the immediate family: his father and mother, Fariba and his other sisters. The family's beloved German shepherd Jolie, meaning "pretty" in French, lay obediently on the floor.

After some casual conversation about what Ahmad had told them about me and what they didn't yet know, his father said, "Well, we love you. You seem to be such a nice girl, and so pretty!" He smiled and leaned across the table, adding, "But so nasty, too. Marrying our son and not letting us throw a party for you!"

"Well, we are going to America. We don't need all the gifts from a party right now to bring across the ocean, and we'd like to save as much money as we can for the United States," I replied. By this time, I was used to taking a little teasing about the unorthodox way I'd gotten married, and I had that little speech about practicality and saving money memorized.

"It's definitely not the way it should go," inserted his mother. She was looking pointedly down into her food, only glancing up at me occasionally from beneath her eyelashes. "A boy should marry a girl his parents approve of and in the traditional way. A woman looks forward to the party and presents of the wedding of her son, you know, even if his strange new bride doesn't care for such things."

The rest of the family continued eating, smiles still on their faces, despite the acidic commentary she'd poured over the atmosphere of welcome. I wondered if they had heard the barbed disapproval in her tone.

Not that I was entirely surprised at his mother's acid tongue or disapproval. Ahmad had told me that his mother was upset she was missing out on all the traditional pageantry of a son's wedding. Ahmad did have an older brother, but he was absent, having gone to Germany to study and remained there. Therefor, Ahmad and his mother were very close and he took after her, much more than after his father.

She had confided to him that what she thought particularly unfair in particular the way we had married: She'd given expensive gifts to so many couples over the years and now would not ever receive in return similar presents for her own son's union. In her mind, there was some scale balancing money/gifts going out with money/gifts coming in, and this transaction slighted her what was only her due reward. With a laugh, Ahmad had gone on to describe her penny-pinching, gift-seeking ways, as if such traits were something silly the family laughed over now and then — an eccentricity, no more. Knowing that so many women exercised their power in the families by controlling money and prestige — much like my mother did — it seemed to be a common enough eccentricity and one I didn't worry about excessively.

And there were other issues his mother took offence about in his choice of bride. After all, Ahmad had chosen a woman that would not only allow him to go to America, away from his doting/controlling mother, but a woman who was just as excited as him about the voyage. With mother-love blindness, she saw this as *my* failing rather than his. But again, I'd thought this emotional response was understandable and that the feeling would ease in time, when we got to know one another and things settled down.

So I looked down at my plate and ignored her twisted lips and searing glances, thinking myself the bigger person for understanding her point of view.

The lunch continued on a celebratory note. I was shown the new room in which they encouraged Ahmad and me to live, and it was as nice as it had been described. There was a pink-satin spread on the bed and pink-satin curtains, which seemed so luxurious to me. I even made a few allowances for Ahmad's mother, telling her that if she wanted to invite important friends and family over for individual dinners or tea parties to celebrate the wedding — and balance her scale of gifts, which seemed to mean so much to her — I would support her in that.

"You are coming to our house soon," he father said. It wasn't a question. "As soon as you can arrange your things, OK?"

I nodded and smiled at this cheerful man who was winning over my heart.

The next day, there was a similar dinner at my family's home and a similar cycle of emotions took place. My father was welcoming and cheerful, while my mother asked pointed questions and hinted her displeasure at the idea of living in America.

Unlike how I had tried to remain meek and accommodating to Ahmad's family, not wanting to push anyone's buttons, I found that Ahmad puffed himself up for the occasion. He took immense pleasure in describing his important university degree and how wonderful he would do academically in America. He spoke of the important job of his father, who had a personal secretary and a driver for the family. I could see the pride in him when he told my family of our upcoming trip to Tehran — our honeymoon — where we would stay with his important uncle, the General. He repeated again the story of the General's fatherly devotion to him, his generosity and the depth of his pockets.

Because he was probably only trying to show my family that he was a worthy husband for me, I tried to ignore the self-important way he was showing off. My mother, however, could never ignore such a thing.

"What the hell are you doing, Maryam?" she asked me when we had a moment alone. "Him going on and on about his family as if they are so important. They're tolerable, I suppose. But we've never respected them. I hope you know that." She clucked her tongue. "And I know I don't respect him personally either now."

"Mother," I warned her. "It's not for you to decide or push your nose in."

"No," she agreed. "You picked your husband. That was your decision. And now you will live with that and go live with them. You made your bed."

Often after a traditional wedding, there was a big ceremony surrounding the bride and the groom retiring to their room for the first time. A little boy would tie a ribbon around the bride's stomach in hope that she would conceive many boys. The couple would have their hands placed together by one of the parents before the whole party left the room. A generation ago, the ceremony even required that one of the bride's relatives stay the night at the couple's new home at the groom's to make sure nothing would happen to the bride. After the first sexual act, the bride's relative would be given the sheet stained by the bride's maiden blood and would then go home, satisfied that the marriage would be honored now that the bride's virginity had been sacrificed.

But there was no such pageantry surrounding our first night together as husband and wife. Instead, I found myself resigned and unexcited about sleeping with my husband. I turned my face from him, presenting him with my back and tried my best to ignore him and keep my eyes closed for whatever it was I was in store for.

Afterwards, I found myself looking at the wall while trying to sleep in the same bed as a man, remembering the time a boy had told me he was going to fly me away, far away from here. I was going to fly far away — it was just another man who was going to make that happen.

We left pretty quickly for our trip to Tehran, which we were calling our honeymoon. For many young people on our background, it was already common to go on longer and more exotic trips for the honeymoon, but we were saving money for a more important trip. Besides, Ahmad was very keen on introducing me to his beloved uncle, the General, and I had always loved visiting the fast-paced, modern capital of the country. Some of the best times of my life had taken place in Tehran, after all.

And in some ways, this trip was no different. Ahmad had the attitude of a waiter or driver, always trying to impress me and give me great service. While in Tehran, we went out to eat at great restaurants, places that I had heard about in magazines. We went to movies. Almost every day, we went shopping at various places around town. Of course, we looked at things that most newlyweds do, like items for a new house and a new life. But we didn't buy many of those items because of our upcoming move. Instead, he took me to see the frivolous and fun things I had always coveted: clothes, jewelry, shoes and such. He bought me a striking leather suit of the style that was so popular that decade. It was an earthy tan and tightly fitted, with a flaring collar and flaring legs. I was so proud of it, and I finally understood in a very small way how the generosity of a husband can fuel the happiness and social standing of a wife.

I knew — and he made sure that I knew — that expensive presents and lots of eating out was normal for a special occasion but wasn't going to be something I could count on all the time. He'd made this almost excessively clear. Unconsciously or not, he hammered the point home by demonstrating his thrift: He wrote down every expense he made in a little book, which he would often go over in the evenings, calculating exactly what was spent and what was in the bank. Everything went into that book. Today I spent $1 on a movie and gave 50 cents to a beggar, he might note in this book. Every penny, every dime was accounted for. Seeing him hunched over these papers with a sharp pencil and a furrowed brow, I could see the resemblance to his mother. Every penny had better prepare to be pinched, and hard.

But the fun parts of the honeymoon trip were mitigated by other factors. In fact, the situation seemed to be the same wherever we went after we were married. The men (like my father and his) were usually cheerful and welcoming to me, trying to make me feel at home in the new family and circumstances. The women (like my mother and his) were skeptical about the conditions of our wedding, doubted my moral character and could be rude — if not downright mean.

The General's wife, Ahmad's aunt, was no different. While the General opened his home to us, introduced me to his friends and family with pride at parties, and told us we should go into the city and have fun, the General's wife found nothing but problems.

"What kind of wedding did you guys have again?" she would ask over tea with a few guests, as if she had forgotten. "Oh yes, you had none at all. What is wrong with you guys?" She asked the last remark in incredulity, thinly veiling the insult as a solicitous question if anything was wrong.

Ahmad's aunt and uncle had no children and treated Ahmad as a sort of adopted child. I, then, was again in the position of unwanted daughter-in-law with the General's wife. She was also accustomed to treating her husband as one of her children, bossing him around and saying or doing whatever she pleased in front of him.

When I got dressed to go out with my new husband, I would wear what I normally would — a short skirt we called a mini jupe, jupe being French for skirt and mini skirts being so popular in the 1970s, even in Iran. The Cultural Revolution that would make such fashion radical was still a twinkle in the country's (then thoroughly modern) eye. But the General's wife and other older women could still find fault with the forward-looking international fashion of youth.

"Her skirt is very, very short, Ahmad," his aunt would say to him, acting as if I wasn't standing at his side, able to hear her words. "Do people on the street really think you are with your wife when going out with such a woman? I don't know, but I would think she was another kind of woman entirely."

She meant a prostitute, of course.

I wanted to speak up and defend myself, telling her about how my family never had a problem with such fashion. My father's philosophy was that if you wear a mini skirt, no cover and whatever else you wanted, but you stand as tall as a soldier in the middle of the street, your actions and intentions obvious to anyone, there is no shame in that.

I wanted to share this with the General's wife, but Ahmad had told me in private to hold my tongue. He would take care of it, he insisted. His women relatives could be difficult and standing up to them would take a certain amount of tact, as well as a bit of time for them to adjust. Leave it up to him, he said, and so I held my tongue and gave it time.

It became obvious that it would take more time than our short stay in the home of the General for the animosity to disappear. Ahmad's aunt simply didn't think I was the type of girl Ahmad should have married, and she wasn't the sort of woman who could let such thoughts go unsaid. One example of this insistence on hating me arose around the dinner table, where we were always served by the General's troops. One solider I had become accustomed to seeing and was very fond of was absent, and I asked where he had gone.

"He went back to his village to get married," the General said. "Very joyous for him, since he has wanted to do so for sometime." She was a village girl from the soldier's hometown, a girl of very humble origins, for sure, but the kind who would make a good wife for a man in the army.

"How exciting for him," I said.

"Yes, he's very excited. He even brought the girl to meet us the other day," the General's wife noted.

"Did you like her? What did she look like?" I asked. Such are the things that women talked about when another got married, after all.

Ahmad's aunt shot an answer back without delay, like a snake striking its prey. "Like you."

"Woman, you stop that," the General responded, raising his voice slightly. She continued eating as if nothing had occurred.

The General defended me from her abuse on many occasions. Often saying, "Stop it, lady" or "I don't want to hear it." But the fact that he didn't want to hear didn't mean such hurtful words couldn't be heard.

So this was the way of being a wife. So this was the world of territorial women, I thought. This was how the power game was played. Perhaps stupidly, I never took my first move, positioning myself as a woman to be respected with firm words and careful actions. In fact, I didn't assert myself at all in the beginning with General's wife, letting her win the all-important first battle. My excuse is that I was a bride in a strange, new family, and I was still very young and had no idea how to act. Petty and silly as it was, this kind of power was the only kind available to women in the home, and my inaction caused me to lose whatever status I might have gained within my new husband's family in those first few weeks. And it certainly didn't help that the men in the family always stood up for me and obviously approved of me, inciting the women's jealousy, too. But at that point, I still trusted that Ahmad would be standing up for me, even if it was behind the scenes where I hadn't yet seen it. I trusted he was easing me in, that Ahmad would take care of all the bitterness in time.

Meanwhile, we were trying to get the ball rolling on our immigration to America. The red tape and paperwork involved was impressive and complex. It began with receiving a student visa from the United States, which required applying to and getting accepted at an American school. A student also had to prove they could pay the tuition and their living expenses so as not to be a burden on the U.S. government.

Once we could qualify for the visa, there were other issues with us entering the country. Both of which to make sure we had translated and certified copies of all our important documents, including our birth certificates and diplomas from high school and Ahmad's from college. We had to prove that we had a certain amount of money in the bank to support ourselves — I think the figure was 50,000 toman or about $7,000 U.S. dollars. My father had given us $10,000 and Ahmad had saved up $2-3,000, but proving that it was all in the bank and safe was another task. The Iranian government also wanted proof that we had family or other investments still in Iran, and were therefore likely to return.

All of the paperwork and red tape took time, and it was Ahmad's sole occupation during the months after the wedding. After a while of wrangling with the government, he'd arranged an important appointment for us a few months away in Tehran, where we would finally sign some forms, get some papers stamped and be assured that our trip would become a reality.

But despite the promises that we would be leaving soon, the situation in the home of Ahmad's family just deteriorated for me. His mother — and increasingly his older sisters, who their mother would recruit to her side — began to keep tabs on my every move. They became a spy network, writing down when I would leave, where I said I was going and when I returned. They'd sometimes go out to see if I actually arrived where I said was my destination, and if I arrived home later than planned, they would run to my husband to inform him.

The family had a servant, an older gentleman, who let me know to lock the transom window over our bedroom whenever I left the house. Otherwise, Ahmad's mother and sisters would put a chair by the door

and heft one another through the rectangular window over the door
to paw through my things, looking for any sign of deception or disreputable behavior they could use as evidence for Ahmad to leave me.
While the picture in my head of these silly women contorting themselves into pretzels to fit through the transom was amusing, the feeling of violation that comes from having no privacy from people who
wished me harm was devastating.

Even when we did have some private time together alone in our
room — where we would laugh and talk and try to have some joy in
our newlywed days — his mother could find it personally insulting. So
extreme was her hatred of me that when she heard us talking or laughing in the evenings, she would take it out on her husband in their own
bedroom. Ahmad's father once pulled up his undershirt one morning
in the kitchen, where he was unlocking the pantry, to show me a smattering of bruises up and down his stomach.

"You see what she does?" he asked. "Every time she hears your voice
from that room, she clamps down on me. Yes, she bites me! Even with
her dentures, she is able to bite me this hard." He sighed in exasperation. "You see how jealous she is of you being with her son?"

I could not believe the extremes of verbal and physical violence this
woman was capable of. I seriously wondered if she might be mentally
ill and not simply eccentric the way her family played it off. But my father-in-law patted my head before I could say anything, as if such behavior were only questionable instead of completely mad. "Of course,
with such a girl there is a lot to be jealous of," he added, chuckling.

I began to fear that Ahmad was being brainwashed by the feelings
of the women in his family. He was constantly hearing about how he
shouldn't let me do this or that, how I was late coming home from
lunch with my family, that I spent too much money. One day we had
our first real fight: about the length of my skirt, or rather, about what
his family thought about the length of my skirt.

"What should I do about them picking on me that way?" I asked
him. "You said I shouldn't talk back to the women in your family, that
you were going to take care of it."

"What should you do? You should make your skirt longer," he replied angrily.

"No," I yelled back at him. "I am going to wear a mini jupe the way I've always worn a mini jupe and that's it. You never had a problem with it before we got married."

"But now I am your husband and I think differently," he said and forcefully nodded his head as if that were the end of the argument.

In the beginning of a marriage, you get to know one another and also the boundaries of the relationship, like who will be responsible for what household chores, who will have the power. He was trying to act like the big man, like he would have all the power he was supposed to as a man, and I was trying my best to keep what power I could for myself. It was hard to keep anything at all, though, in an environment where so much was stacked against me.

And Ahmad, of course, didn't seem to see the irony in the fact that he was learning how to be a powerful husband from his *mother* — a tyrannical, irrational, jealous and greedy *female*. If he'd taken an example from his father, perhaps we wouldn't be screaming at one another.

Day after day, I noticed more and more of his mother's scheming, manipulation and, most importantly, her ways with money in my new husband. I once asked him for money to have my eyebrows plucked and shaped, a very common and necessary beauty ritual for any Persian girl.

"Hold on," he said, reaching for his wallet. Before he opened the billfold, he turned his back to me to make sure I couldn't see how much money he had in his wallet. Then he turned back to me and offered the equivalent of one dollar, about half the amount I would need to have my eyebrows done.

How queer to me! What would my father have done? Given me more than I needed if the thing I asked for was one that he approved of. A man's worth as a husband was often measured in the generosity he poured on his wife. Women gathered to compare everything from diamond rings and vacations to cuts of lamb and winter coats, measuring up their husbands and fathers.

But Ahmad's conception of being a husband was taking a turn I didn't understand, and it was a development that I feared. His promised support in standing up to the women of his family had never happened, and because I didn't stand up for myself either, I was doomed to be walked over and spit upon in the family forever more. I crossed my fingers, closed my eyes and counted down the days until we left for America, when maybe I could turn things around more in my favor — or at least make things more tolerable.

Chapter Eleven

It took six or seven months for all the formalities and technicalities of moving to America to be arranged. At that point, we packed up everything we could, and flew to Tehran, where we again stayed with the General.

"So have you decided where you are going to go within America, my Ahmad?" he asked us before our appointment with immigration.

I had wanted our move to be to California, to have Ahmad go to Berkeley like Dustin Hoffman's character in the recent movie "The Graduate." Ahmad leaned toward New York, to experience the same things his uncle had, but he didn't care too much one way or the other.

The General had other ideas.

"No, no," he said, shaking his head. "You will go to Washington D.C. It's all arranged." Apparently, Ahmad's uncle was good buddies with the Iranian ambassador in Washington D.C. They played cards together since the time they were young, and the General knew that having one powerful friend in a new place could make all the difference to a couple getting their start in a foreign land. "This man is going to be good in your life," he continued. "You should go to Washington."

We shrugged and went along with it. Having never been out of the country, let alone to America, we had little conception of the wide divide between the culture and climate of Berkley, California and Washington, D.C.

Everything went great with our appointment at the American Embassy in Tehran, smooth as could be expected. In that time, America's relationship with Iran was healthy, well-oiled with oil money and a favorable trade relationship. The Shah of Iran was on very good terms with President Nixon and was considered one of the most respected leaders in the Middle East. People traveled back and forth between the two countries relatively freely.

In fact, after all the gathering of paperwork and data over the months was complete, the appointment Ahmad scheduled two months prior was cut and dried. We presented a paper to a kindly man with salt-and-pepper hair. He stamped it, and our visa was valid. The final thing to do was buy a plane ticket and we were on our way to "The Land of Opportunity," "The Land of Hollywood" and the land I had dreamt about since I was a little girl.

"You guys must be so happy," the General exclaimed when we returned with the good news. Of course, I could tell that he was just as excited. "You are going to be American students. Do you know what that means?"

Ahmad and I both shook our heads, knowing that he couldn't wait to tell us.

"In America, you are not even going to have to wash your clothes anymore," he continued, his mustache twitching with the strength of his smile. He was directing this part of his speech at me, the wife, because I would be the one washing the clothes, of course. "In America, they have these places called laundry mats. You go there and you put a coin in the machine along with your clothes. You can just read your book and your clothes will be washed."

I thought to myself, "My God! What a country."

The General had been in New York for his studies in the 1930s and 40s, when America was offering training to Iranian soldiers, who were allies in certain theaters of the war.

"When I was in New York," he continued, "all you have to have is a few coins for anything. You can even use coins to get apples and sandwiches and drinks out of machines. And these machines are everywhere."

I had to smile. I had seen such machines in the movies, though not in person, so they were not quite the novelty the General believed. But on the other hand, to see something from the movies — something so futuristic and unknown — was so exciting that I couldn't help but share the General's grin.

"I'm going there," I thought. "I'm going to the country of the movies and snack machines."

"You are not flying commercial, are you?" the General was asking my husband.

"I thought so," Ahmad replied. "We don't have any other option, I thought."

The General threw his arm around his nephew's shoulders and smiled. "Ha!" he laughed. "You have me and I have connections. I can get you on a military flight for just $100 American dollars — for both of you!"

"Only that?" Ahmad asked. "That's amazing."

I was distracted with thoughts of washing machines and gossip and parties. If I had known how important this decision about choice of air was going to be to me, I would have paid more attention.

We were lavished with gifts the day before we were to depart during many small parties hosted in Tehran on our behalf at the General's and at my aunt's house. But when we arrived at the airport to leave for America, we carried only two suitcases full of clothes and documents. The presents we gave to my mother-in-law — not that we had a choice in the matter — who took them as her just reward for not receiving any goodies from the celebration of our marriage. It meant so much to her, and I took pride in the fact that it didn't matter one bit to me whether we got to keep the presents or not. I was getting in a plane, and that was present enough.

The one gift I retained was thrown over my forearm as we boarded the plane leaving Iran, the arm I didn't use to wave goodbye to the family and friends who accompanied us to the airport. It was a yellow, velvet blanket from Kashan — reversible, with a floral print on one side containing designs of roses and birds— given to me by my oldest aunt's son-in-law. Soft as fur, it was something to hold on to and comfort over the long voyage.

So we got on the plane for the first act of this play of immigration. I don't say that I was getting onto a plane "to America" because that wouldn't be true in the slightest. This leg of our journey wouldn't even come close to our new country. We were getting on that plane for the first leg of a five-day odyssey across two continents and an ocean. And I even use the word "plane" lightly. This was no ordinary airplane with emergency exits, flight attendants serving soda and tray tables. Instead, the General had arranged for us to fly on a military plane that was making the journey for official reasons, but had room for a few passengers of military families and friends at the same time.

Upon walking up the stairs of the tiny vessel, which was only the size of a large, commercial truck, you entered the belly of the beast. There were no seats — only benches, two benches running along each wall. Ahmad and I and the few other passengers — two single men who were also going to be students in America and two families — sat on the hard, metal benches with our backs against the curving, metal wall of the plane's body, the same wall the circular windows were cut in.

I was reminded of war movies that showed parachuters, where brave British or American troops were flown over enemy territory to jump out of a plane, a plane just like this one. Looking around, I knew that this very plane had been used for that very type of thing on other voyages.

Once the plane was in the air, it was chilly and drafty in the cabin. The small plane was unable to keep a smooth path of travel like larger planes as it gained speed. Every cloud and air pocket — perhaps even every large bird — caused it to bounce and shake, rattling the bones of my spine and clanking my teeth together in my mouth. I began to ache in all of my joints and into my body, where I thought my internal organs were slamming against one another, as if they'd decided after all these years that they couldn't get along anymore.

Halfway through the eight-hour flight to Athens, Greece, I'd shoved the yellow blanket between myself and the metal bench to alleviate my discomfort. The only way to keep my mind off of the hard, metal on all sides of me that wanted to shake my bones into powder was the view out of the few, porthole-shaped windows that looked out on the bright blue water of the Mediterranean.

Ahmad, on the other hand, didn't seem to have any problems with the flight. A smile seemed to be plastered to his face. Occasionally, he would glance over at me and say, "Only $100! Can you imagine?"

Once we'd disembarked, the pilots let us know that we would fly the next day to London and what time to meet back at the hanger. The other families mentioned that they were going to head out for the evening, trying to find a little restaurant on the ocean to relax and enjoy the rest of the day.

"Would you like to come?" the father of the family asked us.

I opened my mouth to answer that the outing would be most welcome, but my husband cut me off before the words could escape.

"Thank you but no," Ahmad said curtly. "I am very tired and we have no money to spend on such things. We are saving our money for the time in the States. "

"Yes, of course," the father said with a curious frown.

The next morning, the five-hour flight to London was a bit more eventful, if only because the other passengers screamed over the engine noise of the tiny plane about the previous evening's fun.

"Lobster!" one woman shouted. "Have you ever eaten lobster?!"

"And the view of the ocean! The Caspian Sea has nothing on this ocean!"

"You should have come!" said the women to my left. Though her mouth was only a foot from my ear, she still had to speak loudly for me to understand her. I smiled and nodded politely, saving myself the trouble of answering in all that noise.

The city of my dreams — London. As I stepped off the plane and took a deep breath of English air, it was nothing as I'd expected. I guess I had always linked the thought of London to the summer day in the garden when Arian made a plane to fly me there, and that memory was redolent of sweet, blooming flowers and moist grass. The military air field in London smelled the same as any other air field.

"There's a charming little hotel for you to stay at here in Swindon," he continued. "And because we will be kept here for two days before journeying on, don't worry, you can travel into London to take in the sights before we go."

I clapped my hands in happiness along with some of the other women. Ahmad shot me a dark look and touched his stomach, a signal to me that we shouldn't be too wasteful. But I informed him in no uncertain terms that we would not be left behind the other passengers on this leg of the trip. London was a city I'd dreamed of my entire life, and him being "tired" (which also meant "cheap") wasn't going to dampen my enthusiasm.

The next day we took the train to London and walked our sore joints around the town that had grown so large with hope in my head all those years. We snapped pictures in front of Buckingham Palace and watched the changing of the guard — mostly because such things were free and Ahmad kept tapping his stomach in displeasure every time we spent a dime. Even so, it was a great day and I felt I was on my way into the world, in my future. It was such hope that made the next night in Swindon bearable. I sat up late into the night listening to the music of my new husband's snores, sitting in the chair by the window and wondering if my Dream Man, Arian, was still in the country, somewhere beneath the same stars.

As far as I knew from what I'd heard from his sister, with whom I still corresponded occasionally, he was still pursuing his graduate degree somewhere in the United Kingdom, although perhaps in Scotland. I couldn't remember. I thought of him with nostalgic love and a bit of wistfulness, wondering if he would wish me well if he knew where I was going, that I was traveling to the land of opportunity. I wondered if he would feel some regret that I was married, that I wasn't still a girl pining away in the garden near the theater, thinking of him. I wondered if he thought of me at all.

I wondered if my obsession with him, even so many years after our friendship, was only because he symbolized to me my need to get out, to be whisked away from my cloistered existence. To make myself happy, I decided that this was probably the case. He was a childhood dream of travel and glamour, a happy memory and nothing more. The love was only another fantasy like so many girlish others, I convinces myself. And if that was the case, I hoped he would be happy for me that I was setting out to America and I hoped he would be happy, too, with his own future. One day we would meet and smile as childhood friends do upon reunion and be glad that all of our old dreams came true.

The next morning, I dreaded the thought of getting back on the uncomfortable military plane but, awash in a new feeling of hope and impatience to arrive at our destination, I decided I was going to be smart about it. In addition to my yellow velvet blanket, which was becoming an extension of my right arm, I wore every single skirt I had packed in my suitcase. Layered with about eight levels of fabric, my backside was plump and cushioned — perhaps not attractive, but a brilliant tactic. Sitting down on the parachuter's bench, I bounced a few times on the built-in padding and smiled at my innovation.

The next stop was Portugal, on a small island with an army base. It was the typical army base, with several hangers and lots of pavement, offering little in the way of scenery. But they had sunshine and the salty smell of the Atlantic.

What I did see on that island in Portugal on our overnight layover were signs that I was slowly entering the new world. I saw my first black person: a woman a bit older than me kneeling down to play with her children at the base, obviously an army wife. I tried not to stare and I thought myself very mature and open-minded when I smiled at her. At a nearby casino where one of the handsome pilots escorted us for entertainment that evening, the lights and noise of the high-style gaming room overloaded my senses. A flash of turquoise directed my attention to a woman in a glittering blue jumpsuit of the 70s style, with legs that bloomed into bells at her ankles and hugged her curves tightly, the neckline showing enough that my uncle would have fainted dead away on the carpet. With her gold necklaces and gold handbag and incredibly short hair, she made me look down at my own clothing in embarrassment, feeling like a creature from the dark ages in my sweater and skirt — at least I was only wearing one now! With her, I didn't succeed in not staring. If this was only halfway to America, I thought, what would we see when we arrived?

We boarded the plane for our longest trip yet: the jump across the ocean. Watching the sea stretch out beneath us from the porthole windows, our little plane seemed so small in the scheme of things, our little lives aloft above the endless ocean. I wondered if my hope alone kept us in the air.

Looking out the window at our next destination, we landed on an island in Canada called Gander. Snow! There was snow on the ground that was beautiful as it reflected the golden color of the sunset. It was Christmas in May in Canada. I watched my breath coming out in clouds into the crisp air and marveled at the beauty of such an exotic cold. Well, I marveled for a moment, until the cold seeped under my skirt and through my skin, making me hold the blanket tighter around my shoulders and hurry into the typical airline hanger nearby.

"We'll have a car to take you to a hotel here soon, but please make sure that you are back by 5 a.m." said one of the pilots. The passengers gathered in the hanger, sitting on the benches of what looked like a waiting room of some sort. One of the other single men on the plane, also traveling to America to attend university, sat down next to Ahmad and me. He slapped the bench next to him, as if testing its solidity, and said, "You know, these benches look just fine to me."

He raised his voice slightly so the pilot could hear him and continued, "I think I am just going to stay on these nice benches here for tonight if that's OK with the base. I don't have the money for a hotel tonight after this long journey, and still more to go until we arrive."

"That's an excellent way to save money," Ahmad said to me, then he turned to the single gentleman and repeated, "That's an excellent way to save money. Do you mind if we join you?"

My jaw dropped open at this announcement, made so casually. Sleeping in public, let alone on a hard, metal bench, didn't only seem uncomfortable but unseemly, too. I nudged Ahmad and gave him a searching look, wondering if he was serious.

"What?" he asked. "These benches seem just fine."

My eyes grew wider and I continued to look at him with incredulity.

"They're fine," he repeated. "You'll be fine."

The other passengers left and I curled into an unhappy ball on a bench. Unable to raise my voice or contradict my husband in public — this idea was ingrained deep in my mind since childhood — I had no recourse but to clam up, hold tight and bear what could be the worst night of my life. I stared hard at the tin-can wall of the hanger, barely closing my eyes. I had only my yellow blanket and my anger to keep me warm.

Morning dawned cold and crisp, and my anger had cooled into sadness. It was not proper to speak up to my husband in front of others and it was him who had all of our money strapped to his stomach — all of my father's money — some $10,000 American dollars. And he didn't want to spend $20 on a hotel. *This* was my husband. *This* was my husband? This was what he thought of taking care of me as a new wife. I didn't feel I had the right to be angry because, as my mother said, this was my choice. This had been what I was willing to do to get out of the country. So a depressive cloud made a home above my head and continued to fog up my head as I washed my face in the public bathroom and climbed back on the plane for our last hop in the air, this time to New Jersey.

It was a grey afternoon in New Jersey when we landed, not the best weather or location for one's first introduction to the country. But how was I to know the difference? I couldn't even conceive of the vast differences between California and New York or Michigan and Florida — weren't they all America? And so I looked around as if the same old pavement and military hangers could show me the greatness of my new country. But they were the same typical army bases I saw in Canada, in Portugal, in England, in Greece and in Iran. Our bags were unloaded and piled around us, and I thought that it was all the same. Five days journey and a marriage for this, I thought, sinking further into my cloud of disappointment.

After so long together in such close quarters, the passengers scattered like freed prisoners. A few goodbyes and we were all off in different directions. Only Ahmad and I and two other students who were headed north from the army base remained together to

take the same bus to Washington D.C. before parting.

We went into a little diner, which they called a hot shop in those days, to plan. Customers took a tray and slid it down the line, pointing to what they wanted. I shirked slowly along, not recognizing any of the food and wondering if I was offending the employees by not taking anything. I settled on some French fries, because we had fries in Iran, but they doused the potatoes in ketchup, which I had never tried. I turned up my nose at that strange red stuff, and tried to scrape it off as much as I could. How strange, I thought. This is America. This hot shop is America.

Fresh from the belly of the plane, our suitcases went into the belly of a Greyhound bus headed for Washington D.C. that afternoon. It was a five hour trip by bus, which at least had individual seats with padding. That small luxury soothed my jangled nerves to some degree. I had a window to look out of, and once we got out of the city, that window showed me some amazing things: huge expanses of land stretching away into the distance, more open land than I had ever seen. Cows, fences and little farm houses. Because of the open spaces, it seemed like such a clean country. No leaning shacks piled into poor villages, no buildings in need of repair. We passed a small, white church that could have been a picture from a postcard, with its pointed steeple and paned windows that looked like friendly eyes.

Once again, I thought that *this* is America. This quaint countryside and this white church is America.

We arrived in Washington D.C in what was obviously not a nice neighborhood. There were no cows or white churches in sight. Instead, there was the smell of exhaust, crowded streets, yelling taxicab drivers, dirty people sitting on the ground near overflowing trashcans. We hustled quickly into a McDonalds, whose bright lights and standard menu offered some comfort and stability in the noisy world that had transitioned into the deeply dark and scary night. A dark and scary night in an unfamiliar place where I couldn't understand a word that anyone was saying.

"Thank you," I said to the clerk at McDonalds when she handed me more French fries, my dietary staple because it was the only thing I was able to recognize and pronounce. I think "thank you" was the only English I uttered my first day in America. But in Farsi, I told Ahmad that this was a silly thing. That we should have stayed in New Jersey in a hotel because now it was night in a strange city. Had he really thought the Iranian embassy, where we needed to check in first thing with the General's important friend (the whole reason we had gone to Washington D.C., after all), was going to be open in the middle of the night? Where were we to go?

"Maryam," he said firmly. "This will be fine." It wasn't a reassurance. The statement was a way of saying that *he* was going to make sure it was fine, and that I should just leave him alone about it.

"Let's at least get a cab into another neighborhood, a nicer place," I said, looking out the window into the grubby, neon-lit night.

"This is fine," he repeated. He touched his stomach briefly to feel for the money belt and continued eating his hamburger.

What turned out to be "fine" in my husband's estimation was a sign advertising rooms outside of a bar. We walked through the door into the smoky room, where men and women — women! In a bar! — were sadly sipping their drinks in the near-dark. Ahmad approached the bartender and spoke to him in English about a room. I held my suitcase in front of me with both hands and looked at the floor, my yellow blanket draped over my arm. I felt like a child, a vulnerable child in an unsafe land. When Ahmad returned, he led me toward and elevator, where a dirty man that was missing one hand — he had a hook instead — pulled the metal cage closed and pressed the button for us.

How do we know there is a room up here? I wondered. Are they going to kill us? If they don't, this creaky old elevator might!

A narrow hallway with a light that flickered on and off led to our room, which was even worse than the hallway. Honestly, it frightened me. There was one tiny bed and a few pieces of furniture that had probably once been white, but were now banged up and smeared with who knew what to be the color of skin that needs a shower. Ahmad went back downstairs to pay, and I stared at myself in the foggy mirror. My tears were sooty with makeup and made black rivers down my cheeks.

This? This is America? This is me in America? How strange… and scary, disappointing, sad and, again, scary.

America is supposed to be a clean country, I thought. Here was a room where I didn't want to touch the walls and hard-shelled bugs with lots of legs scurried into the drain of the sink when I turned on the light. I stood frozen, unhappy that my feet had to touch the ground and certain that I didn't want any other part of my body to touch any other part of that room.

"Why are you crying?" Ahmad asked when he returned. "What is it?"

"Let's get out of here," I said, my voice quavering. "This is awful. Please, let's just go."

He huffed in frustration at me and plopped himself down on the bed, obviously sharing none of my reservations about touching the dirty room.

"We are staying here," he said. "I can't do better than this."

I knew that if I said another word, the tears building up in my throat would never stop. So I took my yellow velvet blanket, spread it out on one side of the bed and laid down upon it, pulling the other side over me so I wouldn't have contact with the questionable covers and pillow. For yet another night, I stared at a wall. I rarely slept that night, but when I did, I dreamt of my red clipped winged friend, hopping around in the middle of the jungle, scared and unable to fly.

This is the best I can do. My husband's words echoes in my head as I tried to rest that first night in America. But in my head, the words became a question: This is the best I can do? This is America.

How strange.

Chapter Twelve

We checked out first thing in the morning, thank God, and with my blanket over my arm, I walked out of that hotel hoping to never see it again. Tired from lack of sleep over the last several days of travel, my entire body from hairline to toenails ached and complained as I walked. And tiredness wasn't my only problem.

Even in this rough area of town, the streets were quiet and the sun was warming up the sidewalks. The early summer day dawned fresher than the night before, even if we weren't. In the same way, I was feeling a little better, too. No longer about to burst into tears, I decided that I was going to give this strange country a little more of a chance, see it in the light of day. Everyone deserved a second chance.

We arrived at the Iranian embassy and checked our suitcases in the front lobby. Just walking into the building was like breathing the air of home, it was decorated with Persian carpets and objects carved of turquoise, all the familiar touches of Persian culture that reminded me of home. However, we were told that the Ambassador, General's good friend who was supposed to be such a help to us in our new lives, was out of the country. Instead, we saw an American man who worked at the embassy and spoke Farsi.

He stamped our papers and took care of the formalities. When we asked for help getting our bearings in the new country, he told us of an international youth hostel nearby where students from all over the world stayed while in the city. Ahmad's eyes lit up when he heard the man say the hostel was cheap and included breakfast. It was located near the famous Dupont Circle, one of the busiest and most important areas of the city. He wrote down the address on a slip of paper for us to give the taxi driver and he smiled.

Outside the embassy, we did run into two young Iranian men, also students, who gave us their phone number and said to call if we needed any help. Though I kept their number, at the time we didn't even have a telephone — or a bed for the night, for that matter — and making friends wasn't the highest priority for me.

The hostel we were directed toward was typical for that type of establishment, which meant that it was going to be an incredibly new experience for me. I had rarely stayed in hotels back in Iran, having always traveled to the houses of family when I traveled at all. Some of the establishments where we had slept since beginning our American odyssey — a room above a bar, a metal bench — had taught me I wasn't always going to be comfortable on the road. The hostel was no different. Students from all over the world provided lots of excitement. I had never met so many people from so many continents before, and that part was interesting. But a breakfast of cereal and the hard beds (which were really more like army cots) wore on me over time.

I thought of Doris Day's apartment in the movie "Pillow Talk," with all its bright colors, the clean kitchen and the maid who came every day to tidy up. I thought of Audrey Hepburn in "Breakfast at Tiffany's." She hadn't been rich, that's for sure, but her rooms were still light and airy, clean and not in need of repair. Sure, she had a bathtub with cushions in it for a couch, but that was whimsical. And now I was sharing a bathroom with dozens of strangers and having no place to spend the day. This was America for the immigrant, so different than the images of the country I had seen while abroad.

I knew that I couldn't expect to find a life as good as the ones I saw pictured in Hollywood movies. I knew that, but perhaps part of me expected it anyway. I was a young and idealistic girl, after all, journeying to the land I had been dreaming about since I was a child, building it up in my head to mythic and unreachable levels.

Living in the hostel, I finally realized that America wasn't as easy as I imagined it to be. Obviously, the good life I wanted to have wasn't going to fall into my lap. But that didn't mean I couldn't have it. You can have anything in America if you are willing to work for it. That's what I had been told and that's what I believed. It took a few days for my cloud of disappointment and depression to dissipate enough for me to change my outlook. If I wanted things to work out the way I wanted them to, I would just have to take matters into my own hands.

After a week in the hostel, I said to Ahmad, "I can't do this anymore." I threw my hands up in the hair and motioned around the room, taking in the hostel. "Either we are finding a real place to live or I am going back to Iran."

"I think it's fine here," he replied.

"Okay then," I said. "I'll find another place by myself then."

He shrugged his shoulders as if to say, "Suit yourself."

The next day I set out from the hostel to walk around the Dupont Circle area, using the little bit of English I'd picked up from the English school library with Ahmad to read the names of buildings. Luckily, it's pretty easy to see that a building houses apartments without have to decipher the sign out front.

I found a stunning building made of white brick about 10 stories high that looked really promising. It was tall and clean, with fresh paint and clipped grass, and when I walked inside, a saw just a little bit of the American movies and the type of living I had expected upon coming to America. The lobby was pretty and decorated well, with soft carpets and flower arrangements and mirrors on the walls. There was a large desk on the far end of the room with a receptionist-type person sitting behind it.

I took a deep breath and approached her armed with the English sentence I had been practicing in my head. "Do you have room?" I asked.

"Excuse me?" she said.

"Do you have room?" I repeated.

She smiled and asked where I was from. Then she very patiently explained that they had a studio apartment and that it rented for $160 a month, then she gave me a tour of the studio, which was basically one big room, except for the bathroom, which did have a door to separate it. Even so, the apartment had sunlight coming in, a kitchen to have a meal to ourselves and a lock on the door. That was enough for me and I told her we'd take it. Ahmad would probably frown at the price, but I didn't care. I knew we had the money my father gave us to set up a new house in America, and this was a new house. This was going to be my first house both in America and in general. I looked out the window over the D.C. skyline and I felt as if I could see myself in this city.

Of course, we had absolutely nothing in this new apartment except our suitcases and an increasingly well-worn yellow velvet blanket. I spread it out on the hardwood floor and we sat down and stared at one another. Then we went to Sears and bought the best Persian-style rug that we could afford, which cost about $35. (Every home needs a rug, I thought. The rug must come first.) We went home, laid down on it and slept. When we woke up, we went back to Sears and bought a bed and two pillows, and when we got home, I spread my red velvet blanket on the new mattress.

So we had some place to lay our heads, and that was a huge comfort to me. However, that meant I had to start thinking more about food — food other than French fries from whatever fast food restaurant was closest. Having been in America a few days now, I was game for having cereal for breakfast. But having no bowls in the house, I was not up for trying to eat it out of my cupped hands.

Again, Ahmad shrugged his shoulders at me when I mentioned our lack of basic items needed to run a house. It's a myth, I decided, that a man takes care of a woman in a marriage. Instead, my husband just assumed that his wife was going to take care of everything for him. That was the power of being a man — he just gave me his "suit yourself" shrug.

So I went out hunting for the things I needed, starting as close to home as I could since I was on my own in an unknown city. The closest store just happened to be the Drug Fair. Like most drug stores of the era, the Drug Fair had a prescription department, photo processing, general food items and a little diner counter that served food and sodas. I wandered the aisles for a while, just checking out what the store offered, and was about to wander off to another store, when I approached the check out. Behind the counter was a very familiar looking girl. Though her badge said her name was Perry, I could have sworn she looked Persian.

I decided to take a chance and greeted her in Farsi. Her face lit up and she said, "You're Persian! Where are you from?"

"Tabriz."

"How wonderful, such a beautiful city," she said. "And when did you get here?"

I told her a little bit about our adventure so far: the long trip, finding an apartment and having nothing. Just being able to speak in my own language and have someone answer back in words I could understand was overwhelming. Suddenly, I felt so homesick and frustrated with my situation, and I started to cry. Sniffing and trying to keep my sobs in check, I told Perry about how our apartment currently held a rug and a bed and two suitcases, and that I couldn't even cook a meal or make a pot of tea in my own home. She came out from behind the counter and put her hands on my shoulders.

"Don't worry," she said. "It's never as easy as they say it is. It's not Doris Day, is it?"

I had to smile, knowing that this girl had similar misguided dreams once upon a time, but that now she seemed happy and well-adjusted in America.

"I came from Iran and I had nothing, too. Now," she paused to wink at me, "I have an American boyfriend and a good job here. It's a good life."

Thinking that Ahmad and I were as poor as she must have been when she came to America, she pointed me across the street to a store called the Goodwill. I had no idea what a Goodwill was. In fact, I had never even heard of a store that sold second-hand goods. The code of generosity in Iran had always been that unused things are simply given away to the less fortunate as charity, so I had no way of knowing that the store I walked in to was selling items that used to belong to other people, that was usually patronized by people who had very little money.

What a strange store, I thought, with all the mismatched kitchenware, none of it the same. And there are no salesmen, I noticed. But I was happy that I spent only a few dollars and walked out of the store with the basics I needed: a frying pan and a large pot, a few cups to drink out of, a tea kettle, and a few dishes, all of them in different colors, of course. Everything I needed fit into two brown bags, which I carried home with pride. I had conquered the city of Washington D.C. for just one day.

Sure, it was a small thing to accomplish, but sometimes winning a battle gives you the confidence to win the war.

Flush with victory, I made my first journey to the grocery store nearest our apartment. I was able to find Feta cheese and bread for a traditional breakfast along with tea to brew in my new (to me) kettle. It's amazing how a tiny thing like breakfast can make all of life seem sunnier and more manageable. I also picked out a whole chicken, which was one of the few things I knew how to cook as a new bride. While many of the little, frozen birds were about 25 cents, I dug through the freezer bin until I found a slightly smaller one for only 17 cents. Remembering my mother-in-law's comments about the thickness of my potato peeling, I felt as if I had done something important in saving my family 8 cents, and I walked out of the store a happy wife, a proud wife who now had tea, a chicken and a key jangling in my pocket that opened the front door of my first house.

I stopped by the Drug Fair again to show my new friend, Perry, the fruits of my accomplishment, showing her my smile after I had revealed to her my tears the day before.

Like an angel dropped out of the sky — again — she said she had spoken to her boss and may have found a job for me in the store, working behind the counter of the diner: a small counter with about a dozen stools with a window behind framing the short-order cook whipping up eggs, hamburgers and other typical fare.

Perry introduced me to the manager, a middle-aged woman with brown hair who seemed equal parts friendly and skeptical about me.

"So you're Perry's friend?" she asked me. "She says you've just moved from Iran."

"Yes," I replied, keeping my response brief so she wouldn't be able to tell the quality of my English.

"We do have a vacancy for a server behind the diner counter," she said. "Do you think you could do that work?"

"Yes," I said, not quite as confident as I tried to seem.

She sighed and looked me up and down. "Okay," she said. "Get yourself some white shoes and come back in tomorrow for your uniform. You can start in two days. That's alright with you?"

"Oh yes," I said. "Thank you."

I smiled and the manager turned away, leaving Perry and me to hug one another in happiness. Then I had to have Perry explain to me what it was that the manager had said. Though I understood that I had the job, words like "uniform" were too complicated and the woman had spoken so fast. I was to buy white what?

My husband was ecstatic about my new job. Only the night before, we had spoken about the local English school, which offered classes to help students study for the TOEFL exam, the English-proficiency test every foreign student needed to pass in order to attend an American university. My husband's English was better than mine, but he still needed quite a bit of practice before he would be able to keep up in a classroom of higher education. The school was expensive, however — about $100 per week per student — and there was no way we could afford to send both of us at the same time. One of us, it has been decided would have to get a job while the other went to English school. It had been obvious even at the time that Ahmad wanted to be the first one to study, and the fact that I had so handily gotten a job made sure that he would be first to go to school.

Yes, we had the $10,000 of my father's money and Ahmad's savings, which was a lot of money in that time. But with rent and tuition money, that wasn't going to last us very long. At least, that's what Ahmad kept repeating. And he handled the money — I had nothing to do with it — so I was scared of becoming poor in a place where we had no family to help us.

His smile was as wide as the ocean he has just crossed, seeing how everything was falling into place so well. But he comforted me by reiterating the bargain he had proposed back in Iran.

"This is all for the best," he said. "Remember, one of us has to work to make going to school possible. But the sooner I am done with my schooling, the sooner you can go, too."

I smiled and nodded my head. I was being a very good little wife, helping my husband. And then he was going to be a good husband of the Iranian model — generous to his wife with money and prestige — once he was finished with his education. The next day, we went together to a department store named Murphy's and he made a big show of spending about $6 on a pair of comfortable white shoes for me.

I went to bed that night with fear in my heart. Going out into the world to buy a chicken was one thing, a small task that I could handle in this strange foreign country. But perhaps I had gotten myself in over my head taking a job where I would be expected to understand more English than I probably did.

This is the ceiling, I said in English inside my own head, looking up from our bed in the dark of the apartment. That is a wall. This is the floor. There is my dress. These were some of the most complicated sentences I could manage, and I was pretty sure my job at the Drug Fair wasn't going to require me to say anything about ceilings and walls. Cup, plate, bowl. Fork, knife, spoon. I reiterated the few words I knew that related to the kitchen, things that would most likely be more fundamental to the job of a diner girl.

Despite my late-night practice, I was still terrified in the morning when I reported to my first day at work in the Drug Fair, my first day of work in America. Actually, it was my first day of work ever, seeing that I had never had a real job while I was in Iran. I wore the uniform I had picked up the day before: a crisp white dress that looked similar to a nurse's outfit, similar to the kinds I had seen on other diner workers the many times I had eaten French fries in America so far.

I think my face might have been as white as the dress when I first came into the store because I as so scared. I felt as if everyone was watching me, that everyone knew that I wasn't going to be able to understand even the most basic of instructions.

Luckily for me, there was a very kind woman assigned to train me my first day. Jill was a smiling, kind woman a few years older than me, but obviously much wiser and more experienced than I.

"Hello. My name is Maryam. My English is not so good," I said to Jill, "and I am sorry. I say thank you for help."

"Don't worry about it, honey," Jill replied. "There's not too much to it around here. I'm sure you'll catch on quick."

I hoped she was right, but as the day wore on, I began to doubt her confidence in me. I was unable to do the tasks that any of the other girls behind the counter were expected to do. I couldn't take an order from a customer, because I had no idea what the words for the menu items were. Even if I did, I didn't have the skill to take those words and write them down on a ticket in the way the cook could understand.

Instead Jill did all the order-taking in exchange for me doing all the food delivery. That much I could handle. When the cook rang the bell that food was ready, I appeared at the window and he pointed toward the person I was to place it in front of. I tried out the phrases, "Here you go" and "Enjoy."

Jill also had to take care of all the handling of money. Sure, I could do math. After all, I was a high school graduate and reasonably intelligent girl. But I was so unfamiliar with American money that it was impossible for me. Which one was the quarter, and how much was it worth again? How many dimes are in a dollar? The foreign currency was also a foreign language I had yet to master.

In exchange, I tried to handle all the bussing of empty dishes, bringing dirty plates and cups back into the kitchen to be washed. I was running around like a chicken with its head cut off, trying to be of as much use as possible, trying not to get in the way. I think "I'm sorry" was the phrase I got the most use out of, saying it to Jill, to the cook and to the customers more times than I could count.

About halfway through the day, a gentleman took a seat at the counter. He was a large man who looked like he did manual labor for a living. There was dirt under his fingernails and dark smudges under his eyes. He plopped down on the stool with an attitude of tired grumpiness and slapped his newspaper down on the counter next to him.

"Give me a coke," he said to me, the girl nearest him at the counter.

I understood the word coke, of course, so I nodded and scurried off to fetch a glass, fill it with ice and use the soda fountain to top it off with soda. This was something — one of the few things — I could handle, and so I went about the job quickly.

When I dropped off the bubbling glass of coke in front of him, he looked at me as if I was stupid, his eyebrows arched up and his lips curled.

"Something missing here, girl?"

"What?" I asked. I wasn't trying to ask what was missing. I was asking him what he just said, because I didn't understand.

"A straw."

"Straw?" I repeated, rolling the unfamiliar word around in my mouth.

"Yes, a straw," he said, pointing to his glass.

"St-raaaw?" I repeated, trying to wrap my tongue around it.

"Where on earth are you from?" he asked. "Don't you know what a straw is?"

If possible, his eyebrows were arching even more violently toward the ceiling — a word that I knew, unlike the strange thing he was asking for so stridently. I shook my head at him and held up a finger, a rudimentary pantomime to tell him that I didn't know what he was saying and to hold on just one moment. I went to grab Jill and asked, "St-roo? What stroo?"

"I don't know, honey," she said. "I don't know the word stroo."

"Maybe straah? What straah?"

"Oh, you mean straw! Sure!"

She grabbed my hand and led me back to the soda fountain. Under the counter were a box of straws and she grabbed one out for me. "Straw," she said. "Every soda needs to have a straw."

"Straw," I said. "OK." I reappeared at the other end of the counter in front of the large man with the dirty fingernails. I handed him the wrapped straw.

"It's about time," he said, rolling his eyes at me. The menu was closed on the countertop by his hands, but I scurried away before he could tell me what he wanted. I didn't want to face the impatience and frustration of that large, stout face again when I couldn't understand him.

"Hey," he said. "Wait."

I pushed open the swinging door into the kitchen and told Jill he wanted to order his food. Then I stood in the kitchen for a moment, trying to breathe. My throat was tight, my heart was racing. I felt as if my brain and body were too slow and clumsy for this world, where everything was moving so fast. People spoke too fast for me to catch their words, expected me to move too fast in my squeaky new shoes. Everyone was watching me, everyone was judging me — even a laborer with dirty fingernails, who thought he was smarter than I was because I didn't know how American's liked to drink their sodas. I was ashamed to go back out there and look him or any of the other customers in the face.

Though I came close, I didn't cry. I took a deep breath and went back out into the fray, trying to help Jill as much as I could with my slow and clumsy self.

All the while, I continued to glance up at the manager's box, an office on the second level of the store that looked out over the vast expanse of aisles, counters, registers and the diner. Inside was the lady manager Perry had introduced me to as well as a few other bosses. I could feel their eyes upon me, which caused my cheeks to blush and my tears to remain just at the edges of my eyes.

At the end of my shift, the lady manager came down from the manager's box. From back in the kitchen, I saw her approach Jill. They spoke for a moment and then looked back at me in the kitchen. When she saw me, the manager smiled and motioned for me to come to her.

"Maryam," she said. "How was your first day?" Her eyes were kind, and she seemed genuinely worried about how I felt.

"Not good," I said, my eyes filling with the tears I had been suppressing all day.

"It's OK," she said. I think she even threw an arm around my shoulder. "It's just not going to work out right now, right?"

I nodded.

"It's OK," she repeated. "You seem like such a nice girl. You just got to learn a bit more English, and when you do, you come back to us. We'll try it again. All right?"

I nodded again, taking some comfort in the woman's obvious kindness. But that small comfort was overwhelmed by my feelings of uselessness and failure. I had to give back my uniform and walk back to my apartment with my new white shoes, a waste of $6. By the time I opened the front door to the apartment near Dupont Circle, tears had created rivers down my cheeks. Ahmad had been studying, bent over a book, but when he saw my tears, he asked, "What happened?"

"I got fired," I said, happy that I could at least express myself in Farsi again.

"Oh no," he said, standing up to come over and hold my hand. I used the other hand to wipe away a few tears from my eyes.

"I don't know what to do in this country," I said.

"Don't cry, Maryam. I don't know what to do when you cry," Ahmad responded.

"I want to go back to Iran."

"We just got here," he said. "No, no, no. We are going to do a lot of things in this country. It's that we're just starting out. We're struggling students. Everyone struggles when they are students."

I sniffed.

"Right?" he asked.

"I guess so."

"There you go. Now stop crying. Something else will come up for us soon. I know it." He went back to studying his books for the remainder of the evening, and I looked over his finished homework, trying to learn what I could of English second-hand, just like my Goodwill pots and pans.

Our next opportunity to make money came from another Iranian couple who lived in our apartment building, which was called the Bristol House. While we may have passed many Iranian couples on the street at home in Tabriz and felt absolutely no obligation to be friendly with them, it was different in America. In a foreign country, any Persian was seen as a lifeline in a foreign land, a link back home. We hung onto one another for dear life and became close right away, our shared language and customs enough in common to create a bond between us.

Like many Iranian women I knew — including my mother and Ahmad's mother — this lady was intimately concerned with the finances of her husband. She had helped him find a job, shopped for bargains like a pro and considered their finances her way to success and respectability not only in America, but also to prove something to their families back home. She was also a gossip and loved to compare material goods, job quality and other markers of success between husbands. If something happened anywhere in the small Iranian community, we were becoming a part of, she was the first to know, especially if the news was a juicy bit of scandal or failure.

One night, Heshmat came over for tea and told me she has found an extra way to make money.

"A job?" I asked. "What job?"

"All we have to do is go to work on Saturday nights, and we get to go together, with our husbands," she explained. "And it's very good money: about $10 each, so $20 for both of you."

At a time when a chicken cost 17 cents, $20 seemed a lot of money to me. Though I didn't have access to our financial records myself, Ahmad had made it seem as if our bank account was draining like a rowboat with a leak, and I was willing to do most anything to make such we wouldn't have to return to Iran with our tails between our legs in failure.

"Tell your husband and come meet us at 9:30 on Saturday night, and we will all go together, OK?"

I agreed, though I was curious why the job would take place so late in the evening. Ahmad had no such reservations when he heard of the $20 waiting for him once the job was complete.

And so, it happened that we walked in the cold of a fall night in Washington D.C. with a group of other Iranian men and their wives, most of them also students and very smart students at that, training to be doctors and other professionals. We arrived at the side door of the Washington Post, the big-time newspaper in D.C., where a line of other people curled against the brick wall, waiting for a job and breathing clouds of fog into the cold night air. It was a motley crew: lots of immigrants of different nationalities and ethnicities, some people I assumed to be deaf due to their use of sign language.

Heshmat and her husband explained that all these people were waiting in line for a chance to help the Post assemble their Sunday editions. Sunday was always the day they put out their biggest paper, with lots of advertising and special inserts. The papers weren't finished printing until the evening, and they needed to be assembled before dawn for the carriers to pick up and deliver around the city in time for subscriber's morning coffee. It didn't sound that difficult, other than that I was tired, so we took our place in line and gave our names to the man inside the door, who assigned us a place to work.

The interior of the building was immense and full of noisy machinery. We were standing up on both sides of a conveyer belt. Papers kept moving down the line and we were supposed to snatch one up, place all the inserts inside in the right order and place the thick bunches on racks to be picked up by the carriers.

It wasn't exactly work that took a lot of brain power, that's for sure, but it took more stamina than I would have expected. My hands became sooty with the ink of the newspaper, followed by my face and my clothes. I realized that a nice blouse and slacks were not exactly the right uniform for such work. I got a few paper cuts, but soon that stinging was nothing compared to the soreness of my muscles from the repetitive movements of picking up the paper, unfolding, refolding and hefting it up onto the racks. There seemed to be a never-ending supply of papers appearing on the conveyer belt from the other room, and the hours crept by until morning slower than a turtle.

I was sleepy and dehydrated. Chatting in Farsi with the other Persian wives was the only thing that kept me going. From time to time, a kind looking American man with grey hair would walk down the assembly line and ask everyone how they were doing. He'd poke at the people who fell asleep occasionally and kindly corrected people when they assembled a few papers incorrectly.

Finally, it was 7:30 in the morning and we each received a check for $9.30 each. Just as the woman had promised, it was about $20 for little family. Ahmad and I were both happy about that as we dragged ourselves home and into bed, promising the other couples that we would go back to the Post again the next Saturday for another $20.

Though I wanted to be able to have a job, even a job for one night a week, to bring some money home for the family, the work at the Post became very hard for me over time. I wondered if it was the late night and lack of sleep, or perhaps the constant noise of the newspaper presses giving me a headache. Maybe it was something about the smell of the ink, I didn't know. But something was definitely making me sick in the Post building over time.

After about two months, I told Ahmad about my headaches and the sick feeling in my stomach when we went to our Saturday night job, but he seemed unsympathetic.

"No, you have to come," he said. "We need money and you are not working anywhere else, are you?"

I felt this remark was an insult about me losing the job at the Drug Fair after one day. Still feeling guilty and incompetent about that debacle, I knew he was right and so I continued going.

One night, my face must have appeared as sickly as I felt on the inside. The nice old man with the gray hair came around and stopped in front of me.

"Are you OK?" he asked.

"I just don't feel good," I admitted to him, weakly lifting a completed paper onto the rack. My husband looked over at me with a look on his face that showed he was worried I was going to be dismissed.

But the old man was sympathetic, saying, "Why don't you take a break for about an hour?"

I looked around the vast, noisy and inky room. "Where?" I asked.

He grabbed a large piece of cardboard that used to be part of a box and laid it on the ground near my feet, under the conveyer belt. "Rest for a while down here," he told me. I looked at my husband and then did as the man said, laying down under the whirring conveyer belt. The moving slats made the light flash dark and light under the assembly line, and I could see the shoes and pant legs of all my friends as I lay there, my hand under my cheek.

The pounding in my head seemed more manageable when I was lying down. I put my other hand over my stomach, trying to calm it, too. After about an hour, Ahmad nudged me with his shoe and I came up to begin working again. The old man came around to check on me and I said I was feeling a little better, even though the difference was minor. I still felt ill.

A few days later, I was doing some shopping downtown. I had mastered some of the bus lines at that point and felt more comfortable on my own. But that day in particular seemed surreal to me. Everything I saw appeared in sharp focus, as if I was wearing super magnifying glasses. My hearing was sensitive, too. I remember hearing the baby-like voice of Michael Jackson over a speaker in a store, a song from his days with the Jackson Five, as if I had never heard it before. Then back on the street, a woman screamed at her child to stop, but I thought she was screaming at me — directly in my ear, that's how amplified it sounded.

I froze in place, wondering what was happening. Had I done something? Was I in trouble? Was a car careening off the street in my direction, about to hit me? I opened my eyes and saw the woman grabbing for her young son, scolding him for running off. But still, I felt as if I was in danger, as if something was wrong. Again, it felt like an unreal world. I even thought that I could smell and taste things in the air that I had never noticed before.

I cried into my hand on the way home on the bus. I'd been told I was quick to tears in the past, but I had no idea why I was crying. I was just thinking about the view of my friends' legs and the noise in my ears during that time I'd rested under the conveyer belt of the Washington Post. I felt as if I was still there on the ground, and that maybe I was sinking through the floor. My head hurt, my back ached, and I went home to fall asleep on a tear-drenched pillow.

I woke up with a warm, wet feeling around my waist to my husband's panicked voice. "What's wrong, Maryam?" he asked with a high-pitched tone. "What's all this?"

I opened my eyes and saw that I was lying in a pool of blood. My back and my entire stomach area were racked with cramps and I felt hot enough to cook an egg on my forehead.

"I don't know. I don't know. I don't know," I said. I was so confused and disoriented. "Do something!" I pleaded. "Please do something."

He ran into the other room to use the telephone. Apparently he called a doctor, because he came back into the room to tell me that he was taking me to the Columbia Hospital for Women. That's what he had been told to do. Wrapping the sheets of the bed around me, I hobbled outside. Thankfully, we had just spent $1,000 of our savings to buy an old but reliable car: a big, long Olympia Chevrolet that barely fit in a normal size parking space.

The trip in the car and into the hospital and up to a bed was a blur to me. I only really came back to my senses after I had been poked with needles, pumped full of liquids and cleaned up by the kind hands of a nurse.

"You've had a miscarriage, dear," a doctor with neat brown hair and glasses told me. "Did you know you were pregnant? You were about 10 weeks along."

I shook my head, unable to speak thanks to the shock of this news.

"You're going to be all right." He patted my hand and left the room, and I fell into a deep, dark sleep.

Chapter Thirteen

Thanks to Heshmat, the gossip, every Persian in the Bristol House and anywhere nearby had learned about my miscarriage. Heshmat had even spread the opinion that perhaps I had caused the loss of the child myself, I was told by others. I shook my head in amazement. Some women have far too much time on their hands to stick their noses in other people's business, I thought. Sometimes a close-knit community can be a blessing as well as a curse.

A few months later, we met a young American girl and her fiancé, Mehdi, who were getting married. They offered us Mehdi's one bedroom, furnished apartment on California Street, near the DC Hilton. With a great a location and cheaper rent, it was here, across from a great little grocery store and near the D.C. Hilton, that Ahmad and I settled into some sort of routine in America. I was feeling better about my new country, a bit more comfortable and confident in my new home, and Ahmad was learning a lot at the language school. He met lots of other international students there, both single and married men, and began going out to lunch or otherwise hanging out with his new friends outside of classes.

But I found something to make myself feel useful at the same time as Ahmad was finding his way. Another Persian woman from the Bristol House told me she was studying to be a beautician at the Beauty Academy in downtown Washington D.C. I had explained to her that my husband's schooling was all we could afford at the moment, but that I really wanted to get an education of my own.

"Why don't you come to the beauty college, then?" she suggested. "It's not quite as expensive as other schooling, and you start earning tips when you get far enough along that you're doing people's hair. And there are other Iranian ladies there, too. You'd be surprised."

"I don't know," I said, and I was being honest. I had never considered being a beautician before, but I admit the thought of such a career had immediate appeal for me. I had always avidly followed the fashion and beauty magazines, and I'd inherited my father's talent for looking beautiful in public, polished and stylish.

"That way when you go back to Iran, you can have some kind of a certificate," the girl continued.

I nodded. That's true. In fact, beauticians in Iran had quite a bit of status and prestige compared to the stylists in America. Women who did hair and make up were powerful, able to make or break their clients futures. Women fought over the services of good beauty aides, and there were never enough to go around. I knew of several women in Tabriz who had set up very successful businesses centered on beauty, who became very rich from the enterprise and were still regarded highly in the community.

"But maybe my English isn't good enough," I said.

"Don't worry about that," she replied. "You have improved so much just since you've been here. Learn from your husband's books and from talking with people in the city. You don't need to spend the money on tuition for your English classes — the world is your classroom."

She took a sip of tea and then smiled, continuing, "You know what the best English teacher is, don't you?"

"What?" I asked.

"A television, of course. You should make your husband buy you a television."

I pictured Ahmad's face when I asked him for money for a TV, hearing already him saying, "We have no money for that.

"It's so expensive," I told her. "I don't know."

"Tell him it's less expensive than school, right?" Again she smiled. Sometimes women who have been married longer know exactly the right way to approach things with a man.

Once we'd moved into the apartment on California Street, sure enough, we'd bought a black-and-white television from Sears that we put on a chair in the corner of the living room and I'd convinced Ahmad to give me the $500 I needed to begin beauty school.

I heard about the expense of it everyday from him, though. If I came home with groceries, he'd wonder where the change was. Because he used the only car we had all day, I'd ask him for bus fare. He would say that I would have to find some way to earn it myself or just walk. "We have no money for that," he'd say. I think that became his most commonly used phrase: "We have no money for that."

While sometimes it seemed he was being inordinately stingy, he did control the money and he was the one who knew how much we had. And I was happy to be going to school and doing something with my life. I was willing to put up with being a bit poor and taking some abuse from my husband if I could be a beautician. I was a young wife, and I wasn't able to switch the dynamics of power, so I learned to deal with it the best I could. Every time I heard "We have no money for that," I sighed and remembered that Ahmad was his mother's son.

I went to beauty school five days a week, traveling on the bus to the academy in the morning. I had bought a fluffy, stocking hat of a style that all the American girls seemed to be wearing. I kept to myself on the bus, still slightly afraid, but once I got to school, I blossomed.

The course of study was divided into two sections, the first of which was mostly studying out of a book and working on the hair of mannequins. We learned how to separate the hair into sections, how to create a nice line with the scissors. We learned how to do an old-fashioned finger wave in the hair of older ladies who still wore that style, and eventually we were taught how to roll up hair for a permanent wave and how to pull off special dyeing techniques.

I was especially drawn toward the little tricks of the trade I learned: what hairstyle suited each face shape, the best shape for eyebrows, using your skin tone to find the best make up and hair color. It seemed that what I had been used to in Iran — my grandmother's way of creating thick, black eyebrows on the moon patio, for instance — was so clumsy compared with the beauty techniques of America. I felt I was really learning an art form.

Our teacher was a woman whose hair reminded me of the coiffed, shadow-dark hair of Elizabeth Taylor. Her nails were long and shapely, always shining with new polish, and her voice was similarly elegant and sharp. She seemed to be an endless fountain of beauty knowledge, as if she could make the world's women attractive with just a smile and the wave of her hand. Yet she was also very kind: understanding when we made mistakes and more than willing to explain how to do something twice or even three times.

And just like my friend had promised, there were lots of international students in addition to the American and European students. We ate lunch together in the school's break room. I either brought little things from home — feta cheese, bread and perhaps some tomatoes — or bought some French fries from a vendor downstairs (with ketchup now that I was more used to it, just like a real American).

We spoke about getting our husbands together for dinner parties and such after school, but I never made any promises. I was still very embarrassed at the state of our apartment. There weren't enough seats to go around for that many people, and I cringed with the thought of the ladies sitting down upon a ratty couch covered by a blanket. My shame brought out my creativity, though, and inspired me to change things up. I bought some flowery fabric and made curtains and a couch cover, and also picked up a new lampshade, making the home feel put together, if not glamorous.

One day when I was walking home from the bus stop, I passed by a Drug Fair, a different location of the same drug store where I'd met Perry and had my first (embarrassing and frightening) job in the United States. It was attached to the back of the Hilton, connected to the hotel by a glass walkway that kept off the winter chill. The plate-glass windows advertised all sorts of specials, warm light spilling out onto the sidewalk. The door made a nice ringing sound as customers went in and out, and the employees I saw through the window were smiling, not just at customers, but as if they were truly content. Something about the place made me stop and think that perhaps I could change the painful, humiliating memory of my first job into a smiling, content memory by trying my hand at this employment thing again. Straw? Well, I knew what a straw was now, and my heart didn't leap into my throat in fear anymore every time I stumbled across something unknown.

I walked right up to the manager's help desk with a smile on my face, feeling a little bit of the confidence that I once felt in Iran. "I'm looking for a job," I told the man behind the counter when he asked if he could help me. He was a rather petite fellow with brown hair parted on one side, and the smile on his face seemed comfortable, like something he wore all the time.

"My name is Tracy," he said. "What kind of a job are you looking for?"

I explained to him that I was a student and would like some part-time work, that anything he had available would do, and he nodded as if that was the perfect answer for him.

"We need some general help," he explained, "Someone who can work here and there and everywhere when we need it." Here and there, he explained, meant the photo developing station, the pharmacy department, the cosmetics counter — all of the different stations of the store.

After giving him my name and some other information, I found myself shaking his hand and walking out the door with a time to return for my first shift and genuine excitement about the new opportunity.

"We'll see you on Saturday morning," Tracy said as I left. I nodded and waved, thinking that — in addition to beauty school — I was finally finding a way to move around in this new country, to stand up and take part in life instead of lurking around the corners.

I was given a six-hour shift on Saturday morning, which suited me just fine. In fact, it felt hopeful to get out of bed early and get dressed, to leave the apartment and venture out into the world. Some men were headed off to drive buses or sell newspapers. Some women were walking to jobs in dress shops or diners. I was one of them — the working masses, going forth to do good work and heading home a few dollars richer. I had joined the ranks of contributing citizens.

I began at the photo counter with an Indian man named Noman. In the beginning, he taught me how to look for client's names on the envelopes of photos, how to tell the difference between packages of film and how to package up used film for Kodak to pick up at the end of each day for developing. Then we moved on to the register. All those keys and buttons and codes for merchandise — plus the taking of money, making change and math with American currency — weren't as complex as I would have guessed a few months before when I was scared of messing up serving a glass of Coke. A dash of self-confidence is often all it takes to jump into the pool of the unknown and swim. Fear freezes you up, making you sink to the bottom.

By the end of my shift, I felt as if I had been swimming in America all my life. I smiled at customers and greeted them. If I didn't understand something, I had no qualms about asking someone to repeat their words. Have a nice day, I'd leave them with, and genuinely hope their day would go well.

The depression of working late nights at the paper began to evaporate. Instead of assembling papers — only objects — repetitively, I was working with people. And I liked it. Busy, I said to myself. I was happy with the thought of not being shut up in the apartment alone, or with no one but Ahmad for company.

And I was happy that Ahmad might be able to put away his favorite phrase: "We have no money for that." I could be the beneficent partner, reaching into her pocket to say, "Here, here is some money that I brought into this house."

When Tracy, the manager, approached me with a possible schedule of 36 hours a week, which meant from 3 to 9 o'clock at night every weekday plus a six-hour Saturday shift, I wanted to agree immediately. But my classes at the Beauty Academy lasted until 5 in the evening. I paused for a moment, thinking that there had to be some way to make this work.

I approached my teacher at the Academy on Monday about having a more flexible schedule. Having seen lots of international students and struggling immigrants, she understood the situation. Thankfully, most of the informational lectures happened in the mornings, and I would be missing only time in the salon in the afternoons.

"If you stay until 2 in the afternoon everyday, it could work," she told me. "But the problem is that instead of finishing the program in nine months, it will probably take about 15 months for you to accumulate the training hours you need to graduate."

"I understand," I replied. "Thank you so much."

She said, "I understand how it is. Now don't work yourself to death, you hear me?"

We smiled at each other, and that was how easy it was to work out a new schooling schedule. It was not so easy to explain the situation to the other students, especially the married women who loved to compare the greatness of their husbands.

"Oh my god," said one. "You are going to be going to school and working?"

"You're crazy," replied another, shaking her head like she was looking at a misbehaving child.

"Let your husband work," they all agreed.

"We're just starting out," I tried to explain, my cheeks blushing and my entire face warm. "We are both students. And we don't have kids, so I can work. I have to work."

"Have to? Ha!" said one of the wives.

As with any job, my initial excitement with my work at the Drug Fair didn't continue. I wasn't just brimming over with anticipation to go to work everyday. In fact, it could be quite tiring. I would walk every morning in my beauty school uniform (a white smock and white shoes) from California Street to Connecticut Street to the bus stop in the freezing wind. I would work at the Beauty Academy until 2 p.m., when I would change my clothes and take the bus back towards home.

Then I would work at one of several stations in the drug store until 9 p.m. Only then would I walk home and make dinner for myself and Ahmad and then go to bed, ready to start the whole routine over again the next day.

I was a very serious cashier, unlike some of the other girls I saw who took their time and floated their way through a shift as if they couldn't care less. Customers would pile up in lines at their registers and they didn't seem to notice. When people began to line up at my station, I would hustle faster and apologize, trying to help people get out and get on about their lives. I was just the kind of person who, if I had a job to do, was going to do the job right. And I tried to make nice conversation — saying "thank you," "have a nice day" or "how are you today" to customers. After all, it made the day happier for me as well as for them if I could be pleasant.

It was inevitable that people were going to ask me questions that I couldn't understand. For instance, a person might approach me and ask, "Where is the suntan lotion?"

While I was well aware of what suntan lotion was, I didn't know the English word yet. So I would reply, "I'm sorry, but I don't know that word in English. You know what? You ask that nice man over there." I'd point at Tracy or another manager. "He will help you. Then please come back here to pay to show me what suntan lotion is. I want to learn."

The customer would come back and I could hold whatever item I didn't know the name of in my hands and say, "Suntan lotion. Yes, I understand now. Thank you so much." In this way, I learned many more useful nouns than I ever had in formal language lessons. The books usually taught you how to say, "Where is the train station? I am looking for a hat." But the drug store customers taught me more useful lessons, like how to use English when I had a headache and needed an aspirin.

When my rudimentary English became obvious, customers would often ask where I came from, usually in very nice and caring way.

"Iran," I would say.

In that time, most people would smile and say something about the land of oil and wealth, then wish me good luck and success in America.

I was bringing home about $63 a week from my job at the Drug Fair, a decent amount when you consider that our rent was about $130 a month. Just like I expected Ahmad was happy that I was now working. He didn't congratulate me or anything. In fact, he made sure that I knew working was something I was expected to do to help our American efforts. But in the manner of a generous sultan, he said I could keep 10 percent of what I earned for my own pocket money, the remainder going into "our bowl," our common fund for the family. Whatever went into "our bowl" I never saw again, except for the money I was given for groceries. My pocket money, however, was enough to buy me lunch at the Beauty Academy from the hamburger place downstairs and an occasional skirt or piece of clothing.

After a couple of months, my hard work around the Drug Fair got me noticed by management. Tracy approached me and said I had been doing so well at all the counters that I was going to be put up front as the main cashier all the time. Because of my speed, I was assigned the register closest the door — a position of honor, I thought — and I thought of the move as a sort of promotion. Tracy couldn't lavish enough praise on me and told me that I was working out better than he ever expected. My English — not the text book, grammatically perfect kind, but the necessary, everyday language — was improving and I was making friends among my co-workers. We even exchanged presents at Christmas time, a novel experience that I found very moving.

I liked the job well enough and I had settled into my schedule. Just in time, it turned out, for everything to change.

Tracy informed me that another branch of the drug store, on the other side of town, was in desperate need of a cashier in the pharmacy section. Although he was sad to see me go, Tracy begged me to accept the job as a favor to him and to help the stores in general. So, I agreed. And instantly my bus commute to my job in the afternoon went from 10 minutes to 45 minutes — at night. I'd often have to wait for 20 minutes in the freezing cold at the bus stop, and would run to the hot shop across the street for a cup of chicken noodle soup for my dinner on my way home. I'd open the door to my husband on the couch, his face lit by the glow of the television. Or sometimes the apartment would be entirely dark, and I'd have to creep around silently to join Ahmad in bed.

I began to resent Ahmad.

Yes, he went to the language school most of the day. He left in the morning about the same time as me and arrived back home at 5 or 6 in the afternoon. Of course, not all of the time he was gone was spent in a classroom. He also hung around town with some of the other students he'd become friends with.

Especially close to him was a young bachelor named Hossin. I have no idea what Ahmad and Hossin did most of the time. Ahmad said they did their language homework together or went for walks around the city. I only know what I saw with my own two eyes, which was usually two olive-skinned men sitting on the couch in the glow of the television with sodas or beers open on the table when I came through the door from a long day at school and work. They would turn their heads towards me, my coat not yet off my back and hung in the closet, and Ahmad would ask me where dinner was. It was usually almost 10 p.m.

Instead of getting angry, which I didn't think I had the right to do, I decided to accommodate my husband and his friend the best I could. I would call Ahmad from the Drug Fair while I was counting the money in my drawer at 9.

"Do we have company tonight?" I asked.

"Yeah." Ahmad was usually curt, as if he had much more important things to be doing than talking to me.

"Well will you do me a favor?" I asked. The line was silent, so I just continued talking. "We have some ground beef in the freezer. Would you please take it out right now and put it in the sink so it will be ready to cook when I come home?"

"Okay," he said gruffly.

I'd put on my fluffy hat and wait for the bus, my hands deep in my pockets. I'd ride the bus home and open the door, only to find the men in their usual positions and no meat thawing in the sink.

"Ahmad, where is the meat?" Because there was no microwave, it was vital that anything frozen was taken out to defrost hours in advance of cooking—something I often begged Ahmad to do.

"Wherever you put it, wife," he said, not turning his eyes toward me.

I'd sigh and start a pot of rice. While it cooked, I held the rock-hard beef under the hot water of the kitchen tap. At first, it warmed my cold hands and relaxed them after a long day. By the time the meat was soft, my skin was usually red and cracked, the water stinging the rough, dry skin.

I threw together a salad, heaped the rice on a plate and spooned the meat on another, sprinkling it liberally with kebab spice. Even in America, we didn't just serve to individual plates. We wouldn't have thought of not serving ourselves from platters, even though it meant more dishes. It was only once those dishes were done that I crawled into bed, trying to think about what kind of customer would walk through the doors of the Beauty Academy salon the next day, what hair cut I would get to experiment with.

Somewhere along the line, Ahmad began to resent me, too.

I only saw this during one excruciatingly long and heartbreaking day. It was a Saturday and I woke up in the night with intense cramping in my torso and in my back. I felt as if my whole middle was in revolt from the rest of my body, angry with my arms, legs and head over something.

But I didn't panic. I knew exactly what pain was working it's way through my body. It was the same malady that afflicted me since I was a teenager. Some months before my period, it was as if my body seized up with the effort of being a woman and made me miserable for one day. I tried to calm myself and go back to sleep, but my back was especially painful. I repositioned myself in bed so my back was against Ahmad, using his warmth like a heating pad. Even so, I would find myself shaking with chills, my jaws chattering.

In the morning, my condition hadn't improved in the slightest. I could barely drag myself out of sleep. I felt Ahmad's hand on my shoulder.

"Maryam, wake up," he said. "You will be late for work."

I couldn't drag myself through the fog of sleep to answer him.

Five minutes later, he shook my shoulder again. "It's 7 o'clock. You have to get up."

With a sigh of pain, I rolled over and told him what was going on with my body, how bad I felt. "I'm sick," I said.

"You have to go to work, Maryam," he repeated.

"I'm sick. Could you please call the store for me and tell them that I won't be in today? I couldn't drag myself there if I tried."

He was silent for a moment and I could feel his weight next to me on the bed. Then he abruptly shifted away and slammed the door to the bedroom. After about 30 minutes of trying to get upright, I stumbled out to the bathroom for an aspirin, the only medicine I was accustomed to taking at that time. Then I returned to bed and slept again.

At mid morning, I crept out to the living room and snuggled into the corner of the couch, where I positioned the pillows just so to try to be comfortable. Moving only occasionally to make a cup of tea or take more aspirin, I just bore the pain as best I could to make it through the day, knowing that the pain had always gone away after about 24 hours.

For four or five hours, Ahmad made a point of not looking in my direction or speaking a word to me. If I spoke to him, he pretended he couldn't hear my words.

Usually he didn't do anything at all on Saturdays. At least, not much more than what I saw him doing: watching TV. So I had no idea what his problem was, if I in his way or what. I could tell something was wrong with him, but didn't know what it was. Finally, he turned to me sometime during the afternoon.

"If you had gone to work today," he said, "you would have earned about $10, after all the taxes are taken out and stuff."

I see, I thought to myself. He had been calculating his malice in that head of his, adding up how much I had cost him with my sickness and pain.

"We lost $10," he said, still not looking at me. Instead he turned only his cheek toward me, a cheek on which he had begun growing large, mutton chop-shaped sideburns.

I hated those scratchy, messy sideburns. But it wasn't hate that I felt toward him for his lack of sympathy, for his pettiness. Instead, I felt as if the pain moved from my stomach to my heart, as if my husband had just stabbed me through the heart. Not saying a word, not making a cup of tea or fetching me aspirin. Not even thinking, with a recent miscarriage in my past, that I might be in severe pain. Worrying only about the wages I lost when my body decided to betray me because I pushed it so hard day after day.

It was this moment on the couch, my abdomen racked with cramps, that I wondered if I had built a life of slavery for myself. I had craved a life of freedom, of modernity. But I hadn't realized that I was going to be forced to give up my femininity, to give up feeling good about myself and to devote myself hand and foot to the man who had offered me the freedom to leave Iran.

I went back into the bedroom and I cried into the pillow. Until dinner time, that is, when Ahmad wanted me to whip something up in the kitchen to feed him.

Chapter Fourteen

"So your father must be in oil then, right Maryam?" The handsome news anchor in his corduroy jacket was a regular visitor to the drug store where I worked, along with many of the other employees of the ABC television station above the drug store. I and my fellow employees were used to their faces and the ABC badges that hung around their necks or were clipped to their jackets. They bought candy bars and sodas and often sat at the lunch counter for a quick meal before appearing again on television screens throughout the city.

And they love to joke. Once it was known that I came from Iran, the jokes were always about oil, which was the extent of what most Americans knew about my home country.

"Oh yes," I replied. "We have a big oil well in the backyard between the trees and flowers, and we used to play around it as kids."

He laughed and returned my smile.

"So are you going to come up to the studios and take that tour I've been promising you?" he asked. "I know how much you want to go back stage."

"Soon," I replied, hoping that my words were true. "My husband has a very busy schedule, and he has not yet been able to make time." I was more traditionally minded than I would have expected in some regards, and this was one of them. Accepting a social engagement without Ahmad in attendance seemed impossible to me. I didn't even question it. I just sighed and promised myself to approach him again that evening about taking the tour with me, probably the tenth time I'd brought it up with him.

Then again, I envisioned my husband with his shaggy sideburns and expression of distaste for the world standing next to this nice man with the white smile and the pressed suit, and I shuddered a bit. For a man who had seemed to want to go to America as much as I did, Ahmad definitely had no goals of living the clean, glamorous life.

While I would have appreciated him agreeing to the ABC tour just because he knew how much it meant to me, I couldn't fault his busyness too much. After all, Ahmad had gotten a job. Through the suggestion of another Persian acquaintance, my husband was working as a waiter in a nightclub in downtown D.C. called Montage. His language classes were coming to their end — he was almost ready to take the TOEFL test he needed to pass to start attending college in the United States. So now, he would study a little during the day, head off the club and work until the wee hours of the morning, and then come home and sleep until noon the next day.

I rarely saw him.

My schedule hadn't changed. I went to beauty school in the morning, where I was beginning to make some money in tips working on the hair of the older women who came into the training salon. Then I went to work at the Drug Fair and made my 40-minute bus commute back to the apartment, making it home after 9 o'clock, only to fall into bed and complete the cycle again. I was pretty honest about handing all my money over to Ahmad at the end of each week, when he would give me 10 percent for my pocket money. But I started saving a dollar or a few dollars of my tips each day for my own savings, which I kept in an Estee Lauder make-up box I'd gotten free thanks to a marketing promotion in cosmetics at a department store.

It took months before I was able to take the promised tour. Ahmad picked me up with the car after my shift ended at 9, and we were led around the studio. I found it fascinating to see the huge cameras, which somehow beamed the scene onto every television screen in the city, and the hustle and bustle of the place thrilled me. Everyone from the boy who fetched coffee to the make-up girls to the camera men wearing big headphones seemed to be busy and happy, wearing stylish clothes, living happy and glamorous lives in the ABC universe. Ahmad seemed bored and yawned often while our guide was leading us around. I smiled all the wider to offset his rudeness and I poked him a few times with my elbow. He just gave me a look that said, "I'm here. What else do you expect from me?"

Yes, my husband seemed to be happy with only the simple things in life: food at home, television and talking with other men. Anything more was wasteful and unnecessary. He did just enough to get by and not a drop more, and I was beginning to classify that attitude as lazy.

Only once can I remember going out with my husband at night. He invited me to see the club where he worked, along with the wife of the other Iranian waiter who'd gotten him the job. The up-beat dance music of the 70s blared out of the speakers and middle-class office workers sat around at tables, mingling after work. I was allowed to order a soda — "The food and drinks are way too expensive," Ahmad had said — and look at the Americans living the kind of life I thought I would have in America.

The feeling of window shopping on the good life continued when, after Ahmad's shift was over, we walked by the fashionable restaurants of downtown. I looked at the people's evening clothes and smelled the delicious odors of food. Ahmad looked at the prices on the menu and explained that standing on the sidewalk looking at the diners through the plate glass window was as close as we were ever going to get to dining inside.

"We have no money for that," he said, and we went home to instant rice and ground beef.

Perhaps because he refused to eat the club's expensive food while he was at work and partially due to a history of stomach problems, Ahmad developed a serious case of ulcers. They were bleeding ulcers that sent us to the hospital on occasion, where I would lurk in the hallway, cringing at the noise of my husband whining to the doctors, nurses and anyone else in earshot about how much pain he head.

"It's just ulcers," the doctor surmised. "Just take it easy."

After that, Ahmad took the doctor's advice very, very literally. He didn't study. He didn't work. He just stayed around the apartment all day with a group of friends: Kaveh, the youngest brother of some friends in Tabriz who was in America as part of an educational exchange with the navy; a young American girl named Patricia, who was about 25 and started dating Kaveh; Patricia's other friend Carlos, who lived with her; and the young wife of an Iranian couple who'd recently moved in upstairs.

It was summer, and they spent hours a day around the apartment complex's swimming pool. One of Ahmad's favorite things was to sunbathe, and he became very tan — and very fat, his belly bulging out above his swimming trunks on his otherwise lanky frame. Still thinking he was a skinny teenager, he even continued his habit of drinking half-and-half instead of milk, something he'd gotten used to when he was trying to gain weight. He never seemed to look down, see his stomach hanging over his bathing suit, and realize that perhaps it wasn't necessary any longer.

I would call the apartment during the day on breaks at school and work — usually to find out if he expected me to make dinner for him or all of his friends — and Ahmad never answered the phone. Later, the meat would be rock-hard frozen, he'd expected me to feed three people and he'd say he didn't answer the phone because they were all hanging out at Patricia's apartment. Then they would laugh at inside jokes as I prepared food for the table.

And then I became pregnant again.

I was a young girl, a girl who'd had little training in how pregnancy occurs and what exactly goes on in the body. Such are not the things that good girls from good families are told about, or are told about in only the broadest possible terms. I knew that babies were created during the time at night when I turned my back to my husband and closed my eyes, of course. And I knew that there was no way to get around going through that whenever he wanted to or from eventually having kids. Both things were wifely duties. And I had always wanted to be a mother, ever since I had played with my younger brothers growing up. My heart swelled at the sight of their pudgy fingers and clumsy smiles, the way they gave you exuberant hugs. I'd loved watching them grow and change, and it was a joy to go out of my way to put nice things into their lives.

But still, I hadn't really expected or planned for how and when pregnancy would happen, and I didn't know what to do. After confiding in an Iranian friend in the building, she laid out the first step: I would go see a Farsi-speaking gynecologist she knew of.

I told Ahmad the morning of the appointment.

"What?" he asked, his voice sliding up in tone with shock and anger.

"I'm probably pregnant," I told my husband, who was sitting on the couch with one hand on his big, round and tan belly.

"Now? Now you're pregnant?!"

"I don't know. I think so. Let's go to the doctor and see what he says."

He stood up and started pacing around the room, his face growing red with anger. If I could have seen in his head at the moment, I was sure I would have seen dollar signs — money cost and money lost — and swimming pools, where he wouldn't be free to dally so much any more.

With his red face and a bad attitude, he dressed and prepared himself to drive me to the doctor. Down the stairs, into the car and down the road, he said not a word to me, but fumed in the driver's seat, his knuckles clenched white on the steering wheel. Only once did he speak, and only to deliver some of the most painful words of my life.

We drove down a road with a view of the Potomac River, and he pointed his finger in the direction of the grey, sluggish water.

"If you are pregnant," he said, "I am going to throw the baby into the Potomac."

There was a silent pause.

"If you keep this baby," he repeated, "it's going in the Potomac."

I stared straight ahead like a statue, the words seeping though my skin and freezing my bones. I was too shocked and scared for my eyes to well up with tears. I just looked through the windshield and clenched my hands until we arrived at the doctor's office.

Ahmad waited in the car.

The doctor came back through the door and closed it behind him, then sat on a stool next to the table where I was perched in a crinkly, paper gown. I held the gown tightly and squeezed my knees together, trying to keep my modesty and my self-control after the reaction Ahmad had in the car.

"Well," the doctor began, speaking in Farsi, "it's positive. You're about four or five weeks pregnant."

He smiled at me. After a split-second pause, I threw my hands towards my face and I erupted into tears.

"Why?" he asked. "Why are you crying?"

I sniffed and blurted out through my tears, "My husband says if I have this baby, he's going to throw it in the Potomac River."

My first reaction was to be embarrassed at the outburst, but then I reconsidered. Oh well, I thought to myself. I have no one else to talk to, at least no one who wouldn't gossip around the whole Iranian community, so I might as well explain myself to my gynecologist.

His jaw set and he clenched his teeth together. He reached out his hand and placed it on my shoulder.

"First of all, you have this baby," he said. "You hear me? You have this baby, and we'll see if he can do anything about it."

I sniffed again and wiped a few of my tears from my cheeks. The doctor caught my eyes with his and smiled, as if to say everything would be alright.

"Men often say things that they don't mean, you know," he continued. "Most likely he is just bluffing. Is your husband a poker player?"

I shook my head to say no, not realizing he was trying to make me smile.

"Now, let's make a plan of what you are going to do," he said. We went over my history, including my recent miscarriage, and how I was supposed to take care of myself now that I knew I was pregnant again.

"What do you do for work? Is your job standing up?"

"Yes."

"Well, you will have to go home and call your work. Quit your job and put your feet up," he said, writing a few notes in the folder on his lap. "We don't want you to lose this baby like you did last time. We have to really watch you until about the fourth month, when we can probably take a deep breath and let you be more active."

By then, I had taken a few breaths and calmed down. I nodded my head along with all his advice.

"And Maryam," he inserted, just before leaving the room. "You are going to have a little son or daughter, and you are going to be an excellent mother. Just let your husband try to stop you, right?"

I offered him a feeble smile and nodded. He'd just spoken the words that were in my heart.

Strangely enough, it was the happiest day of my life, even after I related the news to Ahmad in the car and he ignored me all the way home, grinding his teeth and squeezing the wheel as if he wanted to strangle it.

Halfway home, I finally summoned up the courage to speak.

"You broke my heart saying you are going to drown this baby," I said. My voice may have been soft, but it was firm, without any trace of the tears I had cried in the doctor's office. "You are not to ever speak about harming our child again. I am its mother and I will defend it from that kind of talk."

It was silent.

"You hear me?" I asked.

He nodded, never moving his flashing-mad eyes from the road.

"And number two," I continued, "I'm told I won't be able to work anymore."

Ahmad's head whipped around toward me, his jaw slightly agape. His chin jutted out in my direction. I could see the dollar signs running around in his head — lost salaries, the cost of diapers, little dollar signs with little feet went pitter patter in his head. Then he met my eyes again and I held his gaze, one hand unconsciously over my stomach.

He closed his mouth and took a deep breath through his nose, puffing it out through his mouth, and he drove on.

One thing I had learned from women in my family and back home in Iran was that a woman's ability to bear children was an important thing. My father, even, had thought of throwing my mother over because it looked like she couldn't produce any sons. A woman's child-bearing ability was also fragile. It was common knowledge that a woman who'd miscarried once was common, but that a woman who miscarried twice might be unable to ever keep a child in her womb. It was as if, having broken twice, my womb would be irreparably broken, and the thought scared me.

If I was not careful with this pregnancy and did everything the doctor said, rumors I had heard informed me that I would never be able to have children and I wanted kids so badly. Children had always seemed like an inevitability, if a distant one. Now, the idea of my future children sat in my lap like an unopened Christmas present.

I was excited and frightened, so frightened that I immediately sat down on the couch and put my feet up. I didn't know if the doctor was just using a phrase for taking it easy when he said to "put your feet up," or whether it was literal, so I figured I'd rather be safe than sorry.

Then I called my boss over at the Drug Fair to tell him what the situation was. My voice quavered a bit as I explained and repeated several times how sorry I was for letting him down, for letting down my co-workers.

"Don't worry, Maryam," he said. "Somehow we'll manage." He sighed. "You take care of yourself and you keep in touch with us. I'll arrange for your check to be sent out later."

"Thank you so much," I told him and let out a breath I didn't realize I'd been holding.

After the fateful trip to the doctor, our lives again shifted slightly. Ahmad went back to work in the nightclub — fatter and grumpier than when he'd left, of course — and he passed his language test. He picked up a few classes at Howard University, where he took just enough courses to be a student but not enough that he would have to work too hard. I did my best to stay busy around our little apartment, with its few pieces of furniture and black and white television. I showered, I cooked a little and I had a few Persian ladies I knew visit from time to time, but other than that, I felt like I only left the couch to use the bathroom.

I started to feel the oppression of being pregnant in a new country.

Back in Iran, a pregnancy was an exciting event, something that both men and women fawned over and celebrated. The house is full of visitors from the time you announced the news to the time of the birth — even at the birth in the case of me and my siblings, who were born with a crowd of family and friends hanging around the house, waiting to party when they heard the baby's first cry. The expectant mother was treated like royalty. If she has a craving, whatever food she wanted would miraculously appear in front of her. The mother herself is babied and pampered.

I, on the other hand, was alone every day until Ahmad came home. I kept in touch with my family back in Iran as much as I always had since moving to Washington D.C. We wrote letters back and forth, of course. Because long-distance calls were so expensive — the rate for a 10-minute call was about $20, a huge amount — Ahmad only allowed me to call my mother once a month and for 10 minutes at a time. My mother and grandmother also called me once a month each, meaning that I got to speak to them about once every 10 days or so.

The few times I got to talk to my friends, it was usually over the holidays. A New Year's party raged loudly in the background as they spoke of their new lives with new husbands. Most of them had houses and furniture, outfitted with the money from their weddings. My wedding money had been spent on language school, pots from Goodwill, an older car for my husband I rarely rode in and who knows what else. I never saw the funds and despaired of knowing what our financial situation was.

Long-distance phone calls sometimes have a way of making your feel more lonely when you're done talking, not less.

"How is everything, my daughter?" my mother asked over the crackling phone line. "How is the American life?"

"Good, mother," I said. "America is a great place." It was the truth, of course, but also halfway a lie, too.

"How is the little life in your tummy? Is your tummy growing?"

"I'm a little sick but it's feeling very good. I'm trying to do everything the doctor says." I felt as if I was telling her a story, a version of my life that was dramatized to keep her happy. Of course, that was the way of phone calls. All the news I received from her was the happy side of life — the good things that my brothers were doing, who was getting married, who was making money.

"So how is your degree going?"

"I can't go to the Beauty Academy because of the doctor's orders, Mom. You know that."

She clicked her tongue at me. "I still don't know about this beauty degree. This is no sort of degree I've heard of. You should go to a real university. You father gave you all that money, you know, and you should be making use of it."

Of course, leave it to my mother to bring up money and use it as a bargaining chip to make me do things her way.

"Do you need more money?" she asked.

"No, no," I assured her. "We are doing fine. We are students and we are not living richly, but we are doing very well. Please don't send money."

I knew my father would send cash at the drop of a hat. I also knew that my mother would hold the gift against me, as if it gave her even more say about how I lived my life because they were supporting it. I also didn't want Ahmad to get used to cash infusions from my family. If that happened, perhaps I couldn't pry his bathing suited body off the couch ever, and he would only get fatter, lazier and tanner until I was married to an unemployed, black blob. No thank you.

"Well, as always, we are excited for you and worried about you. Your father goes around telling people you are studying beauty, and he comes home to tell me about every lady in every neighborhood who makes good businesses that way." She sighed. Obviously, they disagreed about my chosen schooling, and I pitied the nagging my mother probably subjected my father to every time the subject came up. Some things never change.

Even though I'd wanted to escape that same-old, stifling family environment for most of my life, I got really homesick thinking of my generous and bragging father, my concerned and manipulative mother, and all of my siblings. Maybe I was emotional because I was pregnant, or maybe it was the two years of separation. But I suddenly desperately wanted to go home.

I was nearing my fourth month of pregnancy; the time my doctor had said I could resume more of my normal life and stop fearing for the baby's safety. And I just happened to hear about a brilliant deal from one of the girls I went to beauty school with: Iranians with student visas could apply for a special fare from Washington D.C. through New York and to Tehran for $250 per person. Yes, $250 was a great deal of money, but when normal airline tickets usually cost twice that amount, I knew that it was sign. It was time for Ahmad and me to visit our home country for the first time.

That night over spaghetti with the television on the background, I brought up the subject with Ahmad.

"I'm pregnant, Ahmad, and it really makes me long to see my family and friends in Iran again," I said. "I'm homesick, and I really want to see my mother."

He flicked his eyes up at me and said nothing.

"Please send me to Iran," I pleaded. "I've found out about a great deal to fly us there."

After I explained the cheap airfare to him, he chewed the thought over for a minute before responding with his typical response. "That would be great, of course," he said. "But we don't have any money for that."

"You would want to go, too, if we had the money?" I asked.

"Sure," he replied, shrugging his shoulders.

"Okay."

I stood up from the table and I went into the bathroom, where I grabbed the little Estee Lauder box where I saved the money I skimmed off my tips. I had also been adding my unused pocket money — whatever I could save of the 10 percent Ahmad allowed me, 10 percent being about $6.30 a week. It had been a year and a half since I began the fund, and the thickness and weight of the make-up bag made me feel hopeful and smart.

I returned to the kitchen and I placed the bag in front of him.

"You may not have $500," I said. "But I do."

He opened the bag and his eyes became wide and white. He was truly shocked and the angle of his shoulder told me his was also slightly disappointed.

"I'll call and make the reservations for the flight tomorrow," I said. I picked up my fork and continued eating. If he had said he would go if the money was there before he knew about my funds, I knew I had effectively made it impossible for him to now refuse. My heart and the baby inside me were happy. On rare occasions like these, I discovered a feeling of self-worth inside of myself that had been hidden for years. I felt the power shift slightly if subtlety, and I thought that maybe this wife thing just took a bit of practice.

I think we came back to Iran with more in our suitcases than the small amount we left with. We were now visitors back from abroad, and as such, we were expected to bring gifts for pretty much everyone we knew: mothers, fathers, siblings, cousins, aunts, friends and neighbors. In anticipation of such a return trip, I had been picking up little American things on sale at the Drug Fair whenever I could: Revlon lipstick in fire-engine red, handkerchiefs, a pretty blouse in several sizes so it could fit anyone, candy. I especially remember picking up several dozen long-stem plastic roses. By that time, there was a great desire for plastic, long-stem roses for some reason, and I knew every girl back home would love to have one. My suitcase was like Santa Claus' sack, stuffed with goodies for all the boys and girls of the world.

We boarded the plane for a six-week trip back home and I think the whole cabin shared our excitement. Word about the Iran Air special for students had spread, and the aisles were full of young Persians — men and women — who chatted up a storm about what they were studying, where they were from.

That trip was nothing like Ahmad's and my first trip across the Atlantic. The seats were small but comfortable, even for my belly, which was starting to show. I could read or talk to the other passengers, and the noise of the engine didn't drone in my ears. It was even possible to sleep the flight away, making it faster than I had ever imagined.

Due to a delay in New York, our plane was about four hours late. Instead of arriving at midnight in Tehran, we finally emerged about 4 a.m. We walked down the stairs from the airplane to the pavement and I took a deep breath of Iranian air.

The sweet air had hardly entered my lungs when I was beset upon by a huge surprise. Screaming voices and waving hands caught my attention. My hand rose to my heart as I saw a group of family and friends gathered on the tarmac, waiting for Ahmad and me as if we were royalty gracing our hometown with our presence. My aunt, my mother's sister I had stayed with in Tehran during the pageant, was there with her husband. The General and his wife waved from beside them. And when the crowd parted slightly, I made out a familiar figure. He was tall and neatly dressed in an impeccable, American-style suit. His hair was shining and his cheeks clean-shaved, and his white smile lit up the night like the sun. I couldn't believe my eyes. It was Arian, standing and waiting for me. For me! He smiled at me, and next to him, his sister that I still exchanged letters with waved enthusiastically.

Shouted words of Farsi were traded back and forth. I would never have imagined how sweet everyone speaking my native language would feel after so long away. How strange for the ordinary to be extraordinary in a different context, a context of homesickness and joy.

There were hugs and kisses and noise everywhere, and in the hubbub, I snuck another look at Arian. I smiled back. How long had it been since I had seen him? I had probably been 16 years old last time I got even the quickest of looks, and much longer than that since we had been alone together. It had been at least two years since his sister had told me anything about what he had been doing. His sister! Of course, that's how he knew to be here. She would have known all about our upcoming visit.

My heart was beating in my chest like a little boy on a drum and I couldn't hold myself back any longer. I nudged through the crowd to Arian and I threw my arms around his neck. His arms closed in a hug around my back. My feet left the ground and I found my lips pressing against his cheek. It was a chaste, friendly kiss, but my lips burned with the skin-on-skin contact. His face was smooth and warm and with a delicious odor that was part sweet, part spicy.

Though my heart caught in my throat and the moment stretched out in my mind, it was only a moment or two before the embrace was broken and I was back among the crowd. I looked around to see if anyone else had noticed that the world had stopped momentarily, but the crowd seemed to be just as happy and disorganized as it had been seconds before. Only me had felt the welling of emotion. No one had seen the deeper meaning in my embrace of Arian, which was a visceral response I couldn't have stopped if I'd tried.

And it was only friendly — directly after, I hugged and kissed his sister with equal emotion and feeling.

And then I turned to see my husband, Ahmad. His shirt bunched and pulled awkwardly around his little belly, which had become thinner but was still obvious. And his cheeks were puffed out with pride at all the attention being poured upon him with his coarse and puffy mutton chop sideburns. I sighed, one hand unconsciously on my swelling stomach, and thought about my lips on the smooth skin of the man I hadn't thought about for years. But then again, he had never left my mind.

The sun began to rise over the city as the whole welcoming party made their way to the General's house. Though everyone in the party had offered to host the group — "Maryam should be with her family first," said my aunt, while Arian said his home was always open to us, too — the General's wife had the winning invitation through pure stubbornness. I was pretty sure the reason for her insistence was that she knew our suitcases were loaded down with gifts and she wanted to take the first crack at the American gifts.

Morning light poured through the window as we gathered for a traditional Iranian breakfast. Never had the familiar tea tasted so sweet on my tongue and never has Feta tasted more pungent. The familiar smells and tastes and the musical Farsi language made me feel as if I was a child again, safe in the arms of my mother culture. I relaxed fully for the first time in what felt like years as the conversation went back and forth over the table.

At first, Arian related how his business was progressing. He'd become rather famous in business circles in recent years, buying up factories all over the country and abroad and revolutionizing their productivity. Though he was making every attempt to be humble, it was obvious that he was one of the richest and most powerful men in Tehran, where he now made his home. Despite his success, however, he seemed to be the same as a man as he was as a boy. I never felt intimidated or uncomfortable. It was as if he fell right back into our old understanding, as if we could read one another's thoughts written on our faces.

Ahmad, on the other hand, was grating on my nerves in all the ways my old friend Arian was soothing. Economics was the area of his college degree and the subject of his current studies, so he tried to insert his own wisdom about business into the conversation whenever possible. And he threw English words and American slang into his language whenever possible — words like "OK" or "no problem" entered his vocabulary as he distastefully showed off. He even took it a step further: He'd begin a sentence in English as if he hadn't meant to, as if it was just second nature to him now. Then he would make a big show of having to think of the Farsi equivalent.

Oh yes, he thought himself a big shot American now. It was strange to me how this little man could puff himself up with hot air, but the man who had accomplished so much on the other side of the table was relaxed, comfortable and friendly.

After a few hours, the party broke up to return to their own homes — and their beds, I hoped, because I knew they stayed up most the night waiting for us. But the party never really stopped the entire six weeks we were in Iran. We stayed a few days with the General, some time with my aunt and uncle, and some time back in Tabriz with our families, too. There was always people coming with good wishes and leaving with plastic roses, which were just as popular as I hoped they would be. I was stuffed with food and love, pampered like a pregnant princess and my homesickness soon vanished with my morning sickness. My sisters and friends all touched my stomach reverently, as if giving me all their blessings and hoping to take some blessing from me for themselves in the future.

Even Ahmad began to warm to my growing stomach once he saw the fuss that everyone made over the new baby. It was as if he finally saw that my having a child raised everyone's opinion of him, too. He was a real man now, and he walked around nodding his head, as if to say, "Yeah everyone, I got her pregnant. That was all my doing."

The best part of our trip was with Ahmad's family. My father-in-law was still the doting, affectionate man I'd come to like so much while we lived with him after our wedding. (His mother hadn't changed either, of course, and I knew she rifled through my suitcases whenever I left the house.) The intervening years had been very good to Ahmad's father. The government office he managed had prospered, along with his bank account. In fact, he now had a vacation home on the Caspian Sea, which was about a 4 or 5 hour drive from Tehran and the favored destination of the well-to-do throughout the country. Throughout the summer, everybody who was anybody spent long weekends near the Caspian, throwing parties and getting tan.

Then near the end of our trip, I was offered another gift. Arian offered to throw a going away party for Ahmad and I, knowing that we probably wouldn't be back again for quite some time. It was typical of the generosity of Iranian men — generosity was the measure of a man's character, after all — but I was deeply touched at how he'd welcomed me back into his life after so long.

And the scale of the party was also typical, because throwing around your money in public was a sure way of letting everyone know how important and rich you were.

So, in that grandiose and expensive fashion, Arian hosted the party at the best restaurant in town: The Chattanooga. Downstairs was an elegant dining area with plate glass windows overlooking one of Tehran's prettiest streets. Thick fabric tablecloths and shining glassware covered the tables, and the waiters treated every diner like royalty. And upstairs was more a gentleman's night club, where scantily clothed woman danced around and served cocktails.

Upstairs or down, the men and women were dressed impeccably in expensive American and European designer labels. The women's faces were uncovered and done up with make-up, and nothing was thought of them indulging in one — or at maximum two — alcoholic drinks over the course of the evening. It was a scene that would be impossible to witness in present-day Iran or even a few years into the future. But none of us knew that, of course. So we danced and sipped wine and ate fabulous food, all paid for with Arian's oversized wallet and oversized heart. There were about 60 or 70 people at the party, celebrating our new life in America and the new life in my tummy and regretting that we had to leave so quickly.

I wondered if they really knew what it was we were going back to: a one-bedroom apartment with hand-me-down furniture, an exhausting schedule of school and work. Though most people knew I was going to beauty school, none of them knew that I got my hands dirty taking other people's money in a common drug store. That sort of thing just wasn't done in Iran, and I knew they wouldn't understand. With all the gifts and goodwill we returned with, how were they to know that my normal life consisted of Ahmad's constant badgering about money and taking the bus across a cold, gray and often dirty city.

In some ways, the familiar generosity of money and spirit Arian showed me made me even sadder to return to America with my husband, who was the opposite of generous emotionally and financially.

But then I cupped my hand around my growing stomach and my heart soared.

Soon I was going to be a mother, the mother of a little American boy or girl, and I was so excited. And now that I'd been back to Iran and my family, I felt as if my batteries had been recharged. I was reminded that I hadn't lost these important people in my life — they were still right there waiting for me, if at a distance. I had the feeling that getting back on the plane to America was another milestone in my life, just as much as leaving the first time was. I was entering into a new era — the era of motherhood — and I couldn't wait for it to start.

Chapter Fifteen

My pregnancy continued to progress well, and my doctor assured me that I shouldn't have to worry about miscarrying any longer. Though I still couldn't work and my beauty schooling was on hold, I found myself happily puttering around the house, indulging in what they call the "nesting" instinct before the baby arrived. I purchased a brown crib and dresser set at a yard sale and set about painting it a crisp new white for the baby. I sewed a new fabric cover for the couch and matching curtains. And I studied the television to improve my English.

Unlike before our trip to Iran, I didn't feel so alone in the world any more. I was comforted with the knowledge my family was out there, and I was so excited with the new part of my family growing inside my body.

As soon as we returned to the city, we were able to find a new apartment. Again, it was another Iranian — a husband and wife with one son, this time — who wanted us to take over a lease, and it couldn't have been more perfect. The apartment had three bedrooms, one of which would be a nursery, and it was located in Arlington Heights near Sherly Park, a suburb of D.C. on the other side of the Potomac, about 20 minutes from the center of downtown. By the time we moved in, I could hardly move with the weight and awkwardness of my stomach. With how easy I was supposed to take things and how hungry I was, my weight climbed from 125 to 197. Not that I minded. Always so careful with how I dressed and how I looked, those concerns suddenly went out the window with the coming of a baby. It just didn't matter as much. Only his or her health mattered.

That and the beauty of the nursery, where I carefully positioned the newly painted furniture and used an old book of carpet samples to create a multi-colored rug for the floor.

Ahmad, still attending a few classes for his master's degree, had begun driving a cab for a living. Like so many other immigrants, he fell into the job because several other Persians we knew were cabbies, and they pulled a few strings for their countryman. And Ahmad really enjoyed the work. It was flexible, he was his own boss and he got to meet new people and see new sights all over the city every day.

While he was out and about at odd hours, I felt like I had an amazing connection to the baby growing in my stomach. Every time I had a bad dream, a kick from the baby would wake me up and bring me back to reality. It was as if the baby was trying to protect me from ever being sad or frightened. And I felt sure the child was going to be a boy, because every time I tried to imagine what the baby would look like or what its personality would be, I thought of my father-in-law. I loved my father, too, but Ahmad's father had shown me that my own dad had always had his attention focused on the outside world — women, parties, fun. My father-in-law focused all his time, energy and money inwards, toward his wife and kids. Every time I thought of my new baby, I saw my father-in-law's warm smile in my head. I would be a loving parent like that, I thought. And this baby will grow up to be the right kind of man, just like my father-in-law.

I was uncomfortable sitting, uncomfortable standing and even uncomfortable in the supposed comfort of my bed at night by the time my ninth month of pregnancy was over. At first, when the baby woke me up with kick at 4 in the morning, I was frustrated because I was so tired, and had only recently gotten to sleep. But then my pain came and I woke up Ahmad excitedly.

"It's time," I said. "Hurry up now. It's time."

It was a freezing cold morning that day — January 4 — when we bundled into the Chevrolet Impala and drove to the Columbia Hospital for Women, where I had a regular doctor on-call, waiting for me. Though the pain was intense, I don't remember it being anything more than I had expected. In fact, I was calm and excited as they settled me into a hospital bed to wait for the labor to continue.

"Well, here you are," said Ahmad as he looked around the hospital room, checking out the view from the window and opening some of the drawers to see what was inside. "It looks like you're OK here. So, um..." He rocked back and forth on his feet, then said, "I have to go out and drive the cab."

"Go. Go," I said. I waved my hand as if sweeping him out of the room. Sure, he was my husband, but it was uncommon for men to hang around waiting rooms in those days. I didn't really care if he was there anyway. Sure, the baby was technically half Ahmad and half me, but I had already bonded so deeply with the unborn baby that I preferred that nothing get in the way of our first face-to-face meeting.

Besides, the environment of the hospital both interested me and soothed me. All the doctors and nurses in their stiff, starched uniforms scurrying back and forth: It seemed like they were worker bees, each with a task and each incredibly suited to their task. Nothing bad could happen to a person in this clean, bright and modern hospital, so different from my memories of dark, dingy hospitals in my home country. I really felt as if I was being taken care of, that I was safer in the hands of these polite, professional strangers than I had even been in my life.

Because I had never given birth before, it took many, many hours for the labor to progress and it was only at 4 in the afternoon that they finally took me to the delivery room.

There was an intense amount of pain and flurry of activity and voices in English telling me to push, that everything was OK and to bear down. With a rush, it was all over and I heard someone shout, "It's a boy!"

Warm tears of happiness filled my eyes, but halted at the brink of pouring over and down my cheeks. The baby made no noise. I held my breath, straining to see over my knees to get a look at what was going on. Those moments were some of the longest of my life. But then there was a noise like a small cough and my son began to cry, a loud and healthy cry of confusion and alarm at greeting the cold world for the first time.

The tears ran over and I couldn't believe how much happiness I was capable of in that moment. I held him for a brief minute while they wrapped me in an electric blanket, which felt like a warm hug from the world. Then I promptly fell asleep.

I gave my boy two names: Omid and John. The first was after a character in one of my favorite serialized stories in a magazine, about a handsome boy who had every quality I thought important in a man. And the second was for his life in America, where he would have everything all the other little boys did, including a common American name.

He was 10 pounds and 10 ounces, a huge baby by most standards. When the nurses brought him into my room after the birth, they teased me.

"Is the father tall?" one asked.

"No," I replied.

"Well your neighbor must be very tall then, huh?" She winked at me and smiled.

I giggled in embarrassment.

Later in the evening, Ahmad finally arrived back at the hospital and he fell in love with our little John immediately. There was no talk of how expensive a baby would be or throwing anyone in the Potomac River. Instead, he took one look at his son and you could see his heart melt.

From that moment on, Ahmad was head-over-heels in love with John. Sometimes in the first few months after the birth, I wondered if he had fallen *too* hard.

For instance, Ahmad had been working for the Airport Cabs, but switched to working for a national airport cab once the baby was born. This switch meant that he picked up the car each morning — or whenever he started his work day — and paid them $40 to use the car for the day. Then he would have to earn $40 throughout the day (plus gas money, so a little more) in order to just break even. But Ahmad would pick the car up in the morning, then get distracted with the baby and never go to work, meaning he cost us $40 of our own money. Or, he would go out to work but come back early in order to play with the baby. Either way, it was as if he was paying a fee in order to stay home. While I attempted to explain how illogical and counterproductive this was, it never seemed to soak into his head.

Strange, I thought, that he could do such a thing and never say a word about how much money it was costing us. When I had to stay home from work because I was sick, however, he acted as if I owed him a debt. Perhaps the experience of being a father had softened Ahmad, I thought, hoping the idea was true.

While he wasn't quite as insistent about me working as before John's birth, Ahmad did still insist that I make money somehow. So I offered to watch the children of other families in the Sherly Park area. It wasn't a formal arrangement at first, just an occasional favor to friends and acquaintances who paid me a bit of money for the babysitting. But it was enough for me, and enough for Ahmad to not bother me too much about money.

I don't think anything could have burst my bubble of happiness in those months after John's birth.

I owned a child, I thought, my heart swelling when his image was in my eyes or his little body in my arms. He was a fragile, precious boy making his precarious way in the big, unknown world. And I alone had the responsibility of preserving him, nurturing him, shielding that valuable little boy from the slightest possibility of harm.

He would be good, this one. He would do well. And I would make sure of it as his mother, as a mother in the Iranian tradition: fierce, passionate and devoted.

There was no idea in my head of spoiling him. I didn't think such a thing was possible, so I lavished all my attention on my son. I prided myself on knowing what he wanted before he even did, being prepared with bottle or diaper or a warm embrace. In that way, he rarely cried and seemed one of the most content and smiling babies on the planet. But of course, I was his mother, so I was probably a bit biased.

By that time, our apartment was nicely outfitted for a little family, with lots of Persian carpets for John to sit on and eventually walk across. We had a stereo for me to play him American or Iranian music, which usually made him laugh and clap his hands.

He was so extraordinary, and he made me feel like a different person. I was a mother now. Mother. It shook me to my core and made me look at the whole world in a different light. I had a duty and responsibility to this little person, and it was the most important job of my life.

And life continued in this pleasant, maternal fantasy until John was nine months old, in October of that year. It was on that morning — while Ahmad was at work — that my old life collided with the new, my own childhood colliding with my son's.

It was a gray day, as most of them are, but for the last nine months, my attention had been focused inward: where silky Persian carpets covered the hardwood floors and my son John permeated every room with his gurgling and the sweet smell of his baby skin, all sugary and warm. I was barefoot, but dressed in a short navy blue skirt and a matching blouse with a thin trim of white and red around the hemlines. John, too, was wearing a blue jumper with a red and white design. It was only later that I realized that I, like so many other immigrants I met who yearned to fit in, unconsciously garbed ourselves in the colors of the American flag. We'd left rich hues of saffron and bright pink and henna behind, in favor of mass-produced fabrics of red, white a blue that were made in the USA.

On a normal day, I would spend most of my hours anticipating what my son would want before he wanted it, making sure he lacked nothing. In exchange, he rarely cried and smiled brighter than the sun. And when he slept, I watched the television to improve my English, hoping to one day to speak as easily as the blond women of the local news stations.

The phone rang, and the man I had known as a child was on the other end of the line. Literally, the man of my dreams I dubbed my Dream Man.

"Maryam," he said, the voice making the small hairs of my ear stand at attention. "I'm here." He explained he was in Washington DC. In fact, he was at the national airport, which was only a few miles from where I was sitting wearing a navy skirt and no shoes. He was in the States for his factories, buying some kind of specialty equipment in North Carolina. In fact, his flight to North Carolina was in two hours, and he was just on a layover. Then, he explained, he would be back through Washington DC in a few days before jetting back to Iran.

Even though it was hard to hear his words over the beating of my heart, I understood what he was saying. He was so near… And yet, he might as well not be because he was turning around to leave again.

"But on my way back, I also stop in Washington DC, and then I will in town for a couple of days," he continued.

I drew my breath in sharply, realizing that I desperately wished this to be true.

"But of course you will stay with us?" The words came out of my mouth quickly, more as a question than the affirmative statement I wished it to be. Adrenaline rushed through my skin, my lips and my tongue as it was trying to form words.

Of course he would, I thought. It would be almost rude in our culture to not partake of a nearby friend's hospitality, especially overseas and especially because Arian had hosted us so graciously when we were recently in Iran, when I was still pregnant.

I reached down to feel my stomach, making sure it wasn't a dream that I'd lost 40 pounds in 40 days following John's birth, making me just as thin as I was before pregnancy. I was relieved to find that I still was.

He asked for our address for when he was back in town and said he would call again in a few days. And then just as suddenly as the phone had rung, it was again on the cradle. My heart was still beating so fast, the adrenaline pumping with the thought of Arian's proximity. So close to me, and my husband away at work. And then another part of me felt jilted. He'd called out of the blue and then disappointed me by making me wait to see him again.

Not five minutes later, the phone rang again.

"Hello?" I said, trying to say the word like an American.

"Yeah," said a male voice, obviously American. "I gotta passenger here and I need to know your apartment number."

"What?" I asked. The man had spoken quickly, and what I did understand seemed to make no sense.

The man repeated his request and said my address into my ear. "Is that right?" he asked. "What apartment? I've got a passenger from the airport for you."

I paused for a moment, knowing and yet not believing who was in the back of this cab headed in my direction. Then I quickly told the cab driver precise directions and said, "Oh please, how long?"

"Till we get there? About five minutes," he said.

"Thank you, sir."

I sprung up from the couch, where I had been feeding John, and I first headed for the kitchen, then the bathroom, then the bedroom, unsure of where to go and what to do first. He is coming, I thought, but repeating the thought didn't help me formulate a plan of action. I rushed John to his nursery, where I wiped his face and combed his dark hair. His smiling eyes were questioning, sensing that his mother had something on her mind. I rushed back to the main living area, where I set him in his playpen with a few toys. He sat on his chubby bottom, a skill he'd only recently perfected, and curiously watched his mom scurry around the apartment.

It was clean, it was always clean, I thought. But I tugged at the fabric slipcover I'd made for the couch to straighten it. I ran to the bathroom and looked in the mirror. He'd last seen me when pregnant, and I put my hand on my stomach, testing to see if it was still true that I'd lost 40 pounds since the birth.

And then the doorbell rang. There was not time to change or fix my face, and it was still in bare feet that I ran out of the bathroom and to the front door as fast as my uncovered toes would take me. I stopped two feet away to smooth my hair and skirt, and found myself unable to move any further. The noise of the bell had dispersed, and it was silence that seemed to stand on the other side of that tall wooden door.

A few moments later, the bell rang again. I took a step forward and my hand reached towards the knob, and then I retreated. My shoulders pressed back against the entryway's wall. I stepped forward and back again.

Though it has been only a year since I'd seen this man who was once the boy I knew so well, I had never seen him alone, without the eyes and ideas of others surrounding us, encroaching on us. How should I act? I wondered. More importantly, how WOULD I act? I was a married woman, yes, but with this man at my door, that marriage seemed as hollow and light as the falling autumn leaves.

I saw a shadow cross in front of the door's peep hole and heard the crunch of shoes only feet away from me, a few inches of wood in between.

The door bell rang a third time. I stepped away from the wall to place my fingers against the door, which was slightly cool to the touch, and I closed my eyes. In the dark of my mind, I saw the little boy of my memory. He had dark brown hair and mischievous ideas, the gentle caretaker of birds and the adventurous dreams of a pilot.

My heart in my throat, I opened the door and there he was: dark brown hair and mischievous eyes, tall and broad shouldered in a dark blue raincoat and a tailored suit. Though I had seen him only months before in Iran, it was still the little boy — and not the successful, factory-owning man — who stood before me. This was the caretaker of birds, a hide-and-seek companion. The boy who traveled around the world with me via the hanging sets backstage in the theater, the boy who made an airplane of rocks to take me to London.

It was as if no time had passed between those days and this grey American afternoon. Or, at least no consequential time. In the locking of our eyes — had we ever been so alone together? I wondered — was another world apart from our own, where there was no time, no commitments, no adulthood.

Obviously, he felt the time shift, as well. He pulled me to him, as if I was a magnet he could no longer resist the pull of. My cheek was against his warm chest, and he placed a crown of kisses on my head.

"Maryam. Maryam," he said, repeating my name again as if to make sure I was not an illusion.

The embrace felt all-consuming, and I don't how much time passed before I cam back to reality. After a few moments, which was more than I had ever hoped for from him and was enough to teach me that there would never be enough, we stepped apart, conscious of what was the appropriate distance to keep between us. It was as if emotion had flooded the room and then drained away, and we were unsure how to proceed. Something needed to be controlled, perhaps. But was it myself or him? What had just happened, and if such things were possible, what might happen next? My eyes darted up from the floor to take in his face piece by piece, memorizing one section at a time to paste together and keep forever in my mind.

Finally remembering myself, I reached forward for his hand — wide and angular, but very warm — to lead him into the house.

He allowed me to take it, but placed his other hand on my shoulder, making me pause for a moment. He opened his mouth to speak, but then paused for a second, before letting his words out in a rush.

"I came to take you home," he said.

"This is John," I said, introducing my son, the light of my life. Right on cue, John smiled and gurgled, and he waved his tiny fist in Arian's direction, getting the adults' smiles in exchange. I set my son back on his chubby bottom in his play pen, where he continued rolling around, from his bottom to his back to his stomach, where he'd attempt to press down with his chubby arms and legs. His first attempts at crawling.

"He's beautiful," he said, and I nodded in agreement.

I told my guest to sit and fetched some orange juice and snacks to spread out on the coffee table. I stammered out a few polite questions about his health and his family.

In other words, I tried to act as if nothing was amiss, as if this was simply another friendly visit in the Persian tradition. But we both knew that was far from the truth. My skin was radiating heat, my heart beat loudly in my ears and I kept reaching up to smooth my hair, as if I was afraid to suddenly find that I'd lost my head. In a way, I had.

I bustled around the room in a flurry, taking care of these pleasantries, until finally I didn't know what I was doing, where I had been going. I stood in the middle of the living room, confused as to what I was supposed to do next. I met my guest's eyes where he was sitting on the sofa, a glass of juice in front of him. He smiled, as if he understood my confusion, then he glanced to the empty cushion next to him on the couch. I was to sit, he told me with his twinkling eyes.

We sat on the couch, our legs distant but angled toward one another. He reached for my hand and encased it between both of his, which were wide and angular yet warm.

"You are probably wondering what I am doing here," he said, pausing a moment to squeeze my hand a bit tighter.

He cleared his throat. "I came to get you," he continued.

I opened my mouth, trying to say something in return, but I found that my mouth and my head were empty of words. I paused, tried again to speak and failed.

Arian took this as a sign that he could continue talking, telling his side of the story, and the flood of emotion that poured from his lips did little to calm my beating heart. He spoke of our childhood together, how he never really forgot the easy friendship we shared. He related how he felt when he was told that I had gotten married, and to a man that was taking me almost immediately across the ocean. Shocked, he said, and somewhat regretful, as if he'd forgotten something important and would now forever regret his inaction.

He told me that he was married.

How had I not known that? I asked myself. I was home in Iran only months before and he had already been a married man, and yet no one had hinted, not one word was said on the subject.

He must have seen my confusion, because he explained that the wedding wasn't exactly the most important or memorable event of his life. A girl he had been seeing became pregnant, and he had to marry her. That was that.

"She *got* herself pregnant," he said. That was his way of describing it, and he had a point. He'd found out that she was a rather manipulative woman — as if that didn't describe so many Persian women I knew. He was a young, handsome playboy, and she'd pretended to be a part of his fun lifestyle. But it was only a ruse to trap him in that most traditional institution of marriage and land herself one of the most eligible, rich men in the country.

All these confessions, all of these memories, all of these emotions rolled out into my normally quiet living room. Having only said a few words while Arian spoke, I felt as if I was being buffeted by a storm of emotion. It was pooling up at feet and threatening to drown me. His held hand felt so perfect inside my own, the only thing holding me above water. I didn't quite know what to do or say, how to swim through this flood.

Who do I need to control? I asked myself. Him, or me?

"I don't know when it was that we lost so much time," he said. "Some where between then and now, we … But now, I feel as if I am back."

I nodded, my eyes heavy with tears.

"And now I have come for you."

I nodded again. Then I paused and I shook my head, finally clearing it of a few cobwebs.

"Come for me?" I asked. "What do you mean you've come for me?" My eyebrows knit together and I looked across the room at John. The baby smiled at me and chuckled, and the mother's heart inside my chest swelled like a mother tiger's.

"I can't go anywhere," I said, a little bit of my brain being heard over the beating of my heart. Not that I didn't want to drop everything at that moment, walk out of the apartment and lock the door behind me, finally fulfilling the fantasy of running off to London and into a happy, rosy future.

An old Persian poem — one of the classics I'd studied so well back in high school — came back to me. It told the tale of a famous prince. This prince was a brave knight, a hero, who was struck down by disease. They frantically try to save him, but he dies. Only later, after the last breath had turned cold on the prince's lips, does a doctor arrive with the very medicine that could have saved the hero.

"You are the medication coming after the prince is dead," I said to Arian, my Dream Man, using a well-known phrase that referred to the famous poem. "I am a mother," I continued. After a pause, I said, "And I am a wife."

I looked down to see my knees were shaking, and I still held onto his hand as if it was the only thing to stabilize me. The holding of hands, I thought, was something so simple, something so chaste and nothing to be ashamed of. But with this man, in this circumstance, it was one of the most intimate and touching moments of my life.

But the prince is dead, I told myself. There is nothing to be done. The prince is dead.

Arian reached out his hand and stroked my cheek. "I know, Maryam. I know darling," he said. "I know you can't come now. I know it's not as simple as all that."

John gurgled happily in the corner to remind us both that he was still there, serving as chaperone. We both smiled at him, delighted with his beauty.

"I have my connecting flight to North Carolina in one hour. I will have to be going," he continued. "And on my way back, I will have several days in here in Washington DC to spend with you — " He paused, and corrected himself. "With your family here."

"You are most welcome in my home."

"But I just wanted to tell you that I still remember our airplane. Do you remember that?"

Tears poured over my cheeks as he brought up one of my most cherished memories, one I brought out often to soothe or inspire myself. That he, too, thought of that day in the park with its summer heat, fragrant blossoms and youthful promises touched me deeply.

"I still feel the same way, wanting to fly you away," he continued. To stop my tears, he linked his thumbs together and moved his hands like the flying of a bird, like the airplane that would one day manage to take us back to the promise of that long-ago summer day. It worked, and I smiled.

A few moments later, another cab arrived to take my Dream Man back to the airport. He kissed me chastely on the forehead in the manner that any old, family friend would do. We both knew it meant more than that, of course, but we stuck staunchly to the protocol. And then he left in his blue raincoat back into the cold, gray American day.

Two untouched glasses of orange juice still sat on the table.

That fateful day was a Tuesday, and when our guest returned to the city on Thursday for his formal visit — meaning visiting my husband and I, instead of only me in secret — the situation was extremely different. Arian was just as dashing, just as caring and just as nice. But it was his public face he was wearing, his public mask, and I couldn't help but see it as a mask now that I'd seen that public face slip while we were in private. He was a successful and polite man, always sure to project the generosity with money and affection that Persian men were known for. But now I felt as if we shared a secret, a secret shared right out in the light of day but one that no one else could sense.

At least, I was sure that Ahmad didn't sense it.

Whenever we were visiting other people or people were invited into our home, Ahmad's character changed slightly. He was less audibly discontent with his life. While most of what I heard on normal evenings was news of mean or cheap customers or how bitter he was at other people's success, Ahmad was a show off in the company of others. How great everything was when he was showing off his life to anyone outside of it.

And of course, a visit from Arian meant a visit with money, and Ahmad was always a man whose pulse sped up when there was the possibility of money entering his pocket.

Always the perfect, Persian gentleman, Arian didn't disappoint.

My little family met him at the National Airport in the early evening, and the first thing he did was lavish attention on my handsome, little John. From his coat, he procured a tiny model of an Eastern Airlines plane. He pretended to fly it in the air toward John and away again, making the baby giggle with joy, and then he winked at me — a secret nod to our thoughts of flying away, much like his hand gesture from the other day. He gave my delighted son the model plane to play with and John, of course, put it happily into his mouth.

Then, Arian reached over and put $500 into the front pocket of my son's overalls, saying, "For his future." My husband nodded and smiled. It was common for family and friends to give gifts of money or gold for a new baby's future, and it was obvious that Ahmad thought the large size of the gift was a compliment about the quality of his son.

"Welcome to Washington D.C.," Ahmad said, shaking our guest's hand firmly. "You are welcome as our guest."

"Thank you," our guest replied sincerely. "But I want you to know that you will also be my guest. Tonight, I am taking you to the biggest and best restaurant in Washington D.C. I'm told the best is the Orleans House. Is this correct?"

"Oh yes," I replied, excited by the thought of fancy food.

"Oh yes," Ahmad agreed. He smiled at the idea in the same way a baby smiles when it's coddled.

In the fashion of the higher classes in Iran, we dined in high style on the fresh seafood and wine of the Orleans House, a restaurant I'd usually only be able to see from through the window, outside on the cold pavement. Whether it was the rich food or the wine that caused the feeling or not, I felt somewhat outside of time sitting at that table, surrounded by three men, one of them in a high chair. We talked of Iranian and American politics, of the economy in Iran and our guest's factories. We talked of unimportant things that always come up when around family and old friends — nothing too close to the bone, nothing too personal. It was slightly awkward, but also pleasantly surreal. Here was an intersection of the hopes I had as a little girl and the realities I'd stumbled into as an adult.

The disconnected, confused feeling continued when we came home that evening. Cold and snowy, Ahmad dropped me and Arian off at the front door before heading off to park the car. I carried the sleeping baby upstairs, thanking our guest again for the fabulous meal, and he followed me all the way into the nursery, where I placed my angelic son in his crib.

I stood and stared at John for a moment, and I was suddenly shaking. My shoulders shook up and down with heaving breath, which usually foreboded tears, but my eyes were dry.

Arian came up behind me and put his arms around me, pressing my back into his body. One hand reached up to smooth my hair. "There, there," he said into my ear. "There, there." Rather than reacting warmly, the way I had throughout his visit so far, I remember shrugging off his hands. He was here now to soothe, certainly. But where would he be tomorrow? Where would he be next year? With his wife, that's where. I can't. I just can't get used to this feeling, I told myself.

Then the front door opened and closed, meaning Ahmad had returned. We slowly stepped apart, but remained at the side of the cradle, watching my son's breath rise and fall in his chest.

It was unspoken and unbreakable tradition that the guest in a Persian home would be given the best of the accommodations, which meant that our guest would be sleeping in the master bedroom, where Ahmad and I normally slept. There was a red lamp and a red blanket on the bed, and I'd made sure everything was clean and neat for him. We didn't have anything luxurious, but I could at least make sure things were clean and neat.

Ahmad and I would sleep down the hall in the guest room, which was separated from the master by the nursery. But I told Ahmad that I wanted to be there for the baby in the night, and set up a sleeping pallet for myself on the couch. I may have lain there, but I didn't sleep.

Instead, I stared out the window at the trees outside. I looked at the stars. I thought of how many different times I'd looked out windows at different trees and stars, thinking of the boy/man who was now in my house, a guest in the house of my husband, a guest like any other old, family friend. And yet, not at all like that.

I got up in the middle of the night and stood in our darkened hallway, where three doors branched off into three rooms. All the doors were open. Through the one directly in front of me, I saw my son — who had changed my life, changed the meaning of my existence, changed the person I was deep inside. Even in sleep, he exuded a sort of promise about the future, that he could be anything when he grew up and travel anywhere he wanted to. I would never cage him within high garden walls and he would never have to deal with the obstacles of being a girl. I would give him everything I'd always wanted, and that thought felt almost as good to me — perhaps better — than if I'd gotten everything I wanted for myself.

I leaned against the wall and looked right and left into the rooms of the other men in my life, in my house. Arian was an unmoving shape under the red blanket, and my husband's chest rose up and down in time to his light snoring in the less comfortable guest bed. Here were three men with power over me. Three men with very important but very different roles in my life. The rooms spun around and around in my head until I felt like I was on a carnival ride, dizzy with emotion.

In each direction lay a different devotion. To my husband, there was legal duty. To my son, there was the lioness' duty to protect and nurture her cubs, to create the next generation of lions to make the world a better place. And then there was our mysterious, powerful guest, and I wasn't quite sure what devotion I gave him. My duty to him was more visceral, more connected with my heart and soul. But it was also a shallower and more selfish devotion, one that would benefit me and only me. Not the world, not my little family. Just me. My need for him was the need of a fairytale princess who wants to be swept away and worshipped to live happily ever after. Even to my hoping heart, there was something flimsy and fake about the emotion, but it was a strong emotion nonetheless.

I sighed and wondered if I had the strength to choose one man over the other. I didn't think it was possible. All were permanently connected to me, pulling me in different directions, and I was unable to sever any of the three cords.

Then I wondered why all these forces were male. I had no choice to make to walk along a path of my own. My only choices were linked to men, my destiny dependent upon men, like if I chose none of the three choices, my very body would disappear in a puff of smoke.

I closed my eyes and leaned my head back against the hallway wall and I sensed the power of those three forces radiating in the dark. I tried to hear my own heartbeat, but instead thought I heard the beat of those three men, pumping loudly in my ears, confusing me.

Arian was in Washington D.C. for a few days, and I tried to make the most of them. The three men and I visited all the major sights of D.C. Ahmad brought along our first-ever movie camera to record a few snippets of all of us on the expansive lawns and clean sidewalks of the capital. We wandered through the soaring, impressive monuments honoring the great men of America's past, and we took pictures in front of the famous buildings to send back to friends and family in Iran, to prove the enviable places we had been.

I felt as if I was showing Arian my new life, my goals for this new life. The downtown tourist area of Washington D.C. was the perfect place to prove the promise of this land, where America still seemed big, beautiful, calm and clean. Where people smile and converse politely. So much of what I had experienced in America so far was dirtier, meaner and harder than this place, but this was the dream. The Washington Monument and the Lincoln Memorial, those were the dream I was showing off to our old friend.

The next day, Ahmad drove off to work in his cab and I was left to entertain our guest alone. We did what any foreigner in America does: We went shopping. One couldn't return home empty handed back to Iran, of course, and there was also the benefit of wearing a wonderful shirt and telling everyone where it came from. Shopping was nonnegotiable for a tourist of any kind, but it was especially important for a man who had money to throw around and people to take care of and impress.

We went around what felt like the entire city, visiting both normal department stores and high-class boutiques. We wandered, me pushing the stroller with John and him guiding the conversation.

First, he pressed me a little more about what my life was really like in America, married to Ahmad. "What do you do for money?" he asked. It was a subject that wasn't usually brought up in polite conversation, but it was the kind of thing that felt comfortable and normal between the two of us. It always had.

I explained what it was like for Ahmad to drive a cab and how I supplemented the budget by babysitting for other kids in our neighborhood. I also explained that we were still living the life of students — Ahmad wasn't yet done with his graduate work and my beauty school work was almost complete, but I couldn't yet return to wrap it up.

"I, too, have lived the life of a student," he told me. "When I was a student in England, I remember one time that I was waiting for my student check from the government and I had absolutely nothing. I had enough for one tomato and I cut it in half, and I had one half for lunch and one half for dinner." He laughed at the memory and shook his head. Then he bought me lunch.

"So tell me about your wife," I goaded him, and he complied. Just as I had told the truth about sensitive issues not usually brought up in polite society, he reciprocated by telling me about how his feelings for her were forced upon him by rules about how men were "supposed to" behave in Iran. They were supposed to marry and have children, and let their wives meddle behind the scenes at home but keep their professional lives separate. He wanted a divorce, he said. But she had given birth to a daughter recently (she was pregnant when they married), and that complicated things.

I nodded. The idea of divorce was still shocking to me, even after all my Americanization, so I knew how difficult it would be to pull off back in Iran. I sympathized with his feelings of helplessness, of being trapped. Even if he was a man, who were so much more powerful in Persian society, he understood that feeling.

We returned to shopping and I helped him pick out a dress to bring back to his wife. It felt strange, certainly, to be helping pick out a gift for a woman who was essentially my rival. But Arian, a fairytale figure in my mind, had this sort of control over me, to make me think that silly things like unwanted marriages and obligations could be brushed aside, at least temporarily. In the end, we chose a sleeveless green dress with a belt of sequins and the store wrapped it up in tissue paper and ribbon.

On the way out, we stopped at the perfume department, drawn by our noses. Like we had been all day, we just browsed around, commenting upon whatever caught our eyes. My eyes caught a certain fragrance bottle with two doves flying around its label along with a fancy French name. I picked it up and traced the doves with my finger, thinking of the doves that Arian had once kept in his parents' home. He cared for them so sweetly and allowed me to help him.

He came up behind me and noticed the doves, too. He put his hand on my shoulder and said, "Would you like that, Maryam?"

I shook my head and put the perfume back on the counter. "No, no. I don't need perfume."

He picked up the bottle and smelled its scent, nodded as if it pleased him greatly. He signaled the salesgirl and told her he'd take one bottle.

"Why are you doing this?" I asked him. "I don't want it."

He winked at me. "You should have this. You should have it as a gift from me."

I only realized after he paid that the small, French bottle of perfume cost $150, about triple the price of the green dress he was bringing home for his wife. I didn't know how I should feel about that, but I had no choice but to accept the gift.

On the way home that day — his last day in Washington — he again said that he wanted to take me away. "But it's not so easy, I know," he said. "So instead, I am going to think that I just want to see you again. That would be possible, right?"

I tilted my head to the side, as if to say that I supposed so but was unsure what he meant. On the one hand, he was so handsome, charming, familiar and safe. On the other, he was a married man, not my man, and I didn't know if I could trust his words and emotions. Had he said these things and acted this way with other women, or with his wife? But I pushed aside the questions in favor of indulging in the dream.

"How about I send you a ticket to come to Iran for the New Year this year," he suggested. "If I sent you a ticket, would you come?"

"Yes," I replied. "I would like to see my family and friends. And you. Yes."

He smiled. "It's settled then."

We walked in silence for a moment, our heads full of our own thoughts. Finally, I spoke what was on my mind. "The prince is still dead, you know," I said.

"I know," he replied. "He is most definitely dead today." In other words, who knew the circumstances of the future? Who knew what would be possible on another day, in another situation.

I had told him it was too late, and I continued to affirm that was the truth. But deep inside my heart, Arian had planted a seed of possibility. The seed of "someday." Someday it might be different. Someday it might be possible. Children grow up, circumstances change. And he was trying to say that he would be there when they did change.

It was a small sliver of hope. One day, I might be able to balance the weight of devotion to the three men in my life. One day, I might be able to find out what it felt like to give into my devotion to the love I felt for this man, the love that offered pure, almost selfish happiness. I had no idea what that would feel like.

The next day, we took Arian to the national airport and wished him well on his journey back home. From any outsiders' point of view, it would have looked like Ahmad and I were sending off any old, family friend. I told Ahmad the airplane ticket that arrived later was from my father, though I don't think he would have cared if he knew its real source. After all, he smelled my fancy French perfume and knew where that came from. Instead of jealousy, all he felt was pride in the fact that his wife was wearing $150 perfume and smugness that he didn't have to pay for it.

Chapter Sixteen

Life went on in America. Ahmad was going to school and taking it as easy at work as he possibly could. As John got older and easier to care for, I began to baby sit more formally. In other words, I would have regular clients that dropped their children off in the morning and picked them up in the evening, paying me a set fee for my time each week.

In January, we invited over all the neighborhood kids and all the Persian families we knew to celebrate John's first birthday. I had planned food and drinks, music and anything else I could think of for the event, and I was very excited to play host to such a momentous occasion. After all, it may have been John's birthday, but it was a party for the adults, too. And I had never had an excuse to throw a larger party in America. Come to think of it, I hadn't really thrown a party since I had become a wife, and that seemed like something I needed to fix right away.

All that was left to do was pick up the cake from the local grocery store, Giant Food.

"Ahmad," I said, "I need you to go pick up John's birthday cake."

Ahmad made a grunting noise and didn't look up from the paper he was writing on.

"It's just down the street. Now go. Our guests will be coming soon."

"How much is this cake of yours?" he asked, finally meeting my eyes.

"It's $18, and it should be ready under my name."

"I don't have $18, so I guess we're not having a cake then."

I paused, my eyebrows scrunching up in disbelief at what my husband was saying. "It's your son's birthday, now go down and pick up his cake, please."

"I'm not paying $18 I don't have for a cake. And that's that."

I laughed in exasperation at this silly man. It was only $18, after all. But there wasn't much I could do. It was early in the week and I didn't get paid from my babysitting clients until Friday, so I had no cash on hand myself. But we had to have a cake, I thought to myself. The whole community was coming over and I would have to tell them there was no cake to put candles in, no cake for the birthday boy to smear all over his 1-year-old face. It just wasn't right.

From the other room, our recent houseguest must have heard my distress. It was Ahmad's older brother visiting us from Germany, where he still lived. And like all the other men in Ahmad's family except himself, my brother-in-law was especially sweet and considerate in his behavior toward me.

"Don't worry, Maryam," he said, patting John's head as he went to grab the car keys. "I'll go get it."

I sighed in relief. "Thank you. Thank you."

"It's no trouble. I'll be back soon," he replied, and left the apartment. Ahmad said not a word and barely looked up from whatever it was he was reading.

The party went well and the cake was a big hit, especially with John, who seemed surprised at the shockingly sweet taste of the frosting. I was a proud mother and in my element surrounded by so many people, so much excitement. I suppose I was a social butterfly and had missed being a part of such gatherings. Whenever someone complimented the party — including the cake — Ahmad would smile and take all the credit, as if they were telling him what an important and impressive man he was. But he never paid his brother back the $18.

Inside my head, the doubting part of my brain felt that seed of hope growing. When things like this happened and I was confronted with my husband's personality, I thought about how easy it would be with

Arian. Money would be no issue; my social life would be blossoming and conversation would never be so harsh and clipped.

But this is the wrong time. This — right now with John — is the right thing. Right and wrong, wrong and right. My brain knew the difference, but my heart continued to question.

With the hope that had been kindled inside my heart, sometimes I didn't know whether I was coming or going. Even so, I still didn't have a choice. I knew where I belonged.

March rolled around and I found myself on a plane to Iran again, away from home for a few weeks to celebrate the New Year with family and friends. It was John and I alone on the airplane, and though he was usually a well-behaved baby, it's hard for any child to be still through so many hours of travel and inactivity. When he wanted to be active, there was little that could stop him. At times, he'd get so frustrated I wouldn't let him toddle up and down the aisles of the plane or the hallways of the airport that he would grab fistfuls of my hair and pull as hard as his little muscles could.

I was relieved to finally get a reprieve in Germany, where my brother-in-law had invited me to stop over on my way to Iran to repay the hospitality, we'd shown him in Washington D.C. Two men of the same family, and yet I was struck again by how different they acted. My brother-in-law met me at the Frankfurt Airport and presented me with a single flower. Then he gave me a tour of the 1930s-era mansion he lived in. It was filled with intricate woodwork and marble statues, exactly like what was shown in the European movies of my childhood.

The home had been divided in two, and the other half was rented out to another Iranian family from Tabriz. They threw me a little party the night John and I arrived, making me feel like a guest of honor. And if I was the queen, little John was the king. Everyone just adored his chubby smiles and light-hearted play.

From there, I traveled on to Iran. And once there, I traveled around in the way that had become my habit on our last visit. I began in Tehran at my aunt's house, went to Tabriz to visit my family, went to the Caspian Sea with my father-in-law to take in the beach, and spent some time at the General's house back in Tehran. Except for the continuing anger and jealousy of the women in Ahmad's family, I had an amazing time soaking up the family news, familiar cooking and relaxing times my home country provided. And celebrating the New Year the way I had all my life, cheered me up and warmed my heart with nostalgia.

But being back in Iran also jogged my memory as to the restrictive social norms — and therefore the secret transactions that happened behind everyone else's backs. For instance, I was again under the protection of male relatives, which was officially the General, because I was staying at his house in Tehran. Of course, it was his sharp and bitter wife, who watched my every move to report back to Ahmad any irregularities. I'm pretty sure she hoped there would be such occurrences, because it would give her a good excuse to tell Ahmad to divorce me.

"Maryam, you have a phone call," I heard the General's wife call from the other room. "It's Mina, she says," my aunt-in-law said, her eyebrows knit with suspicion because she didn't recognize the name. "Do you know a Mina?"

I waved my hand at her and smiled. "Of course," I replied. But honestly, I had no idea who was on the other end of the line and I was amazed at my ability to play it so cool. I placed the receiver to my ear. "Hi, Mina," I said casually. "How are you?"

"Hello, Maryam," said a female voice, older than mine but still kind and fresh. "I'm calling from the office of ..." She was Arian's secretary. What an amusing ruse! "I'll connect you to his office now," she continued.

"Oh, really? That's great," I said. My aunt-in-law was still lurking at the top of the stairs, so I kept my phrasing very general. While I was on hold for a moment, I marveled at how some of the skills of my childhood were still serving me well. Here I was an adult, a married woman and a mother, and there was still always someone listening at the top of the stairs.

"Hello, Maryam." Arian's voice appeared on the line. "Your visit is going well so far, I assume?"

"Oh, it's been fabulous," I replied. "I'm having a great time."

"Are you too busy to meet me for lunch this week? I'd like to see you," he said. "Just to talk, of course."

"Of course," I echoed.

"How about the Chattanooga? Remember, we threw that party there last time you were home?"

"But of course. That'd be great."

"I'll see you there."

"Sure, Mina. I'll see you there. Bye."

He laughed lightly at the name and signed off.

There was a lot of secret footwork that went on behind the scenes of traditional Persian culture. Everyone espoused certain ideas and modes of behavior, but the gossip factory that told stories of who didn't follow the rules never lacked for material. The modern world crept in, and we all made room for it within the old way of life. It's just few people were able to cut those ancient ties completely. So many secrets — even honest, open secrets that were nothing to be ashamed of.

I was just having lunch. That was completely permissible. There was nothing untoward in our conversation, our actions or our behavior. And there was an entire restaurant of chaperones, and a plate glass window overlooking the street, where anyone in the world could walk by. We hid nothing. We didn't have to. Again, it was just lunch. Not that I told Ahmad about it. But I didn't tell him about every little friend whose path I crossed while back in Iran, I justified.

Over one gin and tonic each, we enjoyed a fabulous lunch and spoke about every little thing. Our families, my trip, his business. We ventured carefully into the subjects of our marriages. Ever the gentleman, he told me he was incredibly unhappy with his wife but never spoke an unkind word about her personally. He never insulted her, but put the blame for unhappiness on his own shoulders or wrote it off to basic incompatibility. He'd asked for a divorce several times, he said, but she simply stated she would not grant it. She'd die first, he said.

All too soon it was over, a normal lunch between friends.

We were leaving the restaurant and he gently took my hand. "I will see you at my birthday party next week?" he asked, applying slight pressure to my fingers. The pressure sent the blood rushing to my head.

"Of course," I replied. "I wouldn't miss it."

He smiled, released my hand and walked away.

Then I shrugged. I felt good finding my old friend again. Yes, he was a friend. What he did or did not do with other women didn't concern me.

The high point of the trip — the reason I had been flown to Iran by Arian — was the huge party he mentioned during lunch, which was at the beginning of April to celebrate his birthday. Arian's sister and I had been in contact about the party. She knew all about the fact that her brother had bought my plane ticket and had wanted to see me, that we went out to lunch. Always the go-between when we were young, she continued to serve as message bearer and cheerleader for both of us, and she agreed to go to the party at my side.

With this occasion in mind, I had saved one of my best silk dresses for the party: a gown with a V neck and a plunging. Leaving John with my aunt-in-law and feeling the old anticipation in the act of combing my hair and doing my make-up, I was transported back to my teenage years. Parties, new people and endless possibilities. Possibilities that ended so quickly when you made a sudden, impulsive choice — into marriage, into adulthood. How little I had known back then. And now that I was an adult, how much more I could read into the subtle gestures of a social gathering.

I arrived with Arian's sister and her husband into the world of Tehran's most privileged. The house was a massive edifice, lit up against the dark of the evening. Light and music spilled out from the visible windows as we walked through a massive arch into the courtyard, a lush and fountain-decked space.

Inside, the silk carpets gave softly beneath my high-heeled shoes. A large color television was on in the hallway, flashing images and words that guests weren't supposed to pay attention to. The television was only a sign of the class of the hosts and their wealth, much like serving a wine whose name automatically told guests how expensive it was.

From there, the party guests meandered from the hall into several living/sitting rooms and into the back garden. They gathered in well-dressed groups or spread the silky fabric of their dresses over cushions or on couches. They held wine glasses and small plates of food, and their laughter tinkled like the ice in the cocktails of some of the men. I took a deep breath, as if I could take such elegance and casual luxury into my body, where it could not be forgotten.

My arm was linked with that of my friend, Arian's sister, when a woman caught my eye and made a beeline across the room toward me, tapping guests on the shoulder to clear her way. Her face was serene and open as she reached over to extend her hand.

"Maryam!" she exclaimed. "You must be Maryam. I know you from the pictures. You know, the pictures that still circulate around here from your days as a beauty queen?" The way in which she said "beauty queen" made me believe she didn't hold the phrase in the highest of esteem. "We do one thing in our youth and it can never be forgotten, right?" She laughed lightly, but I suspected she ardently wished such thing could just be swept under the rug and erased forever.

I smiled graciously back, and she formally introduced herself — Arian's wife.

"It's such a pleasure to finally meet you," I said. "I've heard so much about you, too."

Her smile flickered.

"My friends here —" I gestured to the host's sister and brother-in-law. "They've said such nice things about you."

"I see," she replied, and she looked me up and down to assess my dress, my beauty and, obviously, my status as a threat to her.

I returned the favor, taking her measure, too. She was shorter than me and I guessed about 10 years older. Her frame was petite and thin, but her face was plain with a wide nose that dominated her other features. Her teeth were also noticeably crooked. But her smile was warm despite that, and always one to try to notice people's positive traits, I noticed her eyes and brows were nicely shaped and lovely.

As we spoke, I also noted that she was very intelligent. Her language was sharp, but veiled. She guided us around part of the house making introductions, and her power over the party, the home and her world was transparent. Here was the puppet master, I thought. The woman who called all the shots, or at least thought she did. What an interesting little bird of a woman.

I had no reason to be jealous of her. Really, I had found a man and gotten married first, with no thought as to my Dream Man. Only recently, we had found that we still shared a childhood connection. A friendship, though, and that was all. This is not a competition, I told myself.

But when she excused herself to attend to other guests and we shook hands once again, I admit that I glanced at her hand. Veined and bony, it was the hand of a woman twice her age. A feeling of superiority rushed over me despite myself.

As she made her way back through the crowd, I exchanged glances with my friend, Arian's sister, and we both raised our eyebrows. Her husband had gone off to another corner of the gathering, leaving us to whisper amongst ourselves.

"What was that all about?" I asked her. "It's as if she's trying to size me up. What have I ever done to her?"

"Nothing. Nothing except be young and pretty and have a connection with her husband," she said.

I blushed up to the roots of my hair. Nothing had happened between the two of us that couldn't be replayed before man and God, I thought to myself. It was only the feelings buried deep inside that were perhaps scandalous, and no one could know that. Or could they read it on my face?

"You see those two girls over there?" She pointed towards two 20-something women sitting on a sofa, obviously people watching. "Those are two of her cousins. They have a mission, believe me. You see, the one on the right is supposed to watch you the whole evening, and the one on the left has the job of watching him."

"What do they think is going to happen?" I asked.

She shrugged. "Who knows? They just want to plot and scheme, so take a deep breath and let them. Besides, it's fun to watch, isn't it?" Her eyes twinkled over her wine glass and I laughed along with her.

Everywhere I went that evening, the cousin in the blue dress was not far behind. Music blared from the speakers and everyone got up to dance. Men, women and children: No one was exempt from dancing and, unlike in America, no one felt any embarrassment or shyness. We let loose to the popular Iranian music of the era — often, the same popular songs played over and over again. I took breaks from dancing for food or to say hi to old friends and acquaintances. I wandered around to take in the glamorous house that surrounded me. The television, the music, the wine and the food: All of this was designed to impress and entertain, and I was both.

I compared this life to my childhood, seeing all the comfortable aspects of my early life mimicked here. It was so familiar and comfortable, so unlike a stark American apartment and riding a bus to a job at a drug store. In America, such things were unavoidable, and I learned to adapt to them. I figured I was a stronger person for doing so. But here, I was reminded of the easy and comfortable life I had unwittingly given up.

It wasn't the money — which bought the house and the rich carpets and the furnishings — that I thought of, though that was a part of it, too. It was the idea of the comfort and easiness of such a life, where you could hire a nanny and a maid, where you not only could, but *were expected to* throw such lavish parties all the time. There was no pressure to earn money, only to spend it and make yourself happy and respected.

How easy! How enviable!

But wasn't that exactly what I had been running away from? I didn't really know anymore. But witnessing the old life now that I had the perspective from my new life shed a different light on my childhood and all my choices. I was a little sad, but also defiant. Arian's wife didn't know what a sheltered, easy life she had. She didn't know her own strength. I was a modern woman, and I took my modern-woman self back to the dance floor. I wasn't going to let this special evening of fun be wasted.

My curly hair floating around my shoulders, I threw myself into the party. Hours later, the husband of my friend who escorted me to the party tapped me on the shoulder.

"You've had three glasses of wine, haven't you?" he asked with a smile that was half paternal and half amused. "I've been watching you."

"So what? What of it?" I asked, also smiling.

"It's probably enough, don't you think?"

I shrugged and looked around. The gathering was winding down. More glasses were empty on tabletops than in hands, and many guests held their coats or purses, taking their leave.

"Yes, it's probably enough," I agreed.

I warmly shook the hands of our host, Arian, on the way out. It was the first time I'd seen him all evening except from across the room, and I smiled.

"I had a fascinating time," I told him, and squeezed his fingers while they were within mine. I repeated the sentiment to his wife and we drove off into the evening. All the way back to General's, all thoughts of the party left my head and I thought only of John. I'd had an evening out and a strange experience confronting that way of life, but my sweet boy was waiting at home for me. If I couldn't figure out where else I belonged, at least I knew I belonged there.

Returning to my life in America felt like wrapping up a lot of loose ends. While things had seemed static for so long — our day-to-day routine rarely varying too much — I felt I had the energy and the ability to change things once I came back.

Of course, the circumstances helped, too.

First of all, my sister had come to live with us for a time in the United States. Not just a short visit, instead she had come to live indefinitely in order to have an operation on her heart that wasn't available or safe in Iran. She had a visa and was seeing any doctor who would give her an appointment. Her condition frightened me immensely. She lost her breath easily and during the worst of times, she said the weight of a bed sheet over her chest was heavy enough to make her heart heave. Because of her heart condition, she was still unmarried — the real condition that worried her — and she was really excited that after surgery, she might be able to move on with her life. Healthy enough for most everyday activities, she was also happy to see America and to have a chance to play with her nephew, who she found adorable.

Finally having a companion and someone to watch John, I was able to go back to the Washington Beauty Academy to finish my certificate. After having slaved part-time there and struggling with keeping a job at the same time, I was amazed at how fast the remaining hours I needed to accumulate to graduate were completed. It took only a matter of weeks.

Certificate in hand, I felt both empowered and disappointed. After all that time, this is what I got? A piece of paper and the ability to work long hours in a little salon somewhere? I suppose I hadn't gotten my mother's advice to get some formal schooling and a bigger degree out of my mind. So, I cast around for some way in which to build upon my beauty school certificate.

What kind of job did I know of that used what I learned in beauty school and brought it up to a different, higher level? Suddenly, I thought of the tour I had taken of the ABC studio over the drug store. Everyone there, from the camera men to the girls in make-up seemed to be so glamorous and professional. I wondered how a girl went about getting started in the fascinating world of professional make up for television.

Through the American University in Washington D.C., I tracked down the woman who was Director of Television Programming at the university, and she was also Television Makeup Consultant at a leading news network CBS News in Washington, DC. Her name was Lillian Brown and she was a sweetheart, an older lady who still looked impeccable and with a true desire to help me out. When I had learned all I could, she offered me to assist her in the television makeup of the CBS

Network Special Broadcast, in particular at Mr. Daniel Schorr's program.

I was very happy.

We did some training out of a book, but most of my lessons in the ways of make up for television were hands-on, which suited me just fine. I was often backstage at the set of famous TV shows that hosted some of the most important and powerful figures of the day. Once Lillian had taught me quite a bit, she allowed me to make up certain famous men — under her watchful eye, of course. I sponged pancake make up onto a famous news anchor and a senator from Washington State. After the latter's appearance on the show, there was a buffet line where I was again thrown together with him.

"Do you want me to clean up your face?" I asked. "To get off that TV make up?"

"No way," he replied. "It looks really nice and I have a special meeting over at the capitol. I think I might just keep it on."

Most every day, I trained with Lillian in the back rooms of the news studios, at least for a couple of hours at a time. Coming in contact with powerful people and them respecting me for a job well done — a job that I truly enjoyed, no less — was a powerful and hopeful experience, and it reminded me that I had a lot more to offer the world than babysitting and being a wife and mother. Not that I didn't value those roles, of course. But I also felt as if I was standing on my own two feet. Not financially, but spiritually.

After a significant teaching period, Lillian set up a sort of graduation test for me, which I passed with flying colors. I think she was even more proud than I was.

"You know, Maryam," she said. "You are the first Iranian woman to ever work at our news network. How does that feel?"

I shook my head. "I don't know. I hadn't even thought of it that way," I replied. But my heart swelled with her praise. This wasn't just a job — this was something to be very proud of.

A few months later, I attended a concert at the Kennedy Center in Washington D.C. The room was filled with diplomats and political figures alike, all there to enjoy a night out with great music and conversation. As I was walking through the crowded lobby, a familiar face was headed my way and I suddenly realized that it was the senator who I once worked with at the TV station.

"Maryam! Hello! How are you?" Asked the Senator.

I explained to him that everything in my life was working out well. After I finished relaying my life to the Senator, he stared at me with a charming smile and asked, "Will you go out to dinner with me?"

"Now, now. I'm married Mr. Senator," I said to him, in my old jovial voice when thrown into a crowd of interesting people.

"Well, I tell you what. You get yourself divorced and marry me, I'll get you a permanent green card," he joked and winked at me.

We laughed together at his joke and enjoyed each other's company for a few more minutes before we went to our separate seats in the music hall.

After I had been certified by Lillian, I would often be called to work. It was a part-time position and very irregular. They would just call you up the morning before recording and ask you to arrive before recording time and — boom — you were expected to be there. My sister's help was the only thing that allowed me to leave the house so often and her surgery was approaching. The National Institute of Health in Maryland, a research hospital, agreed to perform the surgery, which was a miracle for her. Without insurance or citizenship, many doctors had refused her and her health was deteriorating all the time.

I was with her in the hospital as much as I could before, during and after the surgery, which was very hard on my sister. But the procedure went well, meaning she would have a very long and normal life once she recovered — that she would be able to marry and have children the way she's always dreamed she would.

But recovery was a slow process that took many months, and so I had the honor of her company in America for a while longer before she had to return home. Ahmad, on the other hand, was glad she stayed on only because my father was sending a few hundred dollars every month in exchange for us taking care of her.

What would I do when she went back to Iran? I wondered. How would I get out of the house to work? Would I end up babysitting for the neighborhood kids again? Not that babysitting was a terrible option, but I had experienced being a working professional, sharp and skilled in high heels and a good attitude, and I didn't want to give that up.

After many years of just scraping by, Ahmad found some joy in his master's work at the university. His old friend Hossin sat down and showed him what he should have learned long ago: how to study. If you just did things the right way, getting good grades was easy, he explained. And Ahmad tackled his studies with newfound excitement. One more set of classes and he would be free to start his thesis, the large research paper that all graduate students had to complete to get their degrees.

With my budding independent spirit and the blessing of my sister's presence, I attended a semester of classes at Northern Virginia College. I knew by now that Ahmad's long ago promise of sending me to school when he was done with schooling was a fantasy — already he spoke about putting my beauty schooling to work in a salon or what kind of job I could get once John was in school. So I seized the opportunity to discover college life for myself while I could. After all, we had some money coming in from my father and even Ahmad would be too ashamed to have my sister report back to our father that he was not allowing me to go to school. My husband was always on his best behavior — or at least better — when there was someone other than me to judge him for it.

At the university, I blossomed in my basic core classes, including English 101, which proved to me that my language skills had become quite good over the intervening years. Television and cashiering, it seems, were excellent tutors. But because of my life-long interest in beauty, make-up and costumes — plus my childhood growing up backstage — my favorite of my classes was theater. We performed the play Anastasia, about the lost Russian princess, and I had a starring role.

At the end of the term, the professor invited all the cast to a graduation party at his house. "Please make sure you'll be there," he said in front of the class. He was a nice, middle-aged man who had brown hair and colorful handkerchiefs tucked into the pockets of his jackets. "It's been a wonderful semester with this class, and it won't be complete without all of you there."

I told Ahmad in advance about the party and he agreed to come, making sure he didn't have to drive the cab that night. Meanwhile, I made sure we had a babysitter and that I had the perfect dress to wear for the celebratory evening. Knowing I probably wouldn't be able to finish a college degree and that this one semester would have to be my only taste of the student life, I took the party very seriously. I was very proud of myself and I wanted to share that feeling with the world.

Ahmad, however, didn't.

"I don't feel good," he replied from the couch when I asked if he was getting ready to go. "I think I have a cold."

"You don't have a cold. You're fine," I said. I came over to the couch and put my hand on his forehead. It was cool to the touch.

"I'm sick and I'm not going," he said. He closed his eyes as if he could shut me out of the world in that way.

"Ahmad," I said, "I told you about this party days ago, and you said it was OK to go. Do you know how important this is to me?"

He grunted, keeping his eyes closed.

"Ahmad, please. Let's go," I pleaded.

"I'm sick," he repeated. "And that's that."

I sat down hard on the arm of the sofa, and felt ridiculous posed that way in the nice dress I'd picked out for the occasion. I sat there for a while staring at my husband, willing him to open his eyes and look at me. If he would only open his eyes, he would see that this one evening meant a great deal to his wife and that giving in would make her happy, now and when she looked back on it in the future. He would sigh, pack away his reluctance to go and get dressed.

Of course, I thought, then he would be at the party — his messy, unkempt, snobbish and negative self — and all of her classmates would whisper, "Him? She's married to that guy?"

Maybe it was for the best he played sick, I thought.

Sitting there, I sighed deeply and gave up, going to the bathroom to take off my dress and party make up. Much like when I felt I couldn't take a tour of the ABC news studio without my husband's permission and chaperoning, it was impossible in my mind to think that I could leave my husband and attend the party by myself. Such things weren't conceivable. They weren't done. There I was resentful and stewing at him, and I never once thought that I could just stand up and walk to the party on my own two feet, the two feet I was so proud of standing on in America. Some American ideals take longer to sink than others, I suppose. Ahmad sat on the couch all evening and not once did I hear him cough or blow his nose.

Two days later, we had our final theater class and I stayed late to personally apologize to our professor for missing the big party. It was obvious from the tightness around his mouth and his sharp eyes that he was a little angry with me. He allowed me to tell my story about my husband being sick and how I was ever so sorry, never once meeting my eyes while he was shuffling papers into his briefcase. But when I'd laid out my tale, he sighed and sat back in his chair.

"I'm sorry," I repeated.

"I didn't miss the party," he replied. "You did. Don't be sorry for me."

He gathered up his things and made ready to go. Before he turned to go, he opened his mouth to speak but then paused. "Maryam," he finally said, "let me teach you a little lesson, a final lesson from your teacher." He smiled just a little, though there was still anger around the edges. "Don't apologize for missing an opportunity or losing out on something to other people. Of course you can apologize for bring impolite, and I accept your apology. But apologize to yourself: The only one losing is you."

I left the room and I cried a little on my trip home, but I was forever thankful. Thankful for the class, the stage experience, the opportunity to see what college life was really like. But most importantly, I was thankful for that lesson, which stuck with me throughout the rest of my life.

Every experience was a gift. And if I allowed someone to hold me back from experiencing it, the only one to lose was me.

Chapter Seventeen

I felt something was missing — my purpose for being in America. My sister had fully recovered from her surgery, I had taken my beauty schooling as far as I could and I knew that I wouldn't be able to continue going to college. I turned my eyes toward the future by turning my back towards my past. I wanted to return to Iran — now. Ahmad agreed that my sister and I could leave to Iran while he stayed in America to finish his thesis, after which he would join us in Iran.

Upon our arrival in Iran, John was also well taken care of. My mother doted on my adorable little man and would watch him for me at the drop of a hat — if I wanted to go shopping or when I took little classes in dressmaking at the Singer sewing shop. John's toy cars had taken over the floor of the sitting room in my parents' house. They bought him a special toy helicopter that glowed in the dark. There was a great kindergarten by the American consulate, where he played happily with other international kids and learned to count in both English and Farsi. Happy to be in the Iranian sunshine and enjoying my freedom, I'd walk the long, meandering way through the city to pick him up from the American Consulate School in the afternoon and then take a taxi back home, the journey being too much for his little legs.

I stayed in Tabriz for a month or two, talking to Ahmad on the phone occasionally. Even from across the ocean, he found reasons to be upset with me and ways to manipulate me. First, the issue was that his family wanted to see John and that I shouldn't keep him cooped up in Tabriz. Then, it was that he didn't know what I was up to while I was staying at my parents' house. Eventually, his nagging was such that I agreed to go back to Tehran and stay at his uncle the General's house, where both John and I could be under the care of his family for the remaining time we'd be alone. A thesis, after all, takes a long time to complete and Ahmad estimated it would be about six months until he was able to join us back in Iran.

If he thought being in Tehran was going to dampen my enjoyment, however, Ahmad was sorely mistaken. In the bustling, busy and exciting capital, I still had lots of friends and family. My father-in-law doted on both John and I and took us to his luxurious oasis of a vacation home near the Caspian Sea. John, who was about 2 years old at that point, ran happily around in his little jean jacket with the American flag on the back. And I was able to visit with Arian frequently.

"Maryam! Mina is on the phone!" Ahmad's aunt would shout.

"How are you, Mina?" I'd say to dead air while his secretary transferred me to his office phone.

"I'd like to see you," his rich voice would say, and we'd meet at the Chattanooga for lunch and one gin and tonic each — enough of a luxury to make it a special occasion but not enough to make us lose our heads, we would joke. And that was all it was: food, a drink and great conversation with a close friend, a friend I felt like I had known my whole life and could tell anything to. We fell into one another like one falls into a comfortable favorite chair. We met once or twice a month in this way.

While the phone calls were clandestine, the fact that I met him wasn't so much of a secret. I'd tell Ahmad that I ran into Arian and that he said hello. Ahmad didn't seem to care about anything except his thesis and his return to Iran.

And money, of course.

"I need $5,000" he said to me over the phone, his voice distant and thin over the long-distance lines.

"What? Why do you need $5,000?" I asked.

He explained that other Iranian students had informed him of a certain duty loophole for returning students. To encourage educated Persians to return to the country, the government was offering a one-time deal to college graduates. They were allowed to import a car into the country duty-free, which saved a whole lot of money.

"We can buy a car for $5,000 in America, and we could sell it for $15,000 to some rich man in Iran," Ahmad said. "We could make so much money."

"Yes, but where are *you* going to get $5,000?" I asked. I pointedly used the word "you" instead of taking some responsibility for the problem by saying "we."

"Well, you need to ask your father for it?"

"Me? Ask my father?" How had he turned this into something that I had to do?

We argued back and forth, Ahmad saying that his parents wouldn't have the money and that my father would give me anything if I just asked. I pointed out that he could ask General, who was very rich, but Ahmad would never ask for a loan from someone he respected, from whom he wanted respect in return. I told him that my father was out of the question. He had just given me $1,600 to import a washer and dryer into Iran after I mentioned how accustomed I'd gotten to the machines in America and none were to be found in Iran.

Then he mentioned Arian.

"You could always just ask him," Ahmad said. "We all know the vast amount of money he has, right? And he's a very generous man."

"Yes. Yes, he is a very generous man," I replied testily. "How come we are never the generous ones, Ahmad? How come we are always the ones asking for money?"

"Oh, be quiet. Just try to get the money, OK?"

I was silent.

"We'll pay him back once we sell the car in Iran," he continued. "It's not like it's a gift. It's a loan."

"I don't want to," I replied. "I just can't do it."

It took three more phone calls of Ahmad badgering me before I finally gave in.

A few days later, Arian's secretary called and we set up another lunch. We sat down at the table and I admired Arian's dark hair and his easy smile. We talked about our lives and our families. We talked about everything. It's just that we never — not once — talked about money. I was stiff and uncomfortable in the plush chair, nervous and fidgeting at the linen-covered table.

"She says that she would rather die than grant me a divorce," he was saying. "I just don't understand why she wants both of us to be so unhappy."

I nodded.

"You seem distracted, Maryam," he said. "What is on your mind?"

"Oh nothing," I replied, waving my hand like I was sweeping away my thoughts.

"Well, what is your husband doing?" he asked.

I swallowed a sip of my drink and braced myself. This was my chance. "Actually, he's been calling me and bothering me on the phone about bringing a car back to Iran from America. Something about students getting to take an automobile into the country without paying duty. He's very excited."

"Wow, that is a good deal. Cars are very expensive here, you know."

"I know," I said. "But he wants to buy a $5,000 car and we don't have that kind of cash on hand. So, he's calling to bug me about finding the money somehow." I sighed. "He's driving me crazy," I told him, being very honest about it.

Arian reached across the table and placed his large, angular hand on top of mine. "Stop it. Stop that worrying right now," he said. "Just give me his account number and I will have my banker transfer $5,000 into his account."

"Really?"

"Just like that," he replied, snapping his fingers to show me how fast and easy it would be.

"Thank you so much," I gushed. "You have no idea how happy he will be — or how happy I will be when he just shuts up about it."

He laughed. "There's no need for thanks."

Some time passed and life went on in the leisurely manner of Persian culture. December past and January was creeping up when I got another call from Mina.

"How are you?" I asked.

Cutting the small talk, Arian got right to the point. "When is he coming back? It must be soon now."

I sighed into the telephone. "Tonight, actually. His plane arrives tonight."

"Have tea with me this afternoon then," he insisted. "It will be a long time before I get to see you alone again and I'm going to miss your friendship so much. Have tea with me."

"Yes," I replied. "Yes."

Bundled into my winter coat — a plush leather jacket with tufts of fur around my neck — I walked into the restaurant at the same time as Arian. We smiled at one another and sat down at a table near the window. Snow drifted down from the sky, swirling and dancing before it hit the clean, cold blanket of snow already on the ground. The sun was beginning to sink in the sky and the clouds were tinged pink and purple with the coming sunset. We drank tea and nibbled on pastries and cake and lost ourselves in conversation. We spoke of our children and our spouses. He talked about an upcoming trip to Pakistan for his business and the opening of a new factory. I talked about how tired I was of living out of a suitcase in someone else's house and how I looked forward to finding a place of my own again, to really create a home for my little family.

"You love him very much, don't you" he asked.

"What?" I responded, confused.

"Your son. John."

I smiled and nodded. "He is the light of my life and my reason for being," I said.

The snow continued to fall, and we lost track of time. By the time we stood up to leave, it was dark as night outside. Teatime and then dinner time had come and gone and my watch told me that it was 9 o'clock.

"Let me take you home," he said while helping me put on my coat. "It's cold and snowy out there."

I agreed. We drove around the city as if in a dream. I don't know if it was the magical quality of the snow or the feeling that a certain window of time was closing, but I felt as if we were hovering above the earth, the tires never touching the pavement. The car was silent, and Arian moved the wheel like a dancer guiding his partner. We spoke of casual but hopeful things, like his suggestions for good neighborhoods to find a home in, good schools for John and job opportunities for my husband.

He parked on the street, which was a good distance from General's house.

"We may not get to talk to one another as much," he said, "but I'll be in touch. We'll see each other around."

"Of course," I replied and smiled at him.

"I'll wait until I see you go inside."

I nodded and opened the car door into the cold. I trudged in my boots through the snow, which had grown to be almost a foot deep, and the feeling of unreality remained. I felt like a figure in a painting walking through that snowy field. I saw the picture in my head as if I was hovering above, standing outside myself. There was my old friend in his car, there was my trail of footsteps, there was the big mansion lit up in the distance. There was a feeling of being suspended between time periods and destination. It was a bittersweet feeling, like a vacation coming to an end, but I wasn't overly sad. I was returning to my normal life and was happy to be moving forward again. A home? A new job for me? Success? I was looking to the future. At that one moment, I had everything.

Of course, I also had nothing at all, just a young woman making tracks in the fresh evening snow. Above my head, I imagined, was the plane carrying my husband, who was heading back home to start his *real* life, to start his adulthood. I had never known him as anything but a student and I wondered if he would look any different when I met him at the airport as a grown up, as a real man.

My husband had a perfect replica of a Mercedes in his pocket for John when we met him at the airport about 11 p.m. In his suitcase, he had a long, leather raincoat for me as well as a set of hot rollers and a lighted make-up mirror — things I had come to love in the United States but that were only available in the correct voltage for Iran by special order. Ahmad was clean shaven and he had lost a little weight. It even looked like he had gotten a haircut.

Immediately after Ahmad's return, I felt we were moving in the adult sphere again, living our lives and interacting with the world. First, we found an apartment: a three-bedroom unit in Geisha area in Tehran, this neighborhood was known as a center for youth recreation and shopping. Finally, I found myself in the heart of the city, feeling myself as a part of the hustle and bustle that I'd looked in on as a tourist when I was a young beauty pageant contestant. Living below us was a Frenchman named Jean-Pierre and, next door to him, the owner's wife, a young woman haggard with the care of a whole hoard of children.

Once again, the place was empty — only a box of echoing space with no carpets, no furniture, not even a glass to have a cup of water when thirsty. How many times would we need to begin again? I wondered. But this time, I took a deep breath and knew I could make this place into something. This time, we were setting up house for keeps, and not as starving students. Instead, I was determined to paint us as a young, well-traveled family just returned from cosmopolitan America, ready to take the capital by storm.

The only obstacle was money. Some things were easy, like the washer and dryer, which arrived from America and were installed right away. Other things were difficult, mostly because anything related to money was difficult with Ahmad. I knew that we had money. A week or two after he arrived, the car did, too. It was delivered to Germany, where a man had been hired to drive it to the Turkish border. Then an Iranian driver was hired to pick it up and bring it to Tehran, where Ahmad sold it for a small fortune.

"I will buy a rug when I want to buy a rug," Ahmad had replied when I asked for the most important accessory in any Persian home: a rug or two to cushion the floors. "Not when you ask me to. Not just because you ask me to," he continued. All my family and Ahmad's family had expensive silk rugs, the kind of rug that was handed down generation to generation and spoke of a family's class the moment a guest's feet touched the ground.

But that's not the way Ahmad saw the purchase of a rug. It was a power struggle like any other in our marriage, like any other dating back to the time we'd lived with his family. And any time his family was nearby to watch over him, he'd put his foot down more often and more arbitrarily just to prove the power he had over me.

The same was true on that occasion, when I was sitting on the floor of our new apartment with John in my lap as Ahmad left to look for work. We had not even truly moved in yet — lack of kitchen utensils meant I couldn't really provide for a family in the space yet. I was talking about the need for some furniture for the place, to really become a part of Tehran life.

"Don't you want to have family over to see how well you are doing?" I asked him. "We can make new friends. We can tell Iran that we have arrived back home."

He seemed to consider this with eyebrows furrowed.

"If you just give me some money, and I can buy stuff," I continued.

"What do you need?" he said.

"We need a sofa and chairs, dining room furniture, bedroom stuff, this and that and everything."

He nodded. "I'll think about it," he said and left the apartment.

Later, I received a phone call and Ahmad said he'd taken care of it. Even over the phone line, I could tell his chest was puffed out with pride. I could expect something to be delivered later that day, he claimed. Curious and a little nervous, I opened the door to group of delivery men who brought up the ugliest sofa set I had ever set eyes on. But this took the prize: a blue velvet sofa set in the modern style, meaning very boxy and plain, and a set of chrome coffee tables.

If it was the last sofa on earth, I thought to myself, I would rather have sat on the floor. And it was so like Ahmad. Instead of understand-

ing that antiques and furniture that hearkened back to our Persian past
were ways of stating that your family was respected, rich and ancient,
he decided to purchase something new, crass, tacky and cheap. It was
the kind of furniture that was bought by those who had just fallen into
money and didn't know any better. It was something that men without the benefit of having a woman in their lives purchased. I shook my
head at the delivery men and tried to hold back tears.

Then I took a deep breath. I could handle this, I thought, thinking
back to how I'd made our American apartments pretty with little
money and a lot of work, or how I'd convinced Ahmad to buy an expensive color TV. I could make this work.

I thanked Ahmad for taking care of the sofa and told him that I
would try to outfit the rest of the house for the same amount of money
that he spent in that one room. He agreed and handed over some cash.
By pure coincidence, I had stumbled across an advertisement in a local newspaper, written in English for foreigners living in the city, that
stated the French ambassador was retiring and would be returning
home. Therefore, all his wife's beautiful and tasteful furnishings were
going to be on sale. I made an appointment to view the items.

Once I arrived, I took in the furniture and accessories with a sweep
of the eye and knew I had struck the jackpot. I agreed to buy almost
everything that was left at that point, including a dining room set made
in Spain with ornate woodwork and little bells hanging from the back
of the chairs, all of her delicate china and shining silverware, a huge,
curving bar of burgundy leather with a mahogany top, a bedroom set
for our bedroom, a desk set, a stylish recliner and more.

By the time we first had family over, the apartment seemed as put
together as if we'd lived there for many years and spent much more
money that we had. People gathered around the bar, which was artfully
placed in the corner. Ahmad enjoyed parting the sheer curtains I'd hung
around the washer and dryer to show guests those gleaming, modern
luxuries. We sat around the Spanish table eating Persian food off fancy
china platters with hand-painted flowers on them. In the corner of the

living room, a set of ugly, blue, modern sofas hid as best they could with new pillows and blankets I'd draped over them.

Our guests couldn't stop raving about the excellent job I had done. Here were a bunch of rich and important people — all the women in Ahmad's family had their own cars to drive around town, for example — and they were admiring my life and my home. My heart swelled that someone could see the good things I was capable of, my value as a wife and a mother. It irked me only a little that my husband puffed up under the flattery, too.

I saw Arian at a few parties and around town once or twice before I was able to meet with him again, to give him back the money that we had borrowed from him for the car. I felt awkward about the situation, partially because of the dirtiness of having to deal with money and also because of the brief interlude we had shared. No, nothing untoward had happened other than some intimate conversation, but it still felt illicit, secret and private, a memory that I didn't want polluted in any way.

Nonetheless, the need to pay back the good deed of my generous friend weighed upon me. Eventually, I called up his secretary and told him that I needed to see him.

As if he, too, didn't want to pollute the memory of our time together at the Chattanooga, we met in a different place, a restaurant equally as nice and well-known but in a different part of the city. He seemed to forget that I'd said on the phone that I needed to speak to him for a specific reason and began conversing as if this lunch was the same as any other.

His wife had given birth to their third child, another son. He spoke of how his wife continued to want to be married and have him serve his duty as a husband, even if he outright said how unhappy it made him. He spent a lot of time away from home for business, and that seemed to suit him fine. It seemed that Arian and his wife were stuck in the same partnership that Ahmad and I were: Neither was able to function well in society without the part that the other half did, making an uneasy partnership better than any place you'd be outside that partnership —

alone, powerless and half a person in the eyes of the traditional society around us.

While we spoke of ordinary things, the $5,000 — folded into an envelope in my purse — was burning a hole on my lap.

Then he started poking fun at my husband, which he did on occasion in a casual way. While perhaps stemming from jealousy, the small jokes weren't cruel.

"So how is the Mister?" he asked. "Still planning on becoming a somebody now that's he's back from big America?"

I smiled and spoke of my husband's new employment, in the budget and planning department of the government. I forgave Arian such subtle jibes at my husband. After all, I would have loved to make similar remarks about his wife but held back out of fear. While I had excellent people skills with the general public or in a workplace situation, with the people I was close with — whose opinion and love I valued — I always watched my step. I thought that words could be like steps across the frozen surface of a lake. One that lands too heavily could fracture the whole surface, ruining a whole relationship, and so I treaded carefully, lightly where I knew the ice was thin. Reserve and politeness were weapons against loss, in my opinion.

But the money was burning, so I gathered up my courage and took a step.

"I called because I have something for you," I said softly. The meal had been cleared away and we were sipping tea.

His eyebrows arched up in surprise. "Yes?" he asked, curious what gift I could have for him.

I reached into my purse and placed the thick envelope on the table cloth near his hand. He continued to look confused. I cleared my throat. "This is the money we borrowed from you," I continued. "To buy a car."

His eyebrows fell, along with his spirits. "We?" he asked, referring to how I'd said "we" to mean Ahmad and me. I opened my mouth to explain but he raised his hand to stop me. "I gave that money to you," he said, emphasizing the word "you" in this little game of words we had to play to express ourselves.

He pushed the money back across the table at me and urged me to put it away, to get it out of sight as quickly as possible. "Put it back in your purse," he said.

"No, I can't take it," I said. I pleaded with him with my eyes, hoping he could see the emotion behind the gesture.

"Don't be crazy," he said. "I don't need it." He took a long sip of tea, as if to give himself some time to think. It also allowed him to avert his eyes until I had hidden the envelope in my purse again.

"Thank you," I whispered.

He reached across the table to put his hand over mine, an intimate gesture we'd rarely attempted outside that one volatile afternoon in my apartment in Washington D.C. He still couldn't meet my eyes, though.

"And don't ever, ever mention it again," he said firmly.

I nodded, my eyes were heavy with tears for a reason I couldn't explain. Unlike other occasions, we left the restaurant quickly and separately that day.

Later, I handed the money back to my husband, whose face lit up like a children's arcade game that had just hit the jackpot.

"He said he couldn't take it back," I explained, my head was still heavy with trying to understand the complex exchange of words and emotion I'd experienced that afternoon.

"Oh, really?" Ahmad responded. He clicked his tongue, his face split open with a smile. "That's nice." The money disappeared into his back pocket, never to be seen or spoken of again.

Only after the weight left my palm did I realize how stupid I was. He would have never known if I'd put it in my own back pocket. When was I ever going to learn? When was I ever going to have some power of my own?

My husband was wearing suits and ties to work, going out to long lunches with the people — especially the pretty ladies — in his office. The house was pretty much in order. This was the time, I told myself. This was the time I had always looked forward to, my whole life spent waiting for the window of opportunity to open. Married, I could move through society freely. Having a child, I had the family off my back about my most important of wifely duties. And my other female responsibilities — supporting my husband through school, finding him a good job, creating a home for family togetherness and social entertaining — were all well in hand.

I woke up one morning to realize that this was one of those golden moments (or perhaps there would be only one?) where I could step up to the plate and live a life that was just for me. It had taken five years since that door shut behind me after high school graduation, a lot of hard work and pain, and a many unconventional choices, but I had arrived on the scene. The girl who had dreamed of standing in front of a judge as a lawyer to defend her fellow females was now a woman, stepping out into the world to defend herself — and make other women beautiful.

Now that I was back in Iran, I realized just how much beauty help was in demand. I always remembered how my father was very proud of me getting a beauty certificate and spoke of how a woman with such training could really succeed in Iran. Now, I was beginning to see where his optimism came from and to adopt that dream as my own.

For starters, I thought I might be able to get a job in Iranian television. While there weren't nearly as many opportunities in the whole country as there were in the one city of Washington D.C., there weren't as many trained make-up artists, either. Soon enough, I was able to find a television station that would hire me. However, the salary for the position was not enough.

Instead, I turned my goals toward the more conventional path of opening my own beauty salon, a brick-and-mortar shop where women could come to have their hair, nails and make-up done. And how many wouldn't love to know their stylist was trained in America, where all the latest styles came from? However, I ran into money troubles on that count, too. Such a shop had to be in a somewhat stylish neighborhood and a good location in order to attract the kind of clients who could make it a success, but such locations were not exactly inexpensive. Everywhere I went in Tehran, I was told rent would be very high.

After such a discouraging search for a location, I returned to our apartment building to find the downstairs neighbor, Jean-Pierre, in the lobby. A dashing and charming Frenchman, he commiserated with my trouble a little before a light appeared in his eyes.

"I have an idea!" he said. He explained that his girlfriend was coming to live him in Tehran, arriving in a few days. She happened to be an Englishwoman, an ex-flight attendant and a professional model. He went into some detail describing her beauty before adding, "You graduated from beauty school and she graduated from modeling school. These are similar things. Perhaps you can figure out something to do together."

I had no idea what that something could be, but I appreciated his enthusiasm. Besides, being the stylish young woman I was, I would want to meet such an interesting and beautiful woman anyway. So, I made plans with Jean-Pierre to meet with his girlfriend, Jenny, once she arrived.

Since he was a bachelor and my husband and son were rarely home during the day, I decided that I would make dinner for Jenny and Jean-Pierre the day Jenny arrived. Perhaps because of all the nice things Jean-Pierre had said about her in the lobby or because of my hope that this woman could help me become a huge success in Tehran, something inside of me wanted to impress this woman. After years of marriage and motherhood, my cooking had improved immensely, and I planned a gourmet spread for the guest of honor. Iranian rice was served along with a rich eggplant dish and special meatballs famous in Azerbaijan: A whole boiled egg was wrapped in meat along with raisins and berries and nuts. And then there was tea and sweets and an immaculately set table of French china.

When there was a knock on the door and Jenny appeared, I was very glad I had gone to such effort to impress her. She was truly everything that her boyfriend had said. Despite her lanky height, she walked gracefully across the room, her figure long and lean and thin. Her dress, I thought, was probably a size zero, but she still had curves in all the right places to show she was a mature woman. In her mid-20s, she was smooth-skinned and green-eyed and had a shaggy cut of blonde hair around her well-shaped features. She smiled with her full lips, and I couldn't picture this beautiful woman walking anywhere in the city without the heads of at least a dozen men snapping her direction. I would find out later that some men would even follow her around for blocks, trying to find out her name or just wanting to be close to her. And her Englishness didn't hurt either. She was the antithesis of most Persian women — tall and lean to their short, blonde to their black, white to their olive.

As we ate, I glanced across the table at her and tried not to stare. My mind was racing. How could I team up with this beautiful — and, I was finding, very personable and friendly — woman? Sure, I had the beauty certificate and training to make women more beautiful, but this Englishwoman was the archetype of beauty, the inspiration and hope of all women everywhere. I knew for a fact that in Iran — or perhaps it was human nature everywhere — customers always were drawn in by outward appearances. It didn't matter what or who was really working behind the scenes, how a person or a business presented itself was all that mattered. This, I thought, this woman was the icing on the cake, the face of the business that would bring people in the door and part them with their money.

But what kind of service would they be paying for?

Throughout the meal, my brain turned over the issue. The evening was more of a getting-to-know-you event than a business brainstorm, so I refrained from airing any ideas out loud. Instead, I simply told Jenny that I would love to team up with her somehow and that we both should be thinking of ideas. After some time to sleep on it, we arranged to meet the next afternoon in my apartment to go over some ideas.

She arrived wearing a mini jupe and her hair in curls, seeming to be effortlessly fresh and stylish. Her posture, whether in bare feet or high heels, was impeccable. In fact, she handled every object from a pencil to a glass of water with grace and poise. For a while, we spoke about our backgrounds. I told her that it had been my childhood dream to go to London, and I soaked up details of her life there gratefully. She was equally fascinated by my upbringing, focusing more on the luxury in-volved than the isolation.

A few hours went by in this way. Although we spoke more about ourselves than about possible money-making schemes, several ideas were bandied about and then shelved. Neither of us had any start-up money, after all, so most traditional businesses seemed out of reach. When we began to get frustrated, Jenny decided to make us a drink.

"Have you ever had one?" she asked of me, saying some fancy-sounding name for a drink that I had never heard before.

I shook my head.

"Well, you're going to love this. I can't believe these haven't made their way to Iran yet," she continued, loping downstairs to her apart-ment for a few ingredients. When she came back, she had a pretty glass pitcher and glasses and mixed vodka, lemon juice, other fruit juices and I had no idea what else. With an elegant flick of the wrist, she stirred the liquid together and poured two glasses.

I took a sip of the sweet mixture and closed my eyes in pleasure. "This is delicious," I exclaimed. "It tastes like dessert." I took another drink. "In Iran, some people don't drink alcohol at all, of course," I said. "But lots of men, when they do drink, just have the alcohol straight."

"They just take shots of it?" she asked, giggling incredulously.

"Oh, yes," I said, miming the action of throwing back a small glass of vodka. She laughed again.

"Well that's a little crass," she replied, sipping her own drink. Relax-ing into the alcohol a little, I watched her as she drank. She was wear-ing pink lipstick that really highlighted her skin tone, which made me think of something else I wanted to share.

"And the women," I continued. "You've seen their heavy, red lip-stick, right?"

"Like there are three or four coats of it? Oh, yes."

"Well, the glasses at parties are just crusted with red lipstick by the end of the night at a gathering," I explained.

Jenny clucked her tongue.

Jenny took another sip of her drink and the thought returned to me that her elegance and grace seemed so natural, as if she'd been born lovely and cultured.

"Who taught you to be so elegant and mannered?" I asked. "Is every English girl taught?"

"Mothers always teach things, just like they do here, I guess. But I was taught many things about how to carry yourself and how to speak in modeling school," she explained. "A few tricks of the trade, if you will. Otherwise, I guess you just learn these things throughout your life, right?"

I froze for a moment to let an idea wash over me. Jenny must have seen the change in my posture, because she stopped and said, "What is it, Maryam?"

"Do you think women would pay to have someone teach them?"

"What do you mean?" Jenny asked.

I explained to her that I had heard about a business in Washington D.C. called the Power School, where ladies could take classes to become better women. In other words, the Power School taught them how to throw dinner parties, educated them on how to be a good conversationalist, and taught different languages in some cases. They also offered beauty, grooming and fashion classes, where experts would help a lady look her best.

"If women in America, who already are so much more connected than Persian woman, still need such instruction, imagine how many Iranian women would want to go to something like a Power School," I thought out loud. "After all, the Shah of Iran is always talking about how going to boarding school in Switzerland helped him learn the manners and traditions of Europe, which makes having good relations with the rest of the world easier. There are a lot of women out there who could use having their eyes opened, too."

"Yes," Jenny agreed. "Their heavily powdered eyes."

We both laughed, thinking of the women we saw everyday whose make-up looked like an overdone version of something on American television, caked with foundation and blue eye shadow.

"This is something we could do," I said to Jenny.

She stopped laughing and looked serious again, a little bit of hope pulling up the corners of her smile. "You mean we could run a Power School?"

"You could teach posture, hostessing and manners, while I could handle the beauty related stuff," I explained.

"It's really quite perfect," she agreed. "I can't believe someone hasn't thought of this before. It's so simple."

"All the best ideas are!"

"A toast then," Jenny suggested. We held up our fruity drinks. "Here's to bringing the worthy ladies of Iran some of our worldly expertise. Cheers!"

Our glasses clinked together and our hearts lifted. I thought we were on to something here, something big. And I didn't think it was just the vodka going to my head, either.

Chapter Eighteen

Excited about our idea, Jenny and I poured over our old school books, mine from the Washington Beauty Academy and hers from her English modeling school. The ideas poured out like rain once we got started. We could give each woman individual attention, making her feel like a princess. We could give Iranian women the same experience and nuance of their fellow women who had spent one or two years abroad.

We crafted posters and took notes, outlining a full curriculum of study that would help an upper class woman be a better asset to herself, her husband and her family. Our eyes and hope grew wide with the thought of how much good such a program could do.

We still ran into some of the same old problems, however: Where would we hold such classes? How would we pay for a high-class location for high-class women? How would we attract clients?

Our hopes sagged back to earth a little bit with the weight of the necessary arrangements and our mutual lack of resources. But I told Jenny that fortune had thrown the two of us together, and that fortune might just throw the other ingredients needed for success into our laps, as well. What we needed, I thought, was a patron of sorts: someone who already had a location or could find us one, or an investor who would help us get the business off the ground. Once airborne, I knew it would really take off.

Because Jenny and Jean-Pierre socialized much more than Ahmad and I did, I told her to keep her eyes and ears open for such a person and such an opportunity. At that time in Iran, oil money had changed life for the richest. While many people, mostly poorer people, continued to be strict Muslims, drank no alcohol and had trouble making ends meet, it wasn't uncommon for the richest of the rich to drive Ferraris and Jaguars around town, patronize clubs where go-go dancers strutted around half naked, publicly drank even hard liquor and attended wild parties that raged into the night. Everything was moving so fast, everything was so flashy, and I threw Jenny into the mix to find someone or something that could help us move our plan forward.

Fate was on our side. Not three days after we'd formulated our plan, Jenny knocked loudly on my door in the early morning hours.

"Open up!" I could hear her say through the thick wood of the door. "I have to tell you something."

I wiped the sleep out of my eyes and let her inside. Her cheeks were bright pink with excitement and the words tumbled out of her mouth, as if she couldn't hold them back any longer.

"I found a place!" she exclaimed. "Yes, they want to take 25 percent of our profits from the start but there's a stage and an office to conduct business in and a big room for the actual classes. And it's no money to start, so 25 percent isn't unheard of. It's just perfect."

"Slow down," I told her. "You found a place? Where?"

She stopped to smile mysteriously, as if I couldn't possibly fathom the quality of location she'd arranged for our fledgling company. She lowered her voice and spoke very clearly, as if afraid I wouldn't believe her words. "The Ice Palace," she said, and her smile widened.

My jaw dropped open. "The Ice Palace?" I asked. In my mind, I pictured the location she was talking about, a beautiful new building — actually, it was more of an arena than a building, a gathering place and a shopping center all in one — centered on Iran's first-ever ice rink. Rich children took ice skating lessons and rich couples floated around the ice for fun on evenings and weekends. Around the ice, luxury shops and boutiques gave mothers something to spend their money on while the kids had fun and nice restaurants offered good food and hot drinks to warm you up after skating. Most importantly, the Ice Palace was very exclusive, meaning members only. You not only had to have money, but also connections in order to ever see the inside of glamorous Ice Palace. People seemed to be willing to do or pay almost anything to see that exotic ice and be a part of one of the most exclusive clubs in the country. "The Ice Palace," I repeated. "Really?"

Jenny nodded and explained how she had met the owner at a party the night before. He'd really taken to the idea of a beauty and grooming school, and thought that he could provide room for the school in the complex. Most importantly, he could see that the idea could be very profitable — and he wanted a 25-percent cut of the pie.

"The Ice Palace," Jenny said.

"The Ice Palace," I repeated.

Then we giggled like school girls, hugged one another and jumped up and down in the entryway of my apartment, walking on air that such a perfect opportunity had found us so fortuitously. John wandered in from the living room and began to jump up and down with us, too young to know what was going on but ready to be excited nonetheless.

That evening, the owner had told Jenny that we should come by the Ice Palace and speak to his manager, the man who handled the day-to-day operations of club. Having only known the club by reputation and never dreaming I would ever see past the doors, I took extra care with my clothes and make-up that day, determined to make a good impression. If these men, very powerful men, were going to take our idea seriously, we needed to look like the type of women who could teach other women to be better. Especially in a culture where women weren't taken very seriously in the public sphere, we had to look, talk, act and be flawless.

From the hot, dirty and bustling street, we walked through glass doors into the Ice Palace. Instantly, it was as if the world outside had disappeared. Air conditioned air filled my lungs and my eyes were greeted with smartly dressed employees at the entrance who politely checked membership credentials. The carpet was thick and every inch of space — the tops of tables placed against walls, tying back the curtains, on every space of brightly painted walls — was some sort of ornamentation. Gold plating, rich mahogany, silk carpets: Everything was of the highest quality and just screamed money.

In English, Jenny explained to the employees who we were and that we were expected by the manager. I just tried to keep my jaw from falling open. Our high heels made no noise in the thick carpet as we were then led down a few hallways, where I could catch a glimpse of the ice arena itself, which was newly polished by the fancy ice machine and gleamed like diamonds. There were doors that led to saunas and rows and rows of exercise equipment.

We introduced ourselves and the manager was kind but efficient, getting right to the point. "I'm told that we will keep track of all the money coming in and that we will get 25 percent of the profits off the top," he began. "We will need a list of all your students to leave at the door, of course, and can't have any non-paying customers enter the facility. If you have need of an office to work in or interview customers, I will allow you the use of this room anytime after 6 p.m. as long as you notify me in advance. Does this all sound correct? I'm afraid we wouldn't be comfortable doing it any other way."

It turned out I was nervous and worried over nothing. Obviously, the decision had been made at the top and approved, and this man simply had to put all the ducks in a row. I should have known better. So much of Iran's business dealings happened over cocktails at fashionable parties.

"No, no," I quickly reassured him. "That's all perfectly acceptable. We don't mind." I translated what the man had said to Jenny, who didn't speak Farsi, and she agreed with me.

"It's settled then," the manager said. How easy it all is, I thought to myself. He reached his hand across the desk to shake each of our hands. Once the handshake was complete and business was done, the manager smiled and relaxed into his chair.

I walked into a dream when I walked into that room. To anyone else, it would have been just a big, empty room. One wall of windows looked down onto the gleaming ice and another wall of windows looked out over the city. In my mind, I was already dressing it up and filling it with excited women — women who would fill my own pocket up with money. I turned to look at Jenny and she, too, was agape and her eyes glazed over with wonder at our luck.

The manager asked in Farsi. "And when do you need this all completed by?"

"Two weeks," I said quickly and confidently, although I hadn't even considered the amount of time we'd need until that very moment.

"Very good," he said. "And how many students do you have?"

"None," I replied in that same easy, confident manner. "But give me two weeks, sir, and we'll have enough students to fill this room and more on the waiting list.

He raised his eyebrows as he made another note. "Very good," he repeated.

I took a deep breath. Finding an opportunity was the hardest part, I reminded myself. Now that we had that firmly in hand, all it was going to take was lots of hard work, and I knew that hard work was something I excelled in.

Where to begin?

We had to advertise.

Of course, I knew very little about advertising in the business sense of the word. I had neither formal business training nor a background in how to market an idea. However, we were trying to target women, and women were something I did know a little bit about. Not only was I a prime female myself, I had also been cloistered among mostly females my whole life, at home and at beauty school and in the beauty salon and even in social situations in Iran, where men stuck with men and women with women. How did I and the women I know find out about things we wanted to try or buy?

An idea rushed into my head with the speed of a train, an idea that brought parts of my life full circle again. We would advertise in Women's Day Magazine. Perfect! Women's Day was the most popular women's magazine in Iran. Almost every female in the country regularly poured over its pages, and the articles and pictures were subjects of girlish conversations for days after each issue arrived. I had named

John — Omid — after a character that appeared in the magazine, and one of the biggest events of my young life, the beauty contest, would never have occurred without Women's Day.

I got on the phone right away and asked to speak to someone about placing an ad. At first the woman I spoke to wasn't very helpful. "You are trying to start what kind of business?" she asked. "I don't understand."

"It depends on what the ad is going to look like and where it's placed in the issue, but, well, yeah," she said. "But I don't know. You must talk to someone else in advertising to get it worked out. Let me take down your name and number and I'll have someone that can help you give you a call back."

"Okay," I said, my voice a disappointed squeak.

Half an hour after I spoke to the girl at the magazine who had bruised my hopes, the phone rang.

"Is this Maryam?" the female voice on the other end of the line asked. The voice was mature and older, but refined and elegant.

"Yes," I said.

"Is this our Maryam? The very Maryam whose picture has been on our pages? Who almost won our beauty contest a few years ago?"

I pressed the phone closer to my ear, wondering what I was hearing. I sat down on the couch in confusion, my eyebrows furrowed over my nose. "Yes," I repeated. "Who is this?"

She laughed. "I just saw your name sitting here waiting for someone in advertising to call back and I knew it was you! I hope you remember me as clearly as I remember you. I judged your pageant, silly girl."

My jaw dropped open. The voice on the other end of the line was none other than the woman I had always thought of as the queen's reporter. She'd once whispered the news that I was a finalist into my ear and dazzled me with her charm and elegance.

"But of course I do!" I exclaimed. "How fortunate. I never even thought I would call the magazine and get to speak to you!"

"It is a happy coincidence," she agreed. She explained that she had seen the message with my name on it and spoken to the girl I had talked to earlier. In exchange, I explained the reason I had called, that I was starting a version of the Power School and wanted to place an ad. I told her all about Jenny and the Ice Palace, and how the cost of placing an ad had really discouraged me.

"I know this. I've heard of this kind of school," she said. "This is such a wonderful idea."

"Forget about a tiny little ad," she said to me. Her tone was conspiratorial, as if she was winking at me over the phone lines. "I can do so much better," she continued. "I just have to clear it with the publisher, but I think they are going to eat this idea up."

"What idea?" I asked.

"Don't pay any money. I want to see both you and Jenny in the lobby of the Continental Hotel tomorrow afternoon to have a cup of coffee and talk. Well, to have an interview. Why have a tiny little ad for so much money when you can have a big, interesting article for no cost at all?"

I didn't know what to say to her generosity. She'd breathed new life into my dream and opened yet another door, continuing our chain of unbelievable luck. Never, ever had a quest for something I wanted gone so smoothly. And of all the women in the world to throw her support behind our idea, the queen's reporter was a writer and a personality that Persian women knew and respected, the perfect spokesperson to introduce the school to the world.

This time, it was my turn to run downstairs and bang on Jenny's door with fabulous news. "Jenny! Get out here!" I yelled. "You won't believe it!"

The door opened a crack and Jenny stood there expectant, her face open to hear anything that I might say. When I told her the news, her jaw dropped open and she began jumping up and down in happiness. We joined hands and jumped together, not caring about how silly we looked. Our happiness bubbled over and had nowhere else to go except our smiles and our exuberant jumping.

The next day, we arrived at the Continental Hotel in high style. Jenny wore a beautiful yellow dress that skimmed the floor and set off the highlights in her golden hair. I was dressed in an elegant white suite with black lining. My shoulders were draped in a silver mink cape to keep off the chill of that Tehran day.

The queen's reporter was exactly as I remembered her, the kind of woman who grabbed your attention and respect in any situation, smooth and polished as a pearl fresh from the ocean. We sipped tea and talked in a very informal way, about what had happened in my life since the pageant, about her career in Iran, about Jenny's background in modeling. And then we got down to business, discussing our school and its chances for success.

"I just think it's such an excellent idea," said the reporter. "I have a heart full of pain for some of these Persian women in Tehran. Just the other day, I was having dinner and a woman was drinking her soup at the table, slurping it up like it was a beverage. And she was such a nice girl when I spoke to her. Just rough is all. And then there are those who think they've picked up manners from the television just because they drink their tea like this." She demonstrated, holding her little pinky up in the air and making a funny face.

We all laughed.

The reporter switched to Farsi so she could speak to me semi-privately. "She's such a beautiful girl," she said about Jenny. "Where on earth did you find her?"

"She's my neighbor, actually."

"Well she's quite a find. She's just the thing for the face of this business."

"I was thinking the same thing," I replied. "If in this article," I continued, "you could not mention my name, I think that would be for the best. Just use Jenny's name and face. That's what will draw them in."

"Of course," she said.

The next week, the article appeared in the magazine. I poured over every word and read it aloud in English for Jenny. "It's in fashion in Iran," the reporter wrote, "for ladies of means to improve themselves in every possible way. They attend French language classes or learn how to play tennis, for instance. But now two young ladies are bringing a new class to the ladies of Tehran, a class from which they will benefit much more than from tennis lessons, a class all about how to be the best possible woman."

The reporter went on to describe some of the tacky and almost rude behavior of some women who don't know the rules of polite society and the beauty mistakes that can be seen all over the city. Tongue in cheek, the reporter was able to namelessly criticize powerful ladies. And yet, her words didn't anger. In fact, the article made the reader wonder if she wasn't the one being described and fear that she was doing something tasteless without even realizing it. In other words, it was perfect.

After describing Jenny and "Jenny's Iranian friend," she talked about how well dressed we were at the interview and how impeccable and attractive our behavior was. "Cosmopolitan beauties were what the ladies were, and if all Persian women could take a page from their book, what a beautiful and charming city ours would be."

At the end, the reporter explained that we were beginning our first round of classes at the elegant Ice Palace in only one week and listed the contact information for anyone interested in signing up.

It was the day of John's third birthday party — January 4— and I was busy cooking and preparing the house for the event, which was going to be a large and festive gathering even by Iranian standards. There was boiling sauces and rattling pans and the clanking of plates and platters being readied. And to top it all off, the phone began to ring.

"Yes, I'm calling about the school I read about in Women's Day," the first woman to call said.

"Yes, of course," I replied, wiping my hands on a nearby towel. "We're holding registration interviews on Thursday and I may be able to squeeze you in. What's the name?"

I wrote down her name and number on the first page of a little notebook I used for phone messages.

"When does the class begin? And how much exactly is the session?" she asked nervously, her voice a little excited.

"It will all be covered in the registration, ma'am," I assured her, trying to sound like a professional receptionist sitting at a desk instead of a harried mother, running around trying to set up a kid's birthday party.

"Thank you," she said. "Until Thursday."

I placed the phone back in its receiver only to have it ring at me before my hand could return to my side.

"Hello?"

"Is this the right number for the Women's Day school?" a female voice asked.

"Yes, ma'am," I replied and repeated the same information about the registration interviews. There were then two names in my little notebook.

Guests began to arrive for the party and still the phone would not stop ringing. So I grabbed a few of my sisters-in-law and made them take turns manning the phone, pretending they were only an answering service for the school and taking down names and numbers. "Thursday," I told them. "Tell them that the school will call them back to make an appointment for Thursday.

The phone continued to ring until almost midnight. At the end of the evening, my little book had a list of 160 names and numbers. I called back every single one of them. Some ladies had changed their minds or were unsure, others couldn't wait to begin the classes, and I made appointment after appointment for Thursday evening after 6 p.m., when the manager said we could use the office for our own purposes.

A few furiously busy days passed in preparation and then Jenny and I dressed up to the nines again to head down to the Ice Palace, butterflies flapping around in our stomachs.

"I'm nervous," Jenny admitted as we walked into the office to prepare.

"Just stay professional and confident," I told her. "The rest will take care of itself." I wished that I had the confidence of my own words in my heart, but as with so many other challenges I'd faced, I just squared my shoulders and took a deep breath. "Professional and confident," I repeated.

We went about making the office look like ours, as if our business had been running and successful for some time and wasn't some shoe-string operation. We took the pictures of the manager's wife and children and slid them into a drawer, replacing them with framed pictures from Jenny's modeling days and other beautiful women from magazines. I took out a few of our new business cards and fanned them out on the desk. Jenny designed the logo — the silhouette of a woman in a graceful, wide-brimmed hat with very delicate features, her chin perched on her gloves — and we'd finally agreed upon a name: Naz-Bonu. The Farsi word Naz-Bonu is difficult to translate, much like the French phrase *savoir faire*. The word connotes a certain sophistication and sexiness, an attraction for sure, but an attraction with an element of coyness or playing hard to get. Naz-Bonu is beauty on a level above everything else, somewhat untouchable. It was the quality that every woman who attended our class was hoping to learn. It was something that every woman strived to be.

Before the first woman arrived, we arranged two chairs behind the desk. I would sit in the center because I would have to translate. Jenny would sit to the side, where she could stand up to answer the door and shake hands, showing herself again as the beautiful face of our school.

Tall and short, fat and thin, young and old, a parade of women came through the Ice Palace office that night. We sat them down and put them at ease, asked them a little bit about themselves. Every single one came forward with some complaint or some little issue they needed help with:

"I'm worried about my hair. It never styles the way I want it to."

"Look at this dress! I have nothing that flatters me."

"I'm sick of looking the same way for the last 10 years!"

"We are going abroad, and I am so worried I'm going to make a fool of myself."

These were women whose names I had known, who circulated in the highest circles of Persian society. They were the wives of government officials, oil men and factory owners. They wore thousand dollar shoes and imported purses from Italy.

We sat down to tell them more about the program — or at least, the few details Jenny and I had worked out in the whirlwind of the last few days. This included that the class would be once a week for three hours for so many weeks and the total fee for the class. Those interested didn't have to pay the whole fee but only a deposit. A large deposit: 2,500 toman. To put the amount in perspective, a normal office worker in that day and age would be happy to pull in a paycheck of 2,000 toman a month. Yet these ladies whipped out the money as if it was nothing. Some counted off the bills from crisp stacks of cash they kept in their purses.

By the end of the evening, Jenny and I had collected 75,000 toman.

And cash in hand, suddenly it was so very real. All the freedom and success and sophistication I had dreamed of since I was a little girl were in my hand, in my power. A window had opened and a fresh breeze blew through my life, making me feel drunk with happiness.

That moment, looking at one another over the money and alternately staring in disbelief and laughing incredulously, belonged only to us. It was our time. It was my time.

It was finally my time.

Chapter Nineteen

"Now, everyone takes a lipstick and finds her own face shape in the mirror," I said in Farsi to our first group of students. They pushed back their chairs from the U-shaped table and arranged themselves in front of the mirrored classroom wall. "Now take the lipstick and outline your own face right on the mirror." Some of the women looked at me curiously, others murmured, but all were enchanted with this strange and novel game. They drew with the concentration of master artists and then stood back from their work, wondering what it all meant.

Jenny walked up to one woman's lipstick shape and outlined it with her finger. Then, she took her own lipstick and made a stylized heart shape.

"You see, every face has a unique shape and a unique way of making that shape beautiful," I continued. I knew many of the women thought I was translating Jenny word-for-word, that she was the real instructor even though this was my area of expertise. But it didn't matter. It was all in the presentation, it was all about selling the glamour.

"Your face is obviously a heart shape," I said, pointing out the tapering to the chin. "Now, this shape over here, on the other hand, is obviously oval." Jenny had moved down the line, making small ovals, triangles and hearts next to each woman's mirror drawing.

"Have you ever tried another person's beauty techniques, just to have them look unattractive on you, even though the same tricks make your friend gorgeous?" Many women around the room nodded in commiseration. "Well, this simple face-shape exercise will help you know which techniques are right for you, including how to shape your eyebrows and where to place your make-up. We're going to help you maximize your personal shape, bringing out your natural beauty from within. Congratulations, ladies. You have the first part of your customized beauty plan."

The women smiled and a few even clapped, pleased to be so entertained and pampered. For each face type, Jenny and I handed out prepared flyers I had created from my Washington Beauty Academy textbooks and experience. Like a paint-by-numbers game, the women could take home the flyer to help them apply their make-up everyday in the most flattering way. And of course, keep their eyeliner and eye shadow within the bounds of taste. Seeing only the overdone stage make-up of television and movie actors, so many of the women applied far too much color on their faces, making them look garish in afternoon sunlight. It was our goal to tone down and soften the edges of these already beautiful women, to take their uncertainty about their status, wealth and beauty and turn it into feminine confidence.

Bringing them the latest in beauty from Europe and America was also a huge component of Naz-Bonu, too. Thanks to all the publicity surrounding the school, Jenny and I made contacts within Estee Lauder and Revlon. We were able to get great prices on products never before imported into Iran, such as the latest in liquid foundation and concealer — a vast improvement over the thick, often irritating powdered mixtures many Persian women still used. And the make-up came in a wide range of skin tones to suit the coloring of any Persian woman, who could run the gamut from dark olive to a light almond color.

We set up a lighted make-up mirrors in front of each of our valued and pampered students — another luxury from abroad that I had ordered through GE in America, which the students would take home as a gift once the class was complete. Each woman was given five or six different shades of foundation. We instructed them to paint a small strip of each foundation on their arms and then examine the colors under the artificial lamps and then in natural sunlight.

"Many women think they should try to change their coloring through make-up," I lectured. "How many of your have tried to use a foundation that's lighter than you're actual skin color?" A few embarrassed hands went up, though I knew from experience that many others were probably guilty of the same beauty sin. I remembered my mother and a friend of hers trying to blend an almost white foundation onto their faces, winding up looking clown-like and silly.

"It's OK to admit it," I continued. "No woman grows up just knowing these things. We have to learn them, just as we learn to read and write or drive a car. That's why we're here, ladies, and this is a place where you will not be judged, only improved."

I walked up to one woman and looked at the strips of color on her arm. "It looks like this shade will be perfect for you," I said, pointing to the third one out of the many shades. The woman picked up the bottle of the color I referred to and looked nervous about the hue. "Don't worry," I told her. "You'll see the difference right away."

I helped her smooth on the new foundation, explaining to the class what tools and techniques I was using as I went along. When I was finished, I allowed her to look in the mirror and she was amazed. Jenny began to talk about how natural and radiant the woman looked, how much younger with just that small step complete. The woman beamed under Jenny's translated comments.

As the rest of the women choose their foundation shades and practiced application, Jenny and I wandered around helping. After a while, I took a moment to look out the glass window down to the ice rink, where John was skating away with the private ice-skating instructor I'd hired to watch him. While they didn't work, all my sisters-in-law and the General's wife claimed to be too busy to watch my son when I taught the three-hour class every Thursday. I suspected they just didn't want to get tied up in the school, with this controversial "women's work" I was involved in. I'd accepted their excuses and turned my head away, my back tall and proud in the knowledge that I would find a way around this obstacle, and I had. John was happy playing on the ice for a few hours and was safe under a watchful eye. I even paid the instructor extra to take him to one of the Ice Palace restaurants for snacks afterwards until I could come pick him up.

Jenny and I had been very nervous about filling up an entire curriculum with beauty, grooming and manners tips, especially once we had all that money. There were so many students and we had no idea what we were going to teach them. But once we set down to our task, I was amazed at how much knowledge we could impart to these women.

From foundation, we moved on to make-up color palates, which shades of eye shadow and blush and lipstick suited each woman. We covered day and evening styles and the importance of not overdoing it. Then, we went into how to take care of the skin underneath the make-up to keep it young, fresh and moisturized. Jenny and I made sure to help each woman individually during each class, and the women loved the personal attention we lavished on them.

We tackled hair next: which products would keep your hair healthy, how to cut your hair to suit your face shape, ways to make it curly or straight, formal styles for special occasions. Many of our students had never attempted to style their own hair, instead keeping with the tradition of going to the beauty shop to have it set in stiff, ornate and old-fashioned styles, which would last for a day or two before needing to be set again. It was an expensive and time-consuming process that often left them with something not quite what they had wanted. We brought in electric hot rollers — another gift ordered from abroad — and put the power back in their own hands.

Most of the beauty lessons were directly from my own experience, but Jenny played a large role, too. We used the Ice Palace's stage to host a sort of fashion show, where the women could try on many things to see what styles and colors suited them. We practiced walking down the stage gracefully and proud, even in the highest of heels.

Jenny introduced topics of manners, such as the correct tone of voice to use at parties, ways to strike up conversation with important people. We set up elaborate tables as if for a party to teach the difference between glasses and forks. One of the best lessons involved a full bar and a fancy cocktail set, when Jenny taught the ladies how to make a few basic drinks that would wow guests.

We always kept in mind that these women were not in need of money or beauty. Most of them had plenty of both, but were simply unskilled in how to use them properly. They had the money to spend on the symbols of power — cars, jewelry and clothes, for example — but so many had become so rich so fast, they had no idea how to do things tastefully at the same time.

After the classes really got off the ground, Jenny and I didn't have a problem with money either. We set aside the 25 percent the Ice Palace was owed from the beginning and divided up everything else in half, fifty-fifty. And because the classes were only held once a week for six weeks, we had plenty of time in which to spend that money.

Jean-Pierre was thrilled for Jenny, but they weren't married, so she had an incredible amount of money for a single girl. She began flying to Europe two or three times a month to go shopping for Italian designer purses or French designer shoes. Estee Lauder not only gave us discounted or free cosmetics, they also invited Jenny to be one of their models, an "Estee Lauder girl" as we called them. She was photographed for advertisements and traveled around the country at their expense for promotions. In England, Jenny's modeling career was hard won — there were so many similar beauties to compete with. But in Iran, she was exotic and one of a kind.

Life in my home didn't change too much, including the fact that I still deferred to my husband on money matters, even though it was *my* money free and clear.

"We're short on funds," he would demand. "Give me some of your cash for expenses for the week." And I would comply.

"My family is coming over for dinner tonight," he'd tell me, knowing that I would have to buy food and refreshments out of my own pocket — and that I would feel compelled to buy nice things to show off for his family. He began to invite them over almost every night, it seemed, to eat us out of lamb and kebabs.

I gave over everything he asked of me, yet I still had money left over with which to indulge in feminine pleasures, the kinds of things that Ahmad couldn't begrudge me if I paid for them myself. I had Jenny bring me a $2,000 purse from Italy and clothed myself in Chanel and Dior. I could attend parties — even the gatherings of a friend who worked in television — and never feel that I was being looked down upon or pitied. In fact, I often felt like the belle of the ball in Charles Jordan shows from France and the newest shade of lipstick, never seen in the country except on my lips.

And I had a passion for jewelry. Every time I visited my family in Tabriz — where the artisans are famous for their beautiful work — I came home with some other expensive bauble: a diamond necklace, pendants, earrings and rings. I cherished the traditional pieces, antiques and hand-crafted items over the size of the stones or the amount of gold, relishing each tiny, hand-forged link in the chain of a bracelet.

But still, they were very expensive and valuable items — an expense I was glad to make. Jewelry and gold, you see, have always been the value of a woman. Girls are given gold coins and rings when they get married, items they are supposed to keep to support themselves in the worst-case scenario that a marriage goes wrong. Husbands shower their wives with jewelry during the marriage, too, and the value of such pieces is indicative of the woman's value in general, to society and among her friends and family.

Ahmad had never given a real gift of this nature and I'd always felt like less of a woman because of it. Now, I was showering myself with worthiness and esteem, which was somehow more rewarding than something given to me by a man. In my mind, I was somehow getting richer by buying more jewelry. I was protecting myself.

I was making it on my own — a woman who ran a business, a business with only female customers. I had family and friends who disapproved, and there had been some negative press about the school, but the jewelry made me feel better, as if I matched on the outside how good I felt on the inside. I felt as if I had taken the hard years in America, my schooling and my experience, and I'd taken what I knew to the highest possible level. I felt the same joy I imagined when I was a young girl, dreaming about what job and what destiny awaited me outside the cloistered walls of childhood and Iranian tradition. And I did it all on my own, without sacrificing my womanhood.

After the first six-week cycle of classes was complete, Naz-Bonu had a graduation party of sorts, a dinner in one of the Ice Palace restaurants. That whole evening of fun and frivolity — the women looking and acting so much more polished and confident than they had when they'd arrived — all Jenny and I heard were compliments about the class. A chorus of unhappy women who'd asked for help had become a group of lovely ladies who couldn't tell us thank you enough. They thanked us for the time and money they saved at the beauty parlor, for how their husbands found them so attractive, how they were going to move up in society by throwing more parties now et cetera.

Jenny and I glowed under their compliments and I honestly told those women that I had enjoyed it just as much as they had. They say when you find the job you are meant to do, you'll realize it because work will feel more like fun. My heart burst with happiness that I could change the lives of so many women — who left with their mirrors and hot rollers to their new, improved lives — and enjoy myself so much in the process.

And yes, the money didn't hurt either. I had the funds to hire a private car just for Thursdays to take John and me to and from the Ice Palace. I'd stare out the window and remember the days I wasn't able to leave the apartment because I didn't have money for a cab, or even the bus. I sat back in the cushy seat and gave thanks for the blessings in my life and the great luck that had allowed me to build something so personal and so successful, something beyond my wildest dreams.

After a few months off, Jenny and I started a second round of registrations. And we continued hosting Naz-Bonu classes into the year 1978.

The first few months of 1978 had other surprises in store, too. Political surprises.

Like many families of the day and of my social standing, we didn't pay too much attention to politics, or religion. Our family followed Islam in theory, but none of us could read or understand the Koran and we rarely attending the mosque. But beginning in January with a few protests against the rule of the Shah of Iran — Mohammad Reza Pahlavi — politics and religion began to be something that permeated life in Iran, something we were not able to ignore.

Around that time, Jenny and I had been approached about planning a series of lessons for the wives of government ambassadors and dignitaries traveling abroad. The queen's reporter had mentioned me to the queen herself, who noted that many of the women who went abroad on their husband's governmental business were woefully unprepared to interact with Western culture. Jenny and I drew up plans to research the customs of the different countries to give each wife a crash course in the manners and decorum that would help her — and Iran's foreign policy, really — when they went abroad.

Over the course of the year, however, little changes crept into even my everyday existence to let me know that my country was changing, turning inward and away from the Western world I'd always loved.

For instance, one day I entered a small grocery store in my neighborhood to find a woman in distress. She was young, probably in her mid to late twenties, with dark brown hair and dark eyes. She was standing in front of the clerk's counter and she seemed frustrated, perhaps even near tears. At first, I thought there was just some misunderstanding. Then I heard her trying to speak Farsi with a heavy accent, as if the language was unfamiliar and heavy in her mouth. I looked at her again. Though she could have passed for Persian with her dark coloring, I thought she might just be American.

I stepped up behind her at the counter to pay for my groceries and — sure enough — I heard her speak a few words of English about how frustrating the situation was. Then she spoke again to the man in her broken Farsi.

"Do you speak English?" she asked. The man shook his head but was smiling, as if taunting her.

"I want ..." She repeated the word two or three times, some word that was not really Farsi, but her mispronunciation of it. But it was very close to the word for asparagus, which it looked like she was pointing to on the shelf behind the clerk.

He continued to smile and shake his head. "I do not understand you. I cannot help you if you can't say what it is you need," he said to her, again with a slight mocking tone.

She sighed in exasperation, and anger leapt in my chest. What right did he have to treat her so dismissively? Just because she was a foreigner — a "meddling American" as some saw them? Here she was trying to give this man business and trying to speak our difficult language, and he was just sadistically watching the young woman squirm.

"Listen, now!" I raised my voice at the clerk, whose smile vanished as he met my angry eyes and perfect Farsi. "The woman just wants some asparagus, and if you had at least tried to understand her and be helpful, you would know that. Just give her a can of asparagus and let her go on her way, please."

He stood frozen looking at me.

"Thank you," I said coolly, even though he'd yet to move. But then he shrugged his shoulders and grabbed the asparagus, rang up the American woman and gave her proper change. She said thank you to him in Farsi.

He rang up the few things I bought with a sour face.

"You speak English?" the woman asked me, still lingering beside me.

"Oh yes," I replied. "I lived in America for a few years while my husband was in school."

She tilted her head, a little shy, but then said, "You really yelled at him, didn't you?"

I took my change from the man and laughed. "Yes. You were just trying so hard and it looked like he was just toying with you for fun. That's no way to treat someone just because they're an American."

She sighed and nodded. "I'm here with my husband, and it's definitely not been easy," she said. She flipped back some of her hair from her face. "It's just so good to be able to talk to someone who understands me, not to stumble over words and feel so embarrassed, you know?"

"Oh yes, I know," I agreed. I put out my hand. "Hello. My name is Maryam," I said.

"I'm Debbie," she said.

We stood out on the sidewalk of the market for some time chatting and comparing notes. She was from South Carolina, had a daughter about John's age as well as a son and lived within a few blocks of my apartment. She also had another American friend named Kristy in the same situation, with a husband working, who had two kids. Both men traveled a lot, leaving their wives to fend for themselves in a foreign and increasingly hostile country. Within moments, Debbie and I had exchanged phone numbers and I promised to make my new American friends a traditional Persian lunch and tea the next time their husbands were out on assignment.

The political situation worsened as the months went by. That summer, an American representative of President Carter's administration visited the Shah to try to dispel the situation, but to no avail. Instead, demonstrations by the Shah's opposition and violence by the SAVAK (real or imaginary) continued. Demonstrations with thousands of participants — most of them not attired or representing themselves as Islamic fundamentalists — crowded the television news almost every night. People were killed during these demonstrations when the Shah ordered the army to fire upon the crowd. Then in the first months of 1979, the Shah left Iran, going into exile at the demand of the prime minister, who declared he would head up a new government by himself.

John was in first grade at that time and I was at home waiting for him to arrive from school. Instead, I heard his voice from downstairs through an open window.

"Mom! Mom!"

Concerned and confused, I anxiously asked, "What's wrong, John? Are you ok?"

"Shah is gone!" he yelled up the two levels of apartment building to me.

"What?"

"Shah is gone!"

"I'll be right down," I said, and popped my head back in the window and grabbed my coat.

I wasn't the only person in street, I soon found out. People from all over the neighborhood — businessmen, shop owners, students, the elderly — were gathering in murmuring groups, exchanging all the latest information. Some were visibly upset, as if they were grieving for a member of their own family. Most were cheering. The bakeries were throwing sugar beets outside. I remember a few people had put dishwashing gloves on the windshield wipers of their cars. When they activated them, the glove waved goodbye to the Shah as the people sang.

At that time, I didn't see many of the religious fundamentals among the celebrants, or at least not that many of them were dressed traditionally or wearing cover. Instead, they talked about a return to the constitutional rights established in 1906, rights the Shah had been circumventing or outright ignoring. They wanted human rights violations to stop. They wanted free and fair elections, and talked about the dawning of a new era of freedom, democracy and fairness. I thought, this democratic idea sounded more like America, despite the fact that many seemed to hate American influence. Freedom and democracy were fine by me.

But the disease of political life continued to fester. Where once I could live my life in peace and ignore such things, it was the talk of the town even in my social circles — perhaps *especially* in those circles, where money and secularism were rampant. Certain verses from the Koran were circulated and discussed, and even painted on walls or hung as flyers in the street. More people were returning to the mosques, pretending they'd been avid attendees all along. Women I'd known since childhood that had never covered their features began to hide themselves in traditional wraps in public.

Then, the new government invited exiled religious leader Ayatollah Khomeini back into the country, and religious extremism seemed to take this political crisis and elevate it to the status of full-blown revolution.

Warning signs began to crop up. Foreigners were leaving the country. Foreign offices and companies were shutting their doors, firing their workers and moving to more hospitable places. The value of toman was falling.

"Down to Shah! Down to America!"

We heard members of Khomeini's party marching through the streets of our neighborhood, their voices reverberating through the window glass.

"Down to Shah! Down to America!"

John and I were home alone. Once he understood what the men were saying outside, he seemed to grow very upset. His face turned red and he stood up with the all the energy and confidence of a six-year-old boy. He ran to the window and slid it open.

"Oh yeah?" he yelled to the crowd of men below. "Down to Khomeini! Up with Carter! Down to Khomeini!"

I grabbed the back of his T-shirt and pulled him inside, slamming the window behind him and pulling him out of view of the men below, who I hoped hadn't heard him.

"What are you doing?" I yelled at him, perhaps a little too roughly. "You don't say that to those men."

I didn't even know how much John was aware of the situation around him. Perhaps I hadn't counted on this constant political conversation working its way into his young head, or that he'd take on such a pro-American point of view — or feel so strongly about it.

"But, Mom — "

"It's too dangerous," I continued quickly and firmly. "You don't say that outside this house. Do you understand me?"

Fear in his eyes at my raised voice and the fabric from his shirt that was still in my hand, he nodded. His eyes were glassy with tears.

"I'm an American, too, Mom. Right, Mom?" he asked.

With a sigh, I realized that Iran was not going to be a safe place for my cosmopolitan family or my modern sensibilities much longer. It was time for us to leave our childhood home and return to the childhood home of my son. It was time to go back to America.

Nothing could have pleased my husband more. Ever since we'd returned home, he'd been hinting that he wanted to head back. Perhaps partially because he was unhappy everywhere he went (the grass always being greener on the other side) and partially because he didn't feel that anyone respected him the way he thought he deserved, he had been ready to pack it in for abroad. He'd get into trouble at family dinners and parties because he'd take the opposite side of whoever he was talking to. If they supported Shah, he's point out the good points of Khomeini. If they were for Khomeini, he'd talk about how he was a dangerous man. Much like his son, I was scared that my husband was going to say the wrong thing. There was little control over the military or police, so the only force in town that would respond would be the Revolutionary Guard, whose reputation for brutality often matched SAVAK's, though you could get in trouble for pointing that out.

It was ultimately my decision to begin the process of getting visas to return to America. Not my husband's or anyone else. I wanted a safe place for my son to grow up. I loved people as a whole, and only wanted to be somewhere that I could live freely and forget about politics. Besides, I missed the ease of Sears and McDonalds, the clean streets and the stocked shelves of America.

To top it off, I received a few phone calls to my home number, which has once been listed as the contact number for Jenny's and my charm school.

"Is this the school where they teach women how to serve alcohol?" a male voice asked.

Thinking quickly, I kept my voice light and airy. "Why no," I replied. "They left the country a few weeks ago I hear. I just moved in."

Another time, a man called asking if I was still teaching women how to paint their faces and flaunt their bodies. I again feigned ignorance.

That was the straw that broke the camel's back. I knew that Iran was not the place for my family to flourish. Not anymore.

My husband's cousin Behrouz, a professor at the Iranian university, led us to his American friend Mr. Michael J. Metrinko in the US Embassy to help us regarding obtaining US visa. I arrived to meet Mr. Metrinko personally. We walked together through the Embassy garden and he advised me of two essential choices: either waiting on line for a visa, but that would take a lot of time because many Iranians were urgently trying to leave Iran to the US, or fly to Canada and get the American visa from there. I really appreciated his advice and him being so generous with his time.

Getting a visa was not an easy task; there were long waiting lists of those who wanted to immigrate. People camped out at the American Embassy to save their spots, papers and documents in hand. My brother, Reza, helped us to get a visa number from the Embassy to make an appointment, he camped out on the sidewalk for my family unit and for himself. He had a sleeping bag, a transistor radio and friends in line who would take turns going to bathroom or coming home to take a shower. They played cards to pass the time. Reza would tell us stories about the variety of people he met in that line: old and young, rich and poor. They were the scared ones, but they were the hopeful ones, the ones with enough foresight to see something truly ominous and repressive was on the horizon.

The Revolutionary Guard and other fundamentalist groups would drive by and taunt the people in line as traitors and pelt them with tomatoes. Ahmad and I would drive by at night to give Reza sandwiches and support.

Two weeks later, he came home with numbers. Each morning, the newspaper would print which numbers could be serviced that day, and anyone holding one of those numbers was supposed to head down to the embassy. Even though Reza had been toward the front of the line, our numbers were high and our wait long.

And just when it seemed that things couldn't get any worse — my business probably illegal under new laws, my life infiltrated by a regime I didn't agree with.

Chapter Twenty

While my family was waiting for our number to be drawn from the American Embassy's hat, the situation in Iran progressed from bad to worse. The foreign companies that had been a part of the booming economy for the last decade — banks, factories, military supplies, import and export businesses, airlines, etc. — began to pull up their roots and abandon their swanky office complexes. The value of the Iranian toman began to fall precipitously, and banks began to stop dealing in foreign money at all, refusing to change toman for dollars or any other currency.

Street scenes in downtown Tehran changed overnight. Where once couples in fancy attire walked to restaurants with music drifting out the doorways, there was now silence. Men with their faces hidden in newly grown beards and women swathed in cover tiptoed silently, or raised their voices to match the chants of the revolutionary protesters, which is kind of the same thing as staying silent, really. But underneath all those new trappings of traditionalism like beards and cover, lurked some of the same faces that used to laugh in fancy restaurants or sneak upstairs at the Chattanooga to see scantily dressed dancers. The wind had changed direction, and there are always those people who blow with the breeze like weightless leaves.

But I was particularly worried about my American friends, Debbie and Kristy. Martial law had been declared and no one was allowed on the streets after 10 o'clock at night. Checkpoints manned by members of the revolutionary guard — the closest thing to a police force or an army the country had — sprung up all over the city. Travel was severely restricted, too, especially for foreigners. It seemed the new government wanted all foreign influence out of the country and didn't want to let those already living there go freely. Stories of imprisonment and even torture worked their way through the grapevine.

Amidst all this, I opened my paper every morning with a cup of tea and sighed, looking for the number that would mean my family would soon be gone, would soon be safe in the arms of our adopted country across the sea.

I feared for my family, I feared for myself and my friend's company, I had heard they may be pulling out of Iran, but somehow my friends were still stuck in Tehran. And they were incredibly alone because their husbands had been out of the city when the revolution occurred. Now they couldn't take the chance of returning to Tehran for fear of never escaping.

So these two young American ladies, so sweet and petite and modern, were trapped in an anti-American revolution backed by Islam. I had become close with the two women over a few months of ladies' teas and other get togethers, helping them navigate Persian life with my English skills and compassion. Now they were being threatened by my countrymen, and I was almost ashamed in myself for what they were being put through. I felt it was my duty to help Debbie, Kristy and their four children, to prove that not all Persians blamed them unfairly as individuals for the country they were born in.

"Why aren't you leaving yet?" I asked Debbie, back when Reza was sleeping outside the Embassy for us. "Even we are trying to get out, and it's much less safe here for you than for us."

Then the news came that the aviation company was pulling up stakes — immediately, with some employees rushing home within hours of declaration. But it wasn't quite so easy for Debbie or Kristy: mothers with husbands, herding a group of kids and a houseful of possessions through dangerous times.

"It's time," Debbie said to me over the phone. "Can you please help us?"

I heard the tension in her voice and agreed immediately, saying, "Anything you need. Anything at all."

"What should we do?"

"Everything, and we need to start right away. We needed to start yesterday."

"I know," she said, her voice full of tears. "Thank you, Maryam. Thank you."

If I knew one thing about immigration in Iran, I knew that they were going to need as much money as they could possibly scrape together — for fees, for bribes, for unexpected delays. If this was true of any traveler, it was doubly true for my American friends. Anti-American sentiment had grown to the point where a visibly foreign person was often hassled on the street or at checkpoints or at the grocery store. The situation at the airport was even worse. Rumors surfaced of Americans being stripped of their possessions or denied boarding. Money, if anything, was a way to navigate the dangerous waters of post-revolution Iran.

To that end, we organized a large moving sale to sell everything that the two families owned. Aside from clothes and a few sentimental items that were already packed in suitcases, all the contents of their two large apartments was carted out, put on display and labeled with bargain prices. Furniture, paintings, dishes, silverware, and bedding: Everything had to go.

And for the most part, everything went. Standing at the front of the sale, acting as its hostess in a way because I could speak Farsi, I mingled with anyone who came by and told them of the high quality merchandise they were looking at.

"This is the American's things?" quite a few people would ask, looking over at Debbie and Kristy.

"Yes," I replied, making a point to hold my chin up proud and confident. "They're my friends."

Some would shake their heads and walk away, their mouths shaped as if they'd tasted something sour, they wished to spit out. Others would smile and nod. Some even approached Kristy or Debbie to try out the few words they knew of English.

Halfway through the sale, Debbie had to watch as her beautiful grand piano was loaded onto a truck to be taken to its new home for a price that was not nearly equal to the piano's value in her life. She had to close her eyes and stop watching, but a few tears crept from beneath her closed lids anyway.

The four American kids and John ran around the apartment building and street like the yard sale was a huge play date for them, ignorant of the larger danger around them and the urgency of the situation. But for Debbie and Kristy, I could see, each sale was both a wound in the heart and a lightening of their burden, making the situation bittersweet and difficult.

All that was left at the end of the day was the two families' suitcases and a stack of toman. A stack of toman may not seem to be enough to balance out the loss of a happy, settled life, but at that turbulent and unknown time, it was comfort enough. It was all the comfort that could be expected.

Having given up their apartments and the mattresses to sleep on, both women and all four kids headed to my apartment to camp out for a few days. The women's husbands, who I'd never met, had my home number and address to let the women know when transport had been arranged. The aviation company was flying them into the Tehran airport, but they wouldn't be able to leave the terminal for fear of never getting back. They needed their wives to make the dangerous journey through checkpoints and curfews and hatred to meet them at the airport to catch the flight back home. We waited for one phone call that would give us the pertinent information. We knew that the phone would ring, and we would have to sprint away. We just didn't know when we would get the signal, although Debbie's husband said it would be in the next couple of days.

Sleeping bags were scattered over the floor of the three-bedroom apartment. The kids ran around and played imaginary games under the kitchen table as if they were granted a trip to summer camp. But Kristy and Kristy sat at the table sipping tea dejectedly, an array of canned goods from the bottom of their pantries arranged around them.

"Thanks so much for all of your help selling our stuff, Maryam," Debbie said. Her chin rested in her hand and her normally sparkly brown eyes were dull and sad. "This will surely be a blessing," she continued, placing the stack of bills from the sale on the table. It was a sizable stack, a small fortune. "But how are we going to get it out of the country? I wonder."

I nodded my head, knowing exactly the trouble she was foreseeing in her mind.

"We can't take it to any bank," said Kristy. "We can't change it into dollars, but toman are going to be nearly worthless once we get home."

"It's certainly true that they're not letting anything of value out of the country if they can help it," I agreed. "I've heard they're searching baggage, every little corner. They are even searching people's bodies. Even the women they are patting down like they have money under their skirts."

The noise of the BBC news was playing in the background that evening, solemn words about Iran spilling out into the kitchen where we sat with our tea. They recited names of people being arrested or detained, and the new government was constantly releasing new information about all the bad things they were discovering that the Shah had done. There were pictures of scary looking bearded men pointing guns at American travelers or even at defenseless women and children who were trying to cross different checkpoints in the city. Despite the victory of the sale today, I could see the spirits of my friends deflating like balloons left out in the scorching sun.

"Let me tell you what I heard about airport security," I said, inserting my own news above the somber news of the BBC. "This neighbor of mine wanted to sell his business here and move to America, but he needed all of his cash in order to succeed on the other side. So he comes up with this scheme."

I went on to tell that this man had an excellent — if eccentric — idea of how to sneak a stack of American dollars through the tight security, who would rob him blind if they found it. He went to a doctor friend of his and had a cast put on his leg. "A big, white cast, you know," I said. "But he didn't have a broken bone or a scratch on him, really."

The morning he was due to leave, he called up the airport to report an anonymous tip: A very rich man was going to try to leave the country today with a fortune hidden in a fake cast on his leg. The revolutionary guard was naturally very interested in this news and spread it to all the other airport security men, so when my neighbor went through, they pulled him aside and violently cut open his cast, their eyes shiny with greed.

"I really don't see why you are doing this," the man said. "I have a broken leg and I need this cast. I'm not supposed to take it off for weeks or the bone won't heal right." He just went on and on about the outrage of the situation, but the men continued to cut until his pasty leg was revealed. Just the leg, no money.

"He just threw a fit at those men," I told my friends. "He hollered up a storm like he was outraged, even though he caused the situation himself." By then he'd missed his plane and been humiliated, and the airport had no choice but to get him a seat on a plane the next day while he went home to have his supposedly broken leg re-cast.

"So, he goes back to the doctor friend and has him cast the leg again, this time putting all of the money — thousands of dollars — in with the leg," I continued. "And the next day, the guards already know him. They've already cut it open and seen nothing, and then dealt with his angry words. So, they let him go through free and clear."

Debbie and Kristy were smiling and chuckling at this point, amused at the man's ingenuity.

"He probably walked off the plane in California and ripped that cast off and is rolling around in his money on the beach right now," I said. "Can you just picture it?"

"Are you saying we need to break our legs?" Kristy asked, joking around. I was so happy to see her mood improved. The children had worn themselves out and were falling asleep right where they were playing, or half-in and half-out of the sleeping bags all over the living room floor. The news had shifted to another part of the world's troubles, and the tea was warming our bellies.

"Of course not," I responded. "I just mean that we will find a way."

I was placing our cups in the sink when the clock struck 10, the evening's curfew. Shots rang out in the streets, first from one direction and then from another. With every shot, my shoulders jerked closer to my ears and my heart froze.

Perhaps they weren't shooting people dead in the street. Perhaps the gun reports were warning shots meant to scare the people into following the guard's rules and restrictions. But when I heard gunshots at 10 p.m., which I did most every night, I just imagined the bodies in the streets, the blood of innocent people — even little boys like John — leaking away in the dark. Bodies that could be people I knew, people I loved. Just the day before, a man who lived across the street and had six kids had been shot in the street, supposedly for once being a member of SAVAK. Who knows if he actually was or not, but his family still had to live with the bloody memories of his execution and without him. The noise of every bullet had the same possible outcome in my mind, making them sound both menacing and tragic.

Our smiles and comfort quickly vanished. We went to bed frightened, nervous and staring at the ceiling, as if the ceiling above had answers to all our questions, solutions for our problems. The full and messy house was silent and waiting, anxious to see if the next day would reveal a way for my friends and their children to return home safely.

And in the back of my own mind, I wondered if my own family would walk that same path next. I ran my hand over my stomach, thinking of the tiny life inside. I still hadn't told Ahmad that I was expecting.

The next morning dawned on the same situation in my crowded apartment. The kids ran around like the best of friends, playing with all the American-brand toys we'd brought for John from America. Debbie and Kristy had the same strained faces over cups of tea. None of us had slept well the night before and our spirits were down as we waited for the possibility of the phone ringing.

I saw Kristy fiddling with her wedding ring, turning it around and around on the ring finger of her left hand. Strange, I thought to myself, that these American women expect only one piece of jewelry from their husbands, when Persian women measure their status and their security in jewels and gold. And I suddenly had an idea.

"Not that I ever need an excuse," I told my friends, "but I think it's time to visit the Geisha jewelry store."

"It's hardly the time for shopping, Maryam," said Kristy.

Debbie, on the other hand, looked like she had an idea of what I was up to. "Jewelry? Why?"

"Iranian money isn't worth the paper it's printed on overseas," I explained. "And no bank will give American money here. But a sparkly, lovely necklace or ring? Women all over the world put their money into such things — and can get their money out of them, too."

I brought out a couple of the handmade pieces I'd collected when I was running the charm school with Jenny, who had left the country months ago. "Jewelry is a Persian woman's bank account," I said. "Because the men run the bank accounts and paychecks, it is what she can fall back on when things go wrong. The same could be true for you. Besides, this kind of bank account is much easier to hide and carry."

"Oh my god, what an idea!" said Debbie.

"The market for gold is the same all around, after all," said Kristy. "It just might work."

If nothing else, I was happy the idea brought excitement into my friend's faces and gave us the excuse to go shopping. We browsed through the aisles of the Geisha market, admiring all the huge, almost tacky gems and precious metal concoctions. After much trying on of different pieces of jewelry they never thought they'd be able to own — diamond-encrusted tiaras, pendants with gems the size of a golf ball — they put their whole lives, or at least all the money that represented their lives, in a piece of jewelry each.

Debbie purchased a large ruby ring surrounded by diamonds and Kristy chose a necklace on a very long chain that could be hidden in her shirt. Both little girls got diamond earrings to wear in their ears. Walking tall like real women of means, we walked home like queens. Debbie couldn't stop holding out her hand to catch the glitter of the ruby and the little girls were constantly tugging on their ears.

That night, we ate Kentucky Fried Chicken around the dining room table and made light of the situation.

"If someone wants to take my necklace from me," said Kristy out of hearing of the kids, "they are going to have to have the guts to reach into my bra to get it."

We all giggled.

Debbie chimed in, too, saying, "My grand piano is on a ring around my finger. How surreal."

"And when you get back home safe and sound," I added, placing my hand over her ringed hand, "you will be able to sell your ruby and get a new piano to play."

She nodded. Still smiling, her eyes filled with tears.

"I never could have had such a gorgeous ring if not for … the strange situation we're in," she said. "Never in my wildest dreams."

"Well, you have it and there's nothing your husband can say now, right?" I quipped.

That night we also got the phone call from my friends' husbands we had been waiting for. Regular passenger flights were being cancelled left and right, though cargo and military planes were going in and out at all hours. The aviation company arranged for one of those cargo planes to transport the families of their remaining employees back to the States. Debbie and Kristy just had to meet their husbands at the airport at 4 o'clock the next afternoon and they could be sure, said the men, that they would be able to fly off in safety.

Safety. What a nice word. But sadly, safety was available only once the Americans were at the airport and on the plane. The hard part was going to be getting there.

Driving around town in any direction was no longer simple but driving toward the cargo airport was almost impossible. Checkpoints were set up on the edges of my Geisha neighborhood (like every neighborhood) at every major street. Soldiers without uniforms but with guns in their hands stopped every car by simply standing in front of it with their weapons. They looked for suspicious people — especially foreigners — and, in the best-case version, wouldn't allow them to pass. In the worst-case scenario, people were dragged from cars to disappear into prisons or shot on sight.

Even away from the checkpoints, people seemed to turn on one another. Some used the revolution as a way to get even with people they'd hated or fought with for completely unrelated reasons. Fundamentalists harassed women who didn't wear cover, sometimes throwing eggs at them where they walked on the sidewalk. I'd taken to wearing longer dresses with long sleeves, packing all my mini jupes and sleeveless clothes in a suitcase, ready to be worn again when we finally made it to America.

But we could not hide inside from the dangerous situation, waiting for it to just get worse. Debbie and Kristy had already waited too long. Seeing that I was the de facto leader of this helpless group of women, I knew I just had to take a deep breath and dive in, facing the situation with as much confidence and poise as I could muster.

"We're just going to get a taxi and go," I said. "If we're careful and lucky, the simplest way could be the best."

We packed up the children's backpacks with jackets for if they got cold and books for if they got bored, hoping they could stay quiet and not get us in trouble. The cab I had called for arrived, driven by a kind-looking old man, and we packed the luggage in the trunk. The Americans all squeezed in the backseat and I leaned into the driver's window to speak to him.

"These are my American friends," I told the man in Farsi. "They are just going back home. I hope you don't think they're spies, right?" I smiled, trying to make a joke out of the conversation.

He looked into the backseat and said, "They don't look like spies to me." He, too, smiled, probably accustomed to trying to get to the airport with various people attempting to flee every day, several times a day. I let out the breath I was holding and went around to get beside him in the front seat.

John grabbed onto my leg from behind.

"I can't take him with me," I said to Ahmad, who was waiting with us. "I can't take you with me," I repeated to John.

He was crying and upset to see his new American friends packed and ready to leave him. "I want to go to Disneyland, too," he wailed. "I want to go to America."

I kneeled down on the sidewalk and cupped his teary face in my hands. "When we get to America, we will go to Disneyland. I promise you that," I told my son. "But it's not our turn yet. This time, it's our friends turn."

He sniffed and nodded, and allowed me to hand him off to his father. But as we drove away, I could see him waving at the receding cab, still crying his little eyes out.

"If you take us safely to the airport," I told the driver, "I will double the money you usually get for such a trip."

He nodded and pulled into traffic.

The back seat was silent as we weaved our way through the streets, making our way toward one of the main roads that would lead to the airport. Never before had I felt so on display inside a car, so exposed to the world. Behind the walls of my apartment, I had been certain I could keep my friends safe. But out here with nothing but the glass of the windows between us and the outside world, it suddenly seemed very treacherous to be seen. I scrutinized the faces of pedestrians and tried to look at other drivers without catching their eyes. Every person was possibly someone who was against us, who would turn us in. Every moment, I thought I might hear gunfire and have to duck for cover.

Although the driver tried to avoid all soldiers and check points, the cab was funneled toward a line of revolutionary guardsmen with long, black rifle barrels slung over their shoulders. We slowed down as if in a traffic jam and the driver turned toward me with a look on his face that showed both apologies and nerves.

We got a little closer, to the point where I could make out the faces of individual guards. Two of them were carrying something down the line in our direction, although they were still at least a dozen yards away. As they turn slightly to move around a car, I was shocked to see that their burden was a person: a woman of about middle age, not wearing a cover but clothed modestly in the sort of long-sleeved dress older ladies wear when doing the marketing. One guard had her arms and the other grasped around her ankles. Her head was thrown back and there was blood all over her forehead.

I gasped and my hand flew to my heart.

The red blood was more than a smear. In fact, it was flowing through her hair and was dripping into a path along the guard's route. The guards hailed an empty taxi. They opened the back door and placed her in the backseat like a bag of rice. The way her body responded to their touch, I knew she was either completely unconscious or dead, and I tried to get myself to believe that it was only the former. One of the guards got into the front seat of the cab and the car drove away. I quickly glanced in the back seat of our own car and saw both Debbie and Kristy looking pale and slack, their eyes following the wounded woman, too. Kristy had covered one of her kid's eyes and Debbie had one child pressed to one shoulder and the second pressed to the other.

Was that woman talking back to the guards or trying to smuggle something? Was she someone important in the time of the Shah, someone close to the former regime? Was she simply in the wrong place at the wrong time? And where were they taking her? Would her family and friends ever hear from her again or know what became of her?

"Turn around, driver," I said softly, not having enough breath to speak above a whisper. "Please turn around."

I heard one of the young girls begin to whimper in the back, but the driver did as I said and backed up until he could steer the nose of the car back toward home. Seeing people on the street, including the guards, look up with curiosity when we left the checkpoint, I finally understood the comfort of anonymity wearing a cover could bring. As soon as the car pulled up to the curb, I hustled my friends out, threw a generous amount of money at the driver and ran back into the relative safety of my building.

Four o'clock came and went, and we knew that their husbands would probably be getting very worried at the airport when their wives and children didn't arrive. And sure enough, the phone rang soon after 4. It was Debbie's husband, Richard, and he was standing with the family's tickets and passports without a family. I heard her try to explain why we had to turn around in a whispered voice, trying not to upset the kids.

"We got scared," she said into the receiver. "It just didn't seem safe to have them see us at all or go through so directly." She paused to listen to him. "Me, too. What? Yes, yes. One moment."

Debbie called out my name and held out the phone in my direction. "He wants to talk to you," she explained.

"Hello?" I said into the phone to this man I had never met, seeing in my head the picture of him Debbie kept on a shelf in her old apartment.

"Maryam, thank you so much for all you are doing to help my family," he began. Then he went on to ask me to explain again what had happened that afternoon. Together, we brainstormed ideas about how to avoid a similar situation. After explaining exactly where our apartment was located, he suggested that we might be able to scurry down a nearby hill a block away to the busy highway, where he would be waiting with a few taxis.

"No, that's not possible," I insisted. "With all those suitcases and four scared children? I don't think so. Besides if the guards in my neighborhood are driving by on the highway and see people running with suitcases, they will assume the worst and just go ahead and ... you know."

I looked around the room at the kids. They were still happily playing together, but in a more subdued manner, as if they could sense the tension of the adults in the room.

He sighed. "You're right," he said. "But we have to try again tomorrow. We have to find a way out."

"We will," I told him. "I promise."

The next day about 2 p.m., we reloaded the kids' backpacks with books and a few cold chicken sandwiches and we got ready to try our intrepid trip to the airport again. This time, we all understood the gravity of the situation — even the kids, who had been told how important it was to remain calm and silent until they saw their fathers again, at which point they were allowed to cry and jump and scream as much as they wanted. In fact, they were told to speak no English at all.

"Today, you are Persian children," I said to the four sets of eyes that looked up at me with trust. "For today, you are Iranian, like my little boy, John."

"I'm American, too, Mom!" John said indignantly.

"You were born there, yes. But for today, you are a little Persian boy through and through. Do you understand?"

He nodded, excited to be let in on the plan and to be allowed to ride along on this trip to the airport.

Today, I had decided that no detail would be neglected and absolutely no chances taken. While I myself never wore a cover, I procured three that morning. Debbie had a darker complexion, so she could leave hers ajar, like I wore mine. But Kristy was blond and blue eyes, so I made sure she was bundled up tightly.

Also different was the fact that I no longer wanted to take a cab to the airport but had asked a friend of the family, Parviz, with a private car to drive us. I don't know if he knew what he was getting into when he agreed to do me this favor, but I saw him become pale at the wheel when I leaned into the back to repeat my warnings: "No English, let me do all the talking, and we'll get to the airport OK. Everyone got it?"

They all nodded silently, showing me that they were starting now.

I turned back around and positioned John on my lap, and then we took off along the same route we traveled yesterday. Again, I felt incredibly exposed, but felt some comfort in the loose fabric that covered my head. Never before had I worn a cover, and I never would have if it wasn't for the benefit of two good friends and their four young children.

The car was silent through the street until we were again slowed by the checkpoint, where they waved some cars through and stopped to check others. There were about five or six guards on duty covering the width of the street. It took what seemed like hours for us to inch through traffic toward the scary men we'd rather avoid. At one point, I turned toward Parviz and said, "If they speak to us, let me do all the talking."

We inched past machine guns and taxis and pedestrians until finally a guard yelled, "Stop." There were no barriers or retractable arms to signal people to stop. Fear alone accomplished that just fine. Fear and the barrel of the gun he carried.

The man was in his early 20s and his beard was relatively neat in comparison with some of the hairy guardsman. He looked at the car up and down and began to approach. I rolled down my window so he would come to my side instead of the driver's. My heart beat in my ears as loud as his footsteps on the pavement and I hoped my smile wasn't twitching with the anxiety that I felt.

"Who are you and where are you going?" he asked. His Farsi was accented to the point that I could tell he was from Azerbaijani, from somewhere near my own home. So I laid on my own accent rather thick, too.

"My name is Maryam. We are going to my aunt's house in the east part of Tehran for a dinner party."

He cocked his head when I said dinner party, seeing that it was only 2 in the afternoon.

"Since it's forbidden to be out past 10 at night because of the martial law," I continued, "we have to leave now or we won't have time."

"Who are these people?" he asked, pointing toward the backseat with one hand while the other was resting on his hip, a pose of a man in charge of the situation.

Pointing at Debbie, I said, "This is my cousin and her children. And this other lady is a relation who has just come from Ankara, Turkey." I had practiced these words all morning, thinking that it would be believable that this blue-eyed woman came from that area of Turkey, where people were known to be much fairer. The fact that this guard came from Azerbaijan only helped the situation, because Azerbaijan was so close to Turkey that we met with Turkish people all the time. Knowing that, I was holding my breath, wondering if he could speak Turkish and would ask her something in that language.

Parviz said nothing, which seemed pretty normal for a Persian man unhappily surrounded by a bunch of women.

The guard paused at my window, seeming to look around at the car and all its occupants one more time. Breathe in, breathe out, I told myself. Breathe in, breathe out. I counted to five and then put an expression on my face like I was annoyed by the delay.

"You know what?" I asked him, speaking in Turkish, which I was sure he understood. "If we don't get going, we are not going to make it to my aunt's and back by curfew. We are just going to have to turn around."

The guard continued leaning on the car, as if he was in no hurry and could wait all day.

"These kids are hungry. Do you want to buy us dinner? There is a nice chicken place they like two blocks over." I was joking around, of course, and made sure that he knew it. I was hoping to come off as any other Persian woman who'd grown tired of having to go through checkpoints all the time. A woman who had nothing to hide.

"I don't want to buy anything," he said. Finally, he stopped leaning on the car and moved back. "Just get out of here," he continued, and motioned us on with his hand.

I saw our driver's eyebrows leap toward his hair line and his eyes grow wide in surprise. Parviz quickly and clumsily put the car in gear and squeaked the tires a little before stopping himself.

"Slowly," I said. "Slowly."

He nodded and then hit the gas in a normal way. Breathe in, breathe out. I took another five deep breaths before looking in the rearview mirror to see if anyone was in pursuit. Instead, there was our Azerbaijani guard, leaning against the car window of a taxi behind us, just like he had done with us, a swagger in his hips and his authority maybe going to his head. "Whew," I said aloud and whistled.

The car remained silent, showing me that Debbie and Kristy had really taken my instructions to heart.

I turned around in my seat to face them. "There are probably a few more checkpoints," I said. "But if they go as well as that last one did, we'll have you out of here in no time."

Kristy nodded. Debbie remained still in fear.

We passed through at least two more checkpoints but were not stopped again. When traffic backed up too far, some of the guards got lazy and just waved you by. Or, no guard would approach the car as we passed, so Parviz slowly and steadily just continued through, ready to halt immediately if one of the men pointed at us or yelled. But somehow we squeaked by without having to speak to another soul.

Within an hour, we were pulling up to the airport terminal, where everything seemed so much more civilized with all the directional signs and glass windows. The kids in the backseat began to yell, "Papa! There's Papa." I had told them they could talk again when they saw their dads, I remembered.

The whole backseat began to fidget and try to get out as Parviz pulled the car up to the curb alongside two tall, fair American men. The families were so happy to be reunited that they all fell to their knees to be the same height as the children, making two big family hugs. My heart warmed to see these people reunited, these families made whole again. And though my system hadn't fully recovered from the fright of the trip to the airport, the rewarding feeling that I delivered these people from harm began to sooth my jangled nerves.

I stood outside the car while the men unloaded all the bags. My sense of humor returning, I leaned in the open window and said to Parviz, "If anyone sees me here with all these white people, they are going to think we are helping a bunch of spies from the American government."

His face was still pale and a few beads of nervous sweat were on his forehead. "Please don't say that, Maryam," he said.

"They are going to get you now for helping spies," I continued, a smile on my face.

"Not funny, Maryam. It's not funny."

"It wasn't fun, but it can be funny," I replied.

I only had a moment to say goodbye to my friends before they went into the relative safety of the airport, where no one could trouble them if they had their passports, business visas to be in the country and plane tickets. They could prove they had legally entered the country, so they would be able to legally leave, too. The husbands herded the kids inside as I gave each of my friends a hug.

"We'll never forget you," said Kristy. "Thank you so much."

"I didn't do anything," I replied.

"Yes, you did," said Debbie. "And when you return to America, make sure that we get back in touch so we can do something in return for you, too."

"It was the least I could do in the circumstances," I said. "So now you can remember that you have Iranian friends, that Iranians are good people as well as bad, right?"

"Very, very good," Kristy said. She still looked pretty frightened, though she'd taken off her cover, her disguise. "Thanks again."

"You're safe now," I assured her.

"Oh no. I'm not counting on anything until that plane is in the sky," laughed Debbie. "Goodbye, Maryam."

"Goodbye," I replied solemnly.

I returned to the car, where Parviz was anxious to be headed home and away from any association with these American friends of mine.

"You want to stop until we see their plane take off?" I asked him.

"Please no. Oh no," he said. "We don't want to be doing anything that's more suspicious than we've done already. I think I'm going to have a heart attack." He started the car and pulled onto the road.

"Well, today you showed you had a lot of heart, Parviz," I said. "You did a very good thing. Thanks."

He nodded, perhaps unwinding just a little. We headed back toward the relative safety of home, feeling safer with our Farsi language and darker skin and no more secrets silent in the backseat.

Chapter Twenty-One

But there were plenty of secrets back home, where I still hadn't told my husband that we were expecting another child. In fact, I planned on never telling him.

Since the moment I had set foot on the floor of the Washington Post, a place that brought up the memory of the deafening machines and the taste of nausea in my mouth, the thought of divorce had been planted in my head. It was a tiny, little seed, whose existence I didn't admit to anyone — even myself. Divorce was so forbidden in the culture I was raised in, at least for women. Men were able to abandon wives, but never vice versa. Any good Iranian woman would never have the thought cross her mind. But then again, I had never been the typical, good Iranian woman.

Life had glued me to this man I'd hastily chosen during a crisis of my youth, this man I'd grabbed onto like he was a life saver, though he'd turned into a dead weight instead, pulling me down to drown.

It had turned out that I was pregnant on the floor of the Washington Post, which meant that I could never dream of leaving. And then I was overwhelmed with mother love when John was born, meaning that my love for him overshadowed the unhappiness of my marriage and I was willing to stay with Ahmad if only because my son needed a father. Then, just when I had reached the pinnacle of my success with the charm school and proved to myself that I could be financially independent, that I might be able to make it on my own, the revolution came along and created more difficulty.

Oh, how wonderful my life could be without my husband, I thought. One of the happiest times of my life was the months I spent in Iran without him, while he was finishing up with thesis for graduate school. In those fleeting days, I had been free of his moods — for instance, we could joke and be pleasant in the evening and I'd wake up the next morning to him treating me like his worst enemy — and I had glimpsed what my life could have been if I'd made different choices. If I'd chosen a different husband. A husband who wouldn't take our son aside after I'd disciplined him for some little thing to tell John that his mother was crazy. "Just don't listen to that crazy woman," he'd say. "Let's go get some ice cream."

And now I was pregnant. What on earth was I going to do?

Yet another radical, untraditional and forbidden thought entered my head. I would not have the baby. I would have an abortion. Then once we left the country — which was easier to do with a man at my side — I could leave my husband while we were in America, where such things were not really easy, but was exponentially simpler and less frowned upon than in ultra-conservative Iran.

While the thought was there in my head, it still frightened me immensely. What a drastic choice! Was this really what I wanted? Was this really the right thing to do, for me and for John? I was so mixed up and confused, and I had no one in the city I could talk to about my feelings, no one who would understand my emotions. Only Ahmad's family lived in Tehran. My mother was still in Tabriz, my sisters all married away.

And the stress of waiting for our number to be called to get our American visas and the anxiety of preparing to leave the country again was wearing my nerves thin, stressing my relationship with my husband to the breaking point.

Ever since I made a lot of money with Jenny through the charm school, his family had been over at our house a great deal, coming for dinners to eat our food or staying in the guest room for weeks at a time. They made a big show of looking down on a woman working and running her own business, but they also made a big show of sharing all the money, food and comfort that stemmed from that business.

Ahmad, meanwhile, never changed his attitude toward money. In other words, he always said he had none, despite the fact that he made a good salary while working for that foreign firm. He bought nice clothes and went to nice restaurants, but when he came home, he claimed his pockets were empty. And he never shared any banking or other financial information with me, so I had to pretend to believe him.

During one of his family's visits, he approached me with his hand out, begging.

"My parents are here," he said, "and I have to go buy the meat and groceries for their stay."

"Yes?" I questioned, knowing what he was leading up to but feigning ignorance.

"So give me some money to go to the store," he said, his tone irritated.

"You don't have any?"

"I know you have the money, Maryam," he said, not answering my question. "Just give me some money."

My blood boiled. Perhaps I was hormonal or moody due to my pregnancy or perhaps this constant financial wrangling had finally gotten to me, like the straw that broke the camel's back. Whatever the reason, his outstretched hand and his attitude that he was entitled to *my* money infuriated me. I threw my hands down to my sides and jutted out my chin.

"You want my money?" I asked. "Fine. Follow me."

I grabbed my purse and flung open the door, striding angrily down the hall and not even turning around to see if he was following me. If there was money at the end of the journey, I knew he would be. I stomped all the way to my bank, where I had every cent not already spent from my business safely saved.

I strode straight up to the first teller and threw my little red deposit book on the counter, where it bounced once.

"Whatever money is in this book, whatever money is in my account, give it to this gentleman," I said. "Please," I added. "Every cent."

"Yes ma'am," said the startled teller, who took the book and began looking it over.

He stacked up the funds in crisp toman notes on the counter and pushed it toward me, as I was the account holder. I guess he was confused about what I was doing giving my money away, but I wasn't. I put the money — which was a pretty large amount, enough to live comfortably on for a few years without any other income — into my husband's hands.

"There," I said to him firmly, almost loud enough to cause a scene. "Leave me alone. I gave you all the money I have. All of it. Now leave me alone."

Tears were gathering in my eyes, threatening to spill over. My heart was thumping in my chest at what I had done, giving my oppressor and my sometimes enemy the fruits of all my hard work and inspiration, giving him all that was left of the most important and fulfilling thing I had ever done in my life. And all Ahmad did was shrug, smile and walk away, headed down the street to the grocery store to buy meat for his visiting family. I walked home alone, my anger evaporating and leaving me empty, as if a stiff breeze could blow me away.

After that, I figured out that I was pregnant. I thought to myself. Let this child be a girl. Let me have another female in my life, someone like me. Someone who will have everything that I cannot. Someone who shares as little with this inscrutable, penny-pinching curmudgeon as humanly possible.

Bit by bit, we sold all of our furniture and household goods, all of the wonderful things I had purchased from the ambassador's wife that meant so much to me as well as the ugly, modern couch that Ahmad had contributed. If we had to empty our lives again, at least I could take pleasure in seeing that monstrosity go. We held onto our life savings nervously, watching the value of Iranian currency go down daily in comparison to the dollar, biding our time.

And then our number came up, after weeks of waiting. It was the last number of that day, the last one to squeak by. It was a Tuesday, I remember, because I was so excited that we wouldn't have to wait for another week, the embassy being closed on Thursdays and Fridays in the Muslim way, much like Americans have their weekends on Saturdays and Sundays. My brother Reza, who had gotten the number for us by sleeping outside on the street and had a number very close to ours, had the number for the next day, Wednesday, and would make the cutoff for this week, too.

Having been through the process of getting a residency visa before, we were all ready to go with the necessary paperwork, a massive list of things we needed to provide in order to be considered. We had bank statements proving we could support ourselves. We showed we had property and family still in Iran (actually, we had our names put on some of our parents' property) and were therefore likely to return someday. And because a student visa was the easiest to get, we'd managed to find a school — any school, it didn't matter — to give Ahmad a letter of acceptance. He didn't really plan on attending, at least not for long, but the Florida Institute of Technology was our ticket back to America, so we went along with the ruse.

Everything was in order, the woman at the embassy told us. At least, everything we provided. They needed to do background checks and security checks and checks of the social security numbers we were given the last time we were in America. If there were no problems, the visa would be issued and could be picked up the next week, on Wednesday.

There shouldn't have been any problems with social security or background checks. My husband and I both knew that, but we were still nervous, holding back from celebrating escaping this now oppressive and unsafe country. We still heard gunshots in the night. Neighbors were turning on one another, claiming they knew who used to work for the Shah or for his SAVEK agency. You couldn't freely travel the city or see friends and family. Going to get groceries was a scary journey, and I'd always sigh in relief when I made it back to the safety of our apartment, pulling shut the curtains so I didn't have to see the scary world outside, the world that had turned upside down. People had celebrated the Shah leaving, thinking that we'd have more freedom and a new democracy. But the revolution had turned into the opposite: a strict, traditional regime that told everyone what was right and wrong, and even what to wear and what to eat and what to say.

We waited for the week to go by, counting the days until Wednesday. Reza was counting, too. His appointment had also gone well, although he needed to have a new passport issued whereas we already had ours. His visa, then, would take a little more time, and he was told to return after the upcoming Thursday/Friday weekend, on Saturday.

On Wednesday, Ahmad went to the embassy alone. An hour later, I received a phone call from him. His voice was scratchy and distant because he was talking on a pay phone.

"Let me talk to John," he said.

"What happened? Is everything OK?"

"Let me talk to John," he repeated.

I called for our son and put him on the phone. "Hello?" he said. Such a serious look crossed his childish face as he listened to his father. Then his smile lit up the room. "We're going to Disneyland, Mom!" he yelled. "We're going to Disneyland!"

My hand went to my heart and I breathed a sigh of relief. We were one step closer to getting back to America. We had our visas, and no one could take those away from us. When Ahmad got home, we immediately went to buy our plane tickets, which left from Tehran and traveled through Paris and then New York to Orlando, Florida.

The next day was Thursday, November 4, 1979, and a group of students called the Muslim Student Followers of the Imam's Line overpowered the security at the American embassy and took 52 U.S. diplomats hostage in one of the most renown stand-offs in modern history. They blindfolded hostages and paraded them in front of the rabid, raving crowds. Graffiti appeared on the embassy walls, walls my husband had just entered the previous day. Smoke poured out of some of the windows, most likely burning my brother's passport and visa.

The television and radio relayed news and pictures all day, both terror and recrimination from the United States and the Western world
and praise and joy from hard-line Muslims in Iran and throughout the
Middle East for striking back at the American imperialists. The television ran endless images of the crowds at the embassy yelling, "Death to
Israel. Death to Carter." I had no idea where these people — men with
beards and ladies in cover — had come from, no idea how so many supported this crazy plan, especially seeing that most people I knew were
scared for their lives and didn't like the direction of the new government.

The reasons for the incident, which would come to be known as the
Iran hostage crisis, are varied. For one, the United States had recently
allowed the Shah to enter America for medical treatment — few people
knew he'd been battling cancer over the last year or more. The Khomeini government demanded that he be returned for trail and, probably,
execution. But America refused. Therefore anti-American sentiment
surged even higher than it had been. Then there was the CIA's involve-
ment in overthrowing the elected prime minister in the 1950s, something many Iranians could never forgive. And of course, there was also
that so many Persians were choosing to leave after the revolution, going to the land of Khomeini's enemies. The fact of the matter was that
tension and anti-American sentiment had been building for decades,
and the hostage crisis was just the way in which that tension finally exploded.

Needless to say, the situation was grim. Those poor hostages. They
were only doing their jobs, trying to help people, when those radicals
came in. They were led blindfolded in front of the crowds and media
cameras, some of them obviously terrified. And us poor Iranians, too.
The American government obviously wasn't issuing any more visas,
and though planes continued to take off and land, air travel was severely restricted and supposedly difficult, with every Iranian passport
scrutinized and its holder sometimes threatened or refused entry to the
U.S.

With our visas and plane tickets in hand, we hoped that the actions of these radical students hadn't ruined our plans, forcing us to stay put in this hostile and dangerous country. The stress of it all took its toll.

My husband began getting rid of all of our possessions more quickly and carelessly, sometimes giving away items that I deeply loved to family and friends. I accused him of burning our lives up for nothing. Unable to carry many possessions with us, he told me to get with the program and get rid of the last of my things, too, mostly clothes — expensive, stylish and beautiful European clothes I'd collected when Jenny and I were riding high on the success of our school. I couldn't bear to give them away but Ahmad insisted. Stressed beyond belief and angry at the world, but especially at my husband, I gathered them in the kitchen and put a match to them.

"If you are burning everything, I'm burning my stuff, too," I told him, hoping that I'd get some sort of reaction from my stone-faced, cold husband. He just shrugged and opened a window for the smoke to escape. The action I thought would make me feel strong and in control instead left me feeling empty, weak and foolish. Of course, I was also two or three months pregnant and incredible emotional at a time of intense turmoil, which is not a great combination.

My jewelry, on the other hand, was not something I could burn. I couldn't bear to part with most of it, seeing that I saw my jewelry as a security blanket, something that made me a woman and could financially protect me if anything went wrong. But I also knew it was going to be difficult to take with us. If I put it in our luggage or wore too much of it, the guards at the airport would simply confiscate it, saying that we were hoarding wealth from the country. So I set to devising a plan of how to carry it through.

First, I thought of hiding it in a bag of cooking herbs I was planning on taking anyway. But I heard through the grapevine (so many people were trying to leave, so the talk got around fast) that they were paying close attention to food stuffs and were cutting open plastic bags to check for valuables. Instead, I decided to hide it in my clothes, the very clothes I would be wearing. I had heard of similar plans working —

families trading in their wealth for diamonds, which they then made into buttons, or people who sewed diamonds or other valuables into their clothing.

I had a black velvet, sweater-like jacket that had a curving, puffy collar. I carefully ripped open the seam and removed some of the padding that caused the volume and stuffed some of my best jewelry in there, tacking some of the pieces in places with a little thread so they wouldn't move around or slip.

The rest of our possessions had been liquidated into cash, but getting that cash out of the country was also going to be a problem. We were definitely taking about $17,000 American dollars worth out of the country, probably to be strapped to my husband's stomach like on our first voyage across the ocean. But we had a great deal more that my husband wanted to leave with General. The toman's value was continuing to drop, from 7 toman to the dollar to 22 and even higher. And Ahmad thought that it was bound to go back up, so we would leave it in the country and take it back out later, when the situation had stabilized. Plus, the General would be able to wire us some of the money once we got there, up to the government's cap of $3,000 every three months.

We gave up our apartment, placed our remaining possession in boxes in the General's basement and went to stay with his parents for a few weeks while we counted down to our flight. We all knew that even if we made it to the plane and to a foreign country, it was not guaranteed that we wouldn't be refused and sent back on the next flight. In fact, it became quite a joke.

"Be sure to go shopping at one of the department stores before they send you back, right?" said my mother.

Everything was as in order as it could be for us to make the trip and leave this scary place, but something still seemed to be unfinished for me. One of the last things I did before taking off was to take care of this unfinished business, letting Arian know that I was leaving.

I called up his sister, who was always one of my closest friends, to tell her we'd gotten some of the final visas out of the country.

"I wish he was here," she told me, explaining that he was in Europe — and would likely be stuck in Europe for quite some time because of the hostage crisis. "He'd be shocked to know you're leaving, that he may never get to have lunch with you or accidentally see you at parties."

I wiped away a tear, remembering the freedom I felt when I was with my Dream Man, Arian, and the ease of conversation and how anything that could happen didn't seem insurmountable in his presence. I hoped she couldn't hear me crying.

"This is how life goes," I said. "Unexpected changes and missing goodbyes."

The weeks passed slowly for me, my fear and stress crippling me, but we did make it to the airport. Much like the first time we left for America, we had very little to call our own, only a few suitcases, a money belt of cash and a lumpy velvet collar full of jewels. Of course, we had John this time around and we kept on brave faces for his sake, promising him that long-awaited trip to Disney World, which would finally be possible because we'd be living in Florida, so nearby.

I hugged my mother and father and my sisters and brothers, the most tearful farewell being with Reza. Poor Reza, who'd slept in the rain and the cold for a chance to get out and had missed his window of opportunity by only one day.

"I'm so sorry," I whispered in his ear as we hugged.

He pulled away but continued to hold both of my shoulders, as if he was supporting me.

"Don't worry," he said. "I'm single and I have a job here. You have so much more to worry about. You deserve to go."

I nodded, tears running down my cheeks.

"I'll make it someday," he said.

Those were the last words spoken before we got on the plane, Ahmad and I being too scared and nervous to talk until we were belted into seats and in the air, traveling away from so much chaos, so much fear, so much success and happiness disappeared.

We drank glass after glass of the free champagne on our way to France, anxious about the reception we'd face when we got there.

Televisions at the airport in Paris displayed Dan Rather, speaking about the hostage situation as it entered day 44, and tension about how Iranian passports was high. At one point as we made our way through customs, I made to grab a bag that looked like mine but was the property of a stylish and haughty French woman nearby. She shouted, "Madam!" and looked at me as if I was a common criminal. Pregnant and moody and my nerves frayed, I burst into tears.

"Don't cry," said Ahmad in a moment of kindness. "She's not yelling at you. She's yelling at your nationality."

We were able to board the plane to New York after a customs official scrutinized our visas, making us sweat as we waited. But then in New York, the situation became even worse.

Holding our bags and keeping our fears in check, we stood in line for entry into the United States. John traipsed in front of us, and was quickly let through thanks to his American passport. But once the official had Ahmad's and my documents in hand, he said, "I'm sorry, folks, but you'll have to proceed to that room over there." He pointed his hand down the hall. Then he motioned for an official to bring John back to us. My son returned with the crushed look of someone shown his dreams, only to have them yanked away again. Despite his youth, he definitely understood the gravity of the situation we faced.

"What room?" asked Ahmad, and the man gave better instructions.

Heavy with bags, we made our way in the direction we were told, only to find ourselves in a large room filled with worried people from all over the world, of all shapes and sizes and colors but all with an air of dejected waiting. Some were slumped in chairs. Kids played on the floor, babbling in different languages. There was no line, only scattered chairs and a counter at one end where officials worked. It felt like we were waiting to be let into jail, scared to continue being in the room but scared of what waited beyond, too. There was also a wall of glass, where the traveling companions of some people exiled to the room stood anxiously, waiting out their separation.

While we sat until it was our turn to speak to the intimidating officials behind the counter, I saw another Iranian woman speaking to a clerk, her face nervous and her skin clammy. She glanced several times to another lady behind the glass — from the resemblance I thought it must be her sister.

On the counter in front of her were some of the woman's possessions, which the official was looking through. He came to a photo album and opened it up, then became upset and pointed at a particular page.

"What is this? Look at your picture," the man said, his voice almost shouting. The picture showed the young woman standing in front of the American embassy in Tehran. From the graffiti and the crowds around her, it was obvious that the picture had been taken while the hostage crisis was raging in the background. She had her hands clasped in front of her and a prim smile on her face.

"We are basically at war with your country and your people are keeping ours hostage," he continued, "and here you are smiling in front of where this terrorism is taking place." He was obviously outraged, as if the picture was of her personally leading one of the blindfolded hostages with a gun over her shoulder.

"I was in Tehran and something so historic was going on. I just had a friend snap a picture."

He sighed in disgust.

"I am coming back to America," she said. "I want nothing else but to go back to America to finish my school." He was silent, looking over some papers. "I don't know why I was smiling," she added. "I'm sorry."

"I'm going to have to do a background check," he replied, not meeting her eyes.

He left the counter for a few minutes while the young woman made eye contact and gestured to her sister behind the glass.

He returned, telling her that he had found she had an outstanding traffic ticket in Maryland before she went back to Iran to visit her family.

"I'm going to cancel your visa," he said matter-of-factly.

Her face fell. "Oh no. Please," she said. "Don't put a stamp on my visa. Don't cancel it."

He didn't reply.

"OK, OK," she said, throwing up her hands like she was backing away, like she wasn't a danger to him. "You can tell me I can't go to America. I can go back to France. But please don't cancel my visa. I have this visa for four years and I can come back later, when everything is … resolved with this crisis. Please. Please."

Oh my god, I thought. I don't want to go back to France. I don't want to go back to Iran. Please don't send my family back to where we came from. Questions rolled through my head: What will happen to me? What will happen to John if we must go back? What about this un-known, unborn child? I started to panic, and I could tell from the sweat on his forehead that my husband was panicked, too.

I tried to send my prayers toward this young Persian woman in such a horrible situation, all over a silly pictured snapped in haste. But I never knew what became of her because, at that moment, we were called over to a different customs official.

I was a little relieved to see that the man who called us wasn't hard and angry like the clerk who'd threatened the woman's visa. He was older, with grandpa-like white hair and a soft smile.

We sat down in front of him.

"Where are you headed?" he asked, obviously going through a checklist of questions he needed to ask.

"The Florida Institute of Technology," said Ahmad quickly.

"And do you have the funds to support yourself during your stay in the United States?"

"Yes," said Ahmad. "We have $18,000 right here." He lifted up his shirt and before any of us could say a word, he had the stack of bills on the man's desk, as if he would be willing to just hand it over if the man in power asked him to.

"Oh no, no, no, no," the man replied, his eyes smiling. He motioned with his hands for Ahmad to remove the money immediately, and my husband quickly tucked it back into his money belt.

He looked over our visa and said, "Everything looks in order. I'm go-ing to give you a two-week visa. You can go to Miami and settle down, and in 14 days, you need to report to immigration." He stamped our visa and handed it back to Ahmad, who held it in midair as if this was all too easy, as if it was a joke.

Just in case it was, I put my hand on Ahmad's for him to put the visa away and stood up, gathering our stuff as fast as possible in case our window of escape closed again. "Thank you," I told the elderly gentleman. "Thank you."

Chapter Twenty-Two

"I'm sorry, sir," said the primly dressed gate agent where our plane to Florida was departing. "We simply can't accept these."

"But the flight number is the same. There is no mistake. These tickets are for this flight and we are not late," said Ahmad, holding out the three tickets to Florida and flapping them around a little.

"That's correct, sir," she replied. "But our airline no longer does any business through Iran Air or any other Iranian carrier. All tickets purchased are invalid."

"And there are no refunds?"

"No. I'm sorry."

"And there is nothing we can do with these worthless pieces of paper?"

"No. I'm sorry."

"And no one we can talk to about this mistake?"

"There's no mistake, sir. I'm sorry you weren't informed of the cancellation earlier. Of course, you always have the freedom to purchase another ticket with a ticketing agent."

Ahmad turned back to me and John and we walked a distance away. "We have the freedom to purchase another ticket. The *freedom*," said Ahmad softly, his tone a mixture of frustration and humor.

Exhausted physically and emotionally, my family sat down at an airport restaurant. John, having heard so long about the tastiness of American French fries and not able to remember their taste, dug into a large plate of greasy potatoes.

"The land of the free," I said, referring back to my husband's statement about freedom.

"Where they void out tickets, which I paid about $400 for," Ahmad scoffed.

"But now we are free," I continued. "Sure, we have to check in with immigration in Florida in two weeks, but we don't have to go there now." I sipped my tea and thought for a moment. "What about your cousin in Texas who wants us to visit? Why don't we fly down there instead? After all of this stress, I could use the time to relax and think."

My husband tilted his head, as if the action helped him think about what I had just said.

"They have a little boy about John's age, and it would be fun for everyone." At that, John turned towards us, ketchup on his face and salt on his fingertips, but a smile on his face.

"The land of the free," Ahmad repeated, and shook his head, although I knew that meant he had agreed to my plan.

Hours later, we were off to Houston.

We spent 10 days in Texas talking about old times, about the revolution and about how lucky we were to be back in America while John frolicked with his cousins and brushed up on his English, which was always the better of his two languages. We were fed and showed around town, given the best quarters in the house. And it was much like visiting friends and family in Iran, where I had grown used to the leisurely life of a well-off wife and the independence of a sometimes entrepreneur.

I laugh to think how entitled to it I felt, because soon enough, I was plunged back into the American life I remembered. A life where I was isolated from family and friends, had only the cold character of my husband for comfort, and fell from feeling I had reached adulthood and security back to feeling like a starving student again. The land of the free.

And other feelings I had almost forgotten began returning. My belly growing large and cumbrous, I was sick in my stomach and in my head all of the time, like someone was grabbing onto these parts of my body and shaking them, spinning them around and around like a carnival ride.

I waited in the hot and humid car with John while Ahmad went to check in with immigration in Miami, our stamped and approved visa form in hand. In the backseat with John, I pressed my clammy forehead against the glass and pondered some of the ancient questions: Where am I going? Who am I anyway? How did I get here? What is here for me? But then again, what was there for me if I hadn't been able to leave Iran? Which was worse: life under a regime of religious extremism or life under a husband of extreme shifts of mood?

My husband came back in a panic as there was some sort of trouble with our visas. The clerk had sent him to a room with "Deportation" written on it, and his blood pressure had gone through the roof. If anything, I felt myself sink. My life was in Ahmad's hands and in the hands of American fate. My fear slid through me like cold water, while my husband's was bubbling like lava.

There was a flurry of emotion and activity as we discussed what to do. Taking over as usual, I grabbed a yellow book from a nearby payphone and picked an attorney at random, who we hired to stop this deportation Ahmad foresaw. Then a few hours later, when we returned to the scary room labeled "Deportation," but the woman behind the desk simply went over our paperwork again, asked to see proof we could support ourselves in this country, and then declared, "I don't know why they sent you up to me. Why are you here?" She stamped our visas before the attorney we hired — at the cost of a nonrefundable $500 retainer — arrived in the building.

I walked out of that official government building and started down the impressive steps to the sidewalk. Only four months along and already my ankles and feet pulsed with discomfort. I heard the door click shut behind me after my son and my husband exited, and a memory suddenly surfaced, like a message in a bottle bobbing to the surface after riding the tides for years. The memory was of when I finished high school — without fanfare, without a graduation ceremony, with only a few oral exams and the click of the door closing behind me.

Another door to the past closed, I thought. Another goodbye to another part of my life. Another choice made — a choice to be a good wife and a good mother. I thought myself so independent and liberal, but when it came down to brass tacks, I had to brush off my tears and get on with it, forgetting the thrill of a single gin and tonic at Chattanooga or of hiring a car to drive John and I home from the glamorous Ice Palace. I said goodbye to the clothes I'd burned, to the friends that had been pulled away, to the dreams I'd had of what life outside my family's garden walls would be like.

Then John burst in front of me, his energy barely contained in the skinny limbs of his six-year-old body. He scampered down the sidewalk, turning around to walk backward to talk to me.

"And are we going to Disneyworld, Mom?" my little boy asked. "Are we finally going to get to go to Disneyworld?"

"Yes, son," I replied. My mood lightened. And in my head, I continued, "And you, my son, are going to an American school and an American college to have all the American opportunities you want."

One eye on my little boy and a hand under my navel, cupping my rounding belly, I knew that sometimes life seemed dark. But here was the sun in John, and whoever in there was the moon, and with them — living for them — I would never be hopeless or alone.

We rented a tiny, one-bedroom apartment in Melbourne, Florida. Once again, I entered this apartment with only the suitcases in my family's hands and this time not even a yellow, velvet blanket to spread upon the ground. The kitchen had no window and John didn't have a bedroom, but the landlady was a kind older woman who allowed us the use a bed, table and chairs, and a patterned green sofa that a previous tenant had left behind.

The next day, I went to K-Mart to shop for home essentials — silverware and salt shakers, dishes, pots and pans, bedding, curtains and rugs. I began to cry in the silverware aisle, holding a poorly made but cheap metal fork in my hand, my chin crushed to my chest.

"What is the matter with you now?" Ahmad asked.

I shook my head, unable to speak through the welling emotion in my throat. The tears were hot on my sweaty face offering me no relief.

I was looking at the fork and thinking about starting over. I had such solid, tasteful forks in Tehran, the kind to entertain anyone from immediate family to important or famous personages, the kind that could have been passed down through generations. Now, I had a crappy fork with a dull finish in my hand, light enough to blow away in a stiff breeze. I thought what I had was permanent. Silly me.

"You know I won't speak to you when you're crying," Ahmad told me, and he walked away.

John was holding on to my leg, always my friend and protector. "You OK, Mom?" he asked.

I nodded and patted his head. Then I sighed and put a set of the K-Mart forks in my cart.

I was me sad when I put away all our cheap, almost disposable new goods. I was sad because the grater was supposed to be in the second drawer from the fridge and because we were supposed to have a set of 24 dishes of French china, not four disposable dishes. Nothing was as it was supposed to be, how I had become used to it being.

I loved America. I truly did.

The people we met were usually so friendly. In fact, our landlady — knowing we had no friends or family in the state or even the country — threw me a lovely baby shower. Despite the fact that we were still building up the essentials for everyday existence, my unborn child now had clothes, diapers, bottles, an adorable bassinet with yellow-and-white checked fabric and little rollers on the feet. And it all came from the good hearts of women in the apartment complex that hardly knew us. I thanked the heavens for such wonderful people and their generosity, thinking of all the times my father had donated money to some poor women in our neighborhood, wondering if the world had come full circle.

I loved the American stores, where anything could be had if only you had the money in your pocket. I loved the fact that there were jobs everywhere: "now hiring" signs visible in the windows of Laundromats, gas stations, grocery stores. On the streets were teachers, lawyers, bankers, doctors, street sweeps, cashiers, salesman and every other conceivable profession. They mingled and talked or hurried along their way, each one contributing something to society, their movement keeping the ball rolling.

Many immigrants think that because there is opportunity in America, opportunity is going to fall into your lap. My hard work during our last residence taught me this wasn't true. It wasn't always easy. In fact, I would guarantee there would be hard work involved. But what was worth having that was so easily gained? I wondered. What excuse was there for laziness when you could see all around you the fruit of labor?

What I didn't love about America was my husband's behavior while living there. Almost immediately, it seemed he reverted to the same attitude he'd had the first time around. Suddenly the money we brought with us had vanished into thin air, or so he claimed, and his pockets were empty. Despite the fact that he would tell me about our poverty every time I needed pocket change for groceries or wanted medicine to soothe my horrible pregnancy heart burn, he laid around the house doing nothing. I'd point out that the 711 on the corner was hiring and he'd say the job was beneath him. Yet in the same hour, I would hear him complain about every important or rich person in the newspaper, how they only "made it" through either dumb luck or some vast conspiracy theory among the rich.

It doesn't take a genius, I thought, to know that most of the them worked for it, that some of those very success stories could probably point to a time in their past where they worked at a gas station or other such menial job to get their start.

Ahmad was blind to the contradiction: He thought those who had money got it too easily and yet that is the way he wanted it to come to him. The only valuable thing he did in Florida other than make a dent in the sofa in front of the television was take a class at the University, which kept up appearances that we were in the country for education.

It seemed we waited every three months for the money — our money, that we couldn't bring with us — that General was able to wire us, sometimes unable to pay for groceries or rent until the check came through. My landlady understood and cut us a break now and then, but fears grew along with my belly. Is this how life would be? Living off the money from the good times in Iran — money that I either earned myself or money Ahmad earned through the job I found him? Would there never be any good times again?

The value of the toman was plunging even further toward zero, and I feared that even this source of funding would run out. I called up my brother in Tehran to go over to the General's house, to pick up a few valuable things we'd stored there, including some of my fashionable purses, the washer and dryer, and little things like silver candle holders I couldn't part with at the time. The General's wife rudely told him that they'd had a break in and all the boxes had been stolen, an obvious lie both my brother and I saw through but could do nothing about.

I felt like a trespasser in my own life, my every need and want subject to the whim of my husband. My every step thought a play for power, my every thought potentially treasonous. I walked quietly and kept my thoughts to myself, packed up like a suitcase I toted along with me. Always living out of suitcase, physically and emotionally. I felt as if a stiff breeze would blow me away. I felt as if that was what Ahmad wanted me to be — quiet, docile, obedient.

And everything that was wrong was always my fault, including money. But big and bulky and as depressed as I'd ever been in my life, I couldn't work. So when Ahmad talked about money, or the lack thereof, I closed my ears and tuned out with my hands on my stomach, concentrating all my energy on the little life inside me, the little life that kept me tethered to this marriage. This little life that kept me tethered to myself, that stopped me from completely giving up hope. The connection between us was tangible and meaningful, and if it took all my strength to live through this terrible time just for this little person, I could do it. Whenever I thought I might not make it, the baby kicked at my stomach as if to say, "Remember me, Mom. It's all for me."

On July 4th, 1980, the most American of holidays, my second child was born — a daughter, an adorable little girl we named Melody. When she cried and then was placed in my arms, I instantly knew that my life had changed. She looked up with her deep black eyes and seemed as if she knew me, as if we had been friends in a former life and knew each other's souls. She was a girl, a brilliant and beautiful little baby girl, and I would now have a chance to mold a world that was perfect for her. My heart beat loud in my chest as I thought of how I would never hide the world away from this child, but throw the doors of the world open for her to explore. This little one would be my soul's second chance. This little girl would be American.

I knew that my personal struggles were little in the face of this new life full of potential. In that inspiring moment after Melody's birth, I had a revelation that reinvented how I saw myself. I was no longer a caged bird, and the sky was for the present no longer my goal. If I was only the earth in which my son and daughter could grow, that would be enough for me. My son the sun, my daughter the moon. If only that, it would be such a valuable contribution to the universe.

She was such a revolution in my life, transforming me from a woman who would run away into a woman that would live to fight another day. She changed the balance of the family, not only because there was now another girl to even the gender balance, but because we all now had a common purpose, a common goal, and that was doting on this beautiful little girl.

But especially for me, especially inside my mother's heart, Melody was a rebirth for me. All of her potential and beauty were also my own, made over young again, my own hope restored. Come on, world, I thought. Throw whatever you have at me, because as long as I have this bundle of joy cuddled in arms, I can take it, my own hope restored.

With the semester over and Ahmad thinking that was enough playing at school for the immigration department, we again pulled up the stakes of our lives like a traveling carnival family. We packed up the bassinet and pots and pans, leaving everything else, into the battered 1973 Maverick Ahmad bought and headed toward Chicago, where one of Ahmad's friends claimed he made $100 a day as a cab driver, the solitary profession Ahmad had once enjoyed in Washington D.C.

"You have to say goodbye," I told John, who cried over the loss of his pet turtle, an animal he'd found, and I'd allowed him to keep in a little terrarium in the apartment. "This is his home."

"But he's my friend," said John, tears running down his cheeks.

"I know," I said kindly, treading lightly on his fragile feelings. "But we all have to learn to say goodbye. It's part of life."

He sniffed. "Goodbye," he whispered, handing the turtle off to a little girl who lived in the building.

Melody bundled in my arms, and we set off on the road.

In Nashville, I heard the news that the Shah had succumbed to cancer and passed away. I was never political and I knew that the Shah had done wrong, though perhaps not to the extent that extremists claimed. But to me, it was still heart wrenching. He was *my* Shah, the man who'd been in power since I was a little girl, the only Shah I ever knew. His family was the one I looked up to as the pinnacle of elegance and success, his wife the model of beauty we all strived for, his the perfect life we all wanted to lead. It was his picture projected on the big screen before every film I ever viewed in Iran.

Though no one could hear me and I knew it made no difference, I whispered a goodbye of my own and I heard the pages turn on another chapter of my life, a chapter to which I would never be able to return.

The first time I arrived in the United States, I may have been legally an adult, but I was far from mature. I was toted from place to place like my husband's suitcase, and when I spoke out an opinion or voiced an objection, I was looked at like just such an inanimate object. My husband seemed as surprised as if the chair or the kitchen table had developed speech. I also learned that I was as expendable a as piece of furniture or a suitcase: Whenever I reached the point of despair, the point where I would yell and cry, I was told that my presence was nothing. I could be thrown out into the cold, "to the street corner" as Ahmad said.

Much had changed over the course of our marriage and our travels. I was far from the naïve and unworldly girl who folded herself into an army aircraft with her yellow velvet blanket. I was a grown-up woman with the responsibility of two children, a responsibility that I loved. I had climbed the mountain of success in Iran all by myself, with no male help, to find jewelry, riches and respect at the peak — and then had that torn away. I'd battled my own ideas of right and wrong, coming a hair's breadth from leaving my husband and charting my own course — only to be pulled back into my old life due to an unexpected, but eventually much beloved, pregnancy.

I now knew what it was like to shine like a star and fall like a comet. I knew what it was to plow over myself to plant the seeds for another life, becoming the fertile earth in which my children could grow.

In other words, I felt like I'd been through the wringer, twisted and pressed and pulled until I felt threadbare. I felt like I'd experienced enough for a whole lifetime in the course of a few years. And yet with all that experience behind me and all those lessons learned, we entered Chicago and I found I was right back in Ahmad's world again. The world of our student days, where every day was a battle for money and survival. After the struggle of that long journey, I again felt like my husband's suitcase.

The first place he deposited his suitcase — namely, me and our two children — was a dingy establishment called the Heart 'O the City motel. It was the sort of place where a "continental breakfast" was a pink box of hard donuts, and you could see your car parked outside when looking out the front window. You could hear the televisions in other rooms — and other more intimate noises — coming through the walls.

Ahmad would leave in the morning to go socialize with his friend in Chicago and the decent-sized community of Iranians living in Chicago, hoping to network in order to find an apartment, a job, a life in this new city. Of course, that meant that the children and I were stuck in the dingy hotel room. We couldn't really leave except to venture to the vending machine or the hotel lobby, because we had no car and I didn't know my way around this neighborhood. Plus, the neighborhood didn't really seem like the kind of place where families would feel safe walking to the park. The streets were dirty, graffiti-tagged and scary.

So we stayed in the stuffy room and watched television. I paced with baby Melody back and forth across the shag carpet, holding the bundle close to my chest. I didn't want to put her down on any surface in that cheap and dirty room, knowing that everything was crawling with germs. She was only a month and a half old, and I was haggard from lack of sleep and still recovering from the birth.

When Ahmad returned home, he was vague about where he had been and who he had met, but I could tell that he'd been eating well by the smell of kebab on his clothes. Taking the family to McDonalds made him feel like a big hero, even if he made us order the least expensive food on the menu. Then he wanted only to watch TV all evening, even though we'd been stuck doing just that all day long.

During what sleep I could grab between Melody's constant feedings and nighttime crying; I began to dream of birds again. A small red-breasted bird — my old friend from the days of my ice-cream tree — was hopping through dense grass and leaves, the tall vegetation making him seem extra small on his dainty feet. Drops of blood followed him across the ground. Then I was the bird myself. I felt my heart racing as I hopped slowly away and the pain in my wing, which kept me from flying. There was something behind me or above me, something coming after me, and I knew I had to keep hopping because my children were just over that ridge. My kids were in danger, and so I plodded on.

I woke with my heart thumping to Melody crying out in hunger. And I stumbled from bed and picked her up to soothe her. I walked her back and forth, plodding along, still feeling like that helpless little bird with the clipped wings. I looked at my husband sleeping in the motel bed, immediately realizing that he was the one who clipped them — or at least one of the people who clipped them.

But where would I fly anyway? I asked myself, bouncing the baby. Where would I go and what would I do? I sighed, resigned, and returned to bed.

After a few days caged up in the motel room, I couldn't take the confinement any longer. I convinced a friend of ours — the taxi driver who made $100 a day and convinced us to move — to take me for a drive.

I wanted an apartment and I wanted one now, and I made him stop at the first "for rent" sign I saw. It was on Touhy Street, a four-story building owned by a nice, grey-haired Jewish man I met in the lobby. The cleanliness and style of the place impressed me, so I didn't even bat an eye when the man said the available apartment was on the fourth floor, that there was no elevator and that rent was $800 per month. In 1980, $800 was practically extortion, but he must have sensed my desperation and I was at the point where I didn't care. I rented the apartment on the spot and we moved in by the end of the summer.

It was truly as if the last few years of my life hadn't happened, that I'd stepped back in time to our first years in America. Far, far away from the life of luxury in Iran — full of drivers, servants, excellent china dishes and high-quality designer clothes — I was back in low-price stores, snapping up pots and pans, furniture and other household goods.

Though expensive, the apartment was still not ideal. It had a wretched view of the brick wall of the building next to us and hauling Melody and her stroller up the stairs several times a day was draining, to say the least. The two-bedroom apartment afforded John his own room, and Melody slept in our bedroom. Often, it was just the two of us, mother and daughter, drifting off to sleep at night. Cab drivers, I began to remember, often become nocturnal creatures and keep odd hours. Frankly, I didn't care and didn't even take the time to notice his presence or absence most of the time.

Dinner was on the table at 6 at night, and if he was there, he ate it without comment. If he wasn't home, I'd put it on the back burner for him to heat up whenever he wanted. Sometimes he ate out. Sometimes he'd put uneaten food back in the refrigerator, sometimes not. I kept my head down to my duties as a mother and kept swimming. You know, I thought, no one ever told me that marriage was such a lonely thing.

John started attending a local private school, a Catholic institution that had a great reputation. We didn't think too much of it, but got him the school uniform and sent him out to the bus, knowing that he would attend mass and learn about Jesus Christ. Ahmad and I didn't even sit down to discuss the religious aspect of it. Certainly, learning about Christianity was simply a part of being an American, and Americans were definitely what we wanted our children to grow up to be. We were looking for the best school, and we'd found it, and that was all that was important. I knew in my heart that our children would be introduced to God — both the Catholic and Islamic depictions of Him — but would find their own way to religion as they matured.

John found his way as one of the three wise men in the school's Christmas play. We sat in the audience, probably the only Persians in the group, and applauded as loud as we could for our little man, whose face split into the biggest smile when he took the stage. That Christmas, we were invited to several neighbors' houses to celebrate, were plied with food and made to feel very welcome. As usual, the kids and I made friends. Ahmad made sarcastic remarks and sat by himself, also as usual.

On New Year's Eve, all the cabdrivers work the whole night through, and Melody was running a burning fever. John was fast asleep in bed, and I rocked the baby back and forth, back and forth, waiting for the fever to break. Her forehead was definitely hotter than my steaming tea, and she scalded my chest where I held her tight. My mother's intuition wouldn't let me rest, so I went down four flights to start the car warming. On a frigid night in Chicago, the vehicle could easily take 20 minutes to warm up. Then, with one last peek in John's room and a check to make sure the oven was off, I wrote a note to my husband, bundled Melody up, locked the door, said a prayer and took off in the car to the hospital's emergency room — driving below the speed limit and extra carefully in the snow the whole way.

A few shots and a few hours later, the fever had been brought down and medicines prescribed. It was a scary but normal childhood sickness, and we headed home. Outside the emergency room where the ambulances pulled up, I stopped for a moment in the pre-dawn darkness. Something on the ground moved to draw my attention.

It was a bird, a city pigeon, which looked hurt and unable to fly. It seemed as if he'd been making his way to the emergency room and had fallen just a few feet short.

Poor thing, I thought. I flashed back to my dreams of the hurt, flightless bird and the abject terror that accompanied the dream. Without stopping to think, I grabbed a paper towel from the car and scooped the wounded bird up, cushioned him on the seat of the warm vehicle and took him home.

I didn't sleep at all that night. I arrived home and deposited Melody in bed where, exhausted from her ordeal, she fell sound asleep. Then I dealt with the other patient, the bird. In front of the radiator where it was nice and warm, I laid out a little blanket, a bowl of water and a crust of bread. He settled right in, as if he knew exactly what I was about, walking around in circles several times and then scooting his tail feathers into the blanket making a warm nest.

A few minutes later, John appeared from his bedroom, ready for breakfast, but he was arrested in his steps when he saw the moving, feathery shape sitting as if on a nest on the carpet.

"What is that?" He practically yelled, taken so by surprise.

I was puttering around in the kitchen, preparing his morning meal. I turned and over the counter, said, "It's a bird, John."

He rolled his eyes. "I know it's a bird, Mom. But what is a bird doing inside our house?" John walked closer to the little bird and saw the strange way the bird was holding his injured wing. "He's hurt!"

"Yes, he's hurt," I said. "We met outside the hospital, where I had to take your sister last night because of her fever." I explained that the bird was right outside the entrance to the emergency room and that I just couldn't bear to leave him there to die. "Instead, we can be his emergency room."

John was quiet, crouching carefully on the floor next to his new friend and moving slowly so as not to startle the weak creature. He reached out a tentative finger and stroked the soft feathers on the bird's head and neck.

"You know, in Iran, it's very popular to keep birds in the house and to breed them or train them," I said. "In fact, my uncle ..." I stopped in mid sentence. I didn't want to go back to that bloody memory. I wanted this bird to live. I wanted to see him fly out the window and return to freedom, somehow making up for the bird my Javad had wounded. I wanted to change the story.

Luckily, John was having too much fun to notice how I had trailed off. He was breaking the bread into tiny pieces and setting the crumbs within pecking distance. "Maybe we should put a bandage of some sort on the bird's little wing," said John, his eyes full of tenderness and empathy. This boy was not going to be one that broke birds — or women — to his will.

I smiled and nodded, getting the first aid kit.

A few days later, John opened a window and offered it to our little friend, and the bird flew away, never to be seen again. John wanted it to go and to thrive.

"He found his ER," he laughed. "The bird got hospital care, but no bill!"

My heart warmed in my chest, seeing his kind eyes alight with laughter.

Chapter Twenty-Three

We celebrated Melody's first birthday in that apartment, and the pictures tell the story. I'd invited 15 or 20 Iranian families we knew from all over Chicago, and the kids were running around like a tornado of excitement as the grown-ups talked and drank tea. There she was in her pink, frilly dress. I'd purchased it at Marshall Fields, still not close to tired of buying clothing for a girl, of getting to dress her up like a living doll. She was a smiling baby, very cuddly, with not a cross bone in her body. She cried when she was hungry or tired, but never out of crankiness. She was an angel, with sunshine beaming from her bright, toothless smile.

In all the photographs, she's never far from me, always on my hip, in my arms, on my lap or hanging on to my leg. And then there was the family unit: John and I holding up Melody on her big present, a bouncing horse. John was having as much fun as she was. He adored taking care of his little sister and went about the task with a stern, adult attitude that made me stifle my laughter. Ahmad was there, but stiff in the photos, as if on the edges.

Except when he touched Melody. His exterior melted away and he gave a rare, genuine smile of happiness, exposing a little bit of his heart. Her life and the joy it gave us pulled the family together like gravity, keeping us rotating around each other like the planets around the sun.

We moved from the expensive but somewhat dingy apartment in downtown Chicago to the suburb of Skokie, Illinois. It was an area known as a Jewish community, and its streets were clean and safe. The apartment was still on the fourth floor with no elevator — and the laundry in the basement — but it had three bedrooms and was fully furnished. And the furniture was so much better than my own, especially the marble coffee table, which I adored. I also loved that I could look out my window to see where John would catch the school bus and also the cute little park where the kids played after school.

Soon enough, money became an issue between me and Ahmad. Now that she could walk and was starting to talk, he found it difficult to see why I would need to stay at home all day to take care of Melody.

"After all," he said, "it's not like she's a baby anymore."

"But she's not in school, and I don't —"

He interrupted. "You Persian women! Lots and lots of American women work, and they leave their kids at daycare or with a babysitter, and they turn out just fine."

A cold wave of fear spread through my body as I imagined the picture in my head: her pudgy arms reaching back for me through a doorway as I tried to hand her to a stranger, her cheeks damp and shiny with tears. And my cheeks damp with tears, too.

"I should have just married an American woman for all the good you are," he grumbled. It was a complaint he had thrown at me often, that he should have married an American. "We spent all that money on beauty school for you, and you've never picked up a comb in this country."

We spent all that money on a master's degree for you, I thought silently, and you've put that knowledge to use driving a cab. There was no point in expressing the thought out loud.

Ahmad had a way of wearing you down. If he got an idea into his head, he found a million little ways to insert that idea into every day, every interaction. Because he wanted me to go back to work, everything became about money. If I bought new socks, he'd ask why I didn't mend the holes in the old ones and didn't care that John had grown too big for them. When I cooked dinner, he'd complain that the type of meat I used was too expensive of a cut and that I should have bought cheaper if I wanted to stay home and live off his money. Haircuts, trips for ice cream, movie tickets: There were no luxuries allowed, and still he found ways to nitpick, even going over my grocery receipts.

One evening in the park, I met our downstairs neighbor, Carol, sitting on the bench while her kids played. Her young daughter was less than a year older than Melody and we had sons who were the same grade at the same school, so we'd run into one another several times. I'd had her up to tea and we'd chat amiably. But this night, something was on my mind.

"So you work in an office, Carol?" I asked. She was a single mother, and I knew that she worked full time.

"Yeah, I'm an administrative assistant," she replied.

"And you like it OK?"

"It pays the bills, and most of the time, I enjoy it."

I paused. "And what about the kids? Is it hard to ..." My words trailed off, stifled by the tears rising in my throat. Ahmad had been putting so much pressure on me that I felt worn and stressed.

"It's never easy," she replied in time, and I could tell from her tone that she took the subject very seriously. "I am lucky that I have my mom. She lives across the street. I pay her $25 a week or so to watch the kids. She's their grandmother, so it's great that they're with family, but I miss them."

The kids shouted from the playground, jerking our attention back to them, but it was only a loud game they were playing.

"My mother is getting older, though, and I don't know how much longer she'll be able to do it."

I nodded. In this whole great big city, I had no family of this kind, no one to depend upon but myself. I shivered.

"So what are you doing?" Carol asked, her voice more cheerful as she tried to change the subject.

"Nothing," I said. "I have a cosmetology degree, and I loved that work, but I don't want to leave Melody. Now that she's not a baby anymore, though..."

She nodded. "I'm sure you're fabulous at cutting hair! You're so creative."

I smiled weakly.

"Look," she said. "Kids are resilient, and there's no way on earth those kids don't know that you love them with all your heart. Being a mother is hard. Harder than any man will ever know, I think."

I laughed, and soon enough, she joined in with me. Before I took the kids inside, I had the name of a local daycare center Carol had heard of, though she hadn't used it herself.

So many mothers do this, have to do this and get through it, I repeated to myself. I can, too.

The daycare was located in a small shopping center, on the corner of the complex. Melody was almost 2 and dressed in a dark blue knitted sweater with flowers on the shoulders, matching the flowers on her pants. I had been here once before to sign up and fill out some paperwork, but Melody hadn't and I thought she'd be scared. But so far, she seemed happy and up for anything.

I carried her bag full of diapers and such, and handed it off to the teacher, who told me about the meal schedule, the other kids and nap time.

"And you can come and pick her up at 5 o'clock?" she asked me.

"That's right. Five." I was watching Melody tentatively getting to know another little boy about her age and my heart beat fast. Part of me was happy she would make friends and have fun, and the other half of me felt slighted, as if she didn't need her mother anymore.

"Don't worry," said the teacher, sensing my mood. "Everything is going to be fine."

I took a deep breath, waved goodbye and left the room as quickly as I could, hoping Melody wouldn't catch on right away. I couldn't have stood her tears.

I then got in the family's car and headed toward the beauty shop I'd been working in part time. This would be my first full day, and Melody's first day in daycare, and I was nervous on both counts.

I didn't need to be nervous about the work, in the end. The Chicago sky opened up and poured rain all day. It seemed that no one wanted to go out and get their hair done only to venture back into the rain, because we had very few customers all day long. By the afternoon, I had $13 in my pocket for the day. The daycare cost $20 per day for Melody.

So I'd lost $7. Maybe I can at least go early and pick up my baby, I thought. There were no customers and other stylists to help customers if they came, so my boss agreed and I went to pick Melody up at 4 p.m. instead of 5 p.m.

I walked into the school and directly into the kids' room, which was still dark for naptime. There were kids arranged all over the floor and only one girl in the room, a young girl who wasn't the teacher I'd spoken to in the morning. The moment she saw me, she strode across the room and quickly yanked Melody from her nap, startling her awake and scaring her to tears.

"What happened?" I asked, unnerved by her actions.

The girl ran Melody into the back room and hurriedly changed her diaper.

"What are you doing?" I asked.

"Hold on," she said.

A few moments later, she returned the crying, startled Melody to me. My hands instantly recoiled: Her pants were soaked through, cold, damp and nasty to the touch.

"What?"

"She's wet," the girl said. Obviously, I thought.

"And where are her extra pants?"

The girl shook her head.

"And where are her diapers? Why was she not changed?" I stripped off the wet pants to see the fresh diaper. Her legs and bottom were covered with tiny red dots, inflamed from being wet for hours at a time.

Anger flamed in my eyes, while at the same time, tears began to well up in my throat. If the two met, steam would certainly come out of my ears. I was instantly mad — not at this young girl, even though she or the whole school deserved it — at my husband, at the life that I was living. Why must I work and leave me children to be neglected? Why can my husband not provide enough that I can raise my family in the best way, by being at home? Why does he not care about these things? And then came a thought that startled me in its honesty: Why can I not be with someone I love, and who loves me?

The girl had gone searching for the extra clothes and the kids were stirring on the floor, waking up.

"Never mind! Never mind!" I whispered loudly. "Give me that!"

I grabbed a blanket to wrap Melody's lower body, her pretty blue sweater looking out of place. In a few hours, they'd managed to make a mess of her. Underneath her sweater, her little undershirt was stained up to the armpits with yellow moisture. They probably hadn't paid a lick of attention to her since I dropped her off.

I stormed out of the room, swearing to myself. Why did I have to go back to work? Why today? Why this place? Guilt flooded over me as I held her cheek-to-cheek, running my fingers through her hair.

I got in the car and resumed my tirade, this time on four wheels. For this, I lost $7, I thought. I must have driven through a stop sign in my distress, because before I knew it, I was pulled over by a policeman. The held back tears were streaming over my face as I blubbered to him about my awful day, the $13 and the $20, the wet pants.

"I'm sorry, ma'am," he said to me through the driver's window, handing me a slip of official-looking paper. "But the law is the law." He tipped his hat.

"And now you're giving me a $40 ticket," I said, shaking my head. I didn't have $40 to spare and Ahmad was not going to be happy at all.

Keeping my emotions under control — which was a huge struggle — I made it home and I knew I could never go back, that I could never again leave Melody in such a place. I did love cosmetology, but I loved my daughter more, in the fierce way of Persian mothers.

But there was still a problem. There was still the overwhelming, aching pressure of Ahmad's financial griping to think about. I took a deep breath.

Later that night, I went down one level to the third floor, where Carol lived. I knocked and waited anxiously in the hallway. When she opened the door, all of the words that I'd been planning in my head for hours came tumbling out.

"You know what? I just can't do it. I can't leave Melody at one of those places, and I'm so upset that I can't even tell you how bad it was today," I said, the words coming out fast and furious. "I can't go back to that daycare, so I can't go back to work. But if I'm home and because I still need the money, how about I watch the kids for you? Little Stacy and Melody are such great friends, and I can watch her all day. Then the boys can come over after school until you get home."

She opened her mouth as if to speak, but I kept going.

"I know they stay with their grandmother now, and if you still want to do that, I'll understand. But I would be so grateful for the $25 a week, and I doing nothing that I wouldn't be doing anyway, and the kids wouldn't have to leave the building at all."

I paused for breath, finally looking up to meet her eyes, which were still as warm and friendly as always.

"Of course, Maryam," she said. "You must have had a horrible day, but this is great news. I'd love to have you watch the kids."

She reached out and hugged me, which was just what I needed after the day I had. "It's going to be great," she said.

For the first time in weeks, if not months, I felt as if I had found a solution, that I could live my life without a great weight on my head. I was very happy.

For a few months, we were the three musketeers: Melody, Stacy and I. Stacy was an absolute doll of a toddler with blond hair and a dimpled smile. It was coming on winter, and to avoid the chill, Carol would cradle the girl in her arms to carry her upstairs in the morning in her pajamas, wrapped in a blanket. She'd doze for a little longer on the couch and then I'd dress her along with Melody a little later.

When I stayed home with Melody, I was doing all the chores a mother does to take care of a child. I dressed her, bathed her, played with her and fed her. I was amazed to find how easy it was to do the same thing for two little girls instead of one.

It helped, of course, that Melody and Stacy were such fast friends. They could play quietly together with a few dolls for hours, or laugh themselves silly splashing one another with water in the bathtub. After bath, they'd stand on a bench to see themselves in the mirror and comb their hair, and they were mirror images. One blond and fair, one black-haired and olive, but the same smile.

There was a walk-in closet in the main room of the apartment, and I took the doors off of it to create a separate space for the kids, but a space where I could still monitor them closely. With string, I hung stuffed animals like birds and bumble bees from the ceiling, and the floor was covered with board books, dolls, blocks and the wind-up toy that spoke, saying, "The cow says moo!"

For lunch there would be macaroni and cheese or vegetable soup, for that was a handy way to sneak vegetables into their diet. Other times, I'd make mashed potatoes and sculpt a stack of the potatoes into a bird — somehow, it was always birds in my life. I'd then make a valley in the bird's back and fill it with green peas.

"I'm going to eat the head first," said Stacy.

"Let's attack it!" I said.

We all seemed to know that we were alone, that this apartment during the day was our own little world. At least, I knew it. I was free to play my favorite role as mother and my husband was off my mind and out of my hair. The extra $25 a week was good money for not having to leave the house, and I didn't have to ask Ahmad for money all the time. He let me take that $25 for groceries and out-of-pocket expenses. I wasn't begging for pocket change to run errands, made to feel guilty because we were out of eggs or milk. The money was a little taste of freedom, of carving out my own space — no matter how small — and I relished it.

Within three months, I knew that I'd found a good solution for my current problem. No, I wasn't doing cosmetology, but I was still being social and creative. And I didn't have to leave my precious daughter with a stranger in order to make money.

Within three months of having the two girls during the day and the two boys after school, I was already formulating plans. I'm just not the sort to take what's given, but always want to know what's possible, how far I can go along a path.

Therefore, with the help of a Persian friend of mine who had undertaken the same plan, I set about becoming a licensed home daycare so I could bring even more children into my home and perhaps earn upwards of $100 per week. I could also provide a friendly and comfortable place for other parents to leave their children without worry, a place unlike that cold, mean daycare I made the mistake of taking Melody to once upon a time.

I called up the state to get the proper paperwork and schedule a home inspection. Then I invested some money in bringing the apartment up to snuff, buying cots for the kids to nap on, plugging electrical outlets, cushioning sharp furniture edges and acquiring a few more toys for the kids to share. I put up flyers at the local grocery store and told everyone I knew — I was always a social one, so that was quite a few — that I was looking for new clients. Within weeks, I was running a profitable daycare from my home for a few toddlers, all similar to Melody and Stacy's age, and a few older kids for after-school care.

"Oh my God," I thought. "I'm really doing this. I'm running my own business again."

Of course, the experience was nothing like running the beauty school in Tehran, far less glamorous. I'd greet the parents dropping off their kids early each morning, thankful that I didn't have to venture out into the cold grey days I saw outside my window. They played with toys and each other while I chatted on the phone or watched a little television. We watched the fish swim in my aquarium or we went across the street to the park to play. It was often difficult to coax the kids out of that converted walk-in closet, which they thought of as their little fort. No grown-ups allowed!

At the end of the day, the parents would come home, tired from a long day at work and missing their children. I'd offer tea and we'd often chat, socializing about this and that and talking about what their children did that day. Then I'd make dinner for my own family — whether Ahmad was there to eat it or not — and go to bed to repeat the cycle the next day.

After the stress of leaving Iran and the feelings of utter helplessness that had surrounded me, the routine and responsibility were comforting. I was on my feet. I was surviving.

John was 8 years old, going to school and blossoming in the American system. Every morning on the school bus, he was as excited as if he was off to Disneyland again. And Melody was growing into a little person, with ideas and a personality of her own. All the while, Ahmad drove a cab — making his own schedule, counting his money, keeping the exact amount he earned a secret from me.

And it was enough.

Every morning, I woke up early to meet with the parents of the kids in my care. I calmed their tears and hugged them. Then I hugged my boy, smoothing his hair and kissing him on the cheek before he set off for school.

And I thought about how long it would be until he was a man, how long it was until I could leave his father. How long until my cage door opened and I could fly again. Ten more years, I told myself, and he'll be 18. There will be 10 more years until this little boy becomes a little man, off to college and into the bright future.

Then every evening when my husband's key scraped in the lock and he pushed the door opened, permeating what I considered my apartment with his bad attitude and cynicism, I repeated my mantra again. Ten more years, I thought, trying to convince myself it wasn't so long a time.

At that point in my life, my perspective narrowed to encompass only what was important: my children. If I stopped focusing on that one thing for very long, I felt the pull of depression and pain lurking just under the surface. If I didn't focus completely on them, I would have to think about myself. About my education, about possible careers I couldn't have, about places I wouldn't go and about the people I wish I could have been with. That was something I couldn't bear to do.

At that point in my life, time began to stream past me like the water of a river. I knew it was there, but I couldn't have picked out each individual droplet. I just let the current wash over me and kept my head above the river. Therefore, many of my memories are vague and indistinct, like watching a movie underwater.

Only once did we try to go on vacation and, amazingly, it was Ahmad's idea. Some of our friends were speaking about taking trips, taking time off, and I think he needed to feel like our family was as important as theirs. I went along with the idea. Why not? It was a vacation, and we'd never really taken John anywhere except to Iran.

We packed up the car with sandwiches and snacks and left Chicago for Lake Geneva, where Ahmad had gotten it into his head to go. "I just want you to see it," he explained, saying no more.

After a scenic drive, we arrived at Lake Geneva in the evening and it was lovely. The lake was a beautiful, still body of water with nice hotels and docks lining the shores. It smelled of the country, without the exhaust or city odors I'd become so used to. For a moment, I thought of the Caspian Sea. But only for a moment.

It turned out that Ahmad hadn't reserved a hotel room, thinking he could just walk in and get one when we arrived. So we drove to one establishment that looked promising and he strode into the lobby while we stayed in the car. John was excitedly looking at all the boats and I jostled Melody on my lap, her young enough to still be in diapers.

When Ahmad came back to the car, John and I started to gather up our stuff, thinking we were heading inside. But Ahmad's face was dark and stormy.

"It's expensive," he said as he slid back into the driver's seat, leaving the door swung open.

"What's expensive?" I asked.

"The hotel. It's $50." In the 1980s, $50 was certainly a lot of money. But this trip was his idea, I thought. Certainly he knew that a hotel room in a nice vacation destination like this one would be a little pricey.

He stared out the windshield, saying nothing. His eyes were focused forward, but I could tell by the tension in his jaw that he was waiting for me to say or do something.

"Fifty dollars," he repeated, nodding his head. Then he again sat waiting, saying nothing.

"Well," I finally said in reply. "And?"

"We cannot spend that kind of money," he said, his voice rising. "I don't have the kind of money for that."

"Then what are we going to do?" I asked.

He waited a little longer, casting one sidelong glance at me. I thought maybe he was looking at my purse, and I thought I understood what this little showdown was all about. He wanted me to pay.

"I don't have the money, either!" I declared, my anger rising.

He grunted. We looked out the window at the water.

"I want the kids to see the lake in the morning, in the sunlight, and get to play."

"But you don't want a hotel?" I asked skeptically.

He was silent.

"This was all your idea, Ahmad," I stated, my voice rising. "You wanted to go on vacation. You wanted to come here. And now you don't have a plan. This is just great." The anger and frustration rose hot in my throat and warmed my blood, a bone-deep anger I had experienced often with this man but never got accustomed to. My lips were heavy and it felt as if my skin was giving off steam, but my brain froze and my throat closed over any words that might have made him understand me. With my anger came my tears, and after the tears came the quiet despair and hopeless feelings of powerlessness.

From experience, I knew my anger would do me no good. Whenever my temper flared, Ahmad would just ignore me until it abated. It was never dealt with, just pushed aside like dust under the rug. I swear, he was a psychological genius in this way, manipulating my moods to make them weapons against me. He'd wait and wait and wait until my anger petered out and I was left feeling like an irrational child, or maybe like an invisible woman. What was the use raging and crying about things if you were invisible?

"Let's just go home, then," I said. "We came and we saw, and now let's go home. What else do you want to do?"

His jaw was clenched and he didn't even look at me. He just left the car, slammed the door and went to the hood, which he popped open so

I could no longer see him. I wanted to cry, but instead I held back my tears and swallowed my anger, not wanting to place the kids in an even more uncomfortable situation.

In 30 minutes, I'd achieved that quiet despair that Ahmad always waited for — that moment when I was subdued, tamed and under his control again — and he seemed to sense it. He slid back into the car and said we couldn't go home because of some vague issue with the motor needing rest.

"We will stay in the car," he declared.

"All night?" I asked.

"Of course," he replied.

My sinuses were dried out and my brain had surrendered. I had no voice anyway, so why speak? Ahmad, on the other hand, seemed slightly smug. In fact, he always seemed slightly smug when I achieved this state of bruised ego and hopelessness, as if he'd won a battle. I just felt like I had banged my head against a brick wall until I had no more strength. He was so calm, as if nothing that happened was of significance. In the end, I felt like I was the crazy one, that I had uncontrollable episodes of anger and sadness for no reason. I always began to doubt myself, that I had a right to my feelings.

So we slept in the car. The baby was uncomfortable, not happy in my lap but not happy alone on the backseat. We allowed John to stretch out in back — he was a lanky boy with long legs. I tried in vain to find a comfortable way to recline the seat. There were no blankets, only jackets to bunch up around us. My head kept slipping off the head rest, and I just waited for the dawn to come.

This, too, will pass, I thought. This has to end at some point. I will just wait.

The kids did get to see the lake in the sunlight and play along its shores, and they seemed to enjoy it. I remember the lapping water reflected in Melody's big eyes as she scampered around, and John splashed and examined the boats with curiosity. Then we went home.

I don't remember speaking a word.

The only amusing part of the debacle was how Ahmad continued to tell friends and family that he'd taken us to Lake Geneva on a family vacation, puffing up his chest and acting like a big man. But I knew that if I ever inserted the fact that we slept in the car into the conversation in order to embarrass Ahmad, it would embarrass me just as much. I had grown up in a world, after all, where a woman was only as valuable as the attention lavished upon her by her husband or father.

I was ashamed in my heart for what Ahmad's behavior said about me. Was this what I was worth?

I had one part time client at my daycare: an elementary schooler named Ahab with an American mother and an Arab father. His mother had lived in the Middle East and knew the culture, and the family was very rich and not afraid of showing it. Ahab's mother, Peggy, would drive up in her Cadillac car and in her designer clothes, her fingers and neck loaded with jewelry, and she'd drop him off for a few hours after school so she could make other appointments or run errands. Other times, I'd watch the boy — a quiet and agreeable kid of no trouble at all — while his parents went out to dinner or a show in the evenings.

I think that Peggy knew how much I was struggling, financially that is. She knew where I came from, what kind of family I had and even of my days as a beauty pageant queen and the head of the beauty school in Tehran. And here I was babysitting her kid. She'd give me $20 for an evening or a few hours of watching Ahab during the afternoon, and she wouldn't hear of me taking any less.

Ahab and John were friends from school, and loved to play together in the neighborhood park. As the sun was beginning to set behind the suburban buildings one evening, she pulled up to my building in the shiny, expensive Cadillac. Peggy saw the kids and me across the street and clicked over on her stylish high heels. I sighed at her glamour.

She sat down next to me for a moment to let Ahab say goodbye.

"Peggy," I said. "You're lucky. You have a rich husband and a Cadillac and everything in the world." I immediately wondered if I had gone too far, stepped into territory where it wasn't polite to ask such things. But

I couldn't help myself. Where I was at that moment, I needed to commit the thought in my head to words.

She turned to look at me very directly, pausing to peer into my eyes to gauge my feelings. Finally she replied.

"You know what? Sometimes I wish I had a Volkswagen and that it was my own."

I sat in thought for a moment, surprised, and then I nodded. She gave me $20 and gathered up her son, hugging him tight before walking back to the car and driving back to their expensive house, with its perfect Persian carpets and perfect furniture. It was both comforting and sad to know that life inside the house — the life of the rich — wasn't perfect either.

At the end of every week, after scrimping and clipping coupons for the grocery store, I gave Ahmad some of the money I made at the in-home daycare. But I took a portion, sometimes a lot and sometimes only a little, and put the money into an account that only I knew about.

"This is my own," I thought to myself. Maybe one day I'd have a Volkswagen, too.

Somehow, my husband deduced that I was saving money, although he didn't know where or how much. I knew nothing about how much he made every day in the cab or what he did with it, other than once a month he'd scowl and curse while making out the bills at the kitchen table. The only answer I ever got from him about money was that there wasn't any.

Once he had his suspicions that I was holding back a little bit of what I made with the daycare, he started casually hinting about it. He'd ask where I got a certain piece of clothing, hoping to catch me spending, only to find out I'd had it for years. He would point out nice things in the store and then remark how nice it would be to have such things, if we only had the money. That man had a nose for money, and once he got on the trail, he wasn't about to give up.

In the end, he decided to try to appeal to me on a level I would understand. While he was always fine with how our life was going and how we lived, I always yearned for better. "We're not students, anymore," I would often say, trying to keep my voice dispassionate and reasonable. "Why are you still driving a cab? What are you doing with your master's degree?" He would shrug and turn back to the TV, happy as long as his dinner was warm.

Instead of devoting himself to television, however, one evening he started to tell me about the finances of driving a cab, something he rarely discussed.

"I'm not making any money lately," he said.

"Oh?"

"They raised the cab rent," he explained, "to $100 a day, and that's so much. I have to make back that $100 and money for gas before I have any money to bring home."

"And that's not possible?"

"It's possible, but very hard, and some nights I end up paying for the privilege of working." He paused, letting that soak in. "But hey, it's a job, right?"

He then pretended to turn back to the TV, that tension in his jaw showing me that he was watching me from the corner of his eye, waiting for a reaction of some sort. It was the look he always got when he was springing a trap.

"Well, if that's the way it's done," I said. "That is what all the other drivers do."

"No," he replied. "Some of the other drivers own their own cabs, so they pay no rent at all. They walk home with all their money after gas expenses." He bit a nail, trying to act like he didn't overly care about what we were discussing. "But it takes a lot of money to buy a cab. I don't have that money."

I bit my lip for a moment, thinking about the money in my savings and the possible increase in income and freedom we could have if Ahmad owned a cab. If you had your own taxi cab, you were really an entrepreneur, a small businessman. That was certainly better in prestige than just being a cabbie, which was the same thing Ahmad did while we were scraping by as students while our friends were working their way up the economic ladder.

"How much would a cab of our own cost?" I asked.

His eyes brightened. "About $6,000," he answered quickly. "Or so I've been told."

"I don't have $6,000," I said. "Hmm."

He shrugged his shoulders. "Oh well," he said. "I don't care if I bring in money, but I know you do. So if you want to do something about it, that's up to you."

Sometime in the next few days, I formulated a plan. I called up some Persian friends of ours in Washington D.C., the husband of which was a hardworking man who'd built up a car dealership to profitability and success. They weren't incredibly rich, but they were both very smart and business savvy, and I knew they'd help me if they could.

After a few preliminaries, I got right to the point. "I need to buy a cab," I told him.

He immediately laughed. He had known us when we lived in Washington, when Ahmad first drove a taxi, so he said, "Ahmad again?"

Not willing to agree and laugh at my husband or stand up for him either, I just continued explaining. As a car dealer, he confirmed that $6,000 would cover the cost of the kind of taxi we wanted to buy. "I have $1,000," I told him, wincing at the thought of giving away that much of my savings. "But if I can borrow $5,000 from you, I can pay you back at about $300 a month until it's done." I had all these numbers written down; my plan drawn up in advance.

"You are doing these things again?" he asked, again almost laughing. The struggle to make ends meet, the battle to improve our situation: He was right. I had been doing the same thing, pushing my husband up in the world with the sweat off my own brow, for many, many years.

"What choice do I have?" I responded.

"Ach, I know, Maryam. I know," he said. He paused for a moment, as if thinking. "I'm sorry, but I just don't have $5,000 to lend you."

I let out the breath I didn't know I was holding in, my spirits sinking. "That's OK," I said. "I understand."

"No, no," he replied. "I don't have the money, but I can borrow it from a friend of mine I think. He has no problem lending money in the Persian community but he will charge you interest."

"How much?"

"It would probably equal an extra $1,000 after all is said and done."

Without hesitation, I said, "I can do that. We can do that."

Within a few days, there was an extra $5,000 in our bank account, wired in from Washington D.C. There were no in-person meetings, no paperwork and no formal agreement. That was just the way things were done. After all, the Persian community was close-knit in America — someone you know knew someone who knew someone — and if the deal went bad, the shame that followed you around the country would be a worse punishment than any violation of contract would be. The lender got the reputation of being a generous man and we were able to buy a taxi cab to improve our station in life, and everybody wins.

"We pay $300 a month?" Ahmad asked, his eyes squinting up as he thought about the weight of that money. "Where do you think I get an extra $300 a month?"

"You will be earning more because you don't have to pay taxi rent," I said, confused at his response.

"Maybe and maybe not. Such things are never certain," he said. "Because it is you who wants this extra income so much, I think you should pay half of that $300 every month, too, just like me."

I pressed my lips together. It was me who wanted the extra money so much? I found that laughable when he was the one for whom money was always on the mind, the one who had been scheming to access my savings for weeks and the one who wouldn't even consider earning more money so his wife didn't have to work. And I was money obsessed? Right.

"Either you pay half, or it doesn't happen," he added, but in his head I could see him already counting every dime, congratulating himself for getting the down payment on a taxi and half of the payments for free. He loved getting something for nothing.

"Fine, Ahmad," I said. "Fine."

The night after we bought the cab and brought in home, we attended a large Persian party of most of the Iranians in the Chicago area, a lot of them our friends and a lot of them fellow cab drivers. Some owned their taxis, and some didn't, but most were shocked and surprised by the sudden change in our affairs.

"How did you get the money?" asked a male friend of ours. I explained the loan I had arranged and the money I'd squirreled away, and he laughed in happiness.

"You should go and live in Hollywood, Maryam," he joked. I must have looked at him quizzically because he continued, "You are a lady that always pulls the winning card out of the air. You should live in Beverly Hills with the other lucky Americans."

I smiled. Though I was proud of myself for making this deal work for me and my family, this was the first piece of praise I'd had from anyone in a long time. I thanked him warmly, told him it was nothing but knowing the right people and putting in some work, and the evening went on.

It looked like Ahmad might be falling asleep in the corner, like he often did as parties ran on into the evening and he ran out of people to argue with about politics, famous people, the economy or anything else he tried to muster a contrary opinion about.

Thanks to some extra payments I made over time, we had the loan paid off within a year and a half, and I was building back up my secret savings account again. Someday a Volkswagen, I dreamed on dreary days. On others, I thought about really owning a home.

When I worked hard and put that little bit of money away, I felt as if it was the one thing I really did for myself. Not Ahmad or the kids, not the kids in my daycare who I watched all day. Just me.

I continued to care for some of the original kids in my daycare over many years, watching them grow up alongside Melody and John. I saw Melody and our neighbor, Stacy, develop language, speak full sentences and learn their letters. They stopped playing their baby games and transformed from toddlers into real kids, full-blown kids who resisted my attempts to cuddle and coddle them. I admitted to myself with both fear and hope that soon they would be ready to go to school.

I don't think the timing could have been better for me.

I still loved watching Melody grow up firsthand and still didn't to entrust her to the care of another person for so many precious hours. Working at home and conversing with the other parents was still pleasurable. But the kids got older and louder and harder to manage. The activities we did and the games we played seemed to be old and tired, ever repeating.

I found myself watching more television and talking on the phone to my friends more during the day, and my patience with the kids decreased.

On winter days, the apartment would become stuffy with the heat of too many bodies and the breathing of too many lungs. I'd crack open the window and reach my head out into the shocking cold Chicago air. The noises and smells of the apartment dampened, I meditated in my own way, pretending I was further separated from my life than I really way. In my head, I was packing my suitcases and getting a divorce. In my mind, I would never have to return to the stuffy room. But in reality, I always did. I could do no different.

The one thing that was within my power was that savings, which had grown into a tidy sum over the course of a few years. My savings was the only power and protection I had, and other than my children, it was one of the most important things in my life.

For a long while, the possibility of the money was abstract: It could be used for anything and I dreamed of a different expensive plan for it most days. Until one day when I just knew, like lightning had struck, what I had been saving for all along.

A friend of mine had heard about an unheard-of opportunity in her neighborhood of Chicago, an area called Willow Heights. There was a community of condominiums being sold for only $30,000 each — a lot of money certainly, but a great deal for real estate — and the best part was that there would be no interest as long as you kept to the seller's strict payment plan. Figuring out the math in my head, I found that with a significant down payment, we could own our own home in the time period of only a few years. I jumped for the real estate agent's phone number and jumped up and down in excitement at the opportunity.

There were only five units left, I told Ahmad that night. Only five! We needed to act fast. My excitement was not contagious, or if so, Ahmad was certainly immune to it. We were talking at the kitchen table, one of the few places our lives ever intersected anymore with our varied schedules, and he shrugged and continued eating.

For the next three weeks, my excitement bounced against the brick wall of his stubbornness. He'd turn a cold shoulder and I'd work myself up to another try, another angle of persuasion. The only responses he made were the typical ones: that we didn't have enough money for the down payment or the rent and that things were fine the way they were. I had hinted that I had some money, that I could personally add funds to make up the down payment, but he didn't take me seriously.

Frustrated by his inaction and by the fact that as he deliberated our perfect condominium could be sold out from under us, I was sitting on the couch with my hands crossed on my chest, my mood growing just as cross. Anger welled up in me, followed quickly by the despair and depression I always expected butting up against Ahmad.

Stop, I told myself. This is what he wants. He wants you to feel powerless and he doesn't like it when you take command. But he does like free money. He just loves getting something for nothing, I reminded myself.

And I knew what to do.

"I have $5,000 for the down payment on that condominium I want and I've been telling you about," I suddenly declared. He started in surprise and looked at me, his eyebrows raised.

"The place you want and your money, huh?" he asked, emphasizing that he saw it as all about me and my desires.

"And when we sign the papers and as we pay the rent and one day sell this condominium, it will be ours," I continued. "Half yours and half mine."

I paused to let this idea sink in, then repeated, "I will put in all the money, but it will be just as much mine as yours."

He half smiled and shrugged. "Call the agent," he said.

By that time there was one unit left in the community, a first-floor place with three bedrooms and a patio looking out on the parking lot, when other units looked over the back grounds with their trees and a lovely pond. There wasn't a window in the kitchen like I always wanted and the floor plan resembled that of our old apartment, but I didn't care.

John was 13 and would be switching schools for junior high anyway and Melody was starting kindergarten, and it was the perfect time and the perfect place to take the next step in our lives. If I had to drag Ahmad kicking and screaming into that better future, I was completely prepared to do that.

Chapter Twenty-Four

We grow with our children. We age with them. So, when Melody was ready to head off to kindergarten, I was just as ready and excited as she was to return to the adult world. Whereas we got her prepared by easing her separation anxiety, purchasing school supplies and buying back-to-school clothes, I prepared by updating my beautician's license and, well, also buying some back-to-work clothes.

For years, I had done nothing except maybe go to the grocery store during my everyday routine. I'd gotten used to throwing on comfortable, messy clothes. Neither the kids nor their parents worried if my hair or make-up was done. And fashion-forward woman that I'd always been, I did worry. I did care. There's something life affirming about knowing you look like yourself outside and in, and I was ready to grasp life.

I think I looked forward to my first day of work as much as Melody looked forward to school. I thought myself very lucky to find a salon that was just opening, that needed all new stylists. There would be no seniority and all the other girls would be getting used to the way the new salon, called Hair Performers, functioned the same way I would. Run by a husband and wife couple, the shop employed stylists of all shapes and sizes, all nationalities.

By the end of my first day back behind the chair in the beauty salon, I was tired and my feet, unaccustomed to standing all day in my stylish high heels, were aching and sore. But I couldn't stop talking at the dinner table, telling John and Melody about the other stylists, the clients, the things I heard and the things I learned.

Lying in bed that night, I remained still and listened to my mind, going around and around in an excited blur like a honey bee after too much coffee. I felt a huge natural high, an adrenaline rush, like I had just jumped into the ocean for the first time. No, the feeling was more the joy of finding out you remember how to swim, and that you're still very good at it. My brain couldn't let go of the feeling that I had reentered the world, or at least found my place in the world again.

Not since I had given birth to Melody, I thought, had I felt this way. Babysitting was treading water, just keeping your head above the surface. But getting out into the world of people, indulging my creative side and carving out a career for myself again was a totally different level of fulfillment. Not since I left Tehran, I thought... but I let the thought drift away. No what ifs, no might have beens. I wasn't going to let the unchangeable circumstances of the past change my happy mood.

I closed my eyes, trying to get some rest for my second day, which would surely be even better.

Just then, the bedroom door opened as Ahmad came in, back from working a night shift with the taxi cab. I pretended to be asleep as he settled himself and started snoring over on his side of the bed, in his territory. I squeezed my eyes shut tighter, noticing that my mood had darkened.

No what ifs, I reminded myself. No might have beens. Tomorrow is another day to seize.

I settled into the rhythm of life at the salon with joy and passion. I got up to speed on all the latest styles and enjoyed flexing my creative muscles to give the clients exactly what they wanted. Whoever sat in my chair, I knew, got the right style advice. Of course, there was a lot of other advice going on, too, with all the social chit chat that happens in beauty salons. The shop was a hive of activity and I was a happy bee among these new friends and colleagues.

After a while working at the salon and enjoying my success, I bought a used canary-yellow Cadillac for driving to and from work and ferrying the kids around town. It was old and rusty on the outside, nothing nice to look at, but the interior was still smooth and well-kept and I had fallen in love with it.

The kids enjoyed sliding around on the back bench seat; I enjoyed my freedom, even if after giving all of my money but my tips to Ahmad, I could usually only put $1 or $2 into the tank. On the rare occasion when I could top it off, I got back in the car and turned to my sweet son, John.

"It's a tankful of hope, baby," I said to him. "A tankful of possibilities."

Ever taller and ever more mature as the days went by, he grinned at me and hugged me. "Let's get out there, then," he'd agree.

There are few things better than feeling that you've found a place for yourself in the world where you are happy and respected by others, that feeling of success on both a financial and self-esteem level. That I felt that feeling of success irked my husband greatly. For if I was on top of the world, he had to be on the bottom, or so was his dark thinking.

I remember walking in the house to find Ahmad at the table, reading a newspaper.

"You know what?" I beamed, setting down my purse and the now empty basket I used to carry my mask supplies. "I won the $50 award again this week!" I stopped to look at myself in the mirror, smiling happily.

"So what?" he growled. "Stop showing off."

There was his cold water, his rain on my parade. My face fell and my hands fell to my sides, then came around to hug myself across the chest. I wasn't showing off. I was proud of my hard work, but hard work it had been. Here I was trying to share in my good fortune and good feelings with my husband, with whom I was supposed to be piloting the raft of our lives — our joint lives — together. Isn't this what couples did? Isn't this how it worked?

I hugged myself tighter and tried to shrug it off. I placed the $50 check on the table beside him. "Here," I said bluntly, and left the room.

It served me right for trying, I reminded myself.

I was in this alone, I thought.

I was in this for the children, I remembered.

The grouchy man in the other room was my cross to bear. I was strong enough to bear him.

While I was beginning to flourish at the salon, I was also continuing to try to manage my husband. Despite the fact that he had a master's degree in economics and we now owned our own house, he still seemed to think that we could and should live as we did when we first came to America — the time when everything we bought was low price and there was no money for anything above what was necessary for everyday life. Also like a student, he still believed that he could drift off to work and make whatever money he could, and then the rest of the time was his to be lazy with.

On his days off and with his time off, he would do nothing but watch TV or scowl at the newspaper, never socializing or making plans. I really thought that he was caught in the bubble of this existence, the rhythm of the life he'd built up. He never wanted things to be any different, I realized. He didn't see anything wrong.

Of course by any standards, there wasn't much wrong with our lives. Our kids were clothed and fed well, and they attended good American schools. We had a nice if small condominium to call our own. But then again, we worked back-breaking jobs. I pictured John attending college; Ahmad shrugged his shoulders and said, "Let the boy decide. He can just go to work if he wants to." My brain clicked along, saying, "How can we improve this? How can we make it even better for ourselves and for our kids?"

Ahmad needed a firm push from me — much like I had propelled him into his great job in Tehran, which was still the most prestigious and adult position he'd ever held — and it was from a friend who worked at a local Holiday Inn hotel. I asked her what working at such a place was like and it seemed so blissfully normal: set hours, benefits, raises, and the possibility of promotion. To my ears, it was too good to be true. Because I knew he'd never approach the subject himself, I asked my friend to arrange an interview for Ahmad for an open position.

After that, the only obstacle besides getting the job was getting Ahmad dressed, ready, and pleasant and prepared for the interview.

"Because it's better, it's more professional," I said for the hundredth time, answering Ahmad's whining.

"But why is it better?" he responded. "It's all about the money for you, isn't it?"

I rolled my eyes, thinking about how much more true it would be if I lobbed that remark back in his face. "You are a college educated man with a master's degree," I said calmly. "You have a family to support, and you have children that look up to you. You should have a job that is something in this world."

He pressed his lips together but didn't say anything. He adjusted his suit around his shoulders, looking in the mirror to assess his appearance.

The management at the Holiday Inn had liked him and given him a position as night auditor, responsible for the books from 11 p.m. to 7 a.m. every night. It was steady, it was regular hours and it was respectable, and I was pleased.

After some time, we were at a party where one of the guests was from another state, where he owned a few Holiday Inns. I quickly ingratiated myself and made small talk, and then politely asked him about how the system of promotion worked at the company. My husband, I explained, was a good employee with a master's degree, but he was only a night auditor.

Apparently, there was a training course called the Holiday Inn University, and every branch was able to send employees down to be trained for management positions. No matter what kind of background Ahmad had, this training was the best way to move ahead at the Holiday Inn. If management backed you as an employee, he explained, the hotel usually fronted the cost of the $500 tuition.

"But my husband has not been chosen," I told the man. "Isn't there any other way to see that he can succeed?"

The man smiled. "I have not heard of it before, but I'm sure if you were willing to pay the $500 tuition yourself, the hotel would send him anyway," he said. "I've never heard of such a thing being done, but it seems reasonable to me."

"And it would show that he's a man that wants to help the company and move ahead," I said, thinking out loud.

"Certainly," he agreed.

My thoughts lit up like a light bulb.

Within the week, I had sold my canary-yellow Cadillac in order to raise $500 for Ahmad's tuition and arranged for him to attend the school. Within a few months, he'd been promoted within Holiday Inn and then offered a job at a very nice hotel in downtown Chicago, where he became the food and beverage manager of their restaurant and room service kitchen. He wore suits and ties, he flirted constantly with the waitresses, and he obviously enjoyed being able to consider himself a big man with a certain amount of power in his own world.

I was glad he had finally reached out to take the world by the shoulders and find his place within it, instead of lazily lolling through life without accomplishing anything of interest. I was glad of the example he could now be to the kids.

But I missed my car. I missed those occasional tanks full of hope. It hadn't been a Volkswagen, but it had been mine. As I continued to work hard and enjoy my job as a stylist, I continued to strive toward that feeling of ownership. Not of possessions, or at least not really.

Ownership of myself, of my work and of my life.

The American dream. I was a big believer in the American dream.

While I may have first been excited to come to America because of the pop culture of Hollywood movies and music, I continued to love my new country because of the freedom for success it offered. No, the success wasn't given away, but I thought that was also wonderful. You had to work hard and push yourself, but no unmovable obstacles of gender, race or religion stood in your way.

By the standards of our families back at home in Iran — our families were certainly upper-middle class, where all of the houses were packed with Persian carpets and none of the women would ever be forced to work — our existence might have been less than they were used to.

We both worked hard to make ends meet, and we were solidly middle class. But we also had the best education system, the best roads, the best stores, and the most popular culture.

To Iranians back home, America was exotic and amazing for such trivial or superficial reasons. I still was in love with all those reasons but also the more important American dream, the one where anyone with a will can put a chicken in their family's pot for dinner or a car in their garage and has the unlimited potential for success and respect.

It's no wonder, then, that I so whole-heartedly supported my sister-in-law's desire to immigrate to America from Iran in the early 1980s. Her name was Fatimah and I sympathized with her situation: As the older sister, she faced a great deal of stress and even ridicule because her younger sister had married before her, leaving her alone in her father's home. Plain in appearance, she had no immediate prospects for marriage, so in order to get out of the family's house and away from an uncomfortable situation, she went to stay with cousins in Turkey.

"I don't know what to do with myself," she told me on the phone long distance. "I don't have the money for school and I don't really know how to go about getting a job. I feel like I'm just stuck, that there is nothing I can do to change this. I'm stuck."

"Is there nothing you can picture that would make your life better?" I asked. "What is it that you want to do with your life?"

She sighed, her spirits obviously down. "I think there would be more opportunity for me in America, certainly," she said. "I could get a job. I might even meet a man to marry. Here, both of those things seem so unlikely."

I totally understood her feelings of being held down, kept out, and pushed down. She was to have gotten married. Period. And now that avenue seemed blocked to her because her family felt shame at her situation. My heart broke for her over the long-distance lines.

"Perhaps that is the best way for you to go," I said. "Perhaps America is the answer."

"You think so?" she asked, her voice picking up slightly. "It's not like immigration is easy. Oh, I just don't know."

"Well, just you think about it and we'll think about it over here, too," I replied. "I'll look into how difficult it would be to have you come to your brother here in Chicago."

"Oh, Maryam," she said. "That is such a nice thought for me to have in my head. America! Wouldn't that be a dream come true."

"We'll see if it's a dream that can be made true," I cautioned her. "But don't give up hope, and you can call us collect from Turkey whenever you need to talk."

"Again, sister-in-law, thank you," she said.

Ahmad took his typical attitude of hostile indifference about the subject.

"Why would you want to help her, to go out of our way like that?" he asked. "You feel too much sympathy."

"She's your sister!" I declared. "And she's in a very difficult position. We can help."

He shrugged. "Helping is sometimes hard work. And expensive," he noted. "If you want to take this on your shoulders, go right ahead."

I began to look into the process of supporting a relative for immigration, and it was just as complex as when Ahmad and I had come to America so many years before. There were stacks and stacks of paperwork and a long list of requirements to be met.

The most onerous for us were certainly the financial obligations: One had to prove to the U.S. government that the family sponsoring the immigrant had $30,000 in the bank, thereby proving that they could support their relative so they'd never become a burden to the American system. While Ahmad was making a little more money as a hotel and restaurant manager and I got by at the salon, that was an astronomical sum to our family in the early 1980s — more than we would make in several years if we never spent a penny on rent or food. We only had a couple thousand in savings, and that was vital for the kids' educations or any emergency expenses.

But Fatimah continued calling, excited by the thought of coming to America. She now saw the immigration as her ticket out of the life she was living, the only place she imagined her future. I had planted the seed of this idea in her head. I also knew in my heart that America had the potential to offer her everything in her dreams and even more, so I continued to fight through the red tape of immigration.

At one point in the battle, I talked to a neighbor about the problem.

"Are you sure you want to bring your sister-in-law over here?" she asked, her eyebrows scrunched and concerned. "Are you sure you know what you're doing, and that she knows what she's doing?"

"It's her choice," I said. "And I understand her position so well." While I didn't speak the words out loud, I thought about all the times that my plans had been wiped away as if they were words on a chalkboard, how many times my dreams had been crushed. I'd always been a hopeful person, and I knew the power of hope in the heart of a woman. We could endure anything if only we had that hope, and it was hope I wanted to give my sister-in-law both for her own sake and for the sake of my past self. That little girl climbed trees and dreamed of airplanes and had her hope jerked out from underneath her feet. I would never be the accomplice of a hope-denying act like that against another woman. Never.

Perhaps this neighbor saw the turmoil in my eyes, saw the determination and the painful past that prompted my undying support.

"I understand," she said firmly. Then she placed down her cup of tea and made as if to get up and leave. "Well, let's go off to the bank then, shall we?"

My jaw dropped. "What on earth do you mean?" I asked.

She put her purse on her shoulder and replied, "My husband and I have $40,000 in our bank account. We will not need it any time soon, of course, and so I suggest that it can be put to better use in your account for a little while."

Her eyes twinkled with mischief and she went on to explain. All that was necessary was to put the money in my account for long enough for the government to check the balance. Then we could transfer the money back to her account and it would be as if the money had never been gone in the first place.

As we looked at each other standing in the lobby of the bank, I could tell that she understood it was something I had to do. She knew that we had to support one another as recent immigrants, as women. There were good people in this world, I confirmed, validating my unspoken belief. I couldn't thank her enough.

I also knew I could never tell Ahmad. He was so strange around money — always wanting more, not really caring where it came from — that I wouldn't dare mention there was so much money in our account for that brief period of time. Luckily, he was also disinterested in what I did most of the time, and he didn't know a thing about it. The plan went smoothly, the affidavit of $30,000 of support went through and Fatimah prepared for her new American life, thanks to Mrs. Shahrzard.

It was winter in Chicago when she landed at the airport and we took her home, and she looked like the abandoned, confused and restrained Persian woman she was. Her clothes were out of date and ill-fitting, her nails were a mess and her hair was dyed blond, a horrible dye job that was obviously done long ago. It desperately needed maintenance and the color of the hair with her olive complexion was awful. Much as I remembered, Fatimah's face was plain and sharp, not unpleasant but reminiscent of a warning sign, telling watchers to be cautious. She held only two suitcases in her hands, her entire worldly possessions.

"Ahmad! Maryam!" she called, obviously overjoyed to finally be in America, the place she'd been dreaming of for months and months.

"Welcome," I said, giving her a polite hug.

"Thanks," she said breathlessly. Then she threw herself into her brother's arms, causing one of Ahmad's rare genuine smiles, and they started a long and involved chat in Farsi. I gathered up the kids, who she hadn't even greeted, put her luggage in the car and drove the family home, all while the siblings talked only to each other.

At home, I explained that Melody and John were sharing a bedroom to give her some private space in the house. I had told John and Melody in advance what polite and caring children they were being by making this sacrifice for their aunt. Perhaps in her excitement, she forgot to thank them for their generosity, but I patted both of them on the head and smiled to compensate.

I'd put so much work into her dream, thinking of the strength of women when they nurture and support one another, imagining the great bond of sisterhood. Instead, I found myself with a polite house-guest who apparently thought that family hospitality was a given and chatted on and on with only her brother whenever he was home.

Within two weeks, I had a customer at the beauty shop, a Greek woman who owned an alteration shop. A light bulb went off in my head. Sewing! Of course Fatimah would know how to sew. The skill was one of the few that every Iranian girl, especially one from a well-off and traditional family, was taught. Sure enough, Fatimah was a talented and enthusiastic seamstress. After speaking with the Greek woman and agreeing that she would be paid 50 percent of the fees for whatever gar-ments she worked on, she immediately had a full-time job. Because she was quick with her hands, she immediately made quite good money, as well.

She had no problem earning the money; but she did seem to have issues about spending it. She came straight home from work without stopping to shop, go to the movies, see friends or anything else. Aside from occasionally watching the kids while I ran to the store, she never offered to help around the house. Our family paid all the bills and bought all the food. I cooked it, and she made quite a fuss of politely do-ing the dishes after each dinner. Her one treat was candy, which she'd bring home occasionally, eating an entire bag of chocolates and doling out two or three to Melody, who always wanted to share.

After six months of having Fatimah live with us, Ahmad asked, "Maybe you should ask Fatimah to help us out a little bit?"

"Do you want me to?" I asked, somewhat nervously. I had no desire to tread on the domain of his family relationships unless he wanted me to. His sister was his responsibility and his choice.

"Nothing large," he said. "But maybe just one thing, like $20 a month on the electric bill. Wow, does she spend a lot of time with that hair dryer every morning or what?"

I smiled, thinking maybe I was the only one who heard that in the morning.

"If you'd like me to do that, fine," I said.

He nodded. "Fine."

Very gently and very politely, I asked my sister-in-law to stay in the kitchen with me as I cooked dinner the next night, saying I had something to talk with her about. I mentioned that Ahmad and I were both very happy that she was able to come to America and to host her in our home, to see that she was making a good start and had a great job. We were very proud, I said.

"It's just… Ahmad wanted me to ask you something," I continued. "It's just that we are not rich people. We have to watch every bill that comes through our home. We thought that it would be nice if you could contribute to our household a little bit, just to…" I continued the thought in my head: just to make us feel like you're not taking advantage.

"Why are you saying that?" she asked, her arms crossed against her chest as she leaned against the kitchen counter. Her face wasn't mad, but obviously controlled. "Did Ahmad ask you to say this?"

"Yes," I affirmed. "We love having you here and we're not asking for you to spend a lot of money in any way. We thought maybe more as a symbolic gesture: perhaps a little money toward the grocery bill —" as I spoke, I stirred the pot of spaghetti for dinner — "or $20 toward the electricity bill. That's all."

She continued looking at me with that stony face and said nothing. Then she turned on her heel and left. I sighed into the spaghetti pot. That had probably not gone well, but I knew I had finally spoken about those lingering feelings that had been poking at me for months.

A short time later, I called to the house that dinner was ready and we gathered around the table. As was my custom, I was the only one standing, dishing out each person's food. When Fatimah's eyes met mine, she was cold and silent. Then we all sat down and began to eat. Other than the regular questions for the kids about school, we were usually content to have little conversation.

But Fatimah spoke up almost at once.

"Maryam was saying that in order to stay here, I should give her money for the bills," she said bluntly.

"That's not what I said," I inserted, making my voice as kind as my intentions were. "You're welcome here, but Ahmad thought — "

"She said that you, brother, told her to ask me this," she continued, bulldozing over my words. "Is this true?"

Ahmad looked up, using the fact that he was chewing to buy some time before he spoke. He looked directly at Fatimah, his eyes never flicking my direction.

"I never said that," he finally spoke.

Fatimah looked at me with eyes sharp as daggers and nodded her head, obviously declaring victory in some family battle.

"Of course you are welcome here," I whispered to my own plate. I knew no one would hear. Even if they did hear, no one would listen.

I felt as if my husband had killed someone, and I was framed for the crime. I felt betrayed yet again. And with the placid and pleased look on both Ahmad and Fatimah's faces, compared with my own roiling emotions, I felt like I was the emotional psychopath.

Chapter Twenty-Five

I am relatively certain this is the point where I began to live large portions of my life underwater. When I had to deal with my husband, there was this murky barrier between us, an alien place where there were strong currents. He looked and sounded as if he was a great distance away from me, and I was satisfied with the cushion of isolation the water in my ears and my eyes — and in my memory, I would find later — afforded me.

I lived my life at work as a stylist, now in a different salon where I managed my own space, therefore keeping all of my profits instead of splitting them with salon owners. I was respected and popular and much liked by coworkers and clients alike, and I still felt the glow of accomplishment.

My children also elicited that glow in me. Picking them up from school, watching them play sports or participate in other school activities, helping with their homework: It felt like anytime I was near them, I was enveloped in a bubble of love, able to breathe and to be myself.

With them and at work, I was able to give of myself. In so many other places in my life, I just shut down, putting my head down and continued to swim.

During dinner, I would often pretend I wasn't hungry or that there was something I really liked on television. Even though I cooked the meal and served it, I was physically and mentally incapable of sitting down at the table at looking Ahmad or Fatimah in the eye. Although Fatimah was making good money and had moved out of our house

— giving Melody back her room — she rented the condominium unit above ours. It had no furniture or utensils but a bed for sleeping; she still came downstairs for all her meals.

When Melody was about 7 or 8 years old, I was offered the opportunity to escape, if only briefly. My parents called from Iran with a proposition. They had still never met Melody — I was pregnant when we left Iran and hadn't returned since — and wanted to get the entire family together. Instead of converging in Iran, however, they had the idea that everyone should meet up someplace fun and new: Japan.

My beloved brother Reza had married a lovely Japanese woman named Keiko. They'd fallen in love while he was studying in the country, and they still went back once a year to visit. Because Keiko had family and was a native, she would make it easy to go around the country and see the sights, eat the food and have a great time. Keiko's sister would let us rent her large house in Osaka for a whole month. It sounded delightfully exotic to my ears and my heart longed to see my family again.

The second part of the proposition was that my father would send out the airline tickets for us as his treat. I don't know exactly to what extent he was aware of our financial situation or Ahmad's attitude toward money, but he knew that we couldn't (or wouldn't) have the money to fly to Japan. He'd send three tickets for me and the kids: Though Ahmad was nominally invited, one small remark about work was all it took for my family to shrug it off and not care whether he was coming. Once we were there, my father assured, the whole trip would be paid for by him, including sightseeing, lodging, and food and even shopping.

My eyes teared up when I heard this, thinking of my father's large heart and generous nature. For a few weeks, I could be back there: among my loved ones, comfortable and safe, taken care of. It seemed far too good to be possible, and yet my heart beat faster with the thought that this dream might come true.

"You want to go to Japan for how long?" Ahmad asked loudly. He knew the answer to the question already. I'd already outlined the vacation plan in detail, but it was as if he didn't believe my words, as if I was trying to trick him in some way he couldn't figure out.

"A month," I replied.

We were in the living room, where I had sat him down to try to have a rational conversation. The trip was paid for and I'd explained the idea in the most neutral way possible, trying to avoid all of Ahmad's touchy buttons. The kids were going to flip with excitement, or be very disappointed if they couldn't go. I didn't know what he was going to object to.

But of course, I knew he would object to something nonetheless.

"And you will not be working."

"No."

"So there will be no paycheck?"

"No. If I don't work, I don't get a paycheck."

"And so how do I get that money that is in the budget?" he demanded. His cheeks were red with anger and his mouth hung open, as if in disbelief at my audacity.

I was silent.

"You cannot go if you do not have that money," he said, bringing his hand down on the table firmly like a judge who has declared a sentence for a criminal.

"Where am I going to get the money?" I asked, my voice rising in distress. "How can I do that?"

"That's not my problem."

"Money is always your problem," I replied.

He was very angry now. "That's because you have no respect for it!" he yelled. "With you, it's always about the money, isn't it? That's the only conversation we ever have. I don't care how you get the money, but you get it." He breathed heavily and leaned back on the couch.

"You got the money for the tickets, after all," he added, lighting a cigarette.

"That was a gift from my father, from the kids' grandfather," I said. "He's never even gotten to meet his granddaughter and he wants to get to know her. It's a noble and loving thing for him to want us to come."

Ahmad snorted.

"You'll figure it out," he concluded.

"I have the tickets," I said softly, almost whispering. "I can go."

"You can go," he replied. "But don't bother coming back if you cannot hand me the money you are stealing from our home with your laziness. You can make the street corner your home."

Ahmad took us to the airport, warmly hugging the children goodbye and telling them how much he would miss them. To me, he said nothing and our eyes never met, all of which told me that he would miss my money. Not me as a person, my voice, my actions. When he was not at work, I thought, he would sit around the condominium with cigarette smoke, watch TV and count his pocket change. I had no doubt.

Once we took off and were hanging like clouds above the ocean, some of my heavy feelings and fear lifted with the excitement of the children. While John had been to Iran — several years before, when he was much younger — Melody had never been out of the country, never met her extended family. She was giddy with the newness of the airport, the plane, the reclining seats, and the food.

It was an incredibly long trip, but their excitement stayed relatively high.

When we arrived in Japan, I knew that my family from Iran would be there to greet us, their plane having arrived only 30 minutes before ours. We'd agreed to meet in the concourse and travel to our new rented home together. I emerged from the plane cautiously, looking around excitedly at every person in the waiting crowd, scanning faces for the familiar smiles of my mother and father.

It was John that saw them first, and holding his suitcase in one hand, he took off in that direction. Melody scampered behind, craning her neck, trying to see which people John was headed toward. There they were, I saw, the same as ever and yet so noticeable different. Older, more faded, like a photograph exposed to the sun. Yet the new lines on their hands and faces softened them in my mind. My parents! My heart warmed.

The exclaimed as they embraced John, who had sprouted up into a lean and lanky adolescent since they'd last seen him. My father ruffled his hair. Then my mother's eyes lit on Melody and her face melted with pure joy and unalloyed love. She dropped to her knees in front of my little girl and began to caress her face, soon followed by my father.

I took a deep breath to cool my cheeks, which had flushed with pride as outsiders viewed and approved of these two magnificent people who were my children. On an everyday basis, it was easy to forget how special they were and how fast they grew. For these children, I would give my life. To these children, I had given my life and would continue to do so.

Next, my parents' eyes settled on me and their happy smiles softened, less excited than for the kids but more familiar. We hugged openly and honestly, sniffing away a few tears. My mother still smelled the same after all these years, the same as when I had buried my face in her lap and cried over every childhood tragedy.

My mother took Melody's hand as we went to pick up the rest of our luggage and then looked pointedly back at me and said: "She is beautiful".

Keiko was a petite and lovely Japanese woman with a very kind heart, and I could tell she loved my brother, Reza, very much. She welcomed us into her sister's empty house, telling us to make ourselves at home — and we quickly did. My parents, me, my two sisters, my two brothers, spouses and kids stuffed the house to the seams with our rambunctious, happy crew. Melody and John dissolved into the crowd of their cousins, who they'd never met but we're instantly connected to. Gossip and news caught the adults in conversation for hours. And as usual, there was food and tea in abundance from the kitchen. The familiar smells tickled my nostrils and made me nostalgic for my grandmother.

For the next few weeks, we thought of Japan like it was our own personal vacation playground. We visited Osaka, Kyoto, Tokyo and all the major cities. We ate at fantastic restaurants and rode the super-fast trains. We breathed in the exotic culture of the Far East, learning a few words in Japanese and taking in their unique art, clothes and culture. All my brothers took joy in secretly feeding Melody chocolate, her favorite treat, in order to sugar her up and make her bounce off the walls.

In terms of shopping, my father had taken care of everything on that front along with everything else. Due to certain customs requirements, tourists were only allowed to leave the country with about $500 worth of goods. We Persians were very dedicated to the idea that we needed to take home lots of souvenirs, not only for ourselves but for everyone back home. Therefore, my father presented each of us with $500 to shop with as we wished over the month-long trip.

I had taken the stack of bills and drawn in my breath, almost holding it inside my lungs. Surely, he would take it back. Surely, this was some sort of joke or trick. But my father's eyes sparkled with the joy of giving, nothing more, and I realized that it was only my financial training with Ahmad speaking softly in my mind. Like a puppy whapped on the nose, I was waiting for the catch to this wonderful generosity.

But there was never a catch with my father. This was who he was, who he'd always been. Again, I took in his swelling of chest and joyful smile as he went about spreading generosity and love among the family. He was a man who enjoyed making the people he loved happy. While his open hand made me smile for him, it also made me sad that I hadn't seen such a free-spirited sharing of both wealth and love for such a long, long time.

What kind of life was I living that such emotion was exiled? Under what rock had I been hiding? Like so many rhetorical questions I asked in my head, I knew the answer. His name sat like a boulder in my brain, all the other thoughts forced to part and flow around his stubborn sharpness.

We walked around the interior of the Forbidden City and learned about the traditions of the Samurai. We bought little trinkets for neighbors and the kids' friends. My mother even insisted upon buying Ahmad a nice Seiko watch because he was unable to join us, despite my objections. Though I had a great time with my family, as the trip wore on and our departure back to America loomed in front of me, my mood became more downcast. I tried to hide these depressive feelings as best I could, but I was obviously unsuccessful.

"What happened?" my sister asked me. We were alone in one of the living areas sipping tea, and I suppose I had lapsed into silence without realizing it.

I looked up, just about to answer that nothing was wrong and change the subject. But her eyes knew. I sighed.

"I'm having problems with Ahmad," I admitted. She nodded, prompting me to continue. "He's very... strong-willed when it comes to money. His whole family is that way. Not like Father, not like Reza or any of these men."

I could tell from her look that this was something she was aware of. I should have known that when, during conversations with my parents about plane fair and such that the fact that Father had to send the tickets would be passed along through the family. They all knew he never gave me money to return to see them, a tradition of most Iranian families. It was custom for a man to graciously buy plane tickets for his wife and children to return to visit family in Iran.

I steeled myself to continue.

"He wants money," I said. "I am not working these four weeks we are away and he says that I must replace that money into the family budget, that there is no way around it. He said that he would... it doesn't matter what he said. But I don't have it, sister."

She stood up and came to sit next to me and put her arms around my shoulders. "Now hush," she said. "It will all work out. We're your family, Maryam. We'll make sure it all works out."

The next morning at breakfast, my parents were in the kitchen. My mother walked up to me like a woman on a mission and put a stack of cash in my hands — $600, approximately the amount I would have earned in the month I had been absent. I was shocked by her brusque and angry manner.

"Take this and give it him," she said, practically spitting the words out of her mouth. I looked over at my father, but he was making a big show of looking down at a newspaper or a book, as if he couldn't hear a word or see a thing. I looked at the tips of his ears, a little bit pink, and knew he was trying to spare me whatever embarrassment and pain he could.

"I don't know what kind of husband you have," my mother muttered, turning away.

I had the money in my hand as we exited the airplane back in Chicago. The kids saw Ahmad waiting by the car in the passenger loading area — too cheap to want to pay for parking, I assumed — and ran up to hug him. After the long trip and airplane ride, they were tired and not as excited as when we arrived in Japan.

I don't know how he talked behind my back, explaining my trip to some of our friends. A few evenings later at a regular Persian-American party, a male friend of ours walked up to me and said, "How was Japan? How much did it cost this poor guy — " he nudged a thumb at Ahmad "to give you such a trip."

"Actually," I replied, "he got $600 and a Seiko watch."

Then I walked away to fill my drink.

I dove back into the murky depths of unhappiness after our return from Japan. The salon I was working for went downhill fast and I decided to turn toward office work, which seemed more stable and somehow adult. I was hired for an administrative job at a training center for flight attendants, where I quickly moved into higher positions. The position was an excellent fit for me. I worked with people, something I always excelled at.

But outside of my pleasurable job and the joy I took in my children, the underwater feeling continued: muffling the sounds I could hear, making my vision blurry and indistinct. My memory began to leak, not keeping track of so many days empty of emotion and forgetting unhappiness.

Only one thought was sharpened during that time period: the idea of divorce. How often did I think of that almost magical word that would shoot me back to the surface of life that would really start the clock over for me again and return to me the world of possibilities I imagined as a young girl?

I was waiting. For 10 years, I had been waiting. For 10 years we had been in Chicago, freezing our bodies and our hearts in the bitter Midwest climate. And mentally, I had been packing my suitcase for all 10 of those years, putting in another T-shirt or set of socks every time I heard his key scrape the lock.

That year, we celebrated our wedding anniversary as we always did, by going out to dinner as a family. It seemed like the best way to celebrate because, for one, I was always cooking and rarely got to enjoy dining on food that someone else prepared. Also, having a romantic dinner without the kids was a thought neither one of us found appealing. Our marriage was what had brought us our wonderful children, and only our children had — and were — still keeping our marriage together. It was only right and proper that the anniversary was celebrated as a family unit.

It was a cozy neighborhood Italian bistro with red-and-white checkered tablecloths and candles guttering in red bowls. We all four ordered food and were eating our pasta happily until the bill for the dinner came, the waiter setting it down tactful in a plain, black book. Like most waiters, he put down the book closest to my husband, thinking that it was the man who usually paid for family meals. Despite our conservative background in Iran, the waiter couldn't have been more wrong about our particular family dynamics.

Ahmad made a show of patting down the pockets of his coat and his pants, a quizzical look on his face.

"I think I have forgotten my wallet," he said, almost as if it was a question.

I couldn't help but roll my eyes skyward, and my gaze came back to earth in time to find Ahmad giving me that familiar look, the look of waiting for something to appear out of the sky and into his lap.

"You think you did, or did you?" I asked.

"I did."

"Well, it's good I have my American Express," I replied. "Gold."

I was proud of that card. It was something I had separate from Ahmad that he had no access to. It was my money, I paid the bill and I worked my way up to qualify for the gold version of the card. What's mine is yours, I thought in my head. But what's yours is yours, too.

I slipped the card into the plastic sleeve in the book and replaced it on the table, this time situated more on my side of table. He frowned slightly at this, but said nothing. Melody was finishing her food and John met my eye casually, saying something about how good the meal was and thanking me for it. I smiled. Such a thoughtful boy, that one.

Plates were cleared and coats gathered and we were ready to head out to the car when I remembered something: I hadn't put down a tip on the credit card for the waiter. I didn't want to leave him nothing — my sense of honor and respect for the job that he did wouldn't let me — but I didn't have any cash.

"Ahmad," I said. "I forgot to put a tip. Can you please leave some cash for the waiter?"

He again patted the pockets of his coat, a gesture that was half embarrassed and half prideful. "I don't have any," he said.

John dug a few dollar bills out of his wallet and placed them on the table. "Here, Mom," he said.

"Thank you, John," I smiled.

"Not a problem."

John helped me on with my coat as Ahmad and Melody already passed through the door. Ahmad's hand was on her shoulder and they were making fresh tracks in the snow. We walked out into the cold and John stopped me by putting a hand on my shoulder. The others were ahead, out of hearing.

He was 17, tall and lanky, with deep and friendly eyes. A baseball cap was pulled over his forehead and he towered over me.

"Mom," he said, adjusting the collar of his coat and shrugging his shoulders.

"What?"

"Aren't you going to leave this guy?" he asked, slicking his thumb toward his father in the parking lot. "When are you going to get rid of him?"

I was shocked at his words and my mouth must have hung slightly agape, but John was smiling. Not a happy smile, or at least not a totally happy smile. More like we were sharing a long-standing joke, clucking in disapproval but amused that, well, here we were again. What a perceptive boy, that one.

After a moment, I caught his smile and we walked arm and arm to the car in the wake of his father and sister.

I never answered his question, I realized, and I don't think I had to.

John knew. He knew I had been waiting and was nearing my breaking point. I just hope he knew I was there for him, for Melody. I hoped he knew that everything, all of it, was for them.

Chapter Twenty-Six

It was the winter of 1989.

My children were growing so quickly, especially my beloved baby Melody. After we had spent so much time together when she was a baby and a toddler, me being her primary caregiver all day long until she was ready for kindergarten, I was beginning to feel like a stranger to her. She had friends and after-school activities that I couldn't remember hearing about. She was getting to the age where she didn't like me kissing her and saying, "I love you" when I dropped her off at school. The baby fat in her face was smoothing, not yet into the face of a young woman, but approaching quickly.

Every time I noticed that she had grown or that she came home with a good grade from school, my heart swelled with pride. Then it froze in my chest as I thought about myself at the same age: sneaking off to go to Girl Scouts, my first hotel wedding, all of the dreams that were violently slapped out of me.

This would not happen to my girl, I thought to myself for the thousandth time. She was American. So quintessentially American. She was chatty and silly, a performer, a girl who had lots of friends and spent hours on the phone. She liked rock music and cable television. She could be whatever she wanted to be when she grew up.

That growing up was happening so fast! I felt like I was missing something. Yes, I was missing her childhood completely.

I left every morning for work in the dark, the sky only beginning to gray with the cold, hard sun. I worked and ate behind the cover of four walls. Then I returned home after the sun had already set, the stars beginning to wink at me mischievously. I'd park my hated car in the driveway and stumble in to cook dinner, which I'd try to eat away from Ahmad.

I was becoming isolated from my children, I thought, and I didn't want that to continue.

"I'd like to not work for a while," I said to Ahmad one evening as I prepared for bed. We shared a room every night but nothing else, unless you counted mutual discomfort. I was rubbing lotion into my hands.

"What?" he asked, not hearing or understanding me.

"I'd like to not work for a while, so I can be home with the kids more," I continued. "I want to make soups and cookies for them to come home to. I want to have time to do things like reorganize my closet or have tea with our friends."

"You can have tea and clean the closet and still work, Maryam," he replied. He raised his eyebrows at me, wondering where I was going from here.

I was silent, trying to show him I was serious and to let the idea soak in.

"What happens if you take time off?" he asked.

"Nothing."

"What happens to the check?"

"I don't get one."

He snorted through his nose. "In that case, you can go stay on the street corner." He turned away from me and busied himself with something. "Under the light."

I'd heard this phrase from him before, and though I knew the horrible thing that he meant, I had never really pressed him on the issue.

"And by that you mean what?" I asked.

There was no response.

"By that you mean that if I don't bring money into the house, I can become a prostitute?" I asked. "You'd prefer your wife to be a prostitute. That's what you mean?"

"Yeah," he almost laughed the words out. "Yeah."

I was still young and I still was complimented about my beauty, so I knew that he didn't mean the comment as an insult, as in he thought I couldn't make money that way. Instead, he knew that I could make money that way and he was laughing at the thought of my debasement.

Had it always been this way? I wondered. Had he always thought nothing of me but the money and opportunities I could provide him? Without a dime to my person, would I be an empty shell to him?

I knew he was wrong. Even if he did follow through on his threats to toss me out on the street, under that street lamp was the last place I would be. In this country, there were support groups, social workers, charities, shelters and assistance programs. There were people to help and places to stay, and a woman thrown out by her husband was not a shame to society or her family. It was the husband who was shameful, and considering how long we'd been in this country, I was amazed that hadn't sunk into Ahmad's head.

In this country, anybody who had the desire and the work ethic to find a job would find work and perhaps success. In this country, he was not my only link to the outside world as much as he would have been back in Iran. Did he really not know this? Him, who sent me out daily into the world in order to bring back money? Did he really think I was a solely dependent on him like that?

Apparently, he did, and the idea burned my brain like acid for the rest of the night. He'd married a beauty queen and a hard worker. That's all he knew in his head and all he cared. I honestly didn't know if he was aware that there could be — that there should be — more to a relationship.

My mother once told me that the kids are always going to grow and grow until they are out of your house and out of your daily life. Your husband, she said, is your investment for that time, and you will get out of him what you put into him. You have to take care of him in order to take care of yourself once you reach that stage of life. How wrong she was in my case. The kids are going to go, they're already one foot out the door in a way, and he is never going to take care of me. If not by now, never.

The yearning voice in my head that had been counting down these last 10 years piped up, saying, "If not now, never."

He said he was sending me to the street corner? He can toss me out, but that's not where I'm going. If I have to go beg or clean houses, I will never be your wife again. If that's what he is promising me for my future, that's it. It's over. It's time.

That was the straw that broke my back that night. I was absolutely and completely done, and I went about deciding how to make that definite thought a definite reality.

In almost 20 years of marriage, I had learned one thing about confrontation with Ahmad and it was that tears would get me nowhere. He was the sort of hunter that just wanted to shoot you and back away, not hearing anything. He could kill, but he wouldn't hear the crying. He tuned it out as if it was interference on the radio frequency of his thoughts. Just white noise.

So over the next few days, I practiced my words and even my gestures, testing out pushing my fingernails into my palm if the tears started to emerge. I recited all my reasoning and my words in the mirror, making sure that I phrased things as objectively as I could to not put him on the defensive, a fortification through which I would never get through to him.

I don't remember how I achieved an afternoon alone with him in the condominium, but we were sitting in the living room with snow falling outside the sliding glass door overlooking the parking lot, because all the good units were taken by the time I'd convinced him to buy. We sat side by side on the sofa and I had my ankles together, my hands in my lap.

I was very calm.

"I'm not happy," I said. "And I don't think you're happy, so I would like to talk to you about getting a divorce."

He said nothing and his face didn't change expression, as if he was soaking this in.

"I know that a divorce can be costly, but I have found that if we use the same lawyer and we can agree to certain things together without fighting," I continued, "that it will only cost $200."

"I see," he said.

"It is time to stop this, to be free of this unhappiness together, so why don't we compromise in this way and get a divorce?" It was the third time I'd said the word divorce out loud in front of him. I dug my fingernails into my palm as I waited for his response.

"John is leaving and someday Melody will, too," I said, following my outlined thoughts. "It's not fair for you and me to continue to live together when they are the only thing between us. Think: You always say to me that you should have married an American woman, and this way you can correct the mistake. Everything is black versus white between the two of us, everything is at odds, and I am very, very tired."

He breathed out, as if he had been holding his breath, and then he ran one hand through his hair. "What about all of the stuff that we have?" he asked.

I had known this might be a point of contention with Ahmad and, again, I made it as easy as possible for him. "Everything belongs to the kids," I said. "I don't want anything." I meant it.

"What about the kids?"

"John is almost 18 and off to college in the spring, so you can have custody of him if that's what you want. I'd like to have custody of Melody because she's young and needs her mother."

He nodded. Then he shook his head slightly as if to clear it, perhaps overwhelmed with the information and the studied way in which I was presenting it. Had he really not seen this coming? Had he really thought that everything was OK?

"Do we have to tell them?" he asked.

"Not until we are ready," I said. "Not until it's the right time."

"But this is the right time for you to ask me this?"

"Yes," I replied without hesitation. "Yes."

He stood up, huffing like an old man when he did so. He went to the sliding glass door and looked out at the falling snow, again running a hand through his hair but keeping it on his head, as if he was afraid it might roll off.

"OK," he said.

I waited for a moment to make sure there wasn't something else.

"So I will start arranging it then?" I asked.

"OK," he repeated.

It was amazing, really, how calmly the conversation went and how easily I extracted agreement from him. Even more amazing was that as I left the room, I looked over to where he was frozen looking out at the snow.

He was crying. It was silent crying, but there were tears on his cheek. I think there was shame, embarrassment and shock in his eyes. Either that or pure regret.

I'd never know, because I never saw him compose himself. But after that brief moment, the only thing I saw in his eyes was scorn, anger and the twinkle of planned manipulation.

We hired an attorney to represent both of us and outlined an agreement. Ahmad was to pay a certain percentage of his income in child support for Melody and our assets — especially the land we'd at one time bought near the Caspian Sea, thinking we'd return and build on it — were put in trust for the kids.

The division of goods at home was another matter.

"What about the house?" Ahmad asked.

"We sell it and split the profits," I answered.

He nodded, then began looking around the condominium.

"What about the TV and the VCR?" Ahmad asked.

"Give it to John when he leaves for school. He'll need those, and I can buy new ones wherever I end up."

His eyes narrowed at the phrase "wherever I end up." I could see that he flinched at the lack of control he had over that outcome, whether he was conscious of it or not. He then cast around for anything that he could control and settled on the kitchen.

"What about the wine? Or the spices? Or the pots and pans?"

"I don't want any of it," I said. I started to distance myself from him, not paying attention. But I heard him banging around and moving things in the kitchen from the other room.

I walked in and out of the kitchen several times, just going about my own thing, and I amazed at what I saw. There he was hunched over the counter top with the contents of the cabinets spread out around him, dividing everything into two piles. And I mean everything: half-full bottles of alcohol, bottles and packets of spices, salt, pepper, toothpicks. Whatever didn't have a container, he was laboriously pouring into Ziploc bags and Tupperware containers.

It was pointless, ever so pointless, I thought. I really didn't want half a bag of saffron strands, and I don't think he even knew what to do with his half of them. But if he wanted to pursue this useless endeavor, let him.

Gradually, he built two cities of stuff, two piles of kitchen goods on the counter top and he called me over.

"Here," he said, his voice steady, as if he'd regained some control over himself with his hard work. "This is mine and that is yours."

I pointed to one pile. "This is mine?" I asked, making sure.

"Yeah," he said, almost prideful, moving toward his own stack.

"OK, then," I said. Then I scooped up the carefully divided pile of my kitchen items and dumped it into the trash. "I said I don't want anything, Ahmad," I said as I left the room. "I mean it."

So much of life happens in between the big events, the big events that make good stories for friends and family. There is so much of life we don't talk about because it seems to stream through our hands, every day the same and nothing of consequence happening. Grain after grain, the sand falls through the hour glass and you see that years have passed, that things have changed although you can't quite say how.

Sometimes I think that for about 10 years, I intentionally let the sands slip, burying my head in them as much as I could. I stayed within the system I imagined to be unbreakable, the system of man and woman, husband and wife, power and subservience. It was a system of punishment, a punishment for the sin of choosing the wrong man impulsively in my childhood. How young I was to make such a choice! And how old I was when I was finally able to release myself from that mistake.

But finally there was a big event in my life in April of that year. The day of the official court hearing for our divorce arrived and I couldn't sleep in anticipation of what would happen. I was told that it would be a simple affair, but I couldn't help but wonder if I was the one that would be judged, if I would be told that I could not leave this man, if I would be told I was a bad woman. This was what my childhood conditioning made me fear.

Ahmad was not there: not in the condominium, not in the city at all. He'd taken the kids on a trip to Disneyworld at the last minute, specifically to get out of the court appearance. Perhaps he thought that I wouldn't go through with it if he wasn't there, or that I wouldn't be allowed to make it formal. He was wrong, I said to myself. It was him that was wrong. I was wrong about some things in my life — mostly my choice of husband — but I was determined that I wasn't going to be in the wrong anymore.

It's going to be right, I thought. It's finally going to be all right.

In my most professional of outfits, I stood before the judge, who sat up behind an elevated desk. She was an older lady with grey hair, and she'd seemed kind but firm with the other couples who'd come in and out, younger people who'd probably been married for a year or two before calling it quits, knowing staying together would only cause more misery. My attorney said I was seeking divorce for mental cruelty and irreconcilable differences. She pronounced us divorced and called for the next case to come forward.

I burst into tears.

"Why are you crying?" the judge asked. "You were the person who wanted out of the marriage, right?"

I nodded. "Yes, I was. But I just want my 17 years back," I replied, my voice cracking. "What happened? Where is that life? Where did it go?"

She shook her head, obviously unable to answer and surprised by this unexpected outpouring of emotion and personal information in her courtroom.

"You'll find it," she finally said. "You can have a good life from now on if you feel that way, if you want to."

"Thank you," I said. "Thank you so much for this gift. I'm so sorry."

"Don't worry about it," she replied. "Now get out there." Her voice was half joking and half firm, and I almost laughed at myself for this display I was making. I couldn't help it, though. Like a cracking dam that had held onto its load for too long under too much pressure, I realized that the tears had to flow. I had to clear the system of the heartache before I could move on.

Wiping my tears, I stood up and left the room, left the building. The door clicked shut behind me, just as it had after high school graduation. No, I could never take back the intervening years, but I could close that chapter and move on as if from that graduation day long ago. A different door was clicking shut but the same opportunities lay in front of me, the same future full of endless possibilities.

How silly I was not to see this before, I thought to myself. How silly of me to let traditions, fear, my culture and a man I disliked hold me back for so long. At that moment, I could finally go to a university. I could start a new career. I could move away. I could do anything I wanted to. For the first time in my adult life, I was free.

Once again, airline tickets arrived from my father in the mail, the formal invitation to another month-long family reunion, this time in Turkey. Though my parents asked, I didn't even invite Ahmad. We were divorced, and though that was a secret — the hiding was difficult for me, because it was good news I wanted to shout to the world — I just didn't want him there.

"It is a vacation on me," my father said over the long-distance phone lines. "I want to treat you all and enjoy my family." Apparently, they'd driven from Tabriz into Turkey, where the country's bank interest rates were very good, and deposited some funds a long while ago. Now, we would go back to collect the original money and have a great time spending only the interest.

"Very smart," I said to my father. "And very generous." This is a real man, despite all his faults, I thought to myself. This is man who shows his love. "We can't wait to see you," I continued.

As expected, we had a wonderful time. The children had grown so much since the last time they saw their uncles, aunts and cousins, and there was a lot of teasing and roughhousing. We stayed in a beautiful, multi-bedroom apartment home in Istanbul, which had a white balcony protruding into the fantastic view of the blue ocean against blue sky. The adults would gather in the mornings and often again in the evenings to chat on the balcony and drink tea.

Turkey is an amazing country, full of beautiful vistas and landscapes, historical sites and water sports, amazing food. The time blurred together, all the restaurants and shopping. I went dancing with my sisters and felt a release that I hadn't experienced in almost 20 years. Like a woman let out of a constraining corset, I could breathe and be myself. I felt as if I was reconnecting not only with my family, but also with my roots and myself.

I knew it wasn't the country that was making me feel so happy. In fact, at times I looked forward to going back to America and I would never have considered moving back to that part of the world. It wasn't America that had been making me sad. It was only a person, and he couldn't take up a whole country. When not reading books or sightseeing, I was formulating a plan in my head of what I would do when I returned home, a step-by-step plan of how I was going to go about starting a new life.

Thanks to the proximity to the water, we spent a lot of time in the sun, on the beach and on various boats and ships. Waiting on the dock for something — a boat to arrive or a tour to start — my sister and I were leaning against a railing. I was turning my face up toward the sun, eyes closed, as if I was diving against gravity into it.

"There's something different about you," I heard her say from be-hind my closed eyes. I opened them and blinked a few times to see her looking at me slantwise, her arms across her chest.

"What do you mean?" I asked. My heart beat a little faster, thinking that the secret might have to come out.

"The look on your face is something that looks like you in high school," she continued. "You're just not like the sister I saw back in Japan five years ago."

"No," I replied, the corners of my mouth turning up. "I'm not."

I paused, unsure of how to go on. She waved her hand, urging me on.

"I divorced Ahmad," I said. "It was final a few months ago. The kids don't know right now, but it's final."

She looked me in the eyes for a moment, then nodded her head quickly, either in support of the news or just in confirmation of it. She hugged me, and said nothing more.

Toward the tail end of our trip, I found myself suffused in a quiet moment on the balcony with only my mother and my sister. Used to the hubbub of all the siblings and cousins running around, it took me totally by surprise. Once I noticed how alone we were, the silence seemed to stretch and grow around us.

I looked over at my sister only to see that she felt it, too. She raised her eyebrows and jerked her head toward our mother. The look said, "Tell her. It's now or never."

Perhaps never would be better, I thought. My mother was the kind of woman who genuinely believed the old Persian phrase: You go to your husband's house in a white dress, and you come out of that house in a white dress. The first meant the wedding gown, the second meant your shroud. Then I remembered the strong and independent person I was — or at least wanted to be — and how I should respect my mother with the truth.

I cleared my throat.

"Mother," I began. "There's something I want to tell you."

She turned toward me. There was her familiar face, the same often intimidating and contrary face that plagued my childhood, but whose genuine smile and love would always be imprinted on my heart. She had more lines around her eyes and her hands were knobbier, her shoulders maybe stooped. But she still had the power to frighten me with her changeable eyes and her often loud, negative response to me and my desires.

"I think that you know I am — was — not happy in my marriage to Ahmad," I said. To placate her, I added, "I know you thought he was a bad choice for me to make when I was so young. I know you had other plans for me, and maybe you were right. But after so many years, I knew it was a choice that I had to change."

There was silence as her eyes bored into me.

"I got a divorce, mother," I said. "It's already final."

She snorted loudly through her nose. "Of course!" she said. "Of course! I should have known that your life would end up this way. I should have known where you would land." She threw her hands up toward the beautiful blue sky and called out to God.

My sister interjected at this point. "Consider this," she said. "Divorce is made for these kind of lives. God created divorce for bad marriages like this. There is a reason for that option to be on earth."

My mother rolled her eyes a little but seemed to listen.

I took the softening of her face as an opportunity to continue, and I spoke about what the marriage had been like. I told them about how in some ways, Ahmad was a sick man, controlling the money, making the decisions and not listening to women's arguments. He completely went against our idea of a good man because his hand was closed, even to his wife, and he forced me out in the world to work, never once voicing a need to take care of me.

"I remember the money and the Seiko watch," my mother said. "What kind of a man..." She trailed off, shaking her head.

"And he didn't even like the watch," I added.

I had been very unhappy, I continued. I had stayed because of my fierce love of my children, and now John was off to college. He had known a father in his childhood. I had given him that. Now, I had to leave.

"I'd like to have your blessing, Mother," I said softly. "I need to have your blessing."

She pursed her lips considering and my sister and I exchanged glances.

Finally, my mother sighed. Looking away from me, she said, "I will be so embarrassed by this. You have completely embarrassed me, Maryam."

I let out a breath I didn't know I had been holding.

"This is not something that happens in Iran, even if it does it your America," she continued. "So I'm not going to tell anyone you're divorced."

My sister started to smile.

"But you go ahead and get divorced if you want to," she said. She put her hands up to the sky and to God, as if she was constantly amazed at what he threw into her path.

I returned to the United States a few days later with little gifts and souvenirs for the kids and for all our friends.

A few days after my arrival home in Chicago, I received a surprising phone call from Arian, who was in China for business. He informed me that he would be making his way to America, with stop in San Francisco and North Carolina. And like his last visit to the states, he wanted to see me again. Always the gentlemen, he called to ask if I was free to see him, telling me that he was ready to schedule a connecting flight in Chicago to see me before heading to his final stop in North Carolina.

We met for lunch at the Westin Hotel, near the O'Hare Airport.

In whispered voices that afternoon, we spoke about my divorce and my plans for the future. I shared that I felt as if a great burden had been lifted off my shoulders, as if I now had a second chance, a blank slate to do things the right way.

In return, he told me how he still longed for a divorce from his wife, using all the same words and all the same emotions that I'd heard from him 10 years in the past. I held his hand, which had changed. I looked in his eyes, and they had changed. But the words coming out of his mouth and things that he could offer me had not.

Melody and I — and the family dog — were off on a larger adventure. We were planning on moving to sunny California, the place my childhood self had always thought I would live if I could immigrate to America. I told Melody something vague about her father perhaps coming out to California later, when everything with his family was settled.

It's not as if the children didn't know that something was wrong between their parents and had been wrong for some time. They were slightly scared of their "underwater" mother and the uncomfortable silence and distance between their parents. Once I had finally gotten the divorce rolling, they started to see out-and-out fights between Ahmad and me.

I told them the truth, leaving out only the part about the official divorce. In particular, John understood all too well.

"I want to taste California," I said to him. "I want to see how it is. I think your father and I need a break from each other, and I need to see how that is, too."

"You're right, Mom," he replied. "Of course, you're right."

One of our last acts as a four-person family group was to take John off to college in Champagne, Illinois. The car was stuffed with duffel bags and boxes, all of the supplies that I'd been working on checking off the college's list of necessities. He had sheets and towels, paper and pens, new clothes, food for the dorm.

He emerged from the car taller than I'd ever imagined, even though I lived with him every day. His face had become stronger over the past year, sharper and more like a man's, but his eyes were still so warm and kind. These were the same eyes that looked out of 2-year-old John's face, back when I dressed him in all red, white and blue. Back when I was new to this feeling of overwhelming pride, love, fear and protectiveness that rises in your stomach: the feeling of motherhood.

I cried my eyes out, more than most of the other parents dropping off their children that day. I cried because we were both growing up. I cried because I wasn't going to be in the room next door, or even in the town next door, where he could come home for weekend visits. There would be thousands of miles between us for the first time in his life. I mourned the loss of his everyday presence in my life. I mourned the loss of his childhood, even as I celebrated the joy of him becoming an adult and fulfilling all his dreams.

We smiled at each other through my tears. Before we left, he hugged me tight and kissed the top of my head, I was so much smaller than him.

"You're going to be fine," I said to him. Like my grandmother once told me during my times of vulnerability, I gave John the best advice I once received myself. "If you have patience in your life, you can witness sour grapes turn into sweet raisins someday."

John smiled at the saying.

"You're going to do so wonderful and make me so proud," I said to him.

He shook hands with his dad, hugged his sister and disappeared into the dorms.

Chapter Twenty-Seven

A few months later, most mornings would find me at my new home, in a condominium complex called the Casablanca in San Diego. I was more likely to be found eating breakfast outside the home: on the lovely balcony overlooking palm trees and a gurgling stream water feature running through the tropical landscaping. The sun warmed my face and shined off the white stucco of the exterior, and I often wondered — my eyes closed — if this is what heaven felt like, all calm and temperate. After 10 years of Chicago winters, it was certainly my heaven.

The rest of the apartment was no different: Everything was perfect. The neighborhood boasted good schools and a large community of Iranian Americans. There were three bedrooms — which I considered necessary for the kids, because I wanted them to have a family life here — a sunny kitchen and this lovely balcony. I had chosen the furniture and the art to hang on the walls. I had picked out every pot and pan.

Best of all, I had paid for every penny. In addition to what I had been awarded in the divorce, I had received a little bit of money from my parents. And staying true to the idea of my childhood that gold and jewelry were a woman's fail safe, something she could turn to when the worst occurred, I had sold some of my older, handmade jewelry and it fetched a handsome price.

I was in another world from the prison I'd been living in for so long. I was in a world of my own making. My body and spirit felt so light that I thought I might have been able to float off the balcony and into the blue California sky. I looked up to see birds soaring below the clouds and it reminded me of my broken bird dreams. The blood on my uncle's hands. The flightless creature hopping through the jungle, so fragile, something dangerous right on its heels. The sense of doom and danger seems so far from here, so far away in distance and in time.

Melody was adjusting to the move better than I ever could have imagined. In the beginning, she hadn't been very excited, although she wasn't against the move either. She was in fifth grade at her new school, which was very close to home, and she was a good student.

Within a few weeks of her starting school, she flew through the door one evening — she was old enough to have her own key, of course — to tell me, "Mom, Alaham is coming over tonight." She threw her backpack on the ground and slouched against the countertop, like any kid in an American sitcom on television. Her cheeks were rosy, and she was smiling broadly.

"Do we have any popcorn?" she asked. "Would you go and buy us some popcorn?"

Of course, I would get them popcorn. I would put together a tray of popcorn and grapes, soda and ice, other snacks. I would have walked across the ocean, I thought to myself, to see my daughter so happy and well-adjusted, so thoroughly American. Most American children didn't have to worry about not having a home or food, about war and politics, about what they couldn't or wouldn't be allowed to do or to be when they grew up. What I wanted for my children was a real childhood empty of major worries where they could enjoy their youth. So I served popcorn to the two loud, gossipy girls sprawled out on the carpet in front of the TV, and I was truly joyous at the sight.

Meanwhile, John was back in Illinois and he had found out the truth, that his father and I were officially divorced. He had accompanied his father to the lawyer's office to arrange some paperwork about leasing the old condominium.

"And the lawyer says, 'your ex-wife said that she wanted it done like this,'" John said to me over the phone.

I was silent, waiting, my heart in my throat. I didn't know if John was going to disapprove of the divorce, if he would be hurt that I hadn't told him or resigned to the news.

"I didn't know you were divorced, Mom," he said.

"I didn't want it to be the big deal it would have been if we'd talked about," I explained. "I thought that it was between your father and me and that we would take care of it, that your lives should go on as normal."

"But it's not normal anymore," he said. He paused, I think to intentionally heighten the dramatic effect. "It's better."

I sighed.

"You're in California and you're happy," he continued. "And... I think I will be soon, too. I'm coming for the summer."

"Oh John, that's wonderful!"

We'd be together again, I thought. The three of us will be all together again. My heart glowed as warmly as the California sun.

It turned out that the reunion was the four of us instead of three: Ahmad, finished with settling his parents in Florida, had gotten an apartment in San Diego. I don't know if he thought that we were going to get back to together. I don't know what he was planning to do. I didn't even know how he was supporting himself. He talked and talked about finding a business, some sort of investment opportunity, but he never seemed to settle on one. And as far as I could tell, he wasn't working or collecting a paycheck.

"We don't have any money for that," I heard ringing through my head. Well, how did he have money to live in that fashion then? This man, who objected to losing two of my paychecks for me to see the family I hadn't visited in a decade, was losing weeks upon weeks of regular pay.

It's not my problem, I thought. I was able to take a deep breath, all the way into the corners of my lungs, and I felt light as a feather. My ex-husband and his money were really not my problem.

On that count, however, I was wrong. Thanks to the child-support agreement arranged during our divorce, Ahmad owed me a certain amount of money each month for the support of Melody. Months had gone by and I hadn't seen a check or a single penny.

Since he had moved to San Diego, Ahmad had begun to schedule visits with Melody, taking her to the movies or the park. He'd knock on the door and I couldn't help but smile, thinking of him standing on the other side of the door — my door — with no key to scrape in the lock and no claim to the interior of the home — or to me. When I opened the door to let him in, I could see that he was feeling that separation, too. He seemed a little dazed and awkward, as if he didn't know if he could touch anything or make comments about anything he saw inside my new home. He usually stood around uncomfortably until Melody was ready to go and I went about my business, not really trying to entertain him.

"You know," I said to him on one of his first visits, "I've been living on my own with Melody for a few months now and I haven't gotten any child-support payments from you yet."

He made some sort of grunt, which acknowledged what I had said but didn't offer anything in return.

"The divorce agreement states that you are supposed to pay it, Ahmad," I went on, my tone the same as when talking to a stubborn child. "I'm not being mean or demanding. It's only what I am owed."

He sighed and reached into his back pocket for his checkbook, then looked up at me, seeking permission to come into my kitchen and use the table. I nodded. Once the check was written out, he set it down on the table.

"There you are," he said, his voice very neutral, not seeming to be upset.

"Thank you, Ahmad," I replied, and I meant it.

Melody tumbled into the room, always a riot of happy words and smiles, and I went to her to help with something. Then I saw them out the front door on their way, told Melody to have fun and blissfully closed the door. My door, separating my little universe from the world.

A while later when I returned to the kitchen, the check was no longer on the table. I looked high and low, anywhere a draft or the dog could have moved the little piece of paper, but to no avail. It was as if my child support had vanished into thin air.

Every time my ex-husband came by, I'd mention it, and every time, he'd say that it would turn up somewhere. After two months, by which time I really should have had the original check and a second one, I called him on the phone to discuss it.

"It's still missing," I told him. "Put a stop on it and just write me out another one."

His voice was more assertive on the phone than when he was in my house, more reminiscent of the old Ahmad. "No, I have to find out if someone cashed it."

"That's what putting a stop on it will do, Ahmad," I said.

"No," he affirmed. "If you don't bring me the old check, I'm not going to give you a new one."

My jaw fell open. "That doesn't make any sense. If I had the old check, I wouldn't need the new one."

"I don't care," he continued. "That's how it is."

Even though he couldn't see me, I shook my head. I was incredulous at the lengths this man would go to control his money and to control me with his money. I remembered the afternoon he'd written the check and the fact that he'd been alone in the kitchen for several moments before he and Melody left.

He'd taken it. He'd turned around and taken back the check that he had just written. I knew it down in my heart and my bones. Yes, he really would do such a thing. My jaw set tight and firm.

"Fine," I said. "But how this is how it is. Those payments are written into our divorce agreement, and there's nothing you can do about that. Don't think that I can't do this without you and your money — I can and I will — but also don't think that you can get away with this."

"I'm not getting away with anything," he said. "You find the old check — "

"I'm tired of this. Just stop," I replied. "Do your duty as a father and do it proudly, or just go away. You do not need to cheat your children like this."

I hung up the phone.

I found out soon afterwards that my ex-husband obviously didn't care much about taking advantage of his children. He'd sold the land we'd bought in Iran near the Caspian Sea, which was officially allotted to the children during the divorce.

He didn't stay in California long and returned to Washington D.C., where he was going to stay in the home of his sister, who was now married with two kids. That's right. With my help in coming to America and the support of our house for several years, she'd fulfilled her dream of becoming a wife and mother, something she feared she'd never find back home. And she never said thank you.

Served them right to live together, I thought. Those two deserve one another.

When we first arrived in California, I cast around to find my new destiny in various places. We stayed for a short time with a Persian friend we knew from Chicago and got to know some people in the Iranian-American community. I worked for a brief period at a silver shop near the high-class La Jolla beach, where I could have taken over management and made a decently successful tourist shop. But I couldn't bear sitting behind a counter all day selling postcards. I thought of bringing my cosmetology degrees up to date for the state of California, but it had been so long and my fire for that work had dimmed.

In the end, I fell into my new career through luck. Or rather, it was really our dog, a little Maltese named Lucky.

I was walking our little canine down the sunny sidewalk pondering where I was in life, a place that wasn't quite solid and yet wasn't yet scary, either. I didn't want to take just any job, I thought to myself. This is a new start and my new life. If I fall directly back into a bad job or something that keeps my spirit caged, I will have gained nothing with all my prison breaking and upheaval. What am I going to do?

Beside me pulled up a shiny convertible car with its top down, the sort of car that men buy when they want other men to know how important they are. At first I thought I wouldn't look at whoever it was that was taking notice of me, but then a slightly familiar voice shouted my name.

"Maryam!" I heeled up Lucky and turned to find that the car at the curb was driven by an acquaintance named Sam, a real estate agent who had shown Melody and me around before we rented our Casablanca property, when we were thinking about buying. Though he was American, he was married to a Persian woman and therefore was knowledgeable about Middle Eastern culture and was very non-threatening to me.

"Hi, Sam," I said, genuinely happy to see a familiar face. I felt as if I was drifting through most of the daylight hours, just casting around for ways to kill time until Melody got home from school in the afternoon. It was always nice to talk to people.

"What are you doing?" he asked, pushing his dark sunglasses onto his head and revealing his eyes.

"Walking the dog," I said. I raised the leash in my hand to indicate Lucky, who was nosing around in the grass. "Yes?"

He laughed. "No, no," he replied. "What are you doing for work? Have you found anything yet?"

"You must be a mind reader, sir, because I was going over that in my head just now." I smiled. How good it felt to be happy, jovial and funny. I didn't realize how much I'd missed being able to be my unadulterated self until I had moved to this sunny state.

He grinned back at me.

"Well, I'm opening up a new office really soon," he explained. "It's a really big new office and I'm going to need lots of people to fill it up and make it successful. I think you just might be perfect."

"You want me to work in real estate?" I asked. The idea was too new and strange for me to have ever considered it, and I was taken aback. "I don't think I could. I mean, sell houses?"

He got out of the car and came around to me and we talked about mortgages. Selling a house was only one side of the real-estate world. The other half dealt with the technicalities of the finances, helping people apply for loans, dealing with banks and completing paperwork with all T's crossed and all I's dotted. So basically, he wanted someone quick and intelligent to follow instructions. It was really office work and I understood that, although it was in real estate rather than with an airline.

"I'm a broker," he explained. "That means I have the license and the experience to supervise a deal from start to finish. Getting a license takes some time and energy, so it makes sense that someone wouldn't want to jump right into it. Instead, you could be a broker's assistant. You can help me with the mortgages in every way except one: You can't quote customers the actual interest rates. But handling everything other than that really makes it easier for me to do the rest of my job and make the company — and you, of course — even more money."

He was certainly smart and business savvy, but Sam also was very genuine and non-threatening. Of anyone in this world, I knew that he was trying to help and not take advantage of me. While my work on any loans would be under his umbrella, I would receive a commission for every loan I brought to the company.

"Try it out and see if you like it, and if you do, you can take the test later and really work your way up. You're the kind of lady who could go really far in real estate."

I liked the idea, and I liked the fact that I could try it on for size like a new dress. If it didn't fit, there was no harm done. But if it did work out, I could be on the path toward a whole new part of my life, a whole new career.

And speaking of dresses, I would again get to wear them on a daily basis. I'd work in an office with lots of other brokers and assistants, and I'd be working with lots of customers every day. I would be among people, where my personality truly blossomed. If I could have, I might have followed him right there to his nice, new office building instead of going back home with only Lucky as company.

Instead, I found myself in the bathroom the next morning putting on my best earrings, wearing a crisp white blouse and high-heeled shoes. It had been a while since I felt that morning sense of purpose and I reveled in that feeling and the smell of my favorite perfume.

I went into the office and met the people who were to be my co-workers, and the glow never seemed to fade. There were such a variety of international people in California: other Iranians, Africans, Europeans, Mexicans and more. There was hustle and bustle like any office, but it also seemed that, unlike a lot of Chicagoans and residents of the East Coast, Californians were warm, friendly and genuinely helpful. Sam made sure that some of his other associates showed me where to work and began to teach me about mortgages — the processes, the vocabulary, the paperwork. Having only owned one property in my life and being a big believer in the power of homeownership, I took to the numbers and intricacies like a fish to water.

It was clear that I was in training. Sam wanted me to get to know the business and see if I liked it before I got too serious. But sometimes things just click into place — bang — overnight.

That first week I went into Sam's real estate office, I had an evening party to go to at a Persian friend's house. A gathering most nights of the week was pretty common in our close-knit and friendly Iranian community. If you felt lonely, you need only pick up the phone to find some friends gathering nearby.

For this particular party, I drove to Rancho Santa Fe, a very wealthy community within San Diego, to celebrate my friend Asharaf's birthday. Her husband was a successful businessman and their home was large, so I often spent the night before coming home the next day when I visited them. Her daughter and Melody had become friends, so they enjoyed having a sleepover.

It was a surprise party, so it fell to me and a few other friends to help Asharaf's husband set up their house with food, music and decorations before she arrived home. As we were doing so, her husband and I chatted a little bit about this and that.

He asked, "So how are you keeping yourself busy now, Maryam? You look like you've had a breath of fresh air in your lungs recently."

I smiled, or perhaps I grinned. I couldn't help it. My enthusiasm was always readily apparent on my face.

"I'm beginning work with a real estate office as an assistant mort-gage broker," I replied. "There's a lot to learn and I'm not licensed right now, but I'm really enjoying it. Thank you."

He nodded his head, pleased.

"Well, that's odd," he said. "It just so happens that I'm looking for a loan."

I was completely taken aback, as if a shaft of light had come through the window to illuminate him and heavenly music had started to play.

While I hadn't before known exactly what he did for a living — I knew he worked with commercial shops and such — he explained that he was a commercial developer. He was currently beginning a project constructing a new shopping center and was looking for a loan.

"Of course," he continued, "I've gotten several loans in the past from several different people, but if I could do business with you and help you in this new career, that would be even better."

"That would be... that would be so wonderful."

He laughed at my speechlessness and looked at me kindly, like an older brother giving his sister a helping hand, encouraging her dreams. There was also a touch of amusement in his demeanor, as if he thought that a woman succeeding in business was akin to a fish with legs, but if I wanted to give it a swim, he thought that was grand.

As the time for Asharaf to arrive drew closer, he explained that he needed a loan for $1 million — a huge amount in the early 1990s — and gave me all of the details I needed for the loan application. I couldn't quote him a rate, I reiterated, but he assured me that as long as the rate was fair, he certainly had my business.

On Monday when I went into the office for my second week of work in mortgages, I had a $1-million loan application in my pocket.

"My god," said Sam, reaching across his desk for the paperwork. "You said $1 million?"

"I certainly did."

"Your first loan will be one for $1 million?" he repeated.

"That's right," I said, my shoulders held high. "Thanks to you bring-ing me on here, of course."

He laughed. "I knew you'd be good at this sort of work, Maryam," he continued. "But I had no idea. Just no idea." He was shaking his head back and forth in the negative, but he overflowed with positivity and praise.

The rest of that week, I immersed myself in this new world of real estate and finance, finding joy in keeping myself productively busy and in a job well done. I looked at titles, got to know escrow representatives, shuffled paperwork, learned to read rates and read up on the different banks and bankers the company dealt with. The real-estate business in California was booming through the ceiling and it seemed like another gold rush, a place that the right person in the right place could strike a gold mine.

A woman that I'd gotten to know pretty well, a lady named Farah who would be a long-time friend, teased me for my reckless abandon and boundless energy.

"What are you doing?" she asked. "Everyone is in mortgages. You're not going to make money."

"You don't know that," I said. "And you're in mortgages, too!" She had her license, however, while I was a broker assistant.

"Go on to something better. With hundreds and thousands of loan officers out there, why do you want to be one of them and have all that competition?"

I gave her a slant-eyed look and said, "You know what? Go tell those hundreds of loan officers that Maryam is coming. You tell them that."

She laughed and squeezed my shoulder.

Within four months, I had my real estate license. Within my first year in real estate, I brought 69 loans to the office, more than any other broker or assistant. John put his studies in Illinois on hold in favor of joining the Marines, where he could be stationed nearby me and his beloved sister. And I was a single mother making it in the world. It seemed at times like I was standing on top of the spinning Earth.

I found out that business is all about networking. I found out, then, that business was all about being myself, my social and people-loving self.

I remember sitting outside at a local sandwich shop for lunch when a Persian acquaintance stopped by and commented on my business clothes, which led to a conversation about what I was doing professionally. Within five minutes, this gentleman had my card in hand and an appointment to talk about a loan. Plus, two or three more gentlemen of our mutual acquaintance had gathered around the table in the meantime, asking questions and showing interest. I handed out business cards like I handed out smiles, and most of them came back to me in the form of appointments set at the office to go over down payments, interest rates and credit scores.

I think that a lot of this business loyalty within the Persian community — the fact that when possible, Iranians did business with other Iranians — was a way to feel less foreign with each other. No matter how long anyone had been in the United States, we all distinctly remember that first time we went out in public and opened our mouths, only to say something inaccurate or inappropriate in English. We'd all felt like fish out of water at one point in time.

Therefore, if you could have an Iranian lawyer, doctor or loan officer, it made you feel like you were getting the same service as if you found a lawyer, doctor or loan officer in Tehran. No one looked down on you or discriminated based on your origins or accent, and you knew that you weren't being taken advantage of while also helping out a fellow countryman.

I don't know how much of the interest in my services stemmed from the fact that I was a woman. Perhaps that caught a man's attention, I admit. But once I opened my mouth and proved I was knowledgeable and talented, most Persian men adopted that look I had first seen on the face of Asharaf's husband, my first client. Their faces looked like they had just seen the housecat get up, sit on the couch and talk, then start to add up some figures on a calculator. Usually, the shock faded into respect and perhaps even grudging admiration, and my business relationships were never anything but business.

My commission for bringing in loans to Sam's firm was increased from 50 percent to 75 percent. I was bringing in so much business, Sam didn't want me to be lured away to the competition with an offer for more money.

In that department, I didn't think I had anything to worry about. In that first year, I made more money that I had in the last several years combined. I won several sales contests with prizes like trips to Las Vegas and airline tickets. When my bank account hit the $30,000 mark, Melody and I bought our dream house in the Rancho Bernardo area.

Even though we moved there when she was already about 12, the Rancho Bernardo house will always be the one we think of as her childhood home. It was really a dream come true, like something built on a cloud in my imagination. It was a two-story house of white stucco and a red tile roof with a balcony backing to the hills. The city lights twinkled at night and the birds swooped down through the air currents during the day, playing in the sunshine. It was freedom itself, that house.

I never once felt sad or upset that I was single after I bought that house. Such a thought never once crossed my mind. Sure, I worked hard at my job and struggled balancing all the juggling balls that all single moms do: working fulltime, picking up the kids from school, dinners, housecleaning, and errands. But I was never lonely.

Instead, I felt as if I finally had a rich husband at home. This is the life that I wanted, full of people but drained of worries about meeting financial obligations on a daily basis. A life where I could spoil my children — I bought John a black convertible car, for instance — and where the people who loved me supported me in what I loved to do. Such was the life I had thought that I could have if I hadn't made a mistake, if I hadn't chosen the right husband. Now, I reaped all the benefits, but the husband was invisible.

In some aspects, it was better that way. We went on stress-free family vacations and gathered around the Christmas tree — all three of us — without a black cloud hanging over our heads. Because I was single, my house was the one where my friends liked to gather and have ladies' nights. Melody and I went to the movies on the weekends, and I went to whatever party I desired whenever I desired. Along the way, I was always making friends and handing out business cards, keeping the cycle of success and happiness moving in the right direction.

John was immensely helpful to me and Melody, when John was in the Marine reserves, also after he was released and started attending San Diego State University with a psychology major. He helped pick Melody up when I wasn't able, and he babysat and cooked for her. With my business, he filled in the gaps when my English language skills weren't quite up to the task. He'd write out letters of explanation to send to lenders, proofreading the text and typing it on the computer. Often at the end of the letters he helped me with, he'd like to add his funny phrase: "Thank you and stop by for milk and cookies!" Every time I would delete the phrase, but every time it would make me smile.

I held my own credit cards. I had a mortgage in my name. I opened the envelopes of bills and was responsible for paying everyone. Now that I was more than 40 years old, I finally had control of my finances and I was determined to do things differently than my ex-husband. I had an open hand with my children, not hesitating to make their lives better or easier with the fruits of my labor.

Yet still, my earnings outpaced my spending and I was able to save responsibly. Always with the drive to climb higher and achieve more, I learned more about real estate in California, not only from the angle of mortgages but also sales and investment. My first investment property was a condominium near La Jolla beach.

A few years later, I owned and rented out several units in the Casablanca, where Melody and I had spent our first months in California. It seemed as if things had rounded a corner and came back to the beginning, completing a circle, closing a chapter. I came back to square one, but so much had improved and changed forever that the person sitting on that Casablanca balcony was not the woman I saw in the mirror in the morning. That current reflection was more like the woman I dreamt I would be as a little girl, when I sat far up in the trees in our backyard in Tabriz, watching the airplanes crisscross in the sky.

Chapter Twenty-Eight

When I was a teenager, I'd roll my eyes and scoff at my parents when they began to lecture me about choices, about how things that I did in my life now would continue to affect me for years. As if one thing I did would ripple like a raindrop's echo in a puddle, rolling out and out forever. Usually when they brought up the subject, it was to forbid me from doing something I desperately wanted to do with all my heart, such as study in France or be a flight attendant. So it's not surprising that I failed to listen, that I didn't understand.

I now look back on those admonitions and sigh, nodding my head at the wisdom I recognized in hindsight. The idea popped into my head as my kids aged, especially as Melody became a teenager. Her life seemed so precariously balanced and I wanted to rush up and steady her, make sure that she was taking the right path and see that everything would turn out good in the end. It's an impossible task as a parent, but we all try.

The idea was redoubled in mind, however, when I realized that no matter how hard I pushed away and how high I had now flown, I simply could not rid myself of my ex-husband's presence in my life. Certainly, he could have a relationship with his children, and I would never stand in the way. But one bad decision — that one choice to kiss the wrong frog, thinking he'd be my prince — hung around my head like a black cloud.

After a few years of being a loan officer, where I was one of the most successful officers in the company, I decided that the real action was in real estate sales. Plus, realtors spent so much time all over town with all sorts of clients, socializing and genuinely helping. I was certainly willing to trade my paperwork for that.

I was more successful at selling real estate thanks to my background in mortgages. I was able to give clients a basic outline of what their loan, payments and general interest rate would be for any given home while we were out in the field and without having to pull in a third party to do calculations. I understood the closing process inside and out, too.

John always said I had excellent negotiating skills, and perhaps that comes from years of wheedling the best out of a bad situation. No matter where it came from, I was skilled at bringing buyers and sellers to an agreement, of dealing with banks and loan officers, and to getting my clients the best possible deal on the house of their dreams. I had all those little balls up in the air at the same time and never dropped one.

I continued to receive prizes and awards through my office for sales, my favorite of which were the vacations. And though I was very busy, I was also very happy just living in the life I had chosen day in and day out.

I had much success in my business life, a success so different than anything I could have dreamed when I was still married. Day-to-day life with my ex-husband was excruciating, a fight for every piece of ground I gained, a tooth and nail battle for financial solvency, not even financial gain.

However, I found that America was the country I always dreamed it was: When I struggled to do my best, even when it was an uphill battle, my skill and hard work often allowed me to come out on top. There were no unmovable barriers, and even doors that seemed locked to me often opened when I returned to knock multiple times. Even better, there were people in this world — most of the people in this world, in my opinion — who supported and encouraged you as you worked toward personal success. Most people didn't challenge you, thwart you or throw down a personal confrontation because you were doing well. It was a refreshing surprise, as you might imagine.

However, not all people I knew reacted well to the success of a single woman in business, and this was especially true within the Iranian-American community. Had I been a man with the same career and the same financial success, every door would have been open to me and my family, every hand open to me in hopes that mine would be open to them. I would have been trusted and respected. Because of my gender, however, that idea was turned on its head: My success often made me the target of snide remarks from women who were offended by my independence.

I began to understand that I was threatening to the normal ways of doing things. I was stepping outside the box, and that made many people uncomfortable. But it was the first time in my life I felt outside of the box, too, the first time I felt as if I could stand up tall, walk around the world and be free.

With my life finally turning into how I had always hoped, it seemed to come full circle at John's law school graduation. John, my little man, his pudgy hands and deep eyes, sitting on the floor of our apartment in Washington D.C., watching Superman cartoons and eagerly yelling "Mom! Mom! Turn on Hooperman!" It's amazing to me, that John, who once had trouble pronouncing Superman, was now the man I had always known he would be. My hope and my glue into life in America. John in the Christmas pageant when we first moved to Chicago. John and our "tanks full of hope," our special drives in that yellow Cadillac of mine, when we'd look at the flowers. I used to tell him that God showed himself in the beauty and the unimaginable colors of those flowers. He called me as an adult years later while he was in law school while he was driving on a highway surrounded by blooming flowers, saying, and "Thank you for introducing me to God in this beautiful way." How had so much happened, so many miles under the tires and so much time past? The memories washed over me, one after another.

On that spring morning of his graduation, he was tall and strapping in his graduation gown, his dark hair peeking out on his forehead under the square hat. His eyes were sparkling, almost giddy with happiness that all his hard work was done and he was graduating from one of the top ten law schools in America, George Washington University. He was already assured a great job with a law firm in Los Angeles, which was quite a feather in his cap. But I don't think he really saw beyond the happiness of that day, that he saw with the same eyes as I did, with the eyes of history.

As he came down off the stage, my heart was beating as if it would take flight out of my chest. As I hugged my adult son, my head rested where I could feel his heartbeat and I closed my eyes and saw for the first time, the lonely clipped wing bird fly.

"Mom? What's wrong?" John asked, ducking his head down to look in my face.

"It's just the flight," I said. "It's flying..." I held one hand on my own beating chest and the other on John's.

Melody came up beside me and put her hands on my shoulders.

"Mom? Why don't we sit down?"

I let her guide me to a table with several chairs. There was a gathering after the ceremony for the graduates and their families, and other happy groups of people wandered about. After reassuring my children that I was perfectly well, just overwhelmed, I began to explain the root of the emotion that swept over me, the images and feelings that streamed through my mind as I watched the sun glint off John's smile up on that stage.

I told my children about my small red-breasted bird friend that I lost in my childhood and how the incident had meant so much to me.

I explained to them that while watching John's face under the sunlight, I experienced happiness as I never have before. I witnessed my son following in my own dreams of becoming a lawyer, and his successes becoming my success. My emotions of joy that day washed away the pain and regret that I experienced early on in life. I no longer felt sorry for myself, but instead, felt a renewal of spirit—a spirit that I once had in my favorite tree, surrounded by the earthy smell of the white berries and my favorite friend. I had a vision of the red clipped winged bird with its beautiful full-grown wings, flying toward me. But as the bird flew closer, I realized that it wasn't my red-breasted bird friend after all, it was me. I was flying once again.

"I touch your heart and I hear the beating of wings. I feel in my heart that the wings finally have air under them, that something is truly flying again, up in the sky. I cannot explain it."

"You don't have to, Mom," said Melody. "I think I understand."

I linked my thumbs together and spread my fingers like wings, moving them slightly like a bird in flight. It was the same gesture I used to share with Arian so long ago, the man I thought might have been my ticket out, and a ticket that blew away at the first stiff wind. Now as I moved my hands, that gesture, too, had transformed meaning.

As I showed them, John grabbed my hands in his and held them tight. He nodded, his lips tight and his eyes moist with emotion. The three of us hugged intensely, perhaps more emotionally than a law school graduation merited in the eyes of other families. But to us, it was more.

Our arms around each other, I don't think any of us felt like our feet touched the ground. I think we all knew that nothing could stop us, that anything was possible.

Not negating the past or correcting mistakes. It was larger than that. It was a symbol that everything I worked for and bled for was worth it. I didn't know how much I feared that it wouldn't be until that moment, when the weight fell away and left me quaking with gratitude and love — for my children, yes, but also for me.

A short while later, I linked my thumbs and flew my fingers at Melody as she crossed a similar stage, graduating from the University of Santa Clara with a Master's degree in psychology. She teared up and blew me a kiss.

Among family — among the three of us tightly connected human beings — we know what this little flutter of the fingers means. We know the story behind it. And we understand the feeling of exhilaration when you know in your bones what you are capable of, believing in the strength of your wings and the buoyancy of hope.

I'd like to think we taught each other that lesson.

A few days after Melody's graduation, we had a mother and daughter day on Rodeo Drive, in Beverly Hills. Melody drove my convertible Mercedes that day as we entered the premiere shopping district. Like they advertise and talk about Rodeo Drive, each shop is like an exciting gift waiting to be opened as you cross its threshold to be greeted by the most artistic and inventive of displays of fashion.

We strolled through Rodeo Drive that day with a handful of bags, taking in the luxurious street filled with beautiful people, designer bags and spas and salons that only celebrities dared to enter.

We recognized the name of every single store...Chanel, Gucci, Valentino, Armani, Versace, Bijan, Cartier and Tiffany. It is an endless parade of glittering jewels and fascinating faces from around the world. As soon as Melody and I walked into the Tiffany's store, I quickly remembered when I was in high school and dreamt about being Audrey Hepburn's character in Breakfast at Tiffany's. I wanted to be independent in London, like Audrey, and eat my breakfast in front of the store. Little did I know, I would surpass my dream and be able to walk into Tiffany's with my daughter and buy her a beautiful heart chained bracelet and a fragrant Tiffany's perfume for myself.

As Melody drove us back us back home, she asked, "Mom, you have a few friends that live in Beverly Hills, don't you?"

"Yes, I do," I replied.

They must have really big houses."

"They do. But remember, a big house doesn't necessarily bring everyone happiness," I said.

Then, on October 28th, 2007, I received a "Louis Vuitton" handbag that was purchased from a Bloomingdale's Department Store. Within the bag were a little red rose and a birthday card from my Dream Man, wishing me a happy birthday and hopes in seeing me soon.

Epilogue

I have a high-rise condominium where I hang all my family pictures and drape the Persian rugs I've collected on the floor. There is a wall of windows overlooking the city leading to my balcony, where I grow a variety of plants in lots of separate pots, the leaves and stems a riot of green going every which way. During the day, I can look out over the hustle of traffic and people on the streets. At night, I can always see the flag. It's an American flag that sits front and center, on the roof of a nearby office building. At night, spotlights illuminate the flapping fabric and I often find myself staring, mesmerized and lost in thought. I think about flags and countries. I think about the past and the future. I think of the fullness of my life and, on occasion, the emptiness of the condominium now that both the kids have grown up and moved on.

I've never reached a place in my life where I could just stand still before. I've always strived, but never reached a real destination until now, a place where I wanted to be and to stay. It's a strange emotion and sometimes I feel as if it can't be real, as if there must be something wrong beneath the surface, as if things could possibly be too good to believe. I still get overwhelmed with the idea that I have no control over my life and over the world, but then remind myself, who does?

You traveled from there all the way to here, from point A to point B. No, not traveled. You flew. That's the only way to describe it. So high above solid ground, buffeted by culture and fate, it's an uncertain world in the clouds. But the only way you move forward is to refocus your eyes and continue beating your wings, up and down, up and down, day by day. Just don't look down, I say. When I get scared and uncertain, I say, just don't look down.

I have my health. I have my children. I have my own business. I have my own home, where at 10 p.m. every night, I no longer hear the gunshots fired due to Martial Law in the streets of Tehran. Instead I hear and see the fireworks from Disneyland. As the fireworks bursts across the sky to create an unforgettable show, I can now replace the images in my head of gunshot victims and a time of terror, with colorful and vibrant fireworks that bring alive hope, magic and amazement. I also have a little garden out on the balcony of my condo, where I drink tea— but this time, it has no walls.

I hope all the American girls can appreciate that absence, can understand the freedom of what's not there to stand in their way.